Java™ Application Development on Linux®

BRUCE PERENS' OPEN SOURCE SERIES

http://www.phptr.com/perens

- ◆ *Java Application Development on Linux*
  Carl Albing and Michael Schwarz

- ◆ *C++ GUI Programming with Qt 3*
  Jasmin Blanchette, Mark Summerfield

- ◆ *Managing Linux Systems with Webmin: System Administration and Module Development*
  Jamie Cameron

- ◆ *Understanding the Linux Virtual Memory Manager*
  Mel Gorman

- ◆ *Implementing CIFS: The Common Internet File System*
  Christopher Hertel

- ◆ *Embedded Software Development with eCos*
  Anthony Massa

- ◆ *Rapid Application Development with Mozilla*
  Nigel McFarlane

- ◆ *The Linux Development Platform: Configuring, Using, and Maintaining a Complete Programming Environment*
  Rafeeq Ur Rehman, Christopher Paul

- ◆ *Intrusion Detection with SNORT: Advanced IDS Techniques Using SNORT, Apache, MySQL, PHP, and ACID*
  Rafeeq Ur Rehman

- ◆ *The Official Samba-3 HOWTO and Reference Guide*
  John H. Terpstra, Jelmer R. Vernooij, Editors

- ◆ *Samba-3 by Example: Practical Exercises to Successful Deployment*
  John H. Terpstra

Java™ Application Development on Linux®

Carl Albing

Michael Schwarz

PRENTICE HALL PTR

Prentice Hall Professional Technical Reference
Boston

The publisher offers excellent discounts on this book when ordered in quantity for bulk purchases or special sales, which may include electronic versions and/or custom covers and content particular to your business, training goals, marketing focus, and branding interests. For more information, please contact:

U. S. Corporate and Government Sales
(800) 382-3419
corpsales@pearsontechgroup.com

For sales outside the U. S., please contact:

International Sales
international@pearsoned.com

Visit us on the Web: www.phptr.com

Library of Congress Cataloging-in-Publication Data:

CIP data on file.

© 2005 Pearson Education, Inc.

ISBN 0–13–143697-X

Text printed in the United States on recycled paper at Pheonix Color in Hagerstown Maryland.

First printing, November 2004

To my mother, for her love of words.
—Michael

To my wife, Cynthia.
—Carl

Contents

Preface

JAVA AND LINUX

Why another book on Java? Why a book on Java and Linux? Isn't Java a platform-independent system? Aren't there enough books on Java? Can't I learn everything I need to know from the Web?

No doubt, there are a host of Java books on the market. We didn't wake up one morning and say, "You know what the world *really* needs? Another book about Java!" No. What we realized was that there are a couple of "holes" in the Java book market.

First, Linux as a development platform and deployment platform for Java applications has been largely ignored. This is despite the fact that the *nix platform (meaning all UNIX and UNIX-like systems, Linux included) has long been recognized as one of the most programmer-friendly platforms in existence. Those few resources for Java on Linux that exist emphasize tools to the exclusion of the Java language and APIs.

Second, books on the Java language and APIs have focused on pedagogical examples that serve to illustrate the details of the language and its libraries, but very few of these examples are in themselves practically useful, and they tend to deal only with the issues of writing programs, and not at all with deploying and maintaining them. Anyone who has worked on a major software project, especially a software project that is developed and deployed in a business for a business, knows that designing and coding are only about half of the work involved. Yes, writing Java code is only slightly affected by the development and the deployment platform, but the process of releasing and maintaining such applications is significantly different between platforms.

To address these missing pieces, we decided to cover development and deployment of a Java application that has command-line, GUI, servlet, and enterprise components on a Linux platform. We're writing the guide book we wish we had had when we started writing and deploying Java applications on Linux. We're going to show you a simplistic enterprise application, "from cradle to grave," but along the way cover issues of design process, production environment, setup, administration, and maintenance that few books bother to cover.[1]

If you are considering buying this book and you are wondering if there is any information in here that you can't get for free on the Web, then, no. There is not. In fact, there is little information in any Java or Linux book that is not available for free on the Internet. In fact, in each of our chapters we will tell you where on the Web to find virtually all of the information we present, and then some. And yet books continue to sell, and we have the *chutzpah* to ask you to buy the book. The reason is that Web information is scattered, unorganized, and of highly variable quality. We will be trying to bring all the relevant information together in this book, in a clearly organized manner (and, we would like to believe, at an acceptably high level of quality). We think that has value.

Also, this book is part of the Bruce Perens' Open Source Series. This book is part of the Web literature. And you may freely read it and use it on the Web. We hope this book will be one of those you use on the Web and buy on paper. We don't know about you, but we like to use Web books for reference, but for reading, we like books. We own at least three books that are available for free on the Web: *Thinking in C++*, *Thinking in Java*, and O'Reilly's *Docbook: The Definitive Guide*. We hope that open publishing will be the new model.

---

1. This is not to say this book is without purely pedagogical examples. Especially in Part I we make use of your typical "throwaway" examples and single classes. To try to illustrate the basics with a complete application would obscure and confuse the points being illustrated.

FREE SOFTWARE AND JAVA

GNU/Linux[2] is Free Software. It is Open Source. I don't even want to start the debate on what each term means and which one is "right." One of the two authors of this book is a Free Software advocate, and the other is of a purely laissez-faire attitude towards the question (we won't tell you which, although we invite you to guess). But even with a deliberate decision to cease-fire, the question remains: Is Java Open Source or Free Software?

The answer is mixed. Neither Sun's nor IBM's Java implementations are Open Source or Free Software. You may download and use them for free, but you do not have the source code to them, nor do you have the right to make modifications to them.[3] This book will cover the GNU Compiler for Java, which compiles Java source code to native machine code. The GNU Compiler for Java (**gcj**) is both Open Source and Free Software. It is, however, supporting differing levels of the Java APIs (some packages are current, some are back at 1.1.x levels) and does not fully support the AWT or Swing GUIs.

However, none of this means that you cannot write your own Java programs and release them under a Free Software or Open Source license. So you can certainly develop Free Software in Java. Staunch Free Software partisans (such as Richard Stallman and the Free Software Foundation) would question the wisdom of doing so. Their argument would be that a Free Software product that depends on non-Free tools isn't really Free Software, since to compile, use, or modify it, you need to make use of a proprietary tool.

There is more than one effort to produce a Free Software Java runtime implementation. None of them is "ready for prime time." It would, in our opinion, be a very good thing for Sun to release their SDK and Java Virtual Machine as Free Software. But so far, they have steadily resisted calls to do so.

---

2. This is the only time we will refer to it as "GNU/Linux." See Section 7.3 for the story of why GNU/Linux is the preferred name of some. We understand Stallman and the FSF's position, but "Linux" is much easier on the eyes and ears than "GNU/Linux." And that, not principle, is how names and words go into the language. For better or for worse, "Linux" is the name of the operating system.

3. As we write this, a very public discussion is taking place between Sun, IBM, and Eric Raymond, founder of the Open Source Initiative, about opening Java under some sort of open source license. At this time, no one knows how this will turn out, but it is possible that Java will be Free Software in the future.

The fact, however, that two distinct vendors (Sun and IBM) produce effectively interchangeable development and runtime environments reduces some of the risk that you face when you select a platform available only from a single vendor who does not provide source code.

So, to put the case firmly: Java is free for use, but it is certainly not Free Software as defined in *The GNU Manifesto*[4] or the GNU General Public License.[5] This is a political and philosophical issue of interest only to those aforementioned Free Software partisans. For the rest of us, this has no bearing on Java's technical or business merits. As for us, obviously we like the language or we wouldn't be writing about it.

YOU CAN HELP!

This book is part of the Bruce Perens' Open Source Series. Shortly after this book is published in dead-tree form, it will be on the Web,[6] free for use, redistribution, and modification in compliance with the terms of the Open Publication License,[7] with no options taken. You can immediately create your own version as permitted in that license.

Naturally enough, we plan to maintain our "official" version of the online book, so we encourage you to send suggestions, corrections, extensions, comments, and ideas to us. Please send any such to `javalinux@multitool.net` and we will try to keep our little tome up-to-date so it continues to serve the needs of the Java and Linux development communities.

ACKNOWLEDGMENTS

First off, we naturally wish to thank Mark L. Taub, our acquisitions editor at Prentice Hall PTR, for believing in the book and in open publishing as the way to put it out there. We also want to thank Bruce Perens for lending his name and powers of persuasion to open-content publishing through the Prentice Hall PTR Bruce Peren's Open Source Series. Thanks, too, to Patrick Cash-Peterson

---

4. `http://www.gnu.org/gnu/manifesto.html`

5. `http://www.gnu.org/copyleft/gpl.html`

6. `http://www.javalinuxbook.com/`

7. `http://www.opencontent.org/openpub/`

and Tyrrell Albaugh, who worked as our in-house production contacts, for all the behind-the-scenes work they did, including overseeing the cover.

In more direct terms of content, we owe major thanks to Kirk Vogen of IBM Consulting in Minneapolis for his article on using SWT with **gcj**, and for his kind help in allowing us to use the ideas he first presented in his IBM developerWorks articles. In more direct terms of content, we owe major thanks to: Kirk Vogen of IBM Consulting in Minneapolis for his article on using SWT with **gcj**, and for his kind help in allowing us to use ideas he first presented in his IBM developerWorks articles; and to Deepak Kumar[8] for graciously allowing us to base our `build.xml` file for EJBs off of a version that he wrote.

Thanks, too, to Andrew Albing for his help in drawing some of our diagrams, and to George Logajan and to Andy Miller for sharing their insights on the more intricate details of Swing.

We also wish to express our great indebtedness to our technical reviewers, especially Andrew Hayes, Steve Huseth, and Dan Moore. A very large thank-you is also due to Alina Kirsanova whose eye for detail, endless patience, and tenacity, and overall talent with proofing, layout, and more added so much refinement and improvement to the book. We are greatful for all their contributions. Any errors or omissions in this text are our fault and certainly not theirs. The book is much stronger for all their efforts.

There are likely many more people we ought to thank, especially those at Prentice Hall PTR, whose names and contributions we may never know, but we do know that this was an effort of many more people than just the authors, and we are grateful to them all.

---

8. http://www.roseindia.net/

Introduction

This book has the unfortunate burden of serving a diverse set of audiences. We realize that this book might appeal to both experienced Java programmers who are new to Linux, and to experienced Linux programmers who are new to Java, with all possible shadings in between.

In addition to balancing these two poles, we are also trying to strike a balance between the size of the book and the range of our topic. Fortunately, there is today quite a range of both book and Web publishing on both Java and Linux, so we are able to do our best within the limits of a book a normal person may lift, and we can make recourse to a number of outside references you might wish to use to supplement our efforts.

WHO SHOULD BUY THIS BOOK

If you are an experienced Java programmer, but quite new to Linux, and you have been looking for information on the tools available to develop and deploy Java applications on Linux systems, this book will provide a lot of useful information.

If you are an experienced Linux user or developer, and you are interested in using the Java language on that platform, this book will guide you through some advanced Java development topics and will present, we hope, some novel uses for familiar Linux and GNU tools.

If you are a rank beginner to either Linux or Java, we still think this book has value, but we would recommend that you use it in conjunction with more introductory books. For a basic introduction to Java and object-oriented programming, we recommend Bruce Eckel's excellent book, *Thinking in Java* (ISBN 0-13-100287-2). For an introduction to Linux and its tools, we can recommend *The Linux Book* by David Elboth (ISBN 0-13-032765-4)[1] as an all-around title. We also list several other books in sections titled Resources throughout this book. Many books we recommend are not actually Linux-specific. Since Linux duplicates (in most respects) a UNIX platform, we do occasionally recommend books that are general to all *nix systems.

If you are a developer, contractor, or MIS development manager with more projects than budget, our book will introduce you to many solid tools that are free of license fees for the development and deployment of production Java applications. We are all being asked to do more with less all the time. In many (but certainly not all) cases, Free and Open Source software is an excellent way to do that.

WHO SHOULD NOT BUY THIS BOOK

Those looking for complete documentation on Java APIs and Linux-based Java application servers will be disappointed. Complete reference material on Free Software and Open Source Software may be found in book form, but it is most certainly out-of-date. And while this is an open-content book, we know full well that we will only be updating it as our "day jobs" permit. In other words, those seeking complete and current reference material should go to the Web.

Those who have a multimillion-dollar budget for applications development will probably be well served by commercial application server products. While we very much believe that Linux and Java on Linux are fully capable of supporting production environments, we recognize that products such as BEAWeblogic and IBM's WebSphere have large support organizations behind them, and

---

1. Note that we do tend to recommend titles from Pearson Education (our publishers), but that we by no means confine ourselves to that publisher.

(at least for now) a larger base of developers and contracting organizations with staff (variably) experienced in writing and supporting applications in these environments. Please note that you can run these products on Linux systems, and that they are part of the Linux-Java world. Our book does not cover them, however, both because they are well-covered elsewhere, and because we have chosen to emphasize the Free and Open Source tools merely to keep the book small enough to lift, while still covering those tools most in need of well-written supporting documentation.

HOW TO USE THIS BOOK

There are many approaches to a book. Some people like to start with the last chapter to see how it all turns out in the end; others like to start at the front and master each topic before moving on; some read through quickly, then reread for detail; still others prefer to skip around, "cherry picking" topics as whim and fancy strike. We hope this book will work for you, whatever your style.

Each chapter is not really free-standing, nor is it intricately tied to the previous chapters. If we were writing in depth on a single topic we might be able to build chapter by chapter. Instead, we've tackled an immense amount of information in hopes of condensing it down to give a good overview, to give you a glimpse of the possibilities, and to whet your appetite for more. Some chapters will be strongly related to previous chapters; others you may be able to read without having read any of the preceding chapters—it will depend on the topic.

Many Paths

What we're describing below are a few possible paths that you might take through the book, depending on what you bring to the task—your experience and skills, your patience and persistence. We have tried to pack a lot of useful and practical information into these few chapters, distilling down the most important topics for each subject area. We hope that, even for the most experienced of our readers, we still offer, if not some new facts, at least some fresh explanations that might give you new insight into familiar topics.

The Linux Newbie Path

If you are new to Linux, then you'll want to start with the first two chapters. If you are already experienced in Java, feel free to skip Chapter 3, but you may want at least to skim Chapters 4 and 5. You will definitely want to check out Chapter 7 as we are almost sure that it is something you didn't know about.

Chapter 8 is another topic you may not have encountered outside of Linux, although CVS is not limited to Linux environments. Beyond that, it will depend on what else you already know. See what other categories, below, might fit your situation.

The Java Newbie Path

If you are new to Java, then be sure to read Chapters 3 and 4, but if you are not already an experienced programmer you should probably bring along another, more introductory text.

Chapters 5 and 10 will give you some good background for choosing your Java development tools. So many Java projects these days are tied to Ant that you should also cover Chapter 9 if you don't already know the tool.

With your experience in other languages you may have done a lot of unit testing; read about the approach most popular with Java developers in Chapter 13.

The Client-Side Path

Depending on what type of Java development that you hope to do, you may want to concentrate on certain parts of the latter half of the book. Those most interested in the front end or client side should focus on the middle chapters. Of most interest to you will be Chapters 16 and 17. Your client-side emphasis should also include Chapters 18 and 19.

The Server-Side Path

For those with an emphasis on the middle and third tier, or those with a general server emphasis, all of Part IV will be helpful. This is in addition to a solid grounding in the previous chapters in Parts I and II.

The Enterprise Path

The final Part V will discuss enterprise scale software. Such software also typically includes JSP and Servlet software, as covered in Chapters 18, 19, and 20.

For those working at this level, the projects are usually large enough to be staffed with a variety of roles. Even if your role doesn't include the deployment of the software, we encourage you to read these chapters (20 and 24) so as to get some understanding of what is needed and how it fits together.

Now, let's get to work, and discover some of the amazing capabilities available to you when you combine two of the most powerful software trends in the history of computing—Java and Linux.

Part I

Getting Started

Chapter 1

An Embarrassment of Riches: The Linux Environment

The reader is introduced to the vast possibilities of the Linux command line, and excuses are made for its eclecticism.

1.1 WHAT YOU WILL LEARN

Some basic shell commands are described in this chapter, especially those related to some common programming tasks. Used as a toolkit, they can be a handy collection of tools for everyday use.

Linux provides an incredible array of such tools, useful for any development effort, Java or otherwise. They will be important not only for the development of your Java code, but for all the hundreds of related housekeeping tasks associated with programming and with managing your development environment. A few tools are described briefly in this chapter, to hint at what can be done and to whet your appetite for more.

We will also describe a command which will help you learn about other commands. Even so, it may be quite worth your while to have another book about UNIX/Linux handy. If there is something you, as a programmer, need to do on a Linux system, chances are there is already a command (or a sequence of commands) which will do it.

Finally, we will discuss the extent of our remaining ignorance upon finishing the chapter.

Let us take a moment to explain that last comment. As readers of computer books ourselves, we are often frustrated when we discover how lightly a topic has been covered, but particularly so when other parts of the same book are found to fully explore their topics. When only some parts of a book are thorough, you often don't know that you don't know it all. We will introduce some basic shell concepts and commands here, and we may expand on some of these in later chapters, but each of our chapters covers topics that could each fill its own book. Therefore we need to leave out lots of material. We will also let you know when we have left things out because they are off-topic, or because we don't have room. We'll also try to tell you where to look for the rest of the knowledge. We try to sum this up in a final section of each chapter entitled What You Still Don't Know. But we do have a lot of information to impart, so let's get going.

1.2 THE COMMAND LINE: WHAT'S THE BIG DEAL?

One of the revolutionary things that UNIX (and thus Linux) did was to separate operating system commands from the operating system itself. The commands to display files, show the contents of directories, set permissions, and so on were, in the "olden days," an integral part of an operating system. UNIX removed all that from the operating system proper, leaving only a small "kernel" of necessary functionality in the operating system. The rest became executables that lived outside of the operating system and could be changed, enhanced, or even replaced individually by (advanced) users without modifying the operating system. The most significant of these standalone pieces was the command processor itself, called the shell.

The shell is the program that takes command-line input, decides what program(s) you are asking to have run, and then runs those programs. Before there were Graphical User Interfaces, the shell was *the* user interface to UNIX. As more developers began working with UNIX, different shells were developed to provide different features for usability. Now there are several shells to choose from, though the most popular is **bash**. Some BSD/UNIX die hards still swear by **csh**, a.k.a. the *C-shell*, though most of its best features have been incorporated into **bash**.

> **TIP**
>
> There are actually quite a few shells to choose from, and several editors for entering text. Our recommendation: If you learn only one shell, learn **bash**. If you learn only one editor, learn **vi**. Some basic shell scripting will go a long way to eliminating mundane, repetitive tasks. Some basic **vi** editing will let you do things so much faster than what GUI editors support. (More on editing in Chapter 2.)

Since commands could be developed and deployed apart from the operating system, UNIX and Linux have, over the years, had a wide variety of tools and commands developed for them. In fact, much of what is called *Linux* is really the set of GNU tools which began development as Open Source long before Linux even existed. These tools, while not technically part of the operating system, are written to work atop any UNIX-like operating system and programmers have come to expect them on any Linux system that they use. Some commands and utilities have changed over the years, some are much the same as they first were in the early days of UNIX.

Developers, encouraged by the openness of Open Source (and perhaps having too much free time on their hands) have continued to create new utilities to help them get their job done better/faster/cheaper. That Linux supports such a model has helped it to grow and spread. Thus Linux presents the first time user with a mind-boggling array of commands to try to learn. We will describe a few essential tools and help you learn about more.

1.3 BASIC LINUX CONCEPTS AND COMMANDS

There are some basic Linux commands and concepts that you should know in order to be able to move around comfortably in a Linux filesystem. Check your knowledge of these commands, and if need be, brush up on them. At the end of the chapter, we list some good resources for learning more about these and other commands. Remember, these are commands that you type, not icons for clicking, though the windowing systems will let you set up icons to represent those commands, once you know what syntax to use.

So let's get started. Once you've logged in to your Linux system, regardless of which windowing system you are using—KDE, Gnome, Window Maker, and so on, start up an xterm window by running **xterm** (or even **konsole**) and you'll be ready to type these commands.[1]

1.3.1   Redirecting I/O

The second great accomplishment of UNIX,[2] carried on into its Linux descendants, was the concept of redirecting input and output (I/O). It was based on the concept of a standardized way in which I/O would be done, called *standard I/O*.

1.3.1.1   *Standard I/O*

A familiar concept to Linux developers is the notion of standard I/O. Virtually every Linux process begins its life with three open file descriptors—standard in, standard out, and standard error. Standard in is the source of input for the process; standard out is the destination of the process' output; and standard error is the destination for error messages. For "old fashioned" command-line applications, these correspond to keyboard input for standard in and the output window or screen for both standard out and error.

A feature of Linux that makes it so adaptable is its ability to redirect its I/O. Programs can be written generically to read from standard in and write to standard out, but then when the user runs the program, he or she can change (or redirect) the source (in) or destination (out) of the I/O. This allows a program to be used in different ways without changing its code.

Redirecting I/O is accomplished on the Linux shell command line by the "<" and ">" characters. Consider the **ls** program which lists the contents of a directory. Here is a sample run of **ls**:

```
$ ls
afile     more.data     zz.top
$
```

---

1. If you're not using a windowing system, these commands are typed at the shell prompt that you get after you log in. But if you're not using a windowing system, either you're not a beginner (and don't need this introduction) or you can't get your windowing system to work, in which case you may need more help that we can give you here.

2. Yes, we are aware that much of UNIX actually comes from the Multics project, but we credit UNIX with popularizing it.

We can redirect its output to another location, a file, with the ">" character:

```
$ ls > my.files
$
```

The output from the **ls** command no longer appears on the screen (the default location of standard out); it has been redirected to the file `my.files`.

What makes this so powerful a construct (albeit for a very simple example) is the fact that not only was no change to the program required, but the programmer who wrote the **ls** program also did nothing special for I/O. He simply built the program to write to standard out. The shell did the work of redirecting the output. This means that any program invoked by the shell can have its output similarly redirected.

Standard error is another location for output, but it was meant as the destination for error messages. For example, if you try to list the contents of a nonexistent directory, you get an error message:

```
$ ls bogus
ls: bogus: No such file or directory
$
```

If you redirect standard out, nothing changes:

```
$ ls bogus > save.out
ls: bogus: No such file or directory
$
```

That's because the programmer wrote the program to send the message to standard error, not standard out. In the shell (**bash**) we can redirect standard error by preceding the redirect symbol with the number 2, as follows:[3]

```
$ ls bogus 2> save.out
$
```

---

3. The use of the number 2 comes from an implementation detail: All the I/O descriptors for a UNIX process were kept in an array. The first three elements of the array, numbered 0, 1, and 2, were defined to be the standard in, out, and err, in that order. Thus in the shell you can also redirect standard out by using "1>" as well as the shorter ">".

Note there is no output visible from **ls**. The error message, `ls: bogus: No such file or directory`, has been written to the file `save.out`.

In a similar way standard input (`stdin`) can be redirected from its default source, the keyboard.

As an example, we'll run the `sort` program. Unless you tell it otherwise, `sort` will read from `stdin`—that is, the keyboard. We type a short list of phrases and then type a `^D` (a Control-D) which won't really echo to the screen as we have shown but will tell Linux that it has reached the end of the input. The lines of text are then printed back out, now sorted by the first character of each line. (This is just the tip of the iceberg of what `sort` can do.)

```
$ sort
once upon a time
a small creature
came to live in
the forest.
^D
a small creature
came to live in
once upon a time
the forest.
```

Now let's assume that we already have our text inside a file called `story.txt`. We can use that file as input to the `sort` program by redirecting the input with the "<" character. The `sort` doesn't know the difference. Our output is the same:

```
$ sort < story.txt
a small creature
came to live in
once upon a time
the forest.
```

1.3.1.2   *Pipes*

The output from one command can also be sent directly to the input of another command. Such a connection is called a *pipe*. Linux command-line users also use "pipe" as a verb, describing a sequence of commands as *piping* the output of one command into another. Some examples:

```
$ ls  | wc > wc.fields
$ java MyCommand < data.file | grep -i total > out.put
```

The first example runs **ls**, then pipes its output to the input of the **wc** program. The output of the **wc** command is redirected to the file wc.fields. The second example runs **java**, giving it a class file named MyCommand. Any input that this command would normally read from keyboard input will be read this time from the file data.file. The output from this will be piped into **grep**, and the output from **grep** will be put into out.put.

Don't worry about what these commands really do. The point of the example is to show how they connect. This has wonderful implications for developers. You can write your program to read from the keyboard and write to a window, but then, without any change to the program, it can be instructed to read from files and write to files, or be interconnected with other programs.

This leads to a modularization of functions into small, reusable units. Each command can do a simple task, but it can be interconnected with other commands to do more, with each pipeline tailored by the user to do just what is needed. Take **wc** for example. Its job is to count words, lines, and characters in a file. Other commands don't have to provide an option to do this; any time you want to count the lines in your output, just pipe it into **wc**.

1.3.2 The ls Command

The **ls** command is so basic, showing the names of files in a directory. Be sure that you know how to use these options:

- ls lists the files in a directory.
- ls -l is the long form, showing permissions, ownership, and size.
- ls -ld doesn't look inside the directory, so you can see the directory's permissions.
- ls -lrt shows the most recently modified files last, so you can see what you've just changed.

1.3.3 Filenames

Filenames in Linux can be quite long and composed of virtually any character. Practically speaking, however, you're much better off if you limit the length to something reasonable, and keep to the alphanumeric characters, period, and the underscore ("_"). That's because almost all the other punctuation characters have a special meaning to the shell, so if you want to type them, you need to *escape* their special meaning, or suffer the results of unintended actions.

Filenames are case sensitive—upper- and lowercase names are different. The files `ReadMe.txt` and `readme.txt` could both be in the same directory; they are distinct files.

Avoid using spaces in filenames, as the shell uses whitespace to delineate between arguments on a command line. You *can* put a blank in a name, but then you always have to put the name in quotes to refer to it in the shell.

To give a filename more visual clues, use a period or an underscore. You can combine several in one filename, too. The filenames `read_me_before_you_begin` or `test.data.for_my_program` may be annoyingly long to type, but they are legal filenames.

> **NOTE**
>
> The period, or "dot," in Linux filenames has no special meaning. If you come from the MS-DOS world, you may think of the period as separating the filename from the extension, as in `myprogrm.bas` where the filename is limited to eight characters and the extension to three characters. Not so in Linux. There is no "extension," it's all just part of the filename.
>
>   You will still see names like `delim.c` or `Account.java`, but the `.c` or `.java` are simply the last two characters or the last five characters, respectively, of the filenames. That said, certain programs will insist on those endings for their files. The Java compiler will insist that its source files end in `.java` and will produce files that end in `.class`—but there is no special part of the filename to hold this. This will prove to be very handy, both when you name your files and when you use patterns to search for files (see below).

1.3.4 Permissions

Permissions in Linux are divided into three categories: the *owner* of a file (usually the user who created it), the *group* (a collection of users), and *others*, meaning everyone who is not the owner and not in the group. Any file belongs to a single owner and, simultaneously, to a single group. It has separate read/write/execute permissions for its owner, its group, and all others. If you are the owner of a file, but also a member of the group that owns the file, then the owner permissions are what counts. If you're not the owner, but a member of the group, then the group permissions will control your access to the file. All others get the "other" permissions.

If you think of the three permissions, read/write/execute, as three bits of a binary number, then a permission can be expressed as an octal digit—where the most significant bit represents read permission, the middle bit is write permission, and the least significant bit is execute permission. If you think of the three categories, user/group/others, as three digits, then you can express the permissions of a file as three octal digits, for example "750". The earliest versions of this command required you to set file permissions this way, by specifying the octal number. Now, although there is a fancier syntax (for example, g+a), you can still use the octal numbers in the **chmod** command. See the example below.

The fancier, or more user-friendly, syntax uses letters to represent the various categories and permissions. The three categories of user, group, and other are represented by their first letters: u, g, and o. The permissions are similarly represented by r, w, and x. (OK, we know "x" is not the first letter, but it is a reasonable choice.) For both categories and permissions, the letter a stands for "all." Then, to add permissions, use the plus sign (+); to remove permissions, use the minus sign (-). So g+a means "add all permissions to the group category," and a+r means "add read permissions to all categories."

Be sure that you know these commands for manipulating permissions:

- **chmod** changes the *mode* of a file, where mode refers to the read/write/execute permissions.
- **chown** changes the owner of a file.[4]
- **chgrp** changes the group owner of a file.

Table 1.1 shows some common uses of these commands.

Table 1.1 Changing permissions

Command	Explanation
chmod a+r file	Gives everyone read permission.
chmod go-w file	Takes away write permission from group, others.
chmod u+x file	Sets up a shell script so you can execute it like a command.
chmod 600 file	Sets permission to read and write for the owner but no permissions for anyone else.

---

4. On Linux the use of this command is restricted to the superuser, or "root."

1.3.5   File Copying

Do you know these commands?

- **mv**
- **cp**
- **ln**

The **mv** command (short for "move") lets you move a file from one place in the hierarchy of files to another—that is, from one directory to another. When you move the file, you can give it a new name. If you move it without putting it in a different directory, well, that's just renaming the file.

- `mv Classy.java Nouveau.java`
- `mv Classy.java /tmp/outamy.way`
- `mv Classx.java Classz.java ..`
- `mv /usr/oldproject/*.java .`

The first example moves `Classy.java` to a new name, `Nouveau.java`, while leaving the file in the same directory.

The second example moves the file named `Classy.java` from the current directory over to the `/tmp` directory and renames it `outamy.way`—unless the file `outamy.way` is an already existing directory. In that case, the file `Classy.java` will end up (still named `Classy.java`) inside the directory `outamy.way`.

The next example just moves the two Java source files up one level, to the parent directory. The ".." is a feature of every Linux directory. Whenever you create a directory, it gets created with two links already built in: ".." points to its parent (the directory that contains it), and "." points to the directory itself.

A common question at this point is, "Why does a directory need a reference to itself?" Whatever other reasons there may be, it certainly is a handy shorthand to refer to the current directory. If you need to move a whole lot of files from one directory to another, you can use the "." as your destination. That's the fourth example.

The **cp** command is much like the **mv** command, but the original file is left right where it is. In other words, it copies files instead of moving them. So:

```
cp Classy.java Nouveau.java
```

will make a copy of `Classy.java` named `Nouveau.java`, and:

```
cp Classy.java /tmp
```

will make a copy of `Classy.java` in the `/tmp` directory, and:

```
cp *.java /tmp
```

will put the copies of all the Java sources in the current directory to the `/tmp` directory.

If you run this command,

```
ln Classy.java /tmp
```

you might think that **ln** copies files, too. You will see `Classy.java` in your present working directory and you will see what appears to be a copy of the file in the `/tmp` directory. But if you edit your local copy of `Classy.java` and then look at the "copy" that you made in the `/tmp` directory, you will see the changes that you made to your local file now also appear in the file in the `/tmp` directory.

That's because **ln** doesn't make a copy. It makes a *link*. A link is just another name for the same contents. We will discuss linking in detail later in the book (see Section 6.2.1).

1.3.6   Seeing Stars

We need to describe shell pattern matching for those new to it. It's one of the more powerful things that the shell (the command processor) does for the user—and it makes all the other commands seem that much more powerful.

When you type a command like we did previously:

```
mv /usr/oldproject/*.java .
```

the asterisk character (called a "star" for short) is a shorthand to match *any* characters, which in combination with the `.java` will then match any file in the `/usr/oldproject` directory whose name ends with `.java`.

There are two significant things to remember about this feature. First, the star and the other shell pattern matching characters (described below) do *not* mean the same as the regular expressions in **vi** or other programs or languages. Shell pattern matching is similar in concept, but quite different in specifics.

Second, the pattern matching is done by the shell, the command interpreter, *before* the arguments are handed off to the specific command. Any text with these special characters is replaced, by the shell, with one or more filenames that match the pattern. This means that all the other Linux commands (**mv**, **cp**, **ls**, and so on) never see the special characters—they don't do the pattern matching, the shell does. The shell just hands them a list of filenames.

The significance here is that this functionality is available to any and every command, including shell scripts and Java programs that you write, with no extra effort on your part. It also means that the syntax for specifying multiple files doesn't change between commands—since the commands don't implement that syntax; it's all taken care of in the shell before they ever see it. Any command that can handle multiple filenames on a command line can benefit from this shell feature.

If you're familiar with MS-DOS commands, consider the way pattern matching works (or doesn't work) there. The limited pattern matching you have available for a **dir** command in MS-DOS doesn't work with other commands—unless the programmer who wrote that command also implemented the same pattern matching feature.

What are the other special characters for pattern matching with filenames? Two other constructs worth knowing are the question mark and the square brackets. The "?" will match any *single* character.

The [...] construct is a bit more complicated. In its simplest form, it matches any of the characters inside; for example, [abc] matches any of a or b or c. So Version[123].java would match a file called Version2.java but not those called Version12.java or VersionC.java. The pattern Version*.java would match all of those. The pattern Version?.java would match all except Version12.java, since it has two characters where the ? matches only one.

The brackets can also match a range of characters, as in [a-z] or [0-9]. If the first character inside the brackets is a "^" or a "!", then (think "not") the meaning is reversed, and it will match anything but those characters. So Version[^0-9].java will match VersionC.java but not Version1.java. How would you match a "-", without it being taken to mean a range? Put it first inside the brackets. How would you match a "^" or "!" without it being understood as the "not"? *Don't* put it first.

Some sequences are so common that a shorthand syntax is included. Some other sequences are not sequential characters and are not easily expressed as a range, so a shorthand is included for those, too. The syntax for these special sequences is `[:name:]` where *name* is one of: `alnum`, `alpha`, `ascii`, `blank`, `cntrl`, `digit`, `graph`, `lower`, `print`, `punct`, `space`, `upper`, `xdigit`. The phrase `[:alpha:]` matches any alphabetic character. The phrase `[:punct:]` matches any punctuation character. We think you got the idea.

1.3.6.1 Escape at Last

Of course there are always times when you want the special character to be just that character, without its special meaning to the shell. In that case you need to *escape* the special meaning, either by preceding it with a backslash or by enclosing the expression in single quotes. The commands `rm Account\$1.class` or `rm 'Account$1.class'` would remove the file even though it has a dollar sign in its name (which would normally be interpreted by the shell as a variable). Any character sequence in single quotes is left alone by the shell; no special substitutions are done. Double quotes still do some substitutions inside them, such as shell variable substitution, so if you want literal values, use the single quotes.

> **TIP**
>
> As a general rule, if you are typing a filename which contains something other than alphanumeric characters, underscores, or periods, you probably want to enclose it in single quotes, to avoid any special shell meaning.

1.3.7 File Contents

Let's look at a directory of files. How do you know what's there? We can start with an **ls** to list the names:

```
$ ls
ReadMe.txt    Shift.java   dispColrs   moresrc
Shift.class   anIcon.gif   jam.jar     moresrc.zip
$
```

That lists them alphabetically, top to bottom, then left to right, arranged so as to make the most use of the space while keeping the list in columns. (There are options for other orderings, single column, and so on.)

An `ls` without options only tells us the names, and we can make some guesses based on those names (for example, which file is Java source, and which is a compiled class file). The long listing `ls -l` will tell us more: permissions, links, owner, group, size (in bytes), and the date of last modification.

```
$ ls -l
total 2414
-rw-r--r--    1 albing     users           132 Jan 22 07:53 ReadMe.txt
-rw-r--r--    1 albing     users           637 Jan 22 07:52 Shift.class
-rw-r--r--    1 albing     users           336 Jan 22 07:55 Shift.java
-rw-r--r--    1 albing     users          1374 Jan 22 07:58 anIcon.gif
-rw-r--r--    1 albing     users          8564 Jan 22 07:59 dispColrs
-rw-r--r--    1 albing     users          1943 Jan 22 08:02 jam.jar
drwxr-xr-x    2 albing     users            48 Jan 22 07:52 moresrc
-rw-r--r--    1 albing     users       2435522 Jan 22 07:56 moresrc.zip
$
```

While **ls** is only looking at the "outside" of files,[5] there is a command that looks at the "inside," the data itself, and based on that, tries to tell you what kind of file it found. The command is called **file**, and it takes as arguments a list of files, so you can give it the name of a single file or you can give it a whole long list of files.

> **NOTE**
>
> Remember what was said about pattern matching in the shell: we can let the shell construct that list of files for us. We can give `file` the list of all the files in our current directory by using the "*" on the command line so that the shell does the work of expanding it to the names of all the files in our directory (since any filename will match the star pattern).

```
$ file *
ReadMe.txt:   ASCII text
Shift.class:  compiled Java class data, version 45.3
Shift.java:   ASCII Java program text
anIcon.gif:   GIF image data, version 89a, 26 x 26,
dispColrs:    PNG image data, 565 x 465, 8-bit/color RGB, non-interlaced
jam.jar:      Zip archive data, at least v2.0 to extract
moresrc:      directory
moresrc.zip:  Zip archive data, at least v1.0 to extract
$
```

---

5. Technically, `ls` (without arguments) need only read the directory, whereas `ls -l` looks at the contents of the inode in order to get all the other information (permissions, size, and so on), but it doesn't look at the data blocks of the file.

The **file** looks at the first several hundred bytes of the file and does a statistical analysis of the types of characters that it finds there, along with other special information it uses about the formats of certain files.

Three things to note with this output from **file**. First, notice that dispColrs was (correctly) identified as a PNG file, even without the .png suffix that it would normally have. That was done deliberately to show you that the type of file is based not just on the name but on the actual contents of the file.

Second, notice that the .jar file is identified as a ZIP archive. They really do use a identical internal format.

Thirdly, **file** is not foolproof. It's possible to have perfectly valid, compilable Java files that **file** thinks are C++ source, or even just English text. Still, it's a great first guess when you need to figure out what's in a directory.

Now let's look at a file. This simplest way to display its contents is to use **cat**.

```
$ cat Shift.java
import java.io.*;
import java.net.*;
/**
 * The Shift object
 */
public class
Shift
{
  private int val;

  public Shift() { }

  // ... and so on

} // class Shift
```

When a file is longer than a few lines you may want to use **more** or **less** to look at the file.[6] These programs provide a screen's worth of data, then pause

---

6. Like any open marketplace, the marketplace of ideas and open source software has its "me-too" products. Someone thought they could do even better than **more**, so they wrote a new, improved and largely upward compatible command. They named it **less**, on the minimalist philosophy (with apologies to Dave Barry: "I am not making this up") that "less is more." Nowadays, the **more** is rather passe. The **less** command has more features and has largely replaced it. In fact, on many Linux distributions, **more** is a link to **less**. In the name of full

for your input. You can press the space bar to get the next screen's worth of output. You can type a slash, then a string, and it will search forward for that string. If you have gone farther forward in the file than you wanted, press "b" to go backwards.

To find out more about the many, many commands available, press ? (the question mark) while it's running.

Typical uses for these commands are:

- To view one or more files, for example `more *.java`, where you can type `:n` to skip to the next file.
- To page through long output from a previous pipe of commands, for example, `$ grep Account *.java | more`, which will search (see more on **grep** below) for the string `Account` in all of the files whose names end in `.java` and print out each line that is found—and that output will be paginated by **more**.

If you need only to check the top few lines of a file, use **head**. You can choose how many lines from the front of the file to see with a simple parameter. The command `head -7` will write out the first seven lines, then exit.

If your interest is the last few lines of a file, use **tail**. You can choose how many lines from the end of the file to see; the command `tail -7` will write out the last seven lines of the file. But **tail** has another interesting parameter, `-f`. Though **tail** normally prints its lines and then, having reached the end of file, it quits, the `-f` option tells **tail** to wait after it prints the last few lines and then try again.[7] If some other program is writing to this file, then **tail** will, on its next read, find more data and print it out. It's a great way to watch a log file, for example, `tail -f /tmp/server.log`.

In this mode, **tail** won't end when it reaches the end of file, so when you want it to stop you'll have to manually interrupt it with a ^C (Control-C— i.e., hold down the Control key and press the C key).

---

disclosure, there is also a paging program called **pg**, the precursor to **more**, but we'll say no more about that.

7. The **less** command has the same feature. If you press "F" while looking at a file, it goes into an identical mode to the `tail -f` command. As is often the case in the wacky world of Linux, there is more than one way to do it.

1.3.8   The grep Command

No discussion of Linux commands would be complete without mentioning **grep**. Grep, an acronym for "generalized regular expression processor," is a tool for searching through the contents of a file. It searches not just for fixed sequences of characters, but can also handle regular expressions.

In its simplest form, `grep myClass *.java` will search for and display all lines from the specified files that contain the string `myClass`. (Recall that the `*.java` expansion is done by the shell, listing all the files that end with `.java`.)

The first parameter to **grep**, `myClass` in the example above, is the string that you want to search for. But the first nonoption parameter to **grep** is considered a regular expression meaning that it can contain special characters for pattern matching to make for more powerful searches (see Section 2.2.3). Some of the most common option parameters for **grep** are listed in Table 1.2.

Here's a quick example:

```
grep println *.java | grep -v System.out
```

It will look for every occurrence of `println` but then exclude those that contain `System.out`. Be aware that while it will exclude lines like

```
System.out.println(msg);
```

it will also exclude lines like this:

```
file.println(msg);     // I'm not using System.out
```

It is, after all, just doing string searches.

Table 1.2 Options for **grep**

Option	Explanation
-i	Ignore upper/lower case differences in its matching.
-l	Only list the filename, not the actual line that matched.
-n	Show the line number where the match was found.
-v	Reverses the meaning of the search—shows every line that *does not* match the pattern.

1.3.9   The find Command

If someone compiled a list of the top 10 most useful Linux utilities, **find** would most likely be near the top of the list. But it would also make the top 10 most confusing. Its syntax is very unlike other Linux utilities. It consists of *predicates*—logical expressions that cause actions and have true/false values that determine if the rest of the expression is executed. Confused? If you haven't used **find** before you probably are. We'll try to shed a little light by showing a few examples.

```
find . -name '*frag*' -print
```

This command looks for a file whose name contains `frag`. It starts looking in the current directory and descends into all subdirectories in its search.

```
find /over/there . /tmp/here -name '*frag*.java' -print
```

This command looks for a file that has `frag` in its name and ends with `.java`. It searches for this file starting in three different directories—the current directory ("`.`"), `/over/there`, and `/tmp/here`.

```
find . -name 'My[A-Z]*.java' -exec ls -l '{}' \;
```

Starting in the current directory, this command searches for a file whose name begins with `My` followed by an uppercase alphabetic character followed by anything else, ending with `.java`. When it finds such a file, it will execute a command—in this case, the **ls** command with the `-l` option. The braces are replaced with the name of the file that is found; the "`\;`" indicates to **find** the end of the command.

The `-name` is called a predicate; it takes a regular expression as an argument. Any file that matches that regular expression pattern is considered `true`, so control passes on to the next predicate—which in the first example is simply `-print` that prints the filename (to standard out) and is always `true` (but since no other predicate follows it in this example, it doesn't matter). Since only the names that match the regular expression cause the `-name` predicate to be `true`, only those names will get printed.

There are other predicates besides `-name`. You can get an entire list by typing `man find` at a command prompt, but Table 1.3 lists a few gems, to give you a taste of what **find** can do.

Let's look at an example to see how they fit together:

Table 1.3 Some **find** predicates

Option	Explanation
-type d	Is true if the file is a directory.
-type f	Is true if the file is a plain file (e.g., not a directory).
-mtime -5	Is true if the file is less than five days old, that is, has been modified within the last five days. A +5 would mean older than five days and a 5 with no sign means exactly five days.
-atime -5	Is true if the file was accessed within the last five days. The + and − mean greater and less than the specified time, as in the previous example.
-newer myEx.class	Is true if the file is newer than the file myEx.class.
-size +24k	Is true if the file is greater than 24K. The suffix c would mean bytes or characters (since b stands for 512-byte blocks in this context). The + and − mean greater and less than the specified size, as in the other examples.

```
$ find . -name '*.java' -mtime +90 -atime +30 -print
./MyExample.java
./old/sample/MyPrev.java
$
```

This command printed out the names of two files that end with .java found beneath the current directory. These files hadn't been modified in the last 90 days nor accessed within the last 30 days. The next thing you might want to do is to run this command again adding something at the end to remove these old files.

```
$ find . -name '*.java' -mtime +90 -atime +30 -print -exec rm '{}' \;
./MyExample.java
./old/sample/MyPrev.java
$
```

1.3.10 The Shell Revisited

Most Linux shells—the command interpreters—can be considered programming languages in their own right. That is, they have variables and control structures—if statements, for loops, and so on. While the syntax can be subtly different between shells, the basic constructs are all there.

Entire books can be—and have been—written on shell programming. (It's one of our favorite subjects to teach.) Programs written in the shell language are often called *shell scripts*. Such scripts can be powerful yet easy to write (once you are familiar with the syntax) and can make you very productive in dealing with all those little housekeeping tasks that accompany program development. All you need to do (dangerous words, no?) is to put commands in a text file and give the file execute permissions. But that's a subject for another day.

Some elements of shell scripting, however, are useful even if you never create a single shell script. Of these, perhaps the most important to know (especially for Java programmers) is how to deal with shell variables.

> **NOTE**
>
> We'll be describing the syntax for **bash**, the default shell on most Linux distributions. The syntax will differ for other shells, but the concepts are largely the same.

Any string of alphanumeric or underscore characters can be used as the name of a variable. By convention shell variables typically use uppercase names—but that is only convention (although it will hold true for most if not all of our examples, too). Since commands in Linux are almost always lowercase, the use of uppercase for shell variables helps them to stand out.

Set the value of a shell variable with the familiar method—the equal sign:

```
$ FILE=/tmp/abc.out
$
```

This has assigned the variable FILE the value /tmp/abc.out. But to make use of the value that is now in FILE, the shell uses syntax that might not be familiar to you: The name must be preceded with a "$".

Shell variables can be passed on to other environments if they are *exported*, but they can never be passed back up. To set a shell variable for use by your current shell and every subsequent subshell, export the variable:

```
$ export FILE
$
```

You can combine the assignment of a value with the exporting into one
step. Since repeating the export doesn't hurt, you will often see shell scripts use
the `export` command every time they do an assignment, as if it were part of
the assignment syntax—but you know better.

```
$ export FILE="/tmp/way.out"
$
```

> **NOTE**
>
> The shell uses the dollar sign to distinguish between the variable name and just
> text of the same letters. Consider the following example:
>
> ```
> $ echo first > FILE
> $ echo second  > TEXT
> $ FILE=TEXT
> $ cat FILE
> first
> $
> ```
>
> The `cat` command will dump the contents of the file named `FILE` to the
> screen—and you should see `first`. But how would you tell the shell that you
> want to see the contents of the file whose name you have put in the shell
> variable `FILE`? For that you need the "$":
>
> ```
> $ cat $FILE
> second
> $
> ```
>
> This is a contrived example, but the point is that shell syntax supports ar-
> bitrary strings of characters in the command line—some of them are filenames,
> others are just characters that you want to pass to a program. It needs a way
> to distinguish those from shell variables. It doesn't have that problem on the
> assignment because the "=" provides the needed clue. To say it in computer
> science terms, the "$" syntax provides the *R-value* of the variable. (Not the
> insulation R-value, but what you expect when a variable is used on the Right-
> hand-side of an assignment operator, as opposed to the *L-value* used on the
> Left-hand-side of an assignment operator.)

There are several shell variables that are already exported because they are
used by the shell and other programs. You may need or want to set them to
customize your environment. Since they are already exported, you won't need
to use the `export` command and can just assign a value, but it doesn't hurt.

The most important shell variable to know is PATH. It defines the directories in the filesystem where the shell will look for programs to execute. When you type a command like **ls** or **javac** the shell will look in all of the directories specified in the PATH variable, in the order specified, until it finds the executable.

```
$ echo $PATH
/usr/local/bin:/usr/bin:/usr/X11R6/bin:/bin:.
$
```

The PATH shown in the example has five directories, separated by colons (":"). (Note the fifth one, the "."; it says to look in the current directory.) Where do you suppose it will find cat? You can look for it yourself by searching in each directory specified in PATH. Or you can use the **which** command:

```
$ which cat
/bin/cat
$
```

Some commands (like exit) don't show up, since they are built into the shell. Others may be aliases—but that opens a whole other topic that we aren't covering here. Just remember that each directory in the PATH variable is examined for the executable you want to run. If you get a *command not found* error, the command may be there, it just may not be on your PATH.

To look at it the other way around: If you want to install a command so that you can execute it from the command line, you can either always type its full pathname, or (a more user-friendly choice) you can set your PATH variable to include the location of the new command's executable.

So where and how do you set PATH? Whenever a shell is started up, it reads some initialization files. These are shell scripts that are read and executed as if they were typed by the user—that is, not in a subshell. Among other actions, they often set values for variables like PATH. If you are using **bash**, look at .bashrc in your home directory.

Shell scripts are just shell commands stored in a file so that you don't need to type the same commands and options over and over. There are two ways to run a shell script. The easiest, often used when testing the script, is

```
$ sh myscript
```

where `myscript` is the name of the file in which you have put your commands. (See Chapter 2 for more on how to do that.) Once you've got a script running the way you'd like, you might want to make its invocation as seamless as any other command. To do that, change its permissions to include the execution permission and then, if the file is located in a place that your `PATH` variable knows about, it will run as a command. Here's an example:

```
$ chmod a+rx myscript
$ mv myscript ${HOME}/bin
$ myscript
... (script runs)
$
```

The file was put into the `bin` directory off of the home directory. That's a common place to put homebrew commands. Just be sure that `$HOME/bin` is in your `PATH`, or edit `.bashrc` and add it.

If you want to parameterize your shell, you'll want to use the variables `$1`, `$2`, and so on which are given the first, second, and so on parameters on the command line that you used to invoke your script. If you type `myscript Account.java` then `$1` will have the value `Account.java` for that invocation of the script.

We don't have the space to go into all that we'd like to about shell programming, but let us leave you with a simple example that can show you some of its power. Used in shell scripts, `for` loops can take a lot of drudgery out of file maintenance. Here's a simple but real example.

Imagine that your project has a naming convention that all Java files associated with the user interface on your project will begin with the letters "UI". Now suppose your boss decides to change that convention to "GUI" but you've already created 200 or more files using the old naming convention. Shell script to the rescue:

```
for i in UI*.java
do
  new="G${i}"
  echo $i ' ==> ' $new
  mv $i $new
done
```

You could just type those commands from the command line—that's the nature of shell syntax. But putting them into a file lets you test out the script without having to type it over and over, and keeps the correct syntax once you've got it debugged. Assuming we put those commands into a file called `myscript`, here's a sample run:

```
$ myscript
UI_Button.java  ==>  GUI_Button.java
UI_Plovar.java  ==>  GUI_Plovar.java
UI_Screen.java  ==>  GUI_Screen.java
UI_Tofal.java   ==>  GUI_Tofal.java
UI_Unsov.java   ==>  GUI_Unsov.java
...
$
```

Imagine having to rename 200 files. Now imagine having to do that with a point-and-click interface. It could take you all morning. With our shell script, it will be done in seconds.

We can't hope to cover all that we'd like to about shell scripting. Perhaps we have been able to whet your appetite. There are lots of books on the subject of shell programming. We've listed a few at the end of this chapter.

1.3.11 The tar and zip Commands

The **tar** and **zip** commands allow you to pack data into an archive or extract it back. They provide lossless data compression (unlike some image compression algorithms) so that you get back out exactly what you put in, but it can take up less space when archived.[8] Therefore **tar** and **zip** are often used for data backup, archival, and network transmission.

There are three basic actions that you can take with **tar**, and you can specify which action you want with a single letter[9] in the arguments on the command line. You can either

---

8. Well, technically, **tar** doesn't compress the data in the file, but it does provide a certain amount of "compression" by cutting off the tail ends of blocks of data; for example, a file of 37 bytes in its own file takes up 4K of disk space since disk blocks are allocated in "chunks" (not the technical term). When you **tar** together a whole bunch of files, those extra tail-end empty bytes are not used (except in the final block of the TAR file). So, for example, 10 files of 400 bytes could be packed into a single 4K file, instead of the 40K bytes they would occupy on the filesystem. So, while **tar** won't compress the data inside the file (and thus is quite assuredly "lossless") it does result in a smaller file.

9. Linux option strings always start with a "-", right? Yes, except for **tar**. It seems there is always an exception to every rule. The newer versions of **tar** allow the leading minus sign, but can also work without it, for historical compatibility reasons. Early versions of UNIX only had single

- c: Create an archive.
- x: Extract from an archive.
- t: Get a table of contents.

In addition, you'll want to know these options:

- f: The next parameter is the filename of the archive.
- v: Provide more verbose output.

Using these options, Table 1.4 shows examples of each of the basic functions.

Now let's do the same thing using the **zip** command (Table 1.5). There are actually two commands here—one to compress the files into an archive (**zip**), and the other to reverse the process (**unzip**).

Table 1.4 Examples of the **tar** command

Command	Explanation
tar tvf packedup.tar	Gives a table of contents, in long (or verbose) form. Without the v, all you get is the filenames; with the v you get additional information similar in format to the ls -l command.
tar xvf packedup.tar	Extracts all the files from the TAR file, creating them according to their specified pathname, assuming your user ID and file permissions allow it. Remove the v option if you don't want to see each filename as the file is extracted.
tar cvf packedup.tar mydir	Creates a TAR archive named packedup.tar from the mydir directory and its contents. Remove the v option if you don't want to see each filename as the file is added to the archive.

letter options. Newer POSIX versions of UNIX and the GNU tools, which means all flavors of Linux, also support longer full-word options prefixed with a double minus, as in --extract instead of x or -x.

Table 1.5 Examples of the **zip** and **unzip** commands

Command	Explanation
`unzip -l packedup.zip`	Gives a table of contents of the archive with some extra frill around the edges, like a count of the files in the archive.
`unzip packedup.zip`	Extracts all the files from the ZIP file, creating them according to their specified pathname, assuming your user ID and file permissions allow it. Add the quiet option with `-q` if you would like **unzip** not to list each file as it unzips it.
`zip -r packedup mydir`	Creates a ZIP archive named `packedup.zip` from the `mydir` directory and its contents. The `-r` tells **zip** to recursively descend into all the subdirectories, their subdirectories, and so on; otherwise, **zip** will just take the files at the first layer and go no deeper.

TIP

Since TAR and ZIP files can contain absolute as well as relative pathnames, it is a good idea to look at their contents (e.g., `tar tvf file`) before unpacking them, so that you know what is going to be written where.

There are many, many more options for **tar** and **zip** that we are not covering here, but these are the most common in our experience, and they will give you a good start.

The **tar** and **zip** commands are also worth knowing about by a Java developer because of their relationship to *JAR files*. If you are working with Java you will soon run across the notion of a Java ARchive file, or JAR file. They are recognizable by name, ending in `.jar`. Certain Java tools are built to understand the internal format of JAR files. For Enterprise Java (J2EE) there are similar archives known as WAR files and EAR files. The command syntax for dealing with the **jar** command that builds these archives is very similar to the basic commands of **tar**. The internal format of a **jar** is the same as a ZIP file. In fact, most places where you can use a JAR file you can use a ZIP file as well. (You will see more about this when we discuss the standard Java tools in Section 5.11.)

> **TIP**
>
> Here's one more handy example we know you'll use:
>
> ```
> find . -name '*.java' -print | zip allmysource -@
> ```
>
> This command starts in the current directory (".") finding every file that ends in
> .java and gives their names to **zip** which will read them from standard in in-
> stead of its argument list (told to do so with the -@ argument) and zip them all
> into an archive named allmysource.zip. To put it simply, it will zip up all
> your Java source files from the current directory on down.

1.3.12 The man Command

Primitive but handy, the **man** command (short for *manual*) was the early
UNIX online manual. While we've come to expect (and ignore) online help,
the idea of online manuals was rather revolutionary in the early days of UNIX.
In contrast to walls of printed documentation, UNIX provided terse but
definitive descriptions of its various commands. When they are done well, these
descriptions are an invaluable handy reference. They are not the best way to
learn about a command, but they can be a great guide to using the command's
options correctly.

The format is simply man followed by the name of the command about
which you want information. So man man will tell you about the **man**
command itself.

The most useful option to **man** is the -k option. It will do a keyword
search in the titles of all the manpages looking for the keyword that you give.
Try typing man -k java to see what commands are available. The (1) means
that it's a user command—something that you can type from the shell prompt,
as opposed to (2) which is a system call or (3) which is a C library call. These
numbers refer to the original UNIX documentation volumes (volume one was
shell commands and so on), and it all fit into a single three ring binder.

> **TIP**
>
> One other way to find out something about a command, if you know the com-
> mand name already, is to ask the command itself for help. Most commands
> have either a -? or --help option. Try --help first. If you need to type -?
> either put it in single quotes or type it with a backslash before the question mark,
> as in -\?, since the ? is a pattern-matching character to the shell.

There are other help systems available, such as **info** and some GUI-based ones. But **man** provides some of the quickest and most terse help when you need to check the syntax of a command or find out if there is an option that does what you need.

1.4 REVIEW

We've looked at commands that will show you where files are in your directory structure, show files' permissions and sizes, change the permissions, show you what is in a file, look for files by searching for strings, and look for files based on names or other properties.

Even so, we've given only the briefest coverage to only a few of the scores of Linux commands worth knowing. Tops among these is the shell, **bash** in our case. Whole books have been written on this subject, and you would do well to have one at hand.

1.5 WHAT YOU STILL DON'T KNOW

The shell is a powerful language in its own right. While you think of it mostly as a command interpreter used for running other commands, it is, in fact, a language, complete with variables, logic and looping constructs. We are not suggesting that you write your application in shell scripts, but you will find it useful for automating many repetitive tasks. There is so much that can be done with shell scripts that we encourage you to read more about this and to talk with other Linux users.

Linux is replete with so many different commands. Some are powerful languages like **awk** and **perl**, others are simple handy utilities like **head**, **tail**, **sort**, **tr**, and **diff**. There are hundreds of other commands that we don't even have time to mention.

1.6 RESOURCES

- Cameron Newham and Bill Rosenblatt, *Learning the Bash Shell*, O'Reilly Associates, ISBN 1565923472.
- Ellie Quigley, *Linux Shells by Example*, 4th ed., Prentice Hall PTR, ISBN 013147572X.

- Rafeeq Rehman and Christopher Paul, *The Linux Development Platform*, Prentice Hall PTR.
- Mark G. Sobell, *A Practical Guide to Linux*, Addison-Wesley, ISBN 0201895498.
- Mark G. Sobell, *A Practical Guide to Red Hat Linux*, Addison-Wesley, ISBN 0201703130.

Chapter 2

An Embarrassment of Riches: Editors

Here the joys of creating and changing text files are introduced, the rudiments of the venerable **vi** editor are presented, and the power of text is exalted.

2.1 WHAT YOU WILL LEARN

Readers are encouraged, but not required, to plumb the depths of **vi**. Other text editor choices are briefly covered.

Remember our recommendation: If you learn only one shell, learn **bash**. If you learn only one editor, learn **vi**. Some basic shell scripting will go a long way to eliminating mundane, repetitive tasks. Some basic **vi** editing will let you do things much faster than you can with GUI editors.

2.2 EYE TO EYE WITH VI

Java programs consist of Java classes. Java classes are text files with Java statements and expressions. In order to write a Java program, then, you need to be
able to enter text into a file. Sounds simple enough.

With Linux and its GNU tools, you have an amazing array of choices for
how to do this. Some are GUI tools not unlike simple word processors. Others,
like **vi** and Emacs, predate GUI tools, but provide much the same capability
without the luxury (or annoyance) of a mouse or menus.[1]

The editor named **vi** (pronounced as you would spell it: "vee-eye") is one
of the most enduring tools in Linux. Its popularity comes from a combination
of power and ubiquity—you can find it on virtually every release of UNIX and
Linux since 1985. But it is a powerful editor that can do a lot with only a few
keystrokes.

There are actually several variants of **vi** from which to choose. Each is
someone's attempt to go one better on **vi**, but all retain the same basic syntax
and what you learn here will work equally well on any of the **vi** clones. You can
choose among

- **elvis**
- **nvi**
- **vim**

Start up **vi** by typing the command name at a shell prompt, followed by
the name of the file(s) that you want to edit:

```
$ vi Account.java
```

Keep in mind that **vi** was developed in the days of character-only video
screens. Keyboards didn't always have arrow keys or other special characters,
which have since been (largely) standardized by the advent of the IBM PC. In
that situation, the authors of **vi** had only the alphabetic characters to use for all

---

1. We realize that **vi** is famous for being difficult to learn and nonintuitive. The UI design of
vi dates back to earliest cursor-addressable display terminals. User interface design has come a
long way since then. The **vi** UI does indeed show its age. But the program refuses to die. Why?
Because while simple GUI editors make the easy stuff easy, **vi** makes the hard stuff easy. You
can fall back on **pico** or **kate** or other GUI editors if you want, but bear with us. Mastering **vi**
really does pay off.

of their commands . . . and did they make good use of those keys! Virtually every letter is used, both lower and upper case, to mean something unique in **vi**. But don't be put off by the large number of commands to learn; they fit some patterns that will make it easy for you to become proficient in a short time by learning a few commands and applying the patterns.

> **NOTE**
>
> If you really can't bear to part with your mouse and menus, try **gvim**. We haven't used it, but we hear that it has support for mice to help with cut and paste and the like. After you learn **vi** and get a little practice, though, you may find that you're never reaching for your mouse any more when you edit.

There are three modes to **vi**: the regular *vi mode*, some extended commands in the *ex mode*, and the *input mode*.

The simplest mode is the input mode. In input mode, every character you type becomes part of the text of the file. It's how you enter the bulk of the text for your Java programs. But **vi** doesn't start up in input mode; you have to "get into" input mode, and then get back out. Once out, you can use other **vi** commands to save the text and exit **vi**. More about those in a bit.

> **NOTE**
>
> Get out of input mode by pressing the Escape key. You can press it more than once, too, just to be sure that you are no longer in input mode. If you are no longer in input mode and you press escape, it will beep at you—with an audible or visual notification, depending on how your terminal window is set to respond.

In both **vim** and **elvis** (two popular **vi** clones) there is a status line at the bottom of the window that will show if you are in input mode. In **vim**, look in the lower left and **elvis**, the lower right. When in input mode, you will see a status word displayed like *insert* or *replace*.

In the vi mode, the default mode that you start in, all the keystrokes are interpreted as commands to the editor. They are *not* displayed as characters. So when we describe a command, such as dt;, you can type those three characters but will not see those characters on your screen. Instead you will see some action taken by **vi**—in this case it will delete text from your cursor up to the first semicolon on that line, if any (otherwise it will just beep).

There are several ways to get into input mode, depending on where you want to do the insert. When the file you're editing is completely empty, all these commands are equivalent, but for nonempty files, each command will begin input mode in a different place in the file:

- i inserts before the cursor.
- I inserts at the beginning of the line.
- a appends after the cursor.
- A appends at the end of the line.
- o "opens" a line for input after the line on which the cursor sits.
- O "opens" a line for input before the line on which the cursor sits.

Remember that this is character-based editing, before the days of mice and I-bars. So there is no meta-character for the cursor to show its position *between* two characters in the file. Instead, the cursor sits on top of a character, and thus inserts or appends will happen before or after that character.

Reminder: Get out of input mode by pressing the Escape key.

Next, let's move the cursor around. The simplest way to do that is one character at a time. Using the (lowercase) h, j, k, and l keys—notice that they're all in a row on QWERTY keyboards—you have the "arrow" keys for left, down, up, and right. One of the common enhancements for **vi** clones is to include support for the arrow keys on standard PC keyboards. Even so, the convenience of having the motion keys on the "home row" for touch typists can be a great speedup.

- h moves left one character.
- j moves down one line.
- k moves up one line.
- l moves right one character; same as a space.

Often, character- or line-at-a-time is too slow. Move to the beginning of the line that you are on with 0 (zero), or to the end of the line with $. Move to the top and bottom of the window with H (think "High") and L (think "Low"). So first type L then hold down j. To move back in a file, first type H then hold down k. That gets the display moving down or up respectively.

- H ("high") moves to the top line of the window.
- M ("middle") moves to the middle line of the window.

- L ("low") moves to the bottom line of the window.
- 0 moves to the beginning of the line.
- $ moves to the end of the line.

This may still be too slow for you, especially if you are working your way through a large file. If you want to page up and down half a page at a time, try ^U and ^D (think "up" and "down"). To move a full page at each keystroke, try ^F and ^B (think "forward" and "back").

This may still take a while, especially if you want to get to the absolute beginning or end of the file. For those locations, type a three-character sequence, starting with a colon—which will jump your cursor to the status line of the window—then type either zero or the dollar sign, then press the Enter key. For example, :$.

So what's with the colon? Just when you thought you were getting the hang of the **vi** keystrokes, this odd pattern appears. It's called *ex mode*, and has to do with the history of **vi** being built atop the **ex** editor. Typing the colon got you back giving commands to **ex**, without the fancier screen-based GUI. (Even editors can have command lines.) There are many powerful search/replace commands that you can do from the ex command line; more on that later. For now, though, remember that you can type the colon, then a line number, then the Enter key and **vi** will position the cursor (and thus what is displayed on the screen) to that line number. The 0 and $ are just special cases of that more generic way to position your place in the file.

Back to our positioning in the file. Recall that h, j, k, and l will move you one unit (char or line) at a time. Now enhance that motion by typing a number first, then the h, j, k, or l. So to move five lines up type 5k (just be sure you use a lowercase letter). You can move way down in a file by typing something like 2000j which will move down 2,000 lines. If the file doesn't have that many lines, you will find your cursor at the end of the file.

The point here is that almost any **vi** command can be preceded by a count, to repeat it that many times.

A few more navigation tips. Another useful way to move through text is a word at a time. You can move your cursor forward by a word with the letter w (for "word"). You can move "back" with the letter b. You can move five words at a time with 5w or 5b. See?

The definition of "word" to **vi** has to do with alphanumerics separated by whitespace, but also by certain punctuation characters. So to **vi**, the following Java code consists of how many words? Seven.

```
myArraylist.doSomething(magical); // cool
```

From the beginning of the line, you'd need to type w seven times (or know to type 7w—but how could you guess seven?) To help out, **vi** uses the uppercase W to skip words defined not by punctuation but solely by white space. Think of it as "bigger" words. And of course B will go "back" by these bigger words. So on our example line, a single W will get you to the start of the comment.

Be sure that you're not just reading these descriptions. Run **vi** on any file that you can find and practice navigating by lines or words or screens. Once you get the hang of it, it can be so much faster than reaching for the mouse and trying to maneuver the cursor into just the right spot between letters.

Sometimes you can see where you want to go based on the characters of text in the document. See that "x"? That's a relatively rare character on any line of text. If you see a character, your cursor can "find" it if you type f and then the character you are looking for. So fx would search forward on the line for an "x". And Fx would search backward from the cursor. To repeat the search, just type a semicolon (" ; ").

Searching for a string is another good way to move your way through a file. To search forward, type a slash (/), then the characters for which you want to search, and end the string with a second slash and then Enter:[2]

```
/myArrayList/
```

To search backwards (towards the first line of the file) use the question mark rather than the slash to bracket your search string. In either case, to jump to the next occurrence, type n, or 27n to jump to the 27th occurrence. Whether you are searching forward (/) or backward (?), using uppercase N will reverse the direction as it searches for the next occurrence. So, you can search forward with /myVar/ and then press n for each next occurrence forward. If you go too far, just type N to back up. Similarly, if you were going backwards looking for an occurrence of a constructor, say something like: ?new HotClass?; then each n will search toward the top of the file, and each N will search toward the end of file.

---

2. The second slash is optional in most **vi** implementations, but used for consistency with the same command in ex mode which has optional suffix characters.

In both cases, when you hit the top or bottom of the file, **vi** will wrap and keep searching from the opposite end, though a warning message will appear in the status bar.

OK, enough navigation. Let's start modifying text.

Copy and paste operations can be done easily on whole lines. Just *yank* and *put* the lines. You can yank a single line or several at a time (e.g., 7y) and then a single put (p) will deposit a copy just after the current line (the line where your cursor sits). If you want to put the text before, not after, the current line, use uppercase P.

Go ahead. Try it on the file you're practicing on. It's the best way to get a feel for what we're describing here.

Cut and paste operations involve deleting the lines, not just copying them. This gets us into our third and final kind of syntax in **vi**, the double letter commands. Use dd to delete a line. Try it and you will find that the line your cursor is on just got deleted, and the cursor now rests comfortably on the next line. To paste that line back, use the same p or P that we used for to put the lines that we had copied (a.k.a. "yanked") above.

But why the dd? What's with the double letters? Think of "delete" for d and then add another letter to describe how much you want to delete—dw for "delete word" or dW for "delete the bigger words" (see above). So why dd for a line? We don't know for a fact, but we suspect that it's just for speed. You can also follow a d with the h, j, k, or l of our cursor movement, and that will delete either a character or a line in the appropriate direction.

A faster way (one keystroke, not two) to delete a single character is with the x key. And of course 5x, or 27x, will delete multiple characters. But if you're deleting many characters you will probably get it done faster by deleting "words" (dw or dW).

Another powerful way to delete text is to delete it from the cursor up *to* a specific character. The sequence dt; will delete from the cursor up to (but not including) the semicolon on the current line. If there is no semicolon, **vi** will beep, and no change will be made. To delete *from* the cursor up to and including the semicolon, use df;.

Everything you've just learned about delete is also true for change, the c in **vi**. You can combine it with itself (cc) to change a whole line. You can combine it with w to change a word (cw), or you can change from the cursor up to the next semicolon (ct;), and so on.

Change does the delete, then puts you in input mode. (Notice the reminder on the status line.) Remember, to get out of input mode and back into vi mode, press the Escape key.

Sometimes you've done too much, and you'd like to undo what you've just done. Typing u will undo the last change that you made. But here's a difference between the classic **vi** and some of the new, improved versions. In classic **vi**, if you type another u, then you are telling **vi** to undo what it just did—which was an undo. So the undo of an undo remakes the change that you had originally made. But in **vim**, "vi improved," typing u again and again will just keep undoing previous changes. If you want to undo the undo, in **vim**, you need to type :redo and then Enter.

The **vi** editor has shortcuts for helping you to change the indentation of your code. Typing two less-than signs (<<) will shift the line to the left; typing two greater-than signs (>>) will shift the line to the right. Typing a number first and then the less-than or greater-than signs will shift that many lines at once. But how far will they shift? The default is usually set at eight, but you can set it to any value you want. In ex mode you can set all sorts of values and flags, customizing **vi**'s operation. The value we're interested in here is shiftwidth which can be abbreviated sw. So the command would be :set sw=4 if you want each shift to move by four characters. For more about this, and how to make it your default, see Section 2.2.4.

Any command that you do may be worth repeating. Say, you just shifted 14 lines and you'd like to shift them further. Or you just deleted five lines, and would like to delete five more. Well, you could just retype the command, but an easier way is just to type the period (.) and let **vi** repeat it for you.

2.2.1 Exiting

There are three ways of exiting **vi** (ZZ, :q, :q!) that you should know. The correct one to use depends on whether or not you *want* to save the changes to the file and on whether or not you *have* saved your changes.

- ZZ saves and quits in one step (three keystrokes).
- :w writes what you've been editing but doesn't quit.
- :w *filename* writes what you've been editing to a new file named *filename*; it will complain (and not write out anything) if the file already exists.

- `:7,.w! filename` writes lines from line 7 up to and including the current line to the named file, clobbering any previous contents (think of the "!" as meaning "and don't argue with me!").

- `:q` quits, provided you've saved your changes (e.g., with `:w`).

- `:q!` quits without saving any changes to the file.

- `:n` doesn't exit **vi**, but moves on to the next file if you started up with more than one file to edit (e.g., `vi Fir.java Pine.java`). When you've reached the last file in the list, you need to quit—for example, with `:q`.

2.2.2   Search and Replace

We've mentioned searching for a string with / or ?, but what about replacing? Once you've located a string with /, you can use `cw` or `C` or `R` or other such commands to effect the change. Search for the next occurrence with n, and then you can repeat your change (the last `c`, `s`, `r`, and so on) by typing the period "." that will repeat that last substitution, insert, and so on.

But what if you want to make 225 substitutions? Typing `n.n.n.n.n.n.` would get old after a while. Here, the ex mode, like any good command line, comes to the rescue to help with repetitive tasks.

If we want to search and replace all occurrences of one string for another, we can use the command

```
:1,$s/one string/another/
```

Almost all ex commands take an *address range*, that is, the lines of the file over which they will operate. If just one line number is given, the command will operate on that one line. Two numbers, separated by commas, represent the start and end lines—inclusive—of the operation. The first line is line 1, so a 0 as line number would mean "before the first line." The line where the cursor is currently located is just "." (a period). The last line of the file can be represented by the dollar sign ($). You can even do some simple math on the addresses—for example, `.+2` meaning the second line in front of the cursor's current line.

> **TIP**
>
> There is a shortcut for the 1, $ address range. Use % to mean "all lines"—for example, `%s/one string/another/`.

Here are a few more substitution examples along with an explanation for each.

```
.,$s/here/eternity/
```
From here to the end of the file, replace here with eternity.

```
27,$-5s/lost/found/
```
From line 27 to the 5th line prior to the end of the file, replace lost with found.

```
s/here/now/
```
Replace here with now, on the current line only.

Each line that has a match will do the substitution on only the *first* occurrence of the string. If you want to change all occurrences on those lines, you append a g (for "global" substitution) to the end of the command. Consider this snippet of Java:

```
class tryout
{
  int tryout;

  tryout(int startval) { // make a new tryout
    tryout = startval;
  } // tryout constructor

  // a tryout-like resetting
  public void
  setTryout(int toval) {
    tryout = toval;
  }
  // willfindtryoutinhere

} // class tryout
```

```
1,$s/tryout/sample/
```
Works as expected except for line 5, where "tryout" appears as the constructor name but also in the comment.

```
1,$s/tryout/sample/g
```
Works better (note the trailing g). But neither command can deal with "Tryout" in the setTryout method name. That's because of the uppercase "T", which doesn't match "tryout".

```
1,$s/Tryout/Sample/g
```
Will make the substitution in that method name.

> **TIP**
>
> Remember to precede these commands with a colon (":") to put you into ex
> mode which puts your cursor on the status bar of the window.

2.2.3   The Joy of Regular Expressions

The substitution command really becomes powerful when you start using regular expressions. Our examples so far have only had plain alphanumeric characters between the slashes of the substitution. But other characters take on special meanings inside the search and replace strings. Table 2.1 shows just a few.

From this small collection we can do some useful things. We show just a few in Table 2.2. All commands begin with :1,$ to say that the substitution will be attempted from the first through the last line of the file.[3] You could use a smaller range for any of these substitutions, as we discussed above.

Table 2.1 Regular expression character meanings

Character	Meaning
^	The beginning of the line.
$	The end of the line.
.	Any single character.
*	Zero or more repetitions of the previous expression.
+	One or more repetitions of the previous expression.
[]	Any of the characters inside the brackets will match—e.g., [abc] matches any of a, b, c. Ranges are allowed too—e.g., [a-z].
&	When used on the right-hand side, stands for whatever was found with the search string on the left-hand side (for an example, see Table 2.2).

---

3. Note that % is valid substitute for 1,$.

Table 2.2 Some useful **vi** substitutions

Command	Explanation
`:1,$s/ *$//`	Removes all (any number of) trailing blanks—that is, looks for zero or more blanks followed immediately by the end of line, and replaces them with nothing (no characters between the last two slashes).
`:1,$s/^.*$/""/`	Puts quotes around the text of each and every line.
`:1,$s/^"//`	Removes the leading quote from any line that starts with one.
`:1,$s/"$//`	Removes the trailing quote from any line that ends with one.

There is so much more that could be said about regular expressions. They are one of the most powerful features for making big changes with few keystrokes. It's an integral part of **sed**, Perl, and other tools. It's in such demand that it has been added to Java for better pattern matching. See Section 2.6 for ways to learn more about regular expressions.

2.2.4   Starting Off Right: `.exrc`

You can preset certain behaviors in **vi** by putting ex commands in a file called `.exrc` in your home directory. Those commands will be read whenever you invoke **vi** and before you begin typing commands.

Here's a simple but useful `.exrc` example:

```
" set my favorite options:
set autoindent shiftwidth=4
set ignorecase
```

As you can see from the example, settings can be combined on one line. Note also that these lines do *not* begin with a colon. A colon *is* needed if you type these lines from within **vi**—because you need to get into ex mode; but since these are assumed to be ex commands (hence the name `.exrc`) they are going straight to the ex side of **vi** and no colon is needed. Comment lines begin with a double quote; the rest of the line is ignored, and doesn't need a matching quote.

The `ignorecase` command tells **vi** to ignore any difference between upper- and lowercase characters when searching for text with the / or ? commands. The single character searches on the current line (`f` and `F`) are not affected by this setting. The default for **vi** is `noignorecase`, which means case is significant.

The autoindent setting (can be abbreviated `ai`) means that when you do an `o` or `O` to *open* a line after or before (`o` versus `O`) the line on which your cursor rests, **vi** will automatically add whitespace so that the text that you enter begins at the same column where the current line begins.

For example, suppose you are editing an `if` statement like this:

```
if (userBalance < minDaily) {
    userAccount.chargeFees();
}
```

With your cursor on the middle line, if you type an `o` or `O`, the new (blank) line will open with your cursor at the fifth character position, right in line with the "u" of `userAccount`. If you find that your cursor is flush left when you try this, then you need to set autoindent. You can do this from within **vi** by typing `:set ai` or the longer `:set autoindent`. The leading ":" is important—it gets you to ex mode. (Don't forget to press Enter at the end of the command.)

The `shiftwidth` setting tells **vi** how many character positions to move text left or right with each `<<` (left) or `>>` (right) command, as well as when typing `^D` and `^T` in input mode. When typing text in input mode, people often use the Tab key to indent their text, for example inside an `if` or `for` statement. You can do this in **vi**, and the actual tab character will be the character in your text. But if you want tighter indenting, use the `^T` (that's Control-T, "T" for Tab, we suppose) to increase your indent and `^D` to decrease your indent while in input mode. The **vi** editor will automatically compute how much whitespace to use and will put an optimal combination of tabs and spaces as needed to line things up. Alternately, you can have **vi** always expand tabs into spaces and not mix tabs and spaces, but just use spaces, with `set expandtab`. (Remember to add a ":" if you want to type this from the command line.)

2.3 EDITORS GALORE

There are many editors available to a programmer on a Linux system. Some are text-based editors, typically antedating GUI interfaces. Many have graphical interfaces, with mouse-based cut and paste and the like. We will mention several here and encourage you to find the one with which you are comfortable.

The list of choices for editors is quite long. One of the beauties of the Open Source approach is that personal choices like favorite editors aren't squashed by arbitrary decisions: If you want, you can write an editor; others can adopt it.

Test drive a few; try them on for size. Remember that there can be a learning curve to climb. Don't necessarily settle for the easiest to learn—it may not be able to handle all that you'll need it to do, which may cost you more in the long run.

Speaking of editors that aren't easy to learn, we can't discuss editors without a mention of Emacs. To quote the GNU Emacs project home page:[4]

> Emacs is the extensible, customizable, self-documenting real-time display editor. If this seems to be a bit of a mouthful, an easier explanation is Emacs is a text editor and more. At its core is an interpreter for Emacs Lisp ("elisp," for short), a dialect of the Lisp programming language with extensions to support text editing. Some of the features of GNU Emacs include:
>
> * Content sensitive major modes for a wide variety of file types, from plain text to source code to HTML files.
> * Complete online documentation, including a tutorial for new users.
> * Highly extensible through the Emacs Lisp language.
> * Support for many languages and their scripts, including all the European "Latin" scripts, Russian, Greek, Japanese, Chinese, Korean, Thai, Vietnamese, Lao, Ethiopian, and some Indian scripts. (Sorry, Mayan hieroglyphs are not supported.)
> * A large number of extensions which add other functionality. The GNU Emacs distribution includes many extensions; many others are available separately—even a Web browser.

There is another variant of Emacs called XEmacs. It came from the same code base but split over differences both technical and philosophical.[5] Now if you thought that **vi** had a lot of obscure key sequences, you ain't seen nothin' yet. With its Lisp interpreter Emacs is incredibly extensible and powerful, but

---

4. This is from `http://www.gnu.org/software/emacs/emacs.html#Whatis`.

5. If you want to read more about those differences, and how they came about, see `http://www.xemacs.org/About/XEmacsVsGNUemacs.html`.

has a huge learning curve—which is why we aren't going to cover Emacs or XEmacs at all in this book.

Our favorite editor is still **vi**—in part, we're sure, because we already know it so well. But like any skilled craftsman, even though you may have a favorite hammer or saw that you use on most of your work, you will still have several others ready in your toolkit, and use specialized ones for certain tasks.

2.3.1 Editing Your Pipes (sed, the Stream EDitor)

One important kind of editor available on Linux is the *stream editor*, or **sed**. It allows you to perform editing on the data that comes in on standard in and writes its result to standard out. Similar to the syntax from ex mode in **vi** (and based on the simple **ed** editor), it can be very useful for making changes to large numbers of files in one go.

You can learn much more about **sed** from its manpage or from the book *UNIX AWK and SED Programmer's Interactive Workbook* by Peter Patsis.

2.3.2 Simple Graphical Editors

Linux comes with a wide range of open source software, not all of which is installed on every installation. You may need to use your Linux installation disks to add these programs to your system. Whether it's RedHat's package manager or SuSE's YaST2 or Debian's **apt-get**, most Linux admin interfaces make it easy to add these extra packages. Of course you can also resort to the Web for finding and downloading additional open source software.

Here's a quick listing of some of the many editors that you might find to your liking. The description of each is largely "in its own words," based on the text that the authors supply with their software.

- **jedit** is a cross-platform programmer's text editor written in Java. The Java-based portability seems appealing. This is a very powerful editor and a popular choice.
- **pico** is a small easy to use editor.
- **mbedit** is a multiplatform editor.
- NEdit is a GUI style text editor for workstations with X Window and Motif. NEdit provides all of the standard menu, dialog, editing, mouse support, as well as macro extension language, syntax highlighting, and a lot of other nice features (and extensions for programmers).

- **xcoral** comes up fast; seems well done. Half of the YaST developers swear by it, not only because of the built-in C/C++/Java browser. This editor provides support for C, C++, Java, Perl, Ada, and Fortran programs, as well as LATEX and HTML documents. With the help of the built-in SMall ANSI C Interpreter (SMAC), **xcoral** can be configured and extended in almost arbitrary ways. Examples can be found in the directory `/usr/lib/xcoral` (or wherever **xcoral** is installed on your system). Further information about **xcoral** and SMAC is available in the detailed online help system (also available in HTML and PostScript format).

- **axe** features multiple windows, multiple buffers, configurable menus and buttons, access to external filters, keyboard macros, comprehensive online help, and more.

- **eddi** is an X editor based on the TiX shell, with syntax highlighting and several other useful features.

- **the**: If you're an IBMer from the heyday of mainframes, perhaps you've used **xedit** from VM/CMS. If so, you might want to check out **the**, whose name is the acronym of "The Hessling Editor."

- JED is an extremely powerful but small Emacs-like editor for programmers that is extensible in a C-like macro language and is able to perform color syntax highlighting. Among the many features: Emacs, WordStar, EDT emulation; C, Fortran, TEX, text editing modes; full undo; Emacs-compatible info reader, and lots more. It claims to be 8-bit clean, so you can even edit binary files.

- Glimmer is the editor formerly known as CodeCommander. It is a full featured code editor with many advanced features, including full scripting integration with either Python or Guile.

- **joe** (Joe's own editor) is a freeware ASCII editor for UNIX. **joe** is similar to most IBM PC text editors. The keyboard shortcuts are similar to WordStar and Turbo C. When **joe** has several files opened at the same time, each file is displayed in its own window. Additionally, **joe** supports shell windows whereby the output of the executed commands is saved in a buffer, automatic filename completion (via Tab), help windows, undo/redo, search and replace using regular expressions.

- gEdit is a small but powerful text editor designed expressly for GNOME. It supports a split-screen mode and plug-ins that make it even more powerful. Developers can develop their own plug-ins if they desire.

- **fte** is an editor "with many features and simple usage for X11 and console."

- **e3** is a very tiny editor (only .07MB) that offers many different modes such as **vi**, Emacs, and WordStar. The default mode is WordStar.

- **asedit** is a simple ASCII text editor for X11/Motif. Mouse support, dialog boxes, hypertext online help, undo/redo. Named for its author, Andrzej Stochniol.

2.4 REVIEW

We've given a good foundation for using **vi**—a set of commands that will help you with much of your daily editing. While not as pretty as a GUI tool, **vi** can be much more productive once you get familiar with the commands. Start with some basic commands, then refer to this chapter or another **vi** resource and learn a new keystroke each week. By next year, you'll be a master at **vi**—and incredibly productive at producing code.

We also described several other editors available under Linux. If you know them already, or are wed to your mouse, then try one on for size. The choice of an editor can be as much about personality and "fit" as it is a technical choice.

2.5 WHAT YOU STILL DON'T KNOW

There is still a lot more to learn about regular expressions. They may take a bit of practice, but it is a skill that can be used in a variety of contexts, in a variety of languages.

2.6 RESOURCES

- Rafeeq Rehman and Christopher Paul, *The Linux Development Platform*, Prentice Hall PTR, especially Chapter 2 on editors **vim**, Emacs, and **jed**.

- Peter Patsis, *UNIX AWK and SED Programmer's Interactive Workbook*, Prentice Hall PTR, ISBN 0130826758.

Chapter 3

An Experienced Programmer's Introduction to Java

Here the reader is rapidly acquainted with the manner in which Java implements the OO (Object-Oriented) concepts. The language's statements are unceremoniously presented. Much deference is paid to other texts in print and on the Web, since this is well traveled ground. We then present a simple sample Java application that will be used throughout the rest of this introductory part as an example that can be easily built in all of the Java environments available for Linux.

3.1 WHAT YOU WILL LEARN

- Java syntax and semantics for the familiar (to an experienced programmer) programming constructs.
- How Java implements the OO: buzzwords of inheritance, encapsulation, and polymorphism.
- How Java deals with the absence of C++-style multiple inheritance.

- Why the absence of templates in Java is not as crippling as a C++ programmer might suppose.

- How `final` is better than `virtual` and how interfaces are often better than multiple inheritance.

This is going to be a whirlwind tour. Our book assumes that you already know programming in general, and have had some exposure to OO programming. We are going to distill into a single chapter material that comprises significant portions of other books. In particular, if there are concepts here that you are not already familiar with, look at Chapters 1–9 of Bruce Eckel's wonderful book, *Thinking in Java*, 3rd ed., published by Prentice Hall PTR (ISBN 0-131-00287-2). It is, genuinely, one of the best books on the market for learning the Java language and the design principles Java embodies.

If you are somewhat new to programming, but technically quite adept (maybe a system administrator or database administrator with little formal programming background), you may want to supplement your reading with a book that, unlike Eckel's, is targeted more toward the novice programmer. We like *Java Software Solutions: Foundations of Program Design*, 3rd ed., by John Lewis and William Loftus, Addison-Wesley, 2003 (ISBN 0-201-78129-8). It will introduce the concepts behind the programming constructs, whereas we will assume that you know these concepts so we can focus only on the Java syntax.

3.2 FUNDAMENTAL LANGUAGE ELEMENTS

Before the object-oriented structures, Java (like C) has a small number of fundamental statements and (again, like C and C++) some fundamental "nonobject" data types.[1]

---

1. The existence of these nonobject data types is another thing that brings up criticism of the Java language. Since Java does not have C++'s operator overloading features, you cannot use objects in standard algebraic expressions. I'm not sure if the inclusion of scalar classes was motivated by speed, or by the lack of operator overloading. Whatever the reason, like any other design compromise, it has both advantages and disadvantages, as we shall see throughout the book.

3.2.1   Scalar Types

Java has a number of built-in scalar (in this context, nonobject) types. We discuss these below.

3.2.1.1   *Integer Types*

Java defines four integer types—byte, short, int, and long. Unlike some languages, Java defines the precision, that is, the bit size, of these types.

- byte: 8 bits
- short: 16 bits
- int: 32 bits
- long: 64 bits

For Java, the goal is "compile once, run anywhere." Defining that int means 32 bits—everywhere—helps to achieve this goal. By contrast, when C language was first defined, its goal was different: to be available quickly on a variety of architectures, not to produce object code that would be portable between architectures. Thus, for C, the choice was up to the compiler developer to choose a size that was most "natural" (i.e., convenient) for that particular architecture.[2] This would make it easiest on the compiler writer. It succeeded—C was an easy language to implement, and it spread widely.

Back to Java. Note that all these values are signed. Java has no "unsigned" type.

Note also that byte is listed here. It can be treated as a numeric value, and calculations performed on it. Note especially that it is a *signed* number (i.e., values range from –128 to 127 and not from 0 to 255). Be careful when promoting a byte to an int (or other numeric value). Java will sign-extend on the promotion. If the value in the byte variable was a character (e.g., an ASCII value) then you really wanted it treated like an unsigned value. To assign such a value to an int you'll need to mask off the upper bits, as in Example 3.1.

You may never encounter such a situation, but if you are ever working with bytes (e.g., byte arrays) and start to mess with the individual bytes, don't say we didn't warn you.

---

2. In fact, C's only rule is that a short int will not be longer than an int and a long will not be shorter than an int. It is both ANSI and K&R compatible for all integer types in a C compiler to be the same size!

Example 3.1 Coercing a `byte` to `int` as if the `byte` were unsigned

```
byte c;
int ival;
...
ival = ((int) c) && 0xFF;   // explicit cast needed
```

3.2.1.2   Floating Point Types

Java provides two different precisions of floating point numbers. They are:

- `float`: 32 bits
- `double`: 64 bits

The `float` type is not very useful at that precision, so `double` is much more commonly seen. For other situations where precision is important, but you can spare some cycles, consider the `BigDecimal` and `BigInteger` object classes.

Java floating point numbers are specified to follow the IEEE floating point standard, IEEE 754.

3.2.1.3   Other Types

Java also has a `boolean` type, along with constants `true` and `false`. In Java, unlike C/C++, `boolean` values are a distinct type, and do not convert to numeric types. For example, it is common in C to write:

```
if (strlen(instr)) {
 strcpy(buffer, instr);
}
```

In this case, the integer result of `strlen()` is used as a `boolean`, where 0 is `false` and any other value is `true`. This doesn't work in Java. The expression must be of a `boolean` type.

Java also has a `char` type, which is *not* the same as a `byte`. The `char` is a character, and in Java, characters are represented using Unicode (UTF-16). They take two bytes each.

For more discussion on the differences between `bytes` and `chars` and about Unicode, read the Java tutorial on the `java.sun.com` Web site or visit `www.unicode.org`, the international standard's Web site.

3.2.1.4 Operators

Before we move on to the topic of arrays (which are sort of a hybrid scalar/object type in Java), let's spend a moment on the operators that can be used in expressions (Table 3.1). Most deal with numeric or boolean operands. For completeness, we'll include the operators that deal exclusively with arrays (the "`[]`") and classes ("`.`", `new`, and `instanceof`), even though we haven't discussed them yet.

Operators listed on the same row in the table have the same precedence. Operators with the same precedence, except for the unary operators, group from left to right. Unary operators group from right to left.

3.2.1.5 Arrays

Example 3.2 demonstrates the array syntax in Java.

Example 3.2 Example array syntax

```
int [] oned = new int[35];              // array = new type[size]
int alta [] = {1, 3, 5, 14, 11, 6, 24}; // alternative syntax plus
                                        // initialization
int j=0;

for(int i=0; i<35; i++) {
  oned[i] = valcomp(i, prop, alta[j]);  // array[index]
  if (++j > alta.length) {              // array.length
    j = 0;
  }
}
```

The array can be declared with the `[]` on either side of the variable name. While our example uses the primitive type `int`, array syntax looks just the same for any objects.

Note that in Java, one doesn't declare the size of the array. It's only in creating the array with a `new` that the array gets created to a particular size. (The `{...}` syntax is really just a special compiler construct for what is essentially a `new` followed by an assignment of values.)

Multidimensional arrays follow the syntax of simple arrays, but with additional adjacent square brackets, as shown in Example 3.3.

Table 3.1 Arithmetic and logical Java operators in order of precedence

Operators	Explanation
[ ] .	array indexing, member reference
- ++ -- ! ~	unary operators: negate, increment, decrement, logical-not, bitwise-not
(*type*) new	coercion, or casting to a different type; creating a new object
* / %	multiplication, division, remainder
+ -	addition, subtraction
<< >> >>>	shift-left, shift-right-sign-extend, shift-right-zero-fill
< > <= >= instanceof	less-than, greater-than, less-or-equal, greater-or-equal, comparing object types
== !=	equal, not-equal
&	bitwise-and (boolean for boolean operands with no short-circuit)*
^	bitwise-xor (with boolean operands it is a boolean-xor)**
|	bitwise-or (boolean for boolean operands with no short-circuit)*
&&	logical-and (with short-circuit)*
||	logical-or (with short-circuit)*
?:	Inline if expression, e.g., a ? b : c says, if a is true, then the value is b, else it is c.
= += -= *= /= %= <<= >>= >>>= &= ^= |=	Assignment; those with an operator, as in a op= b will perform the operation a op b then assign the result back to a.

---

*   In Java there are two ways to do a boolean AND operation: using & or &&. Remember that for "a AND b", if either is false, then the result is false. That means that if "a" is false, there is no need to evaluate "b" because it will not affect the result. Skipping the evaluation of "b" in this case is called *short-circuiting*. Java will use short-circuit evaluation when using the && operator, but not &. The same applies to the OR operators || and | where Java can short-circuit on a true evaluation of the first operand for ||. This is an important distinction when "a" and "b" are not just simple variable references but rather method calls or other complex expressions, especially ones with side effects.

**   XOR is exclusive or, where the result of "a XOR b" is true if "a" or "b" is true, but not both. For bitwise operands, "a" and "b" refer here to bits in the operand; for boolean operands it is the one value. Examples: 5^6 is 3; true^false is true but true^true is false.

Example 3.3 Example two-dimensional array syntax

```
int [][] ragtag = new int[35][10];

for (int i=0; i<35; i++) {
  for (int j=0; j<10; j++) {
    ragtag[i][j] = i*j;
  } // next j
} // next i
```

Multidimensional arrays are built as arrays of arrays. Therefore, we can actually allocate it in a piecemeal fashion and have *ragged-edged* arrays, where each row has a different number of columns, as shown in Example 3.4.

Example 3.4 Ragged two-dimensional array syntax

```
int [][] ragtag = new int[17][];

for (int i=0; i<17; i++) {
  ragtag[i] = new int[10+i];
} // next i

for (int i=0; i<17; i++) {
  System.out.println("ragtag["+i+"] is "+ragtag[i].length+" long.");
} // next i
```

For a fuller discussion of arrays, see Chapter 9 of Eckel or Chapter 6 of Lewis&Loftus.

3.2.2 Object Types

The real power in Java, or any object-oriented language, comes not from the scalar types, cool operators, or powerful control statements it provides (see below), but from its *objects*.

Object-oriented programming is a relatively recent innovation in software design and development. Objects are meant to embody the real world in a more natural way; they give us a way to describe, in our programs, the real-world objects with which we deal. If you are programming a business application, think of real-world business objects such as orders, customers, employees, addresses, and so on. Java is an object-oriented programming language and thus has some significant syntax related to OO concepts.

If you are new to object-oriented programming, be sure to read Chapter 1 of Eckel's *Thinking in Java*.

In Java, we define a *class* to represent the objects about which we want to program. A class consists of the data and the methods to operate on that data. When we create a new instance of some class, that instance is an object of that type of class. Example 3.5 shows a simple class.

Example 3.5 Simple class

```
class
PairInt
{
  // data
  int i;
  int j;

  // constructors
  PairInt() { i=0; j=0; }
  PairInt(int ival, int jval) { i=ival; j=jval; }

  // methods
  setI(int val) { i=val; }
  setJ(int val) { j=val; }
  int getI() { return i; }
  int getJ() { return j; }
}
```

Note that this class defines both data (`i`, `j`) and methods (`setI()`, `getJ()`, and so on). We put all this into a file named `PairInt.java` to match the name of the class definition.

If some other Java code wanted to create and use a `PairInt` object, it would create it with the `new` keyword followed by a call to a constructor (Example 3.6).

This example shows only a snippet of code, not the entire `PairInt` class. That class, though, would likely reside in its own source file (named for its class name). In Java you normally create lots of files, one for each class. When it's

---

Example 3.6 Using simple class

```
// declare a reference to one:
PairInt twovals;

// now create one:
twovals = new PairInt(5, 4);

// we can also declare and create in one step:
PairInt twothers = new PairInt(7, 11);
```

---

time to run the program, its various classes are loaded as needed. We'll discuss grouping classes together and how Java locates them in Section 3.3.1.

In Java, each source file contains one class and the file is named after that class. It is possible to define *inner* classes located inside another class definition and thus inside its file, but that introduces other complexities that we wish to avoid discussing at this point. Most importantly, an inner class has access to even the private members of the enclosing class. (Read more about inner classes in any of the Java books that we recommend at the end of this chapter.)

For each of the class methods, class data declarations, and the class itself, Java has syntax to limit the *scope*, or visibility, of those pieces. The examples above didn't include those keywords—that is, they took the default values. Usually you'll want to specify something. See Section 3.4.1.

3.2.2.1 Objects as References

So far we have not explained something important about object type variables. These variables can all be thought of as pointers or references to an object. When you declare a variable of an object type, what you are declaring is a variable that is capable of referring to an object of that type. When declared, it does not point at anything. It has a value of *null* and any attempt to use it will result in a null pointer *exception* (more on those later).

Before an object variable might be used, it must be made to refer to an instance of an object. This is done by assignment. You can assign an existing object, or you can use the `new` operator.

Any new class will have a *constructor*, that is, a method whose name is the name of the class. There can be many different constructors for the same class, each with unique types of parameters. For example, the `String` class has many different constructors, including one which constructs a new `String` from a different `String` and another that constructs a new `String` from an array of bytes.

```
String strbystr = new String(oldstr);
String strbyarr = new String(myByteArray);
```

3.2.2.2   Strings

One of the most commonly used classes is the `String` class. It comes already defined as part of Java and has some special syntax for initialization which makes it look familiar. Whereas other objects need a `new` keyword and a constructor call, a `String` object can be created and initialized with the intuitive double quotes, as in:

```
String xyz="this is the stringtext";
```

The compiler also makes a special allowance for `Strings` with respect to the plus sign (+). It can be used to concatenate two `Strings` into a third, new `String`.

```
String phrase = "That is"
String fullsent = phrase + " all.";
```

It is worth noting that `Strings` do not change—they are *immutable*. When you assign a `String` the value of one `String` plus another, there's a lot of `String` object creation going on behind the scenes. If you need to do a lot of concatenation of `Strings`, say inside loops, then you should look into the use of the `StringBuffer` object. See Appendix A of *Thinking in Java*, 3rd ed., the section titled Overloading "+" and the `StringBuffer`, for a full discussion of the tradeoffs here.

There are a variety of methods for `String`—ones that will let you make substrings, search for substrings at the start or end or anywhere in the string, or check for equality of two strings.

Table 3.2 shows some of the most useful methods associated with `String` objects.

Table 3.2 Useful `String` methods

Return type	Method	Description
`int`	`length()`	Returns the length, i.e. number of characters, in the `String`.
`boolean`	`equals(Object obj)`	Returns `true` if the object is a `String` object and is equal to the `String`. (Aside: the argument takes a generic `Object` type rather than only a `String` object because it's meant to override the `equals()` method in the class `Object` of which `String` is a descendant.) This is the way to compare two `Strings` to see if they are both holding the same sequence of characters. Using `stringA == stringB` will only tell you if `stringA` and `stringB` are referencing the same object (pointing to the same location in memory). What you typically want is `stringA.equals(stringB)`.

`boolean`	`equalsIgnoreCase(String str)`	Similar to `equals()`, but this one only allows a `String` parameter, and it ignores the upper/lower case distinction between letters. For example:
		
		`String sample = "abcdefg";`
		`String sample2 = "AbCdEfG";`
		`sample.equalsIgnoreCase(sample2)`
		
		returns `true`.

`String`	`toLowerCase()`	Returns a string with all characters converted to lowercase.
`String`	`toUpperCase()`	Returns a string with all characters converted to uppercase.
`boolean`	`startsWith(String substr)`	Returns `true` if the `String` starts with the given substring.
`boolean`	`endsWith(String substr)`	Returns `true` if the `String` ends with the given substring.
`String`	`substring(int index)`	Returns a string starting at position `index` to the end of the `String`.

Table 3.2 *(Continued)*

Return type	Method	Description
String	substring(int first, int last)	Returns a string starting at position `first` and up to, but not including, character position `last`. If `last` is greater than the length of the `String`, or `last` is less than `first`, it throws an `IndexOutOfBounds` exception.

3.2.2.3   Other Classes: Reading Javadoc

Java comes with a huge collection of existing classes for you to use. The simplest ones are just wrappers for the primitive classes. There is an `int` primitive data type, but Java provides an `Integer` class, so that you can have an integer as an object. Similarly, there are classes for `Long`, `Float`, `Boolean`, and so on. Such classes aren't nearly as interesting as the myriad other classes that come with Java. These others provide objects for doing I/O, networking, 2D and 3D graphics, graphical user interfaces (GUIs), and distributed computing. Java provides ready-to-use classes for strings, math functions, and for special kinds of data structures like trees and sets and hash tables. There are classes to help you with the manipulation of HTML, XML, and SQL, as well as classes for sound, music, and video. All these objects can be yours to use and enjoy if you just learn the magic of reading *Javadoc*—online documentation for Java classes. The documentation for all these classes is viewed with a Web browser. (In a following chapter we'll describe how you can make Javadoc documents for the classes that you write, too.)

The online version of the API documentation can be found at

```
http://java.sun.com/j2se/1.4.2/docs/api/
```

for Java 1.4.2. (Similarly, put 1.5.1 or whatever version you want at the appropriate place in the URL.) When displayed, it shows a three-frame page, as seen in Figure 3.1, except that we've overlaid the image with three labels: A, B, and C.

The upper left frame of the Javadoc display, the area labeled with A in our figure, lists all the packages that are part of Java 2 Standard Edition (J2SE). While there are many other packages of classes available for Java, these classes are the standard ones available without any other class libraries, with no

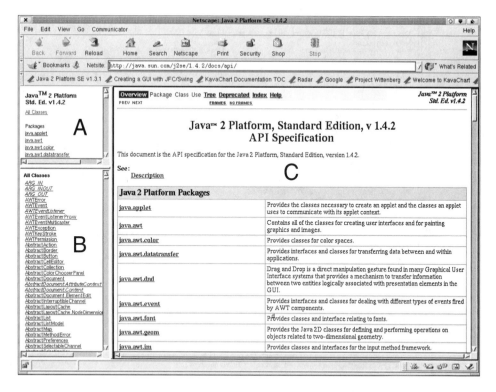

Figure 3.1 The three frames of a Javadoc page

additional downloads necessary. Other classes are documented in the same way—with Javadoc—but they are downloaded and displayed separately.

Frame B initially lists all the classes and interfaces available in all of the packages. When you select a package in A, B will display only those interfaces and classes that are part of the chosen package.

Frame C starts out with a list and description of all packages. Once you have selected a package in A, C will show the overview of that package, showing its classes and interfaces with descriptions.

But C is most often used to display the detailed description of a class. Choose a class or interface in B and you will see C filled with its description—some opening information followed by a list of the visible members of that class, followed by the possible constructors for that class and all the methods in that class (Figure 3.2). Each method is shown with its parameters and a one-sentence description. Clicking on the method name will open a fuller description (Figure 3.3).

Figure 3.2 Javadoc display of class information

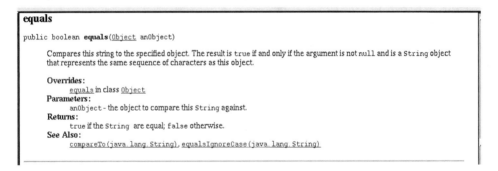

Figure 3.3 Javadoc display of a single method

Since you will likely be referencing the Javadoc pages regularly, you may want to download a copy to your hard drive. From the same page on the `java.sun.com` Web site where you can download the Java SDK you can also download the API documentation.

If you agree to the licensing terms, you will download a large ZIP file. Installing the documentation, then, is just a matter of unzipping the file—but it's best if you put it in a sensible location. If you have installed your Java SDK into a location like `/usr/local/java` then `cd` into that directory and unzip the file that you downloaded. Assuming that you saved the downloaded file into `/tmp`, a good place to put temporary files, and assuming that you have installed your version of Java into `/usr/local/java` and that you have write permission in that directory (check the permissions with `ls -ld .`) then you can run these commands:

```
$ cd /usr/local/java
$ unzip -q /tmp/j2sdk-1_4_2-doc.zip
```

There may be quite a pause (tens of seconds) while it unzips everything. The **unzip** command will spew out a huge list of filenames as it unpacks them unless you use the `-q` option ("quiet") on the command line (which we did, to avoid all that). The files are all unzipped into a directory named `docs`. So now you can point your browser to

```
file:///usr/local/java/docs/api/index.html
```

Now you have your own local copy for quick reference, regardless of how busy the network or Sun's Web site gets. Be sure to bookmark this page; you'll want to reference it often. It's your best source of information about all the standard Java2 classes.

3.2.3 Statements

This section is not intended to be a formal presentation of Java syntactic elements.[3] Our purpose here is merely to show you the Java way to express common programming constructs. You will find that these are fundamentally similar to the analogous statements in C and C++. For much more detail on these subjects, see Chapter 3 of *Thinking in Java* by Bruce Eckel.

Like C, Java has a very small set of statements. Most constructs are actually *expressions*. Most operations are either assignments or method calls. Those few statements that are not expressions fall into two broad categories:

- Conditional execution statements
- Loop control statements

By the way, you may have already noticed one of the two kinds of *comments* that Java supports. They are like the C/C++ comments—a pair of slashes (`//`) marks a comment from there to the end of the line, and a block

---

3. For those so inclined, Sun has a BNF language grammar (`http://java.sun.com/docs/books/jls/second_edition/html/syntax.doc.html`) on their Web site, and the Lewis and Loftus book, Appendix L, has a good set of syntax diagrams.

comment consists of everything from the opening /* to the closing */ sequence.

3.2.3.1 *Conditional Execution*

An experienced programmer probably only needs to see examples of if and other such statements to learn them. It's only a matter of syntax. Java breaks no new ground here; it adds no new semantics to conditional execution constructs.

The if-else statement.   The if can take a single statement without any braces, but we always use the braces as a matter of good style (Example 3.7).

Example 3.7 A compound Java if-else statement

```
if (x < 0) {
    y = z + progo;
} else if (x > 5) {
    y = z + hmron;
    mylon.grebzob();
} else {
    y = z + engrom;
    mylon.kuggle();
}
```

> **TIP**
>
> An important thing to remember about the Java if statement (and all other conditional tests, such as while, do-while, and for) is that, unlike C/C++, its expression needs to evaluate to a boolean. In C/C++, numeric expressions are valid, any nonzero value being considered true, but not so in Java.

The switch statement.   For a multiway branch Java, like C/C++, has a switch statement, though the Java version of switch is a bit more restrictive. Example 3.8 shows the syntax.

In Java, the expression in the switch statement must evaluate to either an int or a char. Even short and long are not allowed.

As in C/C++, be sure to put the break statement at the end of each case, or else control will flow right into the next case. Sometimes this is the desired behavior—but if you ever do that deliberately, be sure to add a comment.

Example 3.8 A `switch` statement in Java

```
switch (rval*k+zval)
{
  case 0:
    mylon.reset();
    break;
  case 1:
  case 4:
    // matches either 1 or 4
    y = zval+engrom;
    mylon.kuggle(y);
    break;
  default:
    // all other values end up here
    System.out.println("Unexpected value.");
    break;
}
```

The `default` case is where control goes when no other `case` matches the expression. It is optional—you don't need to have one among your switch cases. Its location is also arbitrary; it could come first, but by convention programmers put it last in the sequence of cases, as a visual "catch all."

> **TIP**
>
> For whichever `case` is last (typically `default`), the ending `break` is redundant because control will continue outside the `break`—but we show it here in the example, and use it ourselves in our code. Why? Well, code gets edited—for bug fixes and for feature additions. It is especially important to use `break` in all the `cases` in `switch` statements that have no `default` case, but even in those that do, we keep the `break` to avoid forgetting it, should another `case` ever be added or this last one relocated. We recommend that you do the same.

3.2.3.2   Looping and Related Statements

The `while` **statement.**   Like the `while` construct in other computer languages, the expression inside the parentheses is evaluated, and if `true`, the statement following it is executed. Then the expression is evaluated again, and if still `true`, the looped statement is again executed. This continues until the expression evaluates to `false` (Example 3.9).

Example 3.9 A Java `while` statement

```
while (greble != null)
{
  greble.glib();
  greble = treempl.morph();
}
```

Technically, the `while` statement consists of the expression and a single statement, but that single statement can be replaced by a set of statements enclosed in braces (you know, the characters { and }). We will always use braces, even if there is only one statement in our `while` loop. Experience has shown that it's a safer practice that leads to code that is easier to maintain. Just treat it as if the braces were required syntax, and you'll never forget to add them when you add a second statement to a loop.

The `do-while` **loop.**   To put the terminating check at the bottom of the loop, use `do-while` as shown in Example 3.10. Notice the need for the terminating semicolon after the expression.

Example 3.10 A Java `do-while` statement

```
do {

  greble.morph();
  xrof = treempl.glib();

} while (xrof == null);
```

Die-hard Pascal programmers should note that Java has no `repeat-until` statement. Sorry. Of course the logic of an `until(condition)` is equivalent to `do-while(!condition)`.

The `for` **loop.**   The `for` loop in Java is very similar to C/C++. It consists of three parts (Example 3.11):

- The initializing expression, done up front before the loop begins
- The conditional expression for terminating the loop

- The expression that gets executed at the end of each loop iteration, just prior to retesting the conditional

---

Example 3.11 A Java `for` loop

```
for (i = 0; i < 8; i++) {
  System.out.println(i);
}
```

Unlike C/C++, Java doesn't have the comma operator for use within arbitrary expressions, but the comma is supported as special syntax in Java `for` loops. It makes it possible to have multiple initializers in the opening of the `for` loop and multiple expressions in the portion repeated at each iteration of the loop. The result is much the same—you can initialize and increment multiple variables or objects in your `for` loop.

More formally, the full syntax of the `for` loop can be described with following meta-language as shown in Example 3.12 (where the `[ ]*` means "zero or more repetitions of").

Example 3.12 Java `for` loop syntax

```
for ( before [, before]* ; exit_condition ; each_time [, each_time]* )
  statement
```

The biggest difference between C and Java `for` loops, however, is that Java allows you to declare one or more variables of a single type in the initializing expression of the `for` loop (Example 3.13). Such a variable's scope is the `for` loop itself, so don't declare a variable there if you want to reference it outside the loop. It is a very handy construct, however, for enumerators, iterators, and simple counters.

Example 3.13 A Java `for` loop with local index

```
for (int i = 0; i < 8; i++) {
  System.out.println(i);
}
```

As in the `if` and `while` statements, the braces are optional when only a single statement is involved, but good practice compels us always to use the braces. Additional code can easily be added without messing up the logic—should one forget, at that point, the need to add braces.

Speaking of the `while` loop: When do you use a `for` and when do you use a `while` loop? The big advantage of the `for` loop is its readability. It consolidates the loop control logic into a single place—within the parentheses. Anyone reading your code can see at once what variable(s) are being used to control how many times the loop executes and what needs to be done on each iteration (e.g., just increment i). If no initialization is needed before starting the loop, or if the increment happens indirectly as part of what goes on in the body of the loop, then you might as well use a `while` loop. But when the initialization and iteration parts can be clearly spelled out, use the `for` loop for the sake of the next programmer who might be reading your code.

The `for` loop with iterators.   As of Java 5.0, there is additional syntax for a `for` loop. It is meant to provide a useful shorthand when looping over the members of an iterator.[4] So what's an iterator? Well, it has to do with collections. Uh, oh, we're surrounded by undefined terms. One step at a time, here. Java has a whole bunch (we won't say "collection," it's a loaded term) of utility classes that come with it. We mentioned these classes in our discussion of Javadoc. While not part of the language syntax, some of these classes are so useful that you will see them throughout many, if not most, Java programs.

Collection is a generic term (in fact, it's a Java interface) for several classes that allow you to group similar objects together. It covers such classes as `Lists`, `LinkedLists`, `Hashtables`, `Sets`, and the like. They are implementations of all those things that you (should have) learned in a Data Structures course in school. Typically you want to add (and sometimes remove) members from a collection, and you may also want to look something up in the collection. (If you're new to collections, think "array," as they are a simple and familiar type of collection.) Sometimes, though, you don't want just one item from the collection, but you want to look at all of the objects in the collection, one at a time. The generic way to do that, the way that hides the specifics of what kind of collection you have (linked list, or array, or map) is called an iterator.[5]

---

4. This feature is related to the topic of templates and generics. See Section 3.5.

5. The earliest versions of Java used an object called an `Enumeration`. It does much the same thing as an iterator, but with somewhat clumsier method names. Iterators also allow for a

The purpose of an iterator, then, is to step through a collection one item at a time. Example 3.14 shows a collection being built from the arguments on the command line. Then two iterators are used to step through the collection

---

Example 3.14 Using iterators

```java
import java.util.*;

public class
Iter8
{
  public static void
  main(String [] args)
  {
    // create a new (empty) ArrayList
    ArrayList al = new ArrayList();

    // fill the ArrayList with args
    for(int i = 0; i < args.length; i++) {
      al.add(args[i]);
    }

    // use the iterator in the while loop
    Iterator itr1 = al.iterator();

    while(itr1.hasNext()) {
      String onearg;
      onearg = (String) (itr1.next());
      System.out.println("arg=" + onearg);
    }

    // define and use the iterator in the for loop:
    for(Iterator itr2 = al.iterator(); itr2.hasNext(); ) {
      String onearg;
      onearg = (String) (itr2.next());
      System.out.println("arg=" + onearg);
    }

  } // main

} // Iter8
```

---

remove() method, something that Enumeration doesn't support. The Enumeration class is still around, but less frequently used. It is only available from certain older utility classes.

and print the objects in the collection to the command window. The first iterator uses the `while` loop, the second one uses a `for` loop, but they both do the same thing.

As of Java 5.0, there is another way to work your way through a collection, one that requires less type casting, but more importantly one that can enforce the type of objects at compile time.

Notice in Example 3.14 that the result of the `next()` is coerced into type `String`. That's because everything coming from the iterator (via the `next()` method) comes to us as a generic object. That way an iterator can handle any type of object, but that also means that it is up to the application program to know what type should be coming back from the iterator. Any typecasting error won't be found until runtime.

With the syntax added in 5.0, not only is there a shorthand in the `for` loop for looping with an iterator. There is also syntax to tell the compiler explicitly what type of objects you are putting into your collection or array so that the compiler can enforce that type.

Example 3.15 may help to make this clearer.

Example 3.15 Using a `for` loop iterator

```
import java.util.*;

public class
Foreign
{
  public static void
  main(String [] args)
  {
    List <String> loa = Arrays.asList(args);

    System.out.println("size=" + loa.size());

    for(String str : loa) {
      System.out.println("arg=" + str);
    }

  } // main
} // Foreign
```

Here we build a `List` from the arguments supplied on the command line. Notice the type name inside of angle brackets (less-than and greater-than signs).

This is the new syntax that tells the compiler that we are putting `Strings` into the `List`. The compiler will enforce that and give a compile time error if we try to add any other type to the `List`.

Now we come to the `for` loop. Read it as "for `str` in `loa`" or "for `String` values of `str` iterating over `loa`." We will get an iterator working out of sight that will iterate over the values of `loa`, our `List`. The values (the result of the `next()` method) will be put in the `String` variable `str`. So we can use `str` inside the body of the loop, with it taking on successive values from the collection.

Let's describe the syntax, then, as

```
for ( SomeType variable : SomeCollectionVariable ) {
}
```

which will define `variable` to be of type `SomeType` and then iterate over the `SomeCollectionVariable`. Each iteration will execute the body of the loop, with the variable set to the `next()` value from the iterator. If the collection is empty, the body of the loop will not be executed.

This variation of the `for` loop works for arrays as well as for these new typed collections. The syntax for arrays is the same. Example 3.16 will echo the arguments on the command line, but without loading up a `List` like we did in our previous example.

Example 3.16 A `for` loop iterator for arrays

```java
import java.util.*;

public class
Forn
{
  public static void
  main(String [] args)
  {
    for(String str : args) {
      System.out.println("arg="+str);
    }

  } // main
} // Forn
```

The break **and** continue **statements.**   There are two statements that will change the course of execution of the while, do-while, and for loops from within the loop. A continue will cause execution to skip the rest of the body of the loop and go on to the next iteration. With a for loop, this means executing the iteration expression, and then executing the test-for-termination expression. With the while and do-while loops, this means just going to the test expression.

You can quit out of the loop entirely with the break statement. Execution continues on the next statement after the loop.

3.2.3.3   *The* return *statement*

There is one more statement that we need to cover. The return statement is optionally followed by an expression. Execution of the current method ends at once upon executing return, and the expression is used as the return value of the method. Obviously, the type of the expression must match the return type of the method. If the method is void, there should be no return expression.

3.2.4   Error Handling, Java Style

Errors in Java are handled through *exceptions*. In some circumstances, the Java runtime will *throw* an exception, for example, when you reference a null pointer. Methods you write may also throw exceptions. This is quite similar to C++. But Java exceptions are classes. They descend from Object, and you can write your own classes that *extend* an existing exception. By so doing, you can carry up to the handler any information you would like. But we're getting ahead of ourselves here. Let's first describe the basics of exceptions, how to catch them, how to pass them along, and so forth.

In other programming languages a lot of code can be spent checking return codes of function or subroutine calls. If A calls B and B calls C and C calls D, then at each step the return value of the called function should be checked to see if the call succeeded. If not, something should be done about the error—though that "something" is usually just returning the error code to the next level up. So function C checks D's return value, and if in error, returns an error code for B to check. B in turn looks for an error returned from C and returns an error code to A. In a sense, the error checking in B and C is superfluous. Its only purpose is to pass the error from its origin in D to the function that has some logic to deal with the error—in our example that's A.

Java provides the `try`/`catch`/`throw` mechanism for more sophisticated error handling. It avoids a lot of unnecessary checking and passing on of errors. The only parts of a Java program that need to deal with an error are those that know what to do with it.

The `throw` in Java is really just a nonlocal "goto"—it will branch the execution of your program to a location which can be quite far away from the method where the exception was thrown. But it does so in a very structured and well-defined manner.

In our simple example of A calling B calling C calling D, D implemented as a Java method can *throw* an exception when it runs into an error. Control will pass to the first enclosing block of code on the call stack that contains a `catch` for that kind of exception. So A can have code that will *catch* an exception, and B and C need not have any error handling code at all. Example 3.17 demonstrates the syntax.

Example 3.17 A simple `try`/`catch` block

```
try {
  for (i = 0; i < max; i++) {
    someobj.methodB(param1, i);
  }
} catch (Exception e) {
  // do the error handling here:
  System.out.println("Error encountered. Try again.");
}
// continues execution here after successful completion
// but also after the catch if an error occurs
```

In the example, if any of the calls to `methodB()` in the `for` loop go awry—that is, anywhere inside `methodB()` or whatever methods it may call an exception is thrown (and assuming those called methods don't have their own `try`/`catch` blocks), then control is passed up to the `catch` clause in our example. The `for` loop is exited unfinished, and execution continues first with the `catch` clause and then with the statements after the `catch`.

How does an error get thrown in the first place? One simply creates an `Exception` object and then throws the exception (Example 3.18).

Example 3.18 Throwing an `Exception`, step by step

```
Exception ex = new Exception("Bad News");
throw ex;
```

Since there is little point in keeping the reference to the object for the local method—execution is about to leave the local method—there is no need to declare a local variable to hold the exception. Instead, we can create the exception and throw it all in one step (Example 3.19).

Example 3.19 Throwing an `Exception`, one step

```
throw new Exception("Bad News");
```

`Exception` is an object, and as such it can be extended. So we can create our own unique kinds of exceptions to differentiate all sorts of error conditions. Moreover, as objects, exceptions can contain any data that we might want to pass back to the calling methods to provide better diagnosis and recovery.

The `try/catch` block can catch different kinds of exceptions much like cases in a `switch/case` statement, though with different syntax (Example 3.20).

Notice that each `catch` has to declare the type of each exception and provide a local variable to hold a reference to that exception. Then method calls can be made on that exception or references to any of its publicly available data can be made.

Remember how we created an exception (`new Exception("message")`)? That message can be retrieved from the exception with the `toString()` method, as shown in that example. The method `printStackTrace()` is also available to print out the sequence of method calls that led up to the creation of the exception (Example 3.21).

The exception's stack trace is read top to bottom showing the most recently called module first. Our example shows that the exception occurred (i.e., was constructed) on line 6 of the class named `InnerMost`, inside a method named `doOtherStuff()`. The `doOtherStuff()` method was called from inside the class `MidModule`—on line 7—in a method named `doStuff()`. In turn, `doStuff()` had been called by `doSomething()`, at line 11 inside

---

Example 3.20 Catching different kinds of exceptions

```
try {
  for (i = 0; i < max; i++) {
    someobj.methodB(param1, i);
  } // next i

} catch (SpecialException sp) {
    System.out.println(sp.whatWentWrong());

} catch (AlternateException alt) {
    alt.attemptRepair(param1);

} catch (Exception e) {
    // do the error handling here:
    System.out.println(e.toString());
    e.printStackTrace();
}
// continues execution here after any catch
```

Example 3.21 Output from `printStackTrace()`

```
java.lang.Exception: Error in the fraberstam.
    at InnerMost.doOtherStuff(InnerMost.java:6)
    at MidModule.doStuff(MidModule.java:7)
    at AnotherClass.doSomething(AnotherClass.java:11)
    at ExceptExample.main(ExceptExample.java:14)
```

`AnotherClass`, which itself had been called from line 14 in the `ExceptExample` class' `main()` method.

We want to mention one more piece of syntax for the `try/catch` block. Since execution may never get to all of the statements in a `try` block (the exception may make it jump out to a `catch` block), there is a need, sometimes, for some statements to be executed regardless of whether all the `try` code completed successfully. (One example might be the need to close an I/O connection.) For this we can add a `finally` clause after the last `catch` block. The code in the `finally` block will be executed (only once) after the `try` or after the `catch`—even if the path of execution is about to leave because of throwing an exception (Example 3.22).

Example 3.22 Use of a `finally` clause

```
try {
  for (i = 0; i < max; i++) {
    someobj.methodB(param1, i);
  } // next i

} catch (SpecialException sp) {
    System.out.println(sp.whatWentWrong());

} catch (AlternateException alt) {
    alt.attemptRepair(param1);
    throw alt;      // pass it on

} catch (Exception e) {
    // do the error handling here:
    System.out.println(e.toString());
    e.printStackTrace();

} finally {
    // Continue execution here after any catch
    // or after a try with no exceptions.
    // It will even execute after the AlternateException
    // before the throw takes execution away from here.
    gone = true;
    someobj = null;
}
```

3.2.5 `print()`,`println()`,`printf()`

We've already used `println()` in several examples, and assumed that you can figure out what it's doing from the way we have used it. Without going whole-hog into an explanation of Java I/O and its various classes, we'd like to say a little more about the three various output methods on a `PrintStream` object.[6]

Two of the methods, `print()` and `println()`, are almost identical. They differ only in that the latter one appends a newline (hence the `ln`) at the end of its output, thereby also flushing the output. They expect a `String` as their only argument, so when you want to output more than one thing, you add the `Strings` together, as in:

---

6. The mention of the `PrintStream` object was meant to be a hint, to tell you that you can find out more about this sort of thing on the Javadoc pages for the `PrintStream` object.

```
System.out.println("The answer is "+val);
```

"But what if `val` is not a `String`?" we hear you asking. Don't worry, the Java compiler is smart enough to know, that when you are adding with a `String` argument it must convert the other argument to a `String`, too. So for any `Object`, it will implicitly call its `toString()` method. For any primitive type (e.g., `int` or `boolean`), the compiler will convert it to a `String`, too.

The third of the three output methods, `printf()`, sounds very familiar to C/C++ programmers, but be warned:

- It is only available in Java 5.0[7] and after.
- It is similar but not identical to the C/C++ version.

Perhaps the most significant enhancement to `printf()` is its additional syntax for dealing with internationalization. It's all well and good to translate your `String`s to a foreign language, but in doing so you may need to change the word order and thus the order of the arguments to `printf()`. For example, the French tend to put the adjective *after* rather than *before* the noun (as we do in English). We say *"the red balloon"* and they say *"le balloon rouge."* If your program had `String`s for adjective and noun, then a `printf()` like this:

```
String format = "the %s %s\n";
System.out.printf(format, adjective, noun);
```

wouldn't work if you translate just the format `String`:

```
String format = "le %s %s\n";
System.out.printf(format, noun, adjective);
```

You'd like to be able to do the translation without changing the code in your program.[8] With the Java version of `printf()`, there is syntax for specifying which argument corresponds to which format field in the format string. It uses

---

7. Remember, you'll need the `-source 5.0` option on the command line.

8. Java has good support for internationalization, another topic for which we don't have the time. The ability to translate the strings without otherwise modifying the program is a crucial part to internationalization, and the `printf()` in Java 5.0 is certainly a help in this regard. In a similar vein, the Eclipse IDE, covered in Chapter 10, includes a feature to take all string constants and convert them to external properties at a stroke, making internationalization much easier to do.

a number followed by a dollar sign as part of the format field. This may be easier to explain by example; our French translation, switching the order in which the arguments are used, would be as follows:

```
String format = "le %2$s %1$s\n";
System.out.printf(format, noun, adjective);
```

The format field %2$s says to use the second argument from the argument list—in this case, adjective—as the string that gets formatted here. Similarly, the format field %1$s says to use the first argument. In effect, the arguments get reversed without having to change the call to println(), only by translating the format String. Since such translations are often done in external files, rather than by assignment statements like we did for our example, it means that such external files can be translated without modifying the source to move arguments around.

This kind of argument specification can also be used to repeat an argument multiple times in a format string. This can be useful in formatting Date objects, where you use the same argument for each of the different pieces that make up a date—day, month, and so on. Each has its own format, but they can be combined by repeating the same argument for each piece. One format field formats the month, the next format field formats the day, and so on. Again an example may make it easier to see:

```
import java.util.Date;
Date today = new Date();
System.out.printf("%1$tm / %1$td / %1$ty\n", today);
```

The previous statement uses the single argument, today, and formats it in three different ways, first giving the month, then the day of the month, then the year. The t format indicates a date/time format. There are several suffixes for it that specify parts of a date, a few of which are used in the example.[9]

> **NOTE**
>
> Don't forget the trailing \n at the end of the format string, if you want the output to be a line by itself.

---

9. There are many more, familiar to C/C++ UNIX/Linux/POSIX programmers who have used the strftime() library call.

The details for all the different format fields can be found in the Javadoc for the `java.util.Formatter` class, a class that is used by `printf()` to do its formatting, but one that you can also use by itself (C programmers: think "sprintf").

In order to implement `printf()` for Java, the language also had to be extended to allow for method calls with a varying number of arguments. So as of Java 5.0, a method's argument list can be declared like this:

```
methodName(Type ... arglist)
```

This results in a method declaration which takes as its argument an array named `arglist` of values of type `Type`. That is, it is much the same as if you declared `methodName(Type [] arglist)` except that now the compiler will let you call the method with a varying number of arguments and it will load up the arguments into the array before calling the method. One other implication of this is that if you have a declaration like this:

```
varOut(String ... slist)
```

then you can't, in the same class, also have one like this:

```
varOut(String [] alist)
```

because the former is just a compiler alias for the latter.

TIP

We recommend that you avoid methods with variable argument list length. You lose the compile-time checking on the number of arguments that you supply (since it can vary). Often the type of the arguments in the list will be `Object`, the most general type, to allow anything to be passed in. This, too, circumvents type checking of arguments, and can lead to runtime class-cast exceptions and other problems. Methods with variable argument list length are often a lazy approach, but were necessary to make `printf()` work, and for that we are grateful.

3.3 Using (and Making) Java APIs

With every class you write, you define a name—the name of the class. But what if someone else has already used that name? Java programming should encourage reuse of existing code, so how do you keep straight which names are available?

This is a *namespace* issue—who can use which names. A classic way to solve a namespace issue is to divide the namespace up into domains. On the Internet, host names are sectioned off into domains, so that I can have a host named `Pluto` or `www` and so can lots of others—because each host is *qualified* by its domain (e.g., `myco.com`). Thus `www.myco.com` isn't confused with `www.otherco.com` or `www.hisgroup.org`. Each host is named `www`, but each is unique because of the qualifying domain.

Java solves the problem in much the same way, but with the names in the reverse order. Think of the "host" as the class name; the "domain" name, used to sort out identical host names, is, in Java parlance, the *package name*. When you see a name like `com.myco.finapp.Account`, that can be a Java package `com.myco.finapp` qualifying a class named `Account`.

Beyond just keeping the namespace clean, Java packages serve another important function. They let you group together similar classes and interfaces to control access to them. Classes within the same package can access each others' members and methods even when they are not declared `public`, provided they are not declared to be `private`. This level of intimacy, sometimes called *package protection*, means that you should group classes together that are related, but avoid grouping too many classes together. It's tempting just to put all your classes for a project into the same package, for example, `com.myco.ourproject`, but you will provide better safety and perhaps promote better reuse by grouping them into several smaller packages, for example, `com.myco.util`, `com.myco.financial`, and `com.myco.gui`.

3.3.1 The `package` Statement

So how do you make a Java class part of a package? It's easy—you just put, as the first (noncomment) line of the file, the `package` statement, naming the package to which you want this class to belong. So if you want your `Account` class to be part of the `com.myco.financial` package, your Java code would look as shown in Example 3.23.

Example 3.23 Use of a `package` statement

```
package com.myco.financial;

public class
Account
{
  // ...
}
```

Making a class part of a package is easy. What's tricky is putting the class file in the right location so that Java can find it.

Think of the current directory as the root of your package tree. Each part of a package name represents a directory from that point on down. So if you have a package named `com.myco.financial` then you'll need a directory named `com` and within that a directory named `myco` and within that a directory named `financial`. Inside that `financial` directory you can put your `Account.class` file.

When Java runs a class file, it will look in all the directories named in the `CLASSPATH` environment variable. Check its current value:

```
$ echo $CLASSPATH

$
```

If it's empty, as in this example, then the only place where it will look for your classes will be the current directory. That's a handy default, because it is just what you want when your class file has no `package` statement in it. With no `package` statement, your class becomes part of the *unnamed package*. That's fine for simple sample programs, but for serious application development you'll want to use packages.

Let's assume that you're in your home directory, `/home/joeuser`, and beneath that you have a `com` directory and beneath that a `myco` directory with two subdirectories `financial` and `util`. Then with your classes in those lower level directories, you can run your Java program from the home directory. If you want to run it from any arbitrary directory (e.g., `/tmp` or `/home/joeuser/alt`) then you need to set `CLASSPATH` so it can find this package tree. Try:

```
$ export CLASSPATH="/home/joeuser"
$
```

Now Java knows where to look to find classes of the com.myco.financial and com.myco.util packages.

3.3.2   The import Statement

Once we have put our classes into packages, we have to use that package's name when we refer to those classes—unless we use the import statement.

Continuing our example, if we want to declare a reference to an Account object, but Account is now part of com.myco.financial, then we could refer to it with its full name, as in:

```
com.myco.financial.Account =
    new com.myco.financial.Account(user, number);
```

which admittedly is a lot more cumbersome than just:

```
Account = new Account(user, number);
```

To avoid the unnecessarily long names, Java has import statements. They are put at the beginning of the class file, outside the class definition, just after any package statement. In an import statement, you can name a class with its full name, to avoid having to use the full name all the time. So our example becomes:

```
import com.myco.financial.Account;
// ...
Account = new Account(user, number);
```

If you have several classes from that package that you want to reference, you can name them all with a "*", and you can have multiple different import statements, as in:

```
import java.util.*;
import com.myco.financial.*;
// ...
Account = new Account(user, number);
```

Here are a few things to remember about import statements. First, they don't bring in any new code into the class. While their syntax and placement is reminiscent of the C/C++ `include` preprocessor directive, their function is not the same. An `import` statement does not include any new code; it only aids name resolution. Secondly, the "`*`" can only be used at the end of the package name; it is not a true wildcard in the regular expression sense of the word. Thirdly, every class has what is in effect an implicit `import java.lang.*` so that you don't need to put one there. References to `String` or `System` or other core language classes can be made without the need for either the `import` statement or the fully qualified name (except as described in the next paragraph).

If you need to use two different classes that have the same name but come from different packages, you will still need to refer to them by their full names; `import` can't help you here. As an example of this, consider the two classes `java.util.Date` and `java.sql.Date` (though with any luck you won't need to refer to both of them within the same class).

3.4 ENCAPSULATION, INHERITANCE, AND POLYMORPHISM

The classic troika of OOP buzzwords is "encapsulation, inheritance, and polymorphism." How does Java do each of these things?

3.4.1 Encapsulation

Encapsulation is the grouping of data and algorithms together into units, and it's also about hiding implementation details that are not important to the users of the unit. The basic unit of encapsulation is the class. All Java code exists in classes. A class is declared with the `class` keyword (Example 3.24).

Example 3.24 A sample Java class declaration that doesn't actually do anything useful

```
public class
Sample
{
  private int id;

  public void method()
  {
    System.out.println(id);
  }
}
```

3.4.2   Inheritance

Inheritance is how a class places itself in a hierarchy of existing classes. In Java, each class inherits from exactly one existing class. A class names the class from which it inherits with the `extends` keyword. We said a Java class inherits from exactly one class, and yet our Example 3.24 doesn't contain the `extends` keyword. What gives?

If a class doesn't explicitly extend an existing class, it implicitly extends the "root" Java class, `Object`. The `Object` class has some interesting features, and the fact that all Java classes directly or indirectly extend `Object` has interesting consequences that we will explore later.

Persons coming to Java from another object-oriented language whose name shall remain C++ might wonder about multiple inheritance. Java has the concept of *interfaces*. An interface is like a class, except that it may not contain data[10] and may contain only method definitions, without any implementation (Example 3.25). An interface may not be *instantiated* (created with the `new` operator),[11] so how do you make use of interfaces? Well, a class extends exactly one existing base class, but it may *implement* any number of interfaces by using the `implements` keyword (Example 3.26).

Example 3.25 An interface

```
public interface
Identifiable
{
   public int getID();
}
```

As you can see, a class that implements an interface must provide an implementation of all the methods defined in the interface. We said that an interface cannot be instantiated, but you can declare a variable of type `Identifiable`

---

10. Actually, an interface may contain `final static` data, but since we haven't introduced these concepts yet, just pretend interfaces cannot contain data for now and we'll put the lie to it later.

11. Although you can do something that looks suspiciously like it with *anonymous inner classes*—but since we haven't introduced these concepts yet, just pretend that you cannot instantiate an interface; you will see such use later.

Example 3.26 A class that implements an interface

```
class
Sample
  implements Identifiable
{
  private int id;

  public void method()
  {
    System.out.println(id);
  }

  public int getID()
  {
    return id;
  }
}
```

---

and assign an instance of the `Sample` class to it. In fact, you could assign an instance of any class that implements the `Identifiable` interface to it.

Interfaces may also have an `extends` keyword. In other words, an interface may inherit from an existing interface. This may be useful if you know you will want to use methods from both the extended and the base interface without having to cast the object reference. Otherwise extending an interface is unnecessary since a given class may implement as many interfaces as desired.

3.4.2.1   *Inheritance and Encapsulation*

Encapsulation and inheritance are related to one another and are controlled by *access modifiers* on classes, data members, and methods. Let's spend a little time talking about these modifiers and what they mean.

The access modifier keywords are `public`, `private`, and `protected`. When a data member or method is `private`, it can only be accessed or called from within this specific class. Neither classes that extend this class, nor classes outside this class may access such a data member or call such a method. However, one instance of a class can access `private` members of another instance of the same class. We don't encourage such use.

When a data member or method is marked `protected`, however, the only classes that can access such a data member or method are either 1) classes that extend this class and their descendants, or 2) other classes in this package (even if they don't extend this class). Classes in other packages (unless they extend this class) can not get at such members.

A `public` data member or method may be accessed by any code in any class.

What if you do not put an access specifier on? Then the item (data member, method, or class) has package visibility. Such an item is accessible to any other class within the package, but no further. Not even derived classes, unless they are in the same package, are allowed to see it.[12]

In terms of how restrictive the access is, you can think of the terms in order of decreasing strictness as:

- `private`
- (package)[13]
- `protected`
- `public`

> **TIP**
>
> Beginner Java programmers often declare everything as `public`, so that they can ignore such issues. But then they get the OO religion, and having experienced reliability issues (others messing with their variables) they go to the other extreme and declare `private` as much as possible. The problem here is that they often don't know how others will want to reuse their code. Restricting everything to `private` makes reuse more narrow. We prefer using `private` for data members but `protected` for those internal helper methods that you might otherwise make `private`; this hides your implementation from most other classes while allowing someone to override your methods, effectively providing a way for them to override your implementation. Allow those who would build on your work the ability to do so without having to reimplement.

Here is a simple example of each type of declaration:

---

12. If you are a C++ programmer, the following description may mean something to you (if not, skip this): All classes within a package are essentially "friends."

13. Remember there is no keyword for package level protection, rather it is the absence of a keyword that denotes this level of protection. We had to write something in that space on the page so you'd know what we're talking about.

```
private String hidn;
String pkgstr;
protected String protstr;
public String wideOpen;
```

3.4.2.2 The static statement

Another keyword qualifier on declarations that we need to describe is the static keyword. When a variable is declared static then there is only one instance of that variable shared among all instances of the class. Since the variable exists apart from a particular instance of the class, one refers to it with the class name followed by a dot followed by the variable name, as in System.out.

Similarly, methods can be declared static as well. This also means that you don't need an instance of the class to call them, just the class name, as in System.getProperties().

Now with Java 5.0, you don't even need the class name, provided that you have a static import statement at the top of your class, for example:

```
import static java.lang.System.*;
```

3.4.2.3 The final statement

Another way that static is often seen is in conjunction with the final keyword. When a variable is declared final then a value can be assigned to it once, but never changed. This can make for good constants.

Since public will make the variable visible to all other classes, static will make it a class variable (available without an instance of that class), and final will keep it from being altered (even though it is publicly available), then combining all of those gives us a good declaration for a constant, for example:

```
public static void long lightSpeed = 186000;    // mps
```

New to Java 5.0 is the explicit creation of enumerated types. Prior to 5.0, programmers would often use static final constants even when the particular value was unimportant, as a way to provide compile-time checking of the use of the constant values. Here is an example of a declaration of a set of enumerated values:

```
enum WallMods { DOOR, WINDOW, VENT, GLASSBLOCK };
```

TIP

A common technique used with `public static final` constants is to put them in an interface definition. (This is the exception to the rule that interfaces define method signatures but contain no data.) When a class wants to use one or more of those constants, it is declared to implement that interface:

```
public MyClass
   extends BigClass
   implements Comparable, LotsaConstants
{
...
}
```

In defining `MyClass` we have declared that it implements `LotsaConstants` (not a name that we recommend you using). That makes all the constants that we have defined inside the `LotsaConstants` interface available to the `MyClass` class. Since classes can implement many different interfaces, this doesn't interfere with the use of other "real" interfaces, such as `Comparable`.

WARNING

The keyword `enum` is new to Java 5.0, so older programs that may have used `enum` as a variable name and will now cause an error when recompiled for Java 5.0.

The `enum` will look very familiar to C/C++ programmers, but there are some important differences. In C/C++ the values of the `enum` elements are, in reality, integer values. Not so in Java. Here they are their own type, but can be converted to a `String` via the `toString()` method, with a value that matches the name, for easy reading and debugging.

Enumerated values can be used in `==` comparisons since they will be defined only once (like other `static final` constants) and it would only be references that are passed around. They would be referenced by the name of the enumeration followed by dot followed by the particular value (e.g., `WallMods.WINDOW`) and used as an object. (We have used uppercase for the names not out of any syntax requirement, but only to follow the typical naming convention for constants.)

3.4.3 Polymorphism

Polymorphism (from the Greek *poly* meaning "many" and *morph* meaning "shape") refers to the language's ability to deal with objects of many different "shapes," that is, classes, as if they were all the same. We have already seen that Java does this via the `extends` and `implements` keywords. You can define an interface and then define two classes that both implement this interface.

Remember our `Sample` class (Example 3.26). We'll now define another class, `Employee`, which also implements the `Identifiable` interface (Example 3.27).

Example 3.27 The `Employee` class

```
class
Employee
  extends Person
  implements Identifiable
{
  private int empl_id;

  public int getID()
  {
    return empl_id;
  }
}
```

Notice that the same method, `getID()`, is implemented in the `Employee` class, but that the field from which it gets the ID value is a different field. That's implementation-specific—the interface defines only the methods that can be called but not their internal implementation. The `Employee` class not only implements `Identifiable`, but it also extends the `Person` class, so we better show you what our example `Person` class looks like (Example 3.28).

To make a really useful `Person` class would take a lot more code than we need for our example. The important part for our example is only that it is quite different from the `Sample` class we saw earlier.

Example 3.29 demonstrates the use of polymorphism. We only show some small relevant snippets of code; there would be a lot more code for this to become an entire, complete example. Don't be distracted by the constructors; we made up some new ones just for this example, that aren't in the class definitions above. Can you see where the polymorphism is at work?

Example 3.28 The `Person` class

```
class
Person
{
  String name;
  Address addr;

  public
  Person(String name, Address addr)
  {
    this.name = name;
    this.addr = addr;

  } // constructor

  // ... lots more code is here

  public String getName()
  {
    return name;
  }
}
```

Example 3.29 An example use of polymorphism

```
//...
Sample labwork = new Sample(petridish);
Employee tech = new Employee(newguy, 27);
Identifiable stuff;

//...
if (mode) {
    stuff = labwork;
} else {
    stuff = tech;
}
id = stuff.getID();
```

The key point here is when the call is made to `getID()`. The compiler can't know at compile time which object will be referred to by `stuff`, so it doesn't know whose `getID()` method will be called. But don't worry—it works this all out at runtime. That's polymorphism—Java can deal with these different objects while you, the programmer, can describe them in a generalized way.

One other related keyword should be mentioned here, `abstract`. When one declares a class as an abstract class, then the class itself is an incomplete definition. With an abstract class you define all the data of the class but need only write method declarations, not necessarily all the code for the methods. This makes abstract classes similar to interfaces, but in an abstract class, some of the methods can be fully written out.

If you'd like to know more about polymorphism, "late binding," and more of this aspect of Java, read Chapter 7 of Eckel's *Thinking in Java*. There is an extensive example there with much more detail than we can cover here.

3.5 O, TEMPLATES! WHERE ART THOU?

Programmers familiar with C++ may be wondering how in the world an OOP language without templates can be useful.

> **NOTE**
>
> Actually, something very much like templates is available in Java 5.0.[14] A new feature, which Sun calls *generics*, looks an awful lot like C++ templates (including similar syntax). It provides compile-time type checking and implicit casting when retrieving objects from a generic container.

Speaking as programmers who worked with C++ before it had templates, we can sympathize. Java's previous lack of true templates does impose some limits on generic programming, but not as much as one might think. Remember that unlike C++, all Java classes inherit from exactly one base class, and that if no base class is specified, they extend the `Object` class. This means that every single Java class either directly or indirectly extends `Object`, and thus all Java classes are instances of `Object`. So if you need, for example, to implement a container, you can guarantee that it can contain any Java class by implementing a container for the `Object` type. Java also has runtime type identification features that are more than a match for anything C++ has, plus it has type-safe

---

14. Java 5.0 will only be out by the time this book is completed.

downcasting[15] so that in the worst case scenario, your program has a nice, clean type exception. You simply do not get the kind of "mystery bugs" that you can get in C++ when you miscast an object.[16]

Thanks to interfaces and a true single object hierarchy, many of the uses of C++ templates go away. We doubt very much that you will miss them. In many cases, such as STL algorithms and other functional programming implementations, you can use interfaces to produce similar results.

Critics of the Java language have a point when they complain that all the type casting of class references in order to expose desired interfaces tends to produce code that violates object-oriented principles. The fact that a class or interface implements all these other named interfaces is hard-coded all over the place in an application's code. Such critics say this is a bad thing, because it violates encapsulation and implementation hiding. These critics have a point. If you find yourself frequently downcasting object references, consider using the Java 5.0 generics, or try to find another way to code what you want to do. There may be a better way. In defense of the original Java approach (before generics), all casts are runtime type safe. An exception is thrown if a class reference is improperly cast. In C++, if you miscast a pointer, it assumes you meant it. Java certainly can be awkward, but errors will get caught. Sometimes that is more important.

3.6 VIRTUALLY FINAL

One difficulty anyone writing about Java faces is whether or not to assume your readers are familiar with C++. In this chapter, we have tried to help those with C++ experience without requiring such knowledge. But it is in the inevitable comparisons between those languages that many subtle Java features are best discussed. We promised you that we would talk about the relative merits of `virtual` (a C++ concept) and `final` (a Java concept). To do that, we have to assume some knowledge of C++. So, let's reverse the pattern and talk about the

---

15. Don't worry if this is all gibberish to you right now. We will revisit these topics in detail when we come upon them in the course of our sample project.

16. Actually, we're being a bit optimistic here. While Java programs are not subject to many mystery bugs, the Java Virtual Machines that run Java code are written in traditional languages, and there have been VMs with bugs. Time and again we see that there is no "silver bullet." But in our experience, Java comes close. So very close.

straight Java facts so we can let the non-C++ folks move on while we go a little deeper with you C++'ers.

In Java, a method or a class may be declared `final`. A method that is declared `final` may not be overridden in classes that extend the class containing the `final` implementation. A class that is declared `final` may not be extended at all.

Now, the comparisons to C++ require us to talk about a language feature that does not exist at all in Java. In C++, unless a method is declared `virtual`, when a class is used by reference to a base class (for example, when using `Employee` as a `Person`), the base class version of the method is called. If the method is declared virtual, the version of the method called is the version for the type of `Person` referenced (in this case, `Employee`). In Java, all methods are virtual. There is no such keyword in Java.

3.7   A USEFUL SIMPLE APPLICATION

We will use the sample application shown in Example 3.30 in other sections of this book to illustrate the use of Java tools. This example is so simple (a single class) that it doesn't demonstrate the object-oriented aspect of development, but it does make use of some APIs that take advantage of it. We will not walk you through this application right here, but present it as a listing of a complete Java class. Not all of the APIs used in this example will be explained, so you may want to refer to the Javadoc pages for explanations of object types or method calls that don't seem obvious.

3.8   REVIEW

We've taken a very quick look at the syntax of Java statements, classes, and interfaces. Much of the syntax is very reminiscent of C, though Java's object-oriented features differ in significant ways from C++. We looked at how to put Java classes into packages, and at the implications of this for locating the `.class` files.

We also showed what the HTML-based Javadoc documentation looks like. These HTML pages will likely be a handy reference for you as you design and write your Java code.

Example 3.30 Single class example: FetchURL

```java
import java.net.*;
import java.io.*;

public class FetchURL {
  private URL requestedURL;

  public FetchURL(String urlName)
  {
    try {
       requestedURL = new URL(urlName);
    } catch (Exception e) {
       e.printStackTrace();
    }
  }

  public String toString()
  {
    String rc = "";
    String line;
    BufferedReader rdr;

    try {
       rdr = new BufferedReader(
         new InputStreamReader(
         requestedURL.openConnection().getInputStream()
         )
       );

       while ((line = rdr.readLine()) != null)
       {
         rc = rc + line + "\n";
       }
    } catch (Exception e) {
       e.printStackTrace();
       rc = null;
    }

    return rc;
  }
```

```
public static void main(String[] args)
{
  int i;
  FetchURL f;

  for (i = 0; i < args.length; i++)
  {
    System.out.println(args[i] + ":");
    System.out.println(new FetchURL(args[i]));
  }
}
}
```

3.9 WHAT YOU STILL DON'T KNOW

We have deliberately avoided file I/O. For Java, it is a multilayered and complex topic—and with version 1.4 of Java, there is a whole new set of additional classes (`java.nio.*`) to consider. We refer you instead to Chapter 11 of Eckel's *Thinking in Java*.

There are also a few Java keywords that we have not yet discussed, notably `synchronize`.

Even if you know all the Java syntax, it may still take a while to get familiar with the way that syntax is typically put to use. Experience and reading other people's Java code will be your best teachers—but don't assume that a particular approach is good just because someone else uses it; much new code has been written in the last several years as people have learned Java. Be sure it's a style worth imitating, and if you find a better way to do it, use it.

3.10 RESOURCES

- Bruce Eckel, *Thinking in Java*.
- Cay S. Horstmann and Gary Cornell, *Core Java 2: Volume 1 Fundamentals*, especially Chapter 3.
- John Lewis and William Loftus, *Java Software Solutions*.
- The Sun Microsystems Java Tutorial.[17]

---

17. http://java.sun.com/docs/books/tutorial/index.html

3.11 EXERCISES

1. Write a simple class with a `main()` method that prints out the arguments supplied on the command line used to invoke it. First use a `for` loop to do this, then a `while` loop, then a `do-while`. What differences do you notice? Which do you find most amenable for this task?

2. Modify the previous class to quit echoing its arguments should it encounter an argument of length 5. (You can tell the length of a `String` object with the `length()` method, e.g., `mystr.length()`.) Did you use `break`, or `continue`, or some other mechanism?

Chapter 4

Where Am I?
Execution Context

Java claims—and rightly so—to be a "compile once, run anywhere" language. But when a program starts, that "anywhere" is now a specific somewhere. When running a Java application on Linux, or any environment for that matter, the question arises, "Where am I?" (context, environment, familiar landmarks). What can a Java program find out about its environment? In particular, on the Linux platform, (how) can we get at:

- Command-line parameters?
- The current shell's environment variables?
- The current working directory?
- The location of data files?

The answers to these questions will depend on what kind of Java application you are creating, and just how portable you want your application to be.

4.1 WHAT YOU WILL LEARN

We'll show you how Java provides access to the command-line parameters and environment variables. We'll also discuss the Java `RunTime` and `Property` classes. Java's use of the standard input/output/error streams is also briefly covered, along with an introduction to those concepts. We'll end with a short word on portability concerns.

4.2 A SIMPLE START

The most basic external information that a program may use is the information supplied on its invocation—simple parameters or arguments, such as filenames or options, that can direct its running and make it a more flexible tool. Let's start with getting at that information from a Java program.

4.2.1 Command-Line Arguments

When a program is run from the command line, more than just the program name can be supplied. Here are some examples:

```
$ javac Hi.java
$ mv Acct.java core/Account.java
$ ls -l
```

In the first example, we invoked a program called **javac** and gave it the parameter `Hi.java`, the name of the file containing the Java program that we want **javac** to compile to Java byte code. (We've got a whole chapter on how to set up and run the Java compiler, see Chapter 5.) The **mv** got two command-line arguments, `Acct.java` and `core/Account.java`, which look a lot like pathnames. The **ls** command has one argument, `-l`, which in Linux usually indicates, by its leading minus sign, that it is an option for altering the behavior of the command. (In this case it produces the "long" version of the directory listing.)

Even point-and-click GUIs allow such parameters to be supplied, though often not visible to the user. In KDE, one can create a new desktop icon that is a link to an application. Such an icon has a property sheet that lists, on the **Execute** tab, the command to be run, including any parameters.

In Java, the parameters supplied on the command line are available to the `main()` method of a Java class. The signature for this method is:

```
public static void main(String args[])
```

From within `main()`, the various parameters are available as the elements of the array of `Strings`. The class in Example 4.1 will display those parameters when the program is run.

Example 4.1 Java program to dump command-line arguments

```
/*
 * simple command-line parameter displayer
 */

public class
CLine
{
  public static void
  main(String [] args)
  {
    for (int i = 0; i < args.length; i++)
    {
      System.out.println(args[i]);
    }

  } // main

} // class CLine
```

We compile and run the example, providing a few command-line parameters:

```
$ javac CLine.java
$ java CLine hello world file.txt blue
hello
world
file.txt
blue
$
```

Not all classes will have `main()` methods, but any can. Even if several classes in a package have `main()` methods, that is not a problem. Which one will be the "main" `main()`? It's the class we specified when we invoked our program. In Example 4.1, the `main()` that is executed is the one in the `CLine` class. Even if `CLine` used other classes (it does—`String` is a class) it doesn't matter if those other classes have `main()` methods or not.

4.2.2   Unit Testing Made Easy

Why all the fuss about `main()` and command-line parameters? Such `main()` methods are a handy way to provide unit tests for a class. The tests can be controlled by the command-line parameters. By testing each class you can reduce the time to integrate the parts of an application. Furthermore, a set of unit tests can be built up (e.g., as shell scripts) to provide automated regression tests for the entire project. As a more rigorous and systematic approach to unit testing, we discuss **junit** in Chapter 13.

4.3 THE `System` CLASS

The Java `System` class provides some of the answers to questions about our environment. What follows is not an exhaustive discussion of all the methods in the `System` class, but only of those areas that touch on our specific focus—input/output (I/O) and environment variables.

   Be aware that all of the methods in the `System` class are `static`. Therefore you never need to (and you can't) call a constructor on `System`. You just use the "class name, dot, method name" syntax to call the method (e.g., `System.getProperties()`). Similarly, the accessible fields in `System` are all `static`, so for some of the I/O-related methods you use the "class name, dot, field name, dot, method name" syntax (e.g., `System.out.println()`). As of Java 5.0, you can shorten this, by using a `static import`, that is:

```
import static java.lang.System.*;
```

Then in your other references you can leave off `System`, for example, `getProperties()` and `out.println()`.

4.3.1   Java and Standard I/O

Java adopted the UNIX concept of standard I/O (see Section 1.3.1.1). The Linux file descriptors are available to a running Java program as I/O streams via the `System` class. The `System` class contains three `public static` fields named `in`, `out`, and `err`. You've probably already seen `out` in Java programs with statements like this:

```
System.out.println("Hello, world.");
```

You can also write:

```
System.err.println("Error message here\n");
```

and

```
BufferedReader in = new BufferedReader(new
                        InputStreamReader(System.in));
while ((line = in.readLine()) != null) {
...
}
```

Java parallels Linux nicely on I/O descriptors. If you redirect any of those file descriptors from the shell command line when you execute a Java program, then that redirected I/O is available to your Java application—with no additional work on your part.

In the example above, if you have `System.in` all wrapped up into a `BufferedReader` from which your program is reading lines, then you can run that program as:

```
$ java MyCode
```

and it will read input as you type it on your keyboard. This may be how you test your program, but when you put this program to its intended use, you may want it to be able to read from a file. This you can do without any change to the program—thanks to file descriptors, input streams, and redirecting input, for example:

```
$ java MyCode < file2
```

which will let the same Java program read from the file named `file2` rather than from keyboard.

Your Java program can also set the values of `System.in`, `System.out`, and `System.err` as it executes, to change their destinations.

One common example is changing the destination of `System.out`, the typical recipient of debugging or logging messages. Say you've created a class

or even a whole package of classes that write log messages to `System.out`
(e.g., `System.out.println("some message")`). Now you realize that you'd
like the output to go somewhere else.

You could redirect standard `out`, as in:

```
$ java SomeClass > log
```

but that requires the user to remember to redirect the output every time the
program is invoked. That's fine for testing, or if the output is intended to go
to a different place each time it is invoked. But, in this example, we always want
the output to go to the same location.

Without changing any of the `System.out.println()` statements, all the
messages can be sent to a new location by reassigning the `System.out` print
stream. The `System` class has a *setter* for `out`—that is, a method which will let
you set a new value for `out`. In your Java program, open the new destination
file and give this to the `System` class:

```
PrintStream ps = new PrintStream("pathname");
System.setOut(ps);
```

It will be used from that point forward in the execution of this program as its
`out` output stream.

> **CAUTION**
>
> Changing standard `out` (or `in`, or `err`) will make the change for all classes
> from here on in this invocation of the Java runtime—they are `static` fields of
> the one `System` class. Since this is so serious a move, the Java Security
> Manager (see Section 5.8.4.2) provides a check for `setIO` to see if the Java
> program is allowed to make such changes. If such a security manager is in
> place and you are not allowed to make such changes, an exception
> (`SecurityException`) will be thrown. Note also that the permission applies
> to setting any of the fields; it doesn't divide the permission into setting one
> (e.g., `out`) but not another (e.g., `in`).

4.3.2   Environment Variables

When Linux programs are run they have the open file descriptors described
above. They also carry with them a list of "name=value" pairs called their
environment. These environment variables allow for context to be shared among

several successively executed programs. Some examples of environment variables are:

- USER is the name you used to log in.
- HOME is the directory where you start when you log in.
- PATH is the list of directories searched for executable files.

To see the environment variables defined in your current shell, type env at the command prompt:

```
$ env
HOME=/home/user01
USER=user01
PATH=/bin:/usr/bin:/usr/local/bin:/home/user01/bin
...
$
```

The names of environment variables, sometimes referred to as *shell variables*, are traditionally uppercase, though that is only a convention. The variable names are treated in a case sensitive fashion (e.g., Home != HOME).

You can set environment variables for use in the current shell with a simple assignment statement:

```
$ VAR=value
```

That will set the value for the duration of this shell, but *not* for any of its subprocesses. Since running another program is a subprocess, such an assignment won't be visible in your running program. Instead, you can export the variable so that it is carried forward to all subprocesses:[1]

```
$ export VAR=value
```

4.3.3 Java and Environment Variables

If these environment variables are available to all Linux processes, then how do we get at them from a Java program? Well, we can't do it quite as directly as you might think. In previous (1.2 and older) versions of Java, the System class

---

1. If you are using **csh** (the C-shell, another Linux command-line interpreter), then the syntax is slightly different. Instead of export name=value use setenv name value (note the different keyword and no equal sign).

Example 4.2 Java program to dump environment variables

```
/*
 * simple environment examiner
 */
import java.util.*;

public class
AllEnv
{
  public static void
  main(String [] args)
  {
    Properties props = java.lang.System.getProperties();
    for (Enumeration enm = props.propertyNames(); enm.hasMoreElements();)
    {
      String key = (String) enm.nextElement();
      System.out.print(key);
      System.out.print(" = ");
      System.out.println(props.getProperty(key));
    }

  } // main

} // class AllEnv
```

had a getenv() method. Its argument was a String name of an environment variable and it returned the environment variable's value as a String. This has been deprecated. In fact, an attempt to use getenv() in more recent versions of Java will result in an exception. Sun decided that this was too platform-specific; not all platforms have environment variables.

Now (Java 1.3 and beyond) the preferred approach is to use the getProperties() and getProperty() methods of the System class. How are these different from the getenv() approach? To a Linux developer, getenv() was easy and straightforward—just not very portable. To accommodate other systems, Java defines a set of properties that are reasonable to expect to be defined on any system, and provides a Java property name for each one.

To see the entire list, call the getProperties() method. It returns a Properties class, which is an extension of the Hashtable class. From this class you can get an Enumeration of the names, as Example 4.2 demonstrates.

Now compile and run this example:

```
$ javac AllEnv.java
$ java AllEnv
```

and you will get a long list of properties—in no particular order. They are kept in a hashtable and thus not sorted. Of course it would be easier to use this list if they were sorted. Linux to the rescue.

```
$ java AllEnv | sort
```

It's often in simple little steps like this that one begins to see the power of Linux. In Linux, not every desirable feature has to be crammed into every possible place where it might be used. Instead, features can be written once and connected to one another as needed. Here what we need is to have the list of properties sorted. We don't need to worry that our class didn't sort its output. In Linux we just connect the standard output of the Java program with a sort utility that Linux provides.

So what are all these properties? Many of them have to do with Java-related information (`java.version`, and so on), but a few are more general. Those that parallel the typical Linux environment variables are:

- `file.separator` is the file separator ("/" on Linux).
- `path.separator` is the path separator (":" on Linux).
- `line.separator` is the line separator ("\n" on Linux).
- `user.name` is the user's account name.
- `user.home` is the user's home directory.
- `user.dir` is the user's current working directory.

But that leaves out so many environment variables, especially the application-specific ones (e.g., CVSROOT). How would a Java program get at these?

Because of this new, more portable way to describe the environment, there is no easy way to get at other environment variables. There are a few approaches, but they are all indirect.

First, you can add to the properties list by defining new properties on the command line when invoking the program, for example:

```
$ java -Dkey=value AllEnv
```

You can list several properties on the line by repeating the `-D` parameter:

```
$ java -DHOME=/home/mydir -DALT=other -DETC="so forth" AllEnv
```

Instead of typing those values, you'd probably want to let the Linux shell put in the values from its environment. So you'd use shell variables, for example:

```
$ java -DHOME="${HOME}" -DALT="${ALT}" -DETC="${ETC}" AllEnv
```

assuming that HOME, ALT, and ETC have already been defined in the shell's environment.[2]

If there are only a few variables that you need to pass to Java, put them on the command line as shown above. Put that command line into a shell script and use the script to invoke the program so that the parameters are supplied every time.

But if you want to access many or all of the environment variables then you may want to do something a little more complex. Notice the syntax of the output of the env command. It is in the same format (name=value) as are properties. So if we use a shell script to invoke our program, we can have it place all these values into a file by redirecting output, then open this file as a Java properties file and thus make all the name/value pairs accessible.

The following commands in a shell script attempt to do just that:

```
env > /tmp/$$.env
java -DENVFILE=/tmp/$$.env MyClass
rm /tmp/$$.env
```

where MyClass is the Java program that you wish to run.

TIP

The shell variable $$ is the numeric process ID of the running process. This provides a unique ID during each invocation of the program. Each run of the script will have its own process and thus its own process ID. Thus a single user could execute this script multiple times concurrently without fear of collision with himself or others.

---

2. The quotations around the shell variables keep any embedded spaces as part of the variable's value. The curly braces are not strictly necessary in this use.

We remove the temporary file with the **rm** command in the last line of the script to avoid cluttering our `/tmp` directory with lots of these files.

But now we have to add code to `MyClass` to open the file defined by `ENVFILE` and read the properties it contains. This leads us naturally to the Java `Properties` class, the subject of our next section, where we'll talk more about this example.

4.4 THE `Properties` CLASS

The Javadoc page for the `Properties` class describes it as "a persistent set of properties . . . saved to . . . or loaded from . . . a stream." In other words, it is a hashtable (a set of name/value pairs) that can be read from or written to a stream—which typically means a file. (Other things can be streams, but for now, think "file".)

The great thing about name/value pairs is how readable and usable they are. When they are written to a file, there's no fancy formatting, no fixed width fields, no unreadable encryptions and special characters; it's just `name=value`. You could say that the "=" and the newline are the special characters that provide all the formatting you need. It means that you can type up a properties file with the simplest of editors, or even generate one quickly as we saw in the previous example (here we use a simple filename):

```
$ env > propertyfile
```

Properties are also easy to use. Since they're based on hashtables, there is no searching code to write. You call a method giving it the name, it returns the value.

If we pass in the name of the file via the `-D` parameter, then we can get that filename in Java with:

```
System.getProperty("ENVFILE");
```

where `ENVFILE` is a name that we made up and used on the command line:

```
$ java -DENVFILE=propertyfile MyClass
```

We could also have used:

```
$ java MyClass propertyfile
```

so that args[0][3] in the Java code to get the name of the file (see Section 4.2.1), but since we want to learn about properties, we'll use the property methods here.

Now let's open that property file (Example 4.3).

Example 4.3 Demonstrating the `Properties` class

```
import java.io.*;
import java.util.*;

public class
EnvFileIn
{
  public static void
  main(String [] args)
    throws IOException
  {
    String envfile = System.getProperty("ENVFILE", ".envfile");

    BufferedInputStream bis = new BufferedInputStream(
                            new FileInputStream(envfile));
    Properties prop = new Properties();
    prop.load(bis);
    bis.close();

    prop.list(System.out);  // dumps the whole list to System.out

  } // main

} // class EnvFileIn
```

Notice the way that we got the value for the environment file's name. This form of the getProperty() call provides not only the name we are looking up (ENVFILE) but also lets us specify a default value in case the name is not found in the properties list. Here our default value is .envfile.

Just as it was a simple matter of using the load() method to read up an entire file of properties, so you can write out the entire list of properties to the

3. In C language, the arg[0] is the command being invoked; not so in Java. In Java, the first element of the array is the first argument of the command line (propertyfile in our example).

screen with the `list()` method. The argument to `list()` is either a `PrintStream` or a `PrintWriter`. `System.out` is a `PrintStream`, so that will work.

The format of the properties file is `name=value`. But it is also possible to put comments in a properties file. Any line beginning with a "#" is ignored. Try it.

It's also easy to (re)write a file of properties with the `store()` method. The parameters are an `OutputStream` and a `String`; the latter will serve as a label for the parameters, written to an opening comment in the properties file.

If your program needs to examine the list of property names, you can get an `Enumerator` of the entire list via the `propertyNames()` method. Modify Example 4.3 to replace the `list()` call with a do-it-yourself version that uses the `Enumerator` returned from `propertyNames()` to list all the names and values. Hint: Use `getProperty()` on each name retrieved via the enumeration.

The Java `Properties` class extends the `java.util.Hashtable` class. This means, in part, that all the other `Hashtable` methods are available to a `Properties` class. Methods such as `containsKey()` or `containsValue()` can be helpful, as can `isEmpty()`. One caution, though. You should use `setProperty()` if you want to add values to `Properties`, rather than the `Hashtable`'s `put()` method. They do largely the same thing, but `setProperty()` enforces that its parameters are `Strings`. This is important if you want to write out the properties to a file, as it's meant for `Strings` only.

4.5 THE `Runtime` CLASS

Let's discuss one last way to get to the underlying (Linux) system information. Be warned, though, that this is the least portable approach of all we have mentioned.

4.5.1 `exec()`

Familiar to C/C++ programmers, the `exec()` call in the Java `Runtime` class does much the same thing. It gives you a way to start another program outside of the current Java Virtual Machine. In doing so, you can connect to its standard in/out/err and either drive it by writing to its standard in, or read its results from its standard out. (Yes, that's correct—we write to its input and read from its output. If that sounds wrong, think it through. Our Java code is on the opposite side of the I/O fence. The external program's output becomes our input.)

Example 4.4 shows a Java program that can invoke an arbitrary Linux program. The output of the program is displayed.

Example 4.4 Java program to execute any Linux program

```java
import java.io.*;

public class
Exec
{
  public static void
  main(String [] args)
    throws IOException
  {
    String ln;
    Process p = Runtime.getRuntime().exec(args);
    BufferedReader br = new BufferedReader(
                          new InputStreamReader(
                            p.getInputStream())));

    while((ln = br.readLine()) != null) {
      System.out.println(ln);
    }
    System.out.println("returns:" + p.exitValue());

  } // main

} // class Exec
```

The command-line arguments are taken to be the command to be executed and its arguments. For example:

```
$ java Exec ls -l
```

Be aware that in this example, only the standard output is captured and displayed from the invoked process. Error messages written to standard `err` will be lost, unless you modify the program to handle this. We leave that as an exercise for the reader.

Check your Linux knowledge—see if you understand the distinction. If you invoke the sample Exec program as:

```
$ java Exec ls -l *.java
```

the shell does the wildcard expansion before invoking the Java runtime. The `*.java` becomes many files listed on the command line (provided that you have `.java` files in this directory). If you try to pass the `*.java` through literally to `exec(ls '*.java')` it will likely return an error (which won't be displayed using our example code) and you'll see a nonzero return status (e.g., 1). That's because **ls** doesn't expand the `*`. The shell does that. So **ls** is looking for a single file named `*.java`, which we hope doesn't exist in your directory.

4.5.2 Portability

Be aware that the more environment-specific code you build, the less portable your application becomes. It's not uncommon to use a properties file as a way to parameterize your program, to customize its behavior in a given installation. But keep these to a minimum to stay portable. Avoid invoking other programs, they are likely not available in all environments where Java can run. Java's claim to "compile once, run anywhere" is amazingly true—provided you keep away from logic in your program that goes looking for trouble.

4.6 REVIEW

Java command-line parameters are not that different from C/C++ command-line parameters. Environment variables are a different story. Most of the shell's environment variables are not readily accessible, and we looked at how you might deal with this situation.

We have discussed, among other things, some uses for these classes: `java.util.Properties`, `java.lang.System`, and `java.lang.Runtime`, but we have only barely scratched the surface. There are many more methods available in these classes with which you can do lots more.

4.7 WHAT YOU STILL DON'T KNOW

The biggest topic in this area that we've avoided for now is the Java Native Interface (JNI), a mechanism whereby you can get outside of the Java environment to make calls to existing (*native*) libraries—for example, Linux system calls. In a coming chapter we'll actually give you an example of such a call.

Then you'll really be able to make your application nonportable and system-dependent. (But sometimes portability isn't your goal, right?)

4.8 RESOURCES

Perhaps the best resource for the specifics that you'll need to work with the topics mentioned in this chapter is the Javadoc documentation on the classes that we have mentioned. Learn to read Javadoc pages (see Section 3.2.2.3), bookmark them in your browser, and keep them handy as you write your Java code.

Chapter 5

The Sun Microsystems Java Software Development Kit

The Sun Microsystems Java Software Development Kit (Java SDK) is the most basic toolkit for Java development. In some ways, it remains the most flexible. Your understanding of Java development should include this very basic toolset, even if you move beyond it to more "hand-holding" Integrated Development Environments (IDEs). This chapter introduces all the major components of the Java 2 Standard Edition (J2SE)[1] development kit. The Enterprise Edition is discussed later. There is a third Java SDK (the Micro Edition) for embedded development which we will not cover in this book.

---

1. What does the "2" in "Java 2" mean? Hoo boy. Explaining product marketing names is not always easy. There was Java 1.0. Then there were several releases of Java 1.1.x. Then Sun released Java 1.2.x, but they started calling it "Java 2". Since then, they have released Java 1.3.x, Java 1.4.x and they still call it "Java 2". But it gets even more confusing. Sun is now releasing what had been preliminarily numbered 1.5, but is now officially called the 5.0 release, though they still call it Java 2. That's what the 2 in "J2SE" refers to. So it is Java 2 platform, version 5.0. Any questions? See http://java.sun.com/j2se/naming_versioning_5_0.html.

5.1 WHAT YOU WILL LEARN

In this chapter you will learn about the purpose of the programs in the Sun Java Software Development Kit. We will provide you with some details of their options and demonstrate their use in compiling our two sample applications. The next step up in tool automation would be the build tool known as Ant (see Chapter 9 for more information).

5.2 ALL YOU NEED, AND NOT ONE THING MORE

These days, many programmers are what we affectionately call "tool junkies." They can only develop software with the support of complex integrated development environments, their supporting classes, and screen painting tools. By this, we do not mean to imply that we are Luddites. The right IDE can indeed be an enormous boost to productivity, but a programmer should be able to work with any tool. The Sun Java SDK is the lowest common denominator; if you can be productive with it, then you can be productive with absolutely any Java development environment. That makes your skills more portable. And that means more jobs are open to you. And that is good for you and your employers.

The Sun Microsystems Java SDK (formerly known as, and often still referred to as the Sun Microsystems Java Development Kit, or JDK) provides you with all the tools you need to compile, document, run, package, debug, and deploy Java applications and applets. It does this with a collection of purely text-based command-line tools. This is no-frills software development. But a lot of us crusty old types really like that.

You should become comfortable and familiar with these tools. Some IDEs are just fancy window dressing that calls these tools underneath (some are not—some have written their own Java compilers, for example). If you can use these tools comfortably to build any kind of Java program, then you know you have a mastery of the basics and are not "addicted" to a particular tool. You also know the "hardest" way to get the job done. This will help you to make good choices about tools that enhance productivity. Some tools, we find, actually slow you down or get in your way in some cases. If you know the lowest level, you can better recognize the merits and flaws of more advanced tools. Enough justification. On to the SDK.

> **NOTE**
>
> By the way, you will notice that we do not cover the installation of the Development Kit in this chapter. That is because we are deferring the discussion of installation for the next chapter, where we also introduce the concept of multiple concurrent Development Kits on a single box. See Chapter 6 for details.

5.3 THE JAVA COMPILER

At the heart of the SDK is **javac**, the Java compiler. The general form of **javac** follows:

```
javac [option...] [sourcefile...] [@optfile...]
```

The *option* list may be zero or more command-line options. We'll detail those later. The *sourcefile* list may be the name of zero or more Java source files. Usually you specify just the "main" class of an application. As we will describe later, **javac** generally will compile all necessary .java files for any classes that main() class references, directly or indirectly. If you prefix a filename with the at sign (@), the contents of the file will be treated as if they had been typed on the command line.

5.3.1 Compiler Behavior, Defaults, and Environment Variables

In the simplest case—compiling a single class, such as our FetchURL.java class—you get no diagnostics on success (Example 5.1).

Example 5.1 Compiling FetchURL.java

```
$ javac FetchURL.java
$
```

There will now be a new file, FetchURL.class, in the directory with the Java source file. Let's run that again with a command-line option we will detail later (Example 5.2).

Boy, our single, simple, one-class application sure uses a lot of classes! It does. Where did they come from? They come from the classes referenced by

Example 5.2 Compiling `FetchURL.java` with the `-verbose` option

```
$ javac -verbose FetchURL.java
[parsing started FetchURL.java]
[parsing completed 479ms]
[loading /usr/java/j2sdk1.4.1_02/jre/lib/rt.jar(java/lang/Object.class)]
[loading /usr/java/j2sdk1.4.1_02/jre/lib/rt.jar(java/net/URL.class)]
[loading /usr/java/j2sdk1.4.1_02/jre/lib/rt.jar(java/lang/String.class)]
[checking FetchURL]
[loading /usr/java/j2sdk1.4.1_02/jre/lib/rt.jar(java/lang/Exception.class)]
[loading /usr/java/j2sdk1.4.1_02/jre/lib/rt.jar(java/lang/Throwable.class)]
[loading /usr/java/j2sdk1.4.1_02/jre/lib/rt.jar(java/io/BufferedReader.class)]
[loading /usr/java/j2sdk1.4.1_02/jre/lib/rt.jar(java/io/InputStreamReader.class)]
[loading /usr/java/j2sdk1.4.1_02/jre/lib/rt.jar(java/net/URLConnection.class)]
[loading /usr/java/j2sdk1.4.1_02/jre/lib/rt.jar(java/io/Reader.class)]
[loading /usr/java/j2sdk1.4.1_02/jre/lib/rt.jar(java/io/InputStream.class)]
[loading /usr/java/j2sdk1.4.1_02/jre/lib/rt.jar(java/lang/System.class)]
[loading /usr/java/j2sdk1.4.1_02/jre/lib/rt.jar(java/io/PrintStream.class)]
[loading /usr/java/j2sdk1.4.1_02/jre/lib/rt.jar(java/io/FilterOutputStream.class)]
[loading /usr/java/j2sdk1.4.1_02/jre/lib/rt.jar(java/io/OutputStream.class)]
[loading /usr/java/j2sdk1.4.1_02/jre/lib/rt.jar(java/lang/Error.class)]
[loading /usr/java/j2sdk1.4.1_02/jre/lib/rt.jar(java/net/MalformedURLException.class)]
[loading /usr/java/j2sdk1.4.1_02/jre/lib/rt.jar(java/io/IOException.class)]
[loading /usr/java/j2sdk1.4.1_02/jre/lib/rt.jar(java/lang/RuntimeException.class)]
[loading /usr/java/j2sdk1.4.1_02/jre/lib/rt.jar(java/lang/StringBuffer.class)]
[wrote FetchURL.class]
[total 3469ms]
$
```

the application, either directly through composition or inheritance, or indirectly because the classes we used are themselves composed of or inherit from other classes. How did the Java compiler know where to find these classes? For this, it used what the Sun documentation calls a *bootstrap classpath*, which is set when the SDK is installed. A classpath is a list of directories and/or JAR files that are searched for classes. We seem to dimly recall that in early versions of Java, there was only one classpath, and if you changed it, you had to remember to put the Java runtime JAR file on it, or none of the standard APIs were available. This, no doubt, is why Sun created the concept of a bootstrap classpath. If you use any third party JAR files or you create your own, you must tell the compiler about it by creating your own classpath.

There are two ways to provide a classpath to the Java compiler. One is through a command-line switch, which we will cover in a moment. The other is through an environment variable. The CLASSPATH environment variable lists

---

Example 5.3 Setting the CLASSPATH environment variable

```
$ export CLASSPATH=/home/mschwarz/java/simpleApp:/var/java/lib/project.jar
$ echo $CLASSPATH
/home/mschwarz/java/simpleApp:/var/java/lib/project.jar
$
```

---

directories and/or JAR or ZIP files that contain classes. Each directory or JAR file is separated from the others by a colon (":"), as shown in Example 5.3.

The classpath for the compiler consists of the bootstrap classpath plus the user-specified classpath. What does the classpath mean in terms of Java class names? Think of the classpath as a list of "package roots." In other words, when you refer to a class like `java.sql.DriverManager` or `net.multitool.SAMoney`, the Java compiler is going to go to each entry in the combined bootstrap-and-user classpath and check there for `java/sql/DriverManager.class` or `net/multitool/SAMoney.class`. If it doesn't find the `.class` file in a candidate directory, it will look for the `.java` file. If it finds the `.java` file, it will compile it and then use the resulting `.class` file. When it has a `.class` file for the class, it stops searching the classpath. In this way, compiling the single "main" class of an application will often compile the whole application (we will get to exceptions to that rule later).

5.3.2   javac Options

The Java compiler has many command-line options that modify its behavior. We will go over the most important ones here. This is not a complete reference! See the Sun SDK Documentation for complete reference information.

`-classpath`

> Sets the classpath. This overrides the CLASSPATH environment variable, if one is specified.

`-d`

> This switch is followed by a directory name. Compiled classes are placed in that directory. Normally, compiled classes are placed in the same directory as the source code.

`-deprecation`

> This causes every use or reference to a deprecated class or method to be displayed on compilation.[2]

`-g`

> Put full debugging information in the compiled class files. See also `-g:` (the next entry in this list).

`-g:keyword_list`

> This switch gives you fine-grained control over the amount of debug information included in compiled class files. The argument after the colon may be either `none`, in which case no debug information is included, or a comma-separated list with any combination of `source`, to include source file debugging information, `lines`, to include line number information, or `vars`, to include information about local variable names. The default, if no `-g` flag of any kind is specified, is to include source file and line number information only.

`-nowarn`

> Disables warning messages.

`-verbose`

> Causes the compiler to output information about each class encountered during compilation. This can be helpful when trying to resolve problems with missing class definitions.

There are also a number of switches that relate to cross-compiling as well as UNIX-specific options, but these are not commonly used. Refer to the Sun Java SDK Tools documentation if you need details on these options.

---

2. In Java, it is rare for APIs to break support for existing code. Rather than remove old methods, it is more common to *deprecate* them. This is done by putting a `@deprecated` tag in a Javadoc comment on the class or method. The Java compiler will issue a warning (if the `-deprecated` switch is on) whenever a deprecated class or method is used. In general, deprecation is a warning that the class or method will be removed in a future version of the code or library. It is interesting to note that the **javac** compiler records that a method or class is deprecated in the binary. Thus the compiler produces different output based on the contents of a comment. As we have written simple compilers and interpreters, this creeps us out. We have always wondered why `deprecated` has not become a Java language keyword.

5.4 THE JAVA RUNTIME ENGINE

You can download and install just the software required to run Java applications without the development tools. This is known as the *Java 2 Runtime Edition.*

5.4.1   The Basics

You run a Java program by invoking the **java** command. Usually, the argument to the command is a class name. That class is loaded, and its `main()` method is run.

Remember, this is not a filename, but a class name! The rest of the command-line arguments that follow the class name are passed as an array of `Strings` to the `main()` method of the named class. Example 5.4 demonstrates running the FetchURL program.

Example 5.4 Running a Java program with **java**

```
$ java FetchURL http://www.yahoo.com/news
http://www.yahoo.com/news:
<html>
<head><title>Yahoo! Directory News and Media</title>
<script type="text/javascript"
  src="http://us.js1.yimg.com/us.yimg.com/lib/common/yg_csstare.js">
</script>
<style>
  li { font-size: 12px; margin-bottom: 2px; }
</style>
<base href=http://dir.yahoo.com/News_and_Media/></head>
<body>
...
... etc.
```

CAUTION

Remember that if you override the classpath, either with the `-classpath` or `-cp` command-line options (detailed below) or with the `CLASSPATH` environment variable, you must include the "`.`" directory somewhere in the classpath if you want Java to include current working directory in the search list. Since "`.`" is the default classpath, many people are surprised when they set a classpath and suddenly can no longer run a `.class` file in their current directory.

The class invoked must be findable on either the bootstrap or user-specified classpath.

5.4.2   java Options

Just as the Java compiler, the runtime program, **java**, takes a number of command-line options. Here are the most commonly used ones:

-classpath **or** -cp
> Sets the runtime classpath. Overrides any value in the CLASSPATH environment variable.

-Dproperty=value
> Allows a system property to be set on the command line.

-jar
> Specifies that the first nonoption command-line argument is not a Java class name, but the name of a JAR file. The JAR file must have a Main-Class: specification in its MANIFEST (see Section 5.11). The main() method of the class named by the JAR's MANIFEST Main-Class: specification will be called as if that class had been named on the command line, rather than the JAR file. This is commonly used in shell scripts and batch files that accompany Java applications distributed in single .jar files.

There are several other command-line options that are less commonly used. We will cover some of them in later chapters when their use will make more sense. Of course, full documentation on all options for this command is in the Sun Java SDK Development Tools documentation.

5.5 COMPLETE, UP-TO-DATE PROGRAM DOCUMENTATION MADE EASY

One of Java's most useful features is **javadoc**, a command that (by default) produces comprehensive HTML program documentation directly from the program source. Since it works from the source, it can be automated, and you may be certain that the documentation is up-to-date. It takes much of the documentation burden off of programmers and permits new programmers to join a project and rapidly come up to speed because there is comprehensive documentation in a standard format. The **javadoc** tool produces HTML documentation by default, but this is because it uses a *doclet* that produces HTML documentation. You can write your own doclet that produces whatever format you wish. Most find the HTML documentation so satisfactory that custom doclets are rare.

Javadoc can be a large topic, because it not only documents all classes, methods, and class variables, but can also use detailed text from specially formatted comments in the source code. We will cover Javadoc comments only briefly here, but you will see examples in our project code throughout this book.

5.5.1 Running javadoc

The **javadoc** command has the following general form:

```
javadoc [options...] [package names...] [source filenames...]
  [@optfile...]
```

Options are covered in the next section. You can specify the classes to document in two ways. First, you can list one or more Java packages on the command line. Source code for the named packages is searched for on the source classpath (see Section 5.5.2). Wildcards are not permitted in package names.

Second, you may list as many Java source files as you like, and you may use wildcards in the names.

As with the **javac** compiler above, the `@optfile` allows you to name a text file whose lines are treated as arguments as if they had been typed on the command line.

Example 5.5 shows how to run **javadoc** on our small multiclass sample.

In this case, we were in the "base directory" of the package when we ran the command. In other words, `net` was a subdirectory of the current working directory when we ran Javadoc. Javadoc uses the same default classpaths and environment variables as **javac** does, so by default " . " is on the path.

Generally, specifying packages is the most convenient way to document a number of classes, since packages are how collections of classes are generally managed in Java development.

Figure 5.1 shows the main screen of the documentation thus produced.

Example 5.5 Running **javadoc** with defaults against a package

```
$ javadoc net.multitool.Payback
Loading source files for package net.multitool.Payback...
Constructing Javadoc information...
Standard Doclet version 1.4.1

Generating constant-values.html...
Building tree for all the packages and classes...
Building index for all the packages and classes...
Generating overview-tree.html...
Generating index-all.html...
Generating deprecated-list.html...
Building index for all classes...
Generating allclasses-frame.html...
Generating allclasses-noframe.html...
Generating index.html...
Generating packages.html...
Generating net/multitool/Payback/package-frame.html...
Generating net/multitool/Payback/package-summary.html...
Generating net/multitool/Payback/package-tree.html...
Generating net/multitool/Payback/Account.html...
Generating net/multitool/Payback/Cost.html...
Generating net/multitool/Payback/DebtAccount.html...
Generating net/multitool/Payback/Payback.html...
Generating net/multitool/Payback/Purchase.html...
Generating net/multitool/Payback/SavingsAccount.html...
Generating package-list...
Generating help-doc.html...
Generating stylesheet.css...
$
```

5.5.2   Javadoc Command-Line Options

As with other options documentation in this chapter, this is not intended to be a complete reference document. We are documenting only the most important command-line switches.

```
-public
```
    Causes only public classes, members, and methods to be documented. You might want this for end-user documentation of a library.

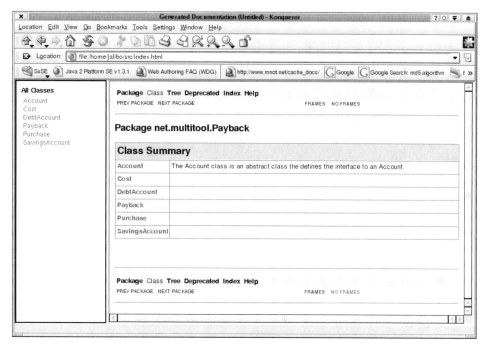

Figure 5.1 Javadoc documentation viewed in Konqueror Web browser

`-protected`

> Causes public and protected classes, members, and methods to be documented. *This is the default documentation level.* This is also the most likely level at which you would want to document code meant for distribution.

`-package`

> We suspect you can see where this is going. This switch causes package, protected, and public classes, members, and methods to be documented.

`-private`

> This switch causes all classes, members, and methods to be documented. In our experience, this is the setting you will want to use for internal projects. It documents everything.

`-sourcepath` **and** `-classpath`

> These are the paths that will be searched for source classes or referenced classes. These switches work like the corresponding switches for the **javac** compiler.

`-verbose` **and** `-quiet`

These switches control how much output is produced as **javadoc** runs. If you choose `-verbose`, detailed information is produced (more than the default; in current versions, this option mostly shows time measurements of the parsing of each source file). If you choose the `-quiet` option, progress messages are suppressed completely.

`-doclet` *starting_class*

We're not going to go into too much detail on this, but this switch allows you to name a doclet (a class that uses the Doclet API) to use in place of the default doclet. See the next paragraph for more information.

All of the switches documented so far are provided by the **javadoc** program itself. Javadoc, like the rest of the Sun Microsystems Java SDK, is written in Java. The authors of **javadoc** took advantage of this. The default behavior of **javadoc** is to produce HTML documentation with a standard look and feel. However, there exists an API, called the Doclet API, which allows you to write a Java class of your own to process the information parsed out of the source by **javadoc**. For details, see the Doclet Overview[3] on Sun's Web site.

Sun provides a default doclet that produces HTML documentation. That doclet takes a number of command-line options as well. We'll cover the most important of those now. Remember, these are provided by the standard doclet. If you use the `-doclet` switch, then these switches will not be available (unless, of course, the alternate doclet just happens to provide them).

`-d` *directory*

By default, the HTML documentation is saved in the same directory as the source. Use this switch to specify an alternate directory into which documentation is to be placed.

`-use`

Causes **javadoc** to generate a "Use" page for each class and package. Such a page is a cross-reference to all uses of the class or package.

`-version`

Causes any `@version` tag data to be included in the documentation. If you are using CVS for source control (and why wouldn't you?) we

---

3. http://java.sun.com/j2se/1.4.1/docs/tooldocs/javadoc/overview.html

recommend adding Id after the version tag, which CVS will automatically replace by its ID string containing the filename, CVS revision number, date/time and the author of last check-in. (For more about CVS, see Chapter 8.)

`-author`

Causes any `@author` tag data to be included in the documentation.

`-splitindex`

Causes the alphabetical index to be broken into multiple pages, one per letter. Can be useful when you have a very large number of classes and/or packages documented in a single Javadoc document set.

`-windowtitle` *title*

Sets the title for the document set. The text that follows this switch will go into the HTML `<title>` element on documentation pages.

`-nodeprecated`

This causes all deprecated methods and classes to go undocumented. Normally they are documented, but marked as deprecated.

`-nodeprecatedlist`

Drops deprecated classes and methods from indexes, lists, and cross-references, but leaves the actual documentation in place.

There are actually many more switches. Some of the most important that we haven't covered are the `-link`, `-linkoffline`, and related tags. If you end up producing many API packages and document them separately, you can use these switches to link your separate Javadoc documentation together seamlessly, so that when you use classes from separately documented packages, the references in the documentation for your code will be live links to that separate documentation. For details on these and other switches, see the Sun documentation on **javadoc**.[4]

---

4. `http://java.sun.com/j2se/1.4.2/docs/tooldocs/solaris/javadoc.html`

5.5.3   Javadoc Comments

There's more to Javadoc than just documenting the types and names of classes, methods, and arguments. A developer can annotate or supplement the documentation by placing specially formatted comments in his or her code.

A Javadoc comment begins with the C-style open comment plus at least one more asterisk. It ends with a C-style close comment. In other words:

```
/* This is a C-style comment, but it
 is _not_ a Javadoc comment. */

/** This is a C-style comment, but it
 is also a Javadoc comment. */
```

This isn't a part of the Java programming language. It is merely a lexical hack to allow the **javadoc** program to recognize a comment it should pick up and process. Javadoc is fairly intelligent about where to place the text extracted from a Javadoc comment. For example, a Javadoc comment placed just before the start of a class will appear in the class summary on the package page and at the top of the class detail page. A Javadoc comment placed just before a method will appear in the method's box on the class detail page, and so on.

We encourage you to discover for yourself the relationship between Javadoc comments and the output of the standard doclet. Use it. Experiment. Or, you can go and read the official Sun Microsystems documentation on Javadoc.[5] That's your choice.

Since comment text is extracted and placed into certain positions in an HTML document, you may use HTML tags in your comments to affect how they are rendered. Be aware that when you do so, you may get unexpected results if you use any custom doclets.

There's more to it than that, however. There are a number of macros that you can place in Javadoc comments to mark data of particular significance. For example, @author should appear just before the name of the author of a particular piece of code.

These *at-tags* must appear after all descriptive text in a Javadoc comment.[6] A tag must be at the beginning of a line within the comment (ignoring any

---

5. http://java.sun.com/j2se/1.4.2/docs/tooldocs/solaris/javadoc.html

6. The exception is embedded tags, which we will discuss in a moment.

Example 5.6 Sample Javadoc comment with at-tags

```
/**
 * addWait - adds in the given wait time to all the counters;
 * we could say much more about the method here, but let me say
 * that we sometimes include HTML tags directly in our comments.
 * Since Javadoc will run all our text together, we may need: <br>
 *        break tags <br>
 *        or paragraph tags <br>
 *        for spacing and separation.
 * <p>We also add <i>other</i> HTML tags for <b>emphasis</b>.
 * <p>You should still try to make the comment readable, though,
 * for the programmer who is editing the source, not
 * just for those looking at the formatted Javadoc.
 * @author John Q. Programmer
 * @version $Id$
 *
 * @param delay - elapsed time, in milliseconds
 * @throws TakesTooLongException
 * @returns total time, in milliseconds
 *
 * @see net.multitool.util.TakesTooLongException, net.multitool.ctrl.Time#count
 *
 */
public long
addWait(long delay)
{
  // ...
}
```

preceding whitespace or asterisks). The tag's data is everything from the end of the tag to the end of the line (Example 5.6.)

Here are the standard at-tags:

`@author`

> Everything from the tag to the end of the line is taken as the name of the code's author.

`@deprecated`

> Marks the method or class deprecated. This tag may be optionally followed by explanatory text. If present, this text should describe when and why the class or method was deprecated and what programmers should use instead.

`@exception` **or** `@throws`

Only valid in the comment for a method or constructor. This tag is followed by the name of an exception class (a descendant of `java.lang.Exception`) and optionally by additional explanatory text. The intent is to list the exceptions that the method throws.

`@param`

Only valid in the comment for a method or constructor. This tag should be followed by the name of a parameter to the method followed by descriptive text. This is used to document method and constructor parameters.

`@return`

Only valid in the comment for a method.[7] This tag is followed by descriptive text meant to document the return value of the method.

`@see`

Populates a "See Also" section in the documentation that will provide hyperlinks to related content. There is a general format for linking to any URL, but the most common use is to refer to other elements in the same Java program. See below for the general format of such links.

In addition to these standard at-tags, there are other at-tags that may be embedded in any comment text—either the comment itself or in text that is an argument to a standard at-tag.

Such tags are placed within curly braces, for example `{@example}`, within a Javadoc comment. The one we use the most is the `@link` tag, which allows you to make a reference to another package, class, method, or class member. The general format is the same as that for the `@see` tag:

package_name.class_name#member_or_method_name

Any of these elements is optional.

The embedded at-tags include:

`@docRoot`

This tag may be used when embedding HTML anchor or image tags (`A` or `IMG` tags) in a Javadoc comment to supply the root part of the

---

7. But not a constructor in this case, because constructors cannot return a value.

documentation path. You should always use this instead of hard-coding the full URL, or a change in directory structure or server configuration might break all of your links.

`@link`

Allows you to embed a cross-reference to another section of the program's documentation directly in comment text. The format of a reference is the same as that for the `@see` tag.

This list is not complete. As always, see the official documentation[8] for details.

5.6 DISPENSING WITH APPLETS

While this book does not cover writing applets, we should mention that, since an applet does not (generally) have a `main()` method, you need something else to launch it outside of a browser. Enter **appletviewer**. This program provides an execution environment for applets.

Why No Applets?

The decision to not cover applets was based both on limited space and on some deployment issues with applets. A surprisingly large number of people are running with either very old browsers that support only Java 1.1.x features, or that support Java runtime plug-ins but do not have them installed or enabled. Also, applets have severe limitations (for sound security reasons), and enabling various features requires a good understanding of the `SecurityManager` Java classes, which could fill a book by themselves. We chose to minimize coverage of applets for these reasons.

---

8. `http://java.sun.com/j2se/1.4.2/docs/tooldocs/solaris/javadoc.html`

5.7 GOING NATIVE

Now we come to the deeper darker mysteries. Let us take a look at **javah**. No, **javah** is not a Hebrew word. It is not some lost mystical text from the days before science supplanted magic. It is the Java C header and stub file generator.

If you are not already fairly experienced in writing, compiling, and building shared libraries in C on a Linux system, we would suggest that you skip this section, at least until you have developed intermediate skills in these areas. Otherwise, feel free to proceed.

We're going to walk you very quickly through building a Java native method here.[9] Don't worry if you don't quite follow it all. We will cover this topic at greater length elsewhere in the book. For now, we're giving you the highlights. Also be sure to check out Section 5.15. We'll point you to many additional resources on JNI (Java Native Interface) in that section.

Sounds pretty intimidating, huh? Well, depending upon your background and experience, it can be a bit intimidating. As much as this will hurt some die-hard Java purists, Java is not the right language for everything. Java's size and semiinterpreted nature in particular make Java ill-suited for the "close to the metal" tasks, such as device drivers and raw socket networking.

Fortunately, Java's designers were of this rocket-scientist breed (and so, for that matter, are your bending authors), so they gave Java programmers a back door: *native methods*. A native method is a class method whose name, arguments, and return type are declared in Java, but whose underlying implementation is written in "native code" (usually C, but it could be any compiled language that can match C's stack frame conventions).

As an example, let's implement a native method that will use the native Linux C library calls to get the current program's effective user ID and the name associated with that user.

First, we will write the Java class (Example 5.7).

You may never have seen code like that at the start of a class definition. The block declared

```
static { ... }
```

---

9. You might be tempted to call our comments in the introduction where we mentioned that we did not like purely pedagogical examples and that we would provide real, useful code. Well, we have to confess that there are some features of the Java language that we couldn't cram into our real-world examples. This JNI sample is one such. We admit our failure, and we apologize.

Example 5.7 Java application with a native method (`GetUser.java`)

```
public class GetUser {
  static {
    System.loadLibrary("getuser");
  }

  public native String getUserName();

  public static void main(String[] args)
  {
    GetUser usr = new GetUser();

    System.out.println(usr.getUserName());
  }
}
```

---

is called a *static initializer* and we'll discuss it in a moment.

Once you have the Java code, compile it with **javac**. You now have the compiled class. The next step is to use the **javah** tool to build the header file for your C code.

```
$ javah GetUser
```

Example 5.8 shows the header file thus produced.

Note that you run **javah** on the class file, not on the source file. The normal class name to classpath mappings apply. The file produced as a result is called, in this case, `GetUser.h`. The next step is to write the C code that implements the method (Example 5.9).

There's a lot going on here. First, the constant, `L_cuserid`, is defined in `stdio.h`; it represents the number of characters required to hold a user name. We're defining a char array to hold that number of characters plus one.[10] We are then calling the `cuserid()` function (see the manpage of `cuserid(3)`) to get the user name of the effective user ID of the process.

That much is familiar C. But what is the argument list? Our method took no arguments. And what's with the functions being called through the pointer argument?

---

10. What can we say? We're paranoid about the trailing null. Sue us.

Example 5.8 Header file for `GetUser` native methods (`GetUser.h`)

```
/* DO NOT EDIT THIS FILE - it is machine generated */
#include <jni.h>
/* Header for class GetUser */

#ifndef _Included_GetUser
#define _Included_GetUser
#ifdef __cplusplus
extern "C" {
#endif
/*
 * Class:     GetUser
 * Method:    getUserName
 * Signature: ()Ljava/lang/String;
 */
JNIEXPORT jstring JNICALL Java_GetUser_getUserName
  (JNIEnv *, jobject);

#ifdef __cplusplus
}
#endif
#endif
```

Example 5.9 Native method's C implementation file (`GetUser.c`)

```
#include "GetUser.h"
#include <stdio.h>

JNIEXPORT jstring JNICALL
Java_GetUser_getUserName(JNIEnv *jenv, jobject obj)
{
  char buffer[L_cuserid + 1];

  cuserid(buffer);

  return (*jenv)->NewStringUTF(jenv, buffer);
}
```

All of the Java class member data and Java class methods may be reached through the JNIEnv pointer argument. There are also methods provided by JNI itself. One of those is `NewStringUTF()`. Remember that Java `String`s are Unicode, not 8-bit ASCII, so you must convert to and from Unicode (UTF-8 is an 8-bit encoding for Unicode that coincides with ASCII in the low 7 bits, so it is often used for such conversions). You can think of the JNIEnv as a C++ class pointer, or you can think of it as a structure of data and function pointers (that's really what a C++ class is, after all). The bottom line is, it provides the means to access and manipulate the Java environment from your native code.

The second argument, jobject, is the "this" pointer. It points to the GetUser class, and it is upcast to the JNI equivalent of the Java Object type. If our method took parameters, they would follow these two constant arguments.

JNI is a huge topic. You can read more about it in the Sun Microsystems JNI Tutorial,[11] or in Java 2 SDK JNI FAQ,[12] or in the JNI 1.1 Specification,[13] or in the associated JDK 1.2 Update[14] or the JDK 1.4 Update.[15]

Even with all of this "We're too busy to explain things to you" going on here, we've got a lot more to cover before we are done. The next step in our little demo is to compile the C program and create a shared library of the code.

```
$ cc -c GetUser.c
$ cc -shared -o libgetuser.so GetUser.o
$ export LD_LIBRARY_PATH=.
```

The first line compiles the native method to a .o (object) file. The second command makes a shared library out of it. Now, refer back to the static initializer in Example 5.7. A static initializer is run before everything else in a class, even before main(). In this case, it uses the loadLibrary() method of the System class to load the shared library we just created. Note that library naming rules of the target OS are applied. The library is named getuser and on a Linux system it is assumed that that library will be in a file named libgetuser.so.

The last line sets an environment variable, LD_LIBRARY_PATH, to provide a path where Java will search for libraries. This is behavior inherited from Solaris. Linux uses **ldconfig** to maintain a list of shared libraries. Usually, a library is placed in a directory named in the file ld.so.conf and a memory cache of

---

11. http://java.sun.com/docs/books/tutorial/native1.1/index.html

12. http://java.sun.com/products/jdk/faq/jni-j2sdk-faq.html

13. http://java.sun.com/products/jdk/1.2/docs/guide/jni/spec/jniTOC.doc.html

14. http://java.sun.com/j2se/1.4.1/docs/guide/jni/jni-12.html

15. http://java.sun.com/j2se/1.4.1/docs/guide/jni/jni-14.html

these libraries is built and maintained with the **ldconfig** program. The library loader in the JVM, however, works as the shared library system in Solaris, where the LD_LIBRARY_PATH is searched for shared libraries. If you try a JNI method and get library errors, check your LD_LIBRARY_PATH first. Here, we used ".", meaning "current directory." In practice, you wouldn't do this. You would deploy your shared library to a standard location and have LD_LIBRARY_PATH preset to that directory or directories. We just wanted to show you how it works here.

Let's see our class in action now.

```
$ java GetUser
mschwarz
$ su
Password:
# export LD_LIBRARY_PATH=.
# java GetUser
root
# exit
exit
$
```

To JNI or Not to JNI

We dislike religious debates. We have no desire to nail down what taints the purity of Java and what does not. A warning we do want to give you is, if you are an experienced UNIX C/C++ developer, you must resist the temptation to use JNI and native methods all over the place. The Java APIs are extensive, and there are probably classes that already do what you want to do. You will be tempted to use native methods because "you know how to do it in C." Resist. Find the Java way. JNI is a great way to introduce subtle and hard to find bugs into your Java programs. Leave that to the API and JVM coders. ;-)

That said, we don't want to discourage you from making use of JNI when it is the right way, or the only way, for what you need to do. The tool is there. Use it. Just remember what it does cost you in portability and what it may cost you in maintenance and debugging. Design decisions have costs and benefits. Try to find the balance.

Here you see the class being run, and, sure enough, it displays our user-name. We then run **su** to become root and (after setting that library path) run it again—and, sure enough, it tells us we are "root."

We'll talk more about JNI later in the book, but now you know enough to be dangerous.

5.8 INTRODUCING RMI

Remote Method Invocation (RMI) is a system for distributing application code over multiple hosts. It is a small part of multitier computing. Much of this book will be devoted to the how's and why's of multitier client/server computing. Here we are concerned only with the SDK tool **rmic**, the RMI compiler.

5.8.1 A Brief Introduction to RMI

Remote Method Invocation is a basic client-server model for invoking Java methods over a network.

5.8.1.1 History and Background

One of the most common problems in computing is how best to make an application available to the largest number of users at the least cost. To this end we have seen the development of "timeshare" systems with dumb terminals all over the place. We have seen the evolution of distributed GUI systems with X Windows and its network display system, and with tools like VNC (Virtual Network Console).[16] We have seen the emergence of the PC, providing autonomous computing at each worker's desktop. And finally we have seen the desktop turning slowly back into a terminal (albeit a prettier one) with the emergence of client-server computing.

What seems to have emerged from this progression is two major kinds of software systems. One is the PC and associated hardware and software. Developments here have dramatically increased the power and productivity of individual work. The PC revolution was indeed a real change throughout the world of business and technology. But even with this, there are a host of applications and business functions that require a collection of data and resources to be available to *multiple* workers at the same time. This is the second major kind

---

16. http://www.realvnc.com/

of software systems. This second kind used to be the only kind, but now it may, in a sense, be the minority of applications, but the most critical to an operation. This second class of system has come to be called *enterprise* systems.

In enterprise computing, we have the same problem we opened with: How do you make the information and resources available to everyone who needs them at the lowest cost? And the answer is (as it always is) "that depends."

These days, one of the most common solutions is to use a Web server to *publish* an application. This works well for a great many applications and it is much easier to do than many other methods. That explains its popularity. The Web interface is quite limited, however, so for more user interface intensive applications, client-server computing evolved. To us techies, all of this stuff is client-server. In this context however, client-server refers to a 2-tier system where the UI and logic exist in a GUI application on a PC and common resources are in an SQL database all the clients share.

This is also commonly used, but becomes expensive in a couple of cases. The first is when the database itself becomes a bottleneck because the number of users grows and grows but only one database can exist. The second is simply the cost of maintenance. Since the logic exists in the client, any change to the logic requires updating the software on all clients. Even when a scheme for automating this exists, it is still time-consuming and costly to get all the changes out to all users simultaneously. There are workarounds for both of these issues, but here we are concerned with a different solution altogether.

So, how can we have a UI richer than with a Web application but avoid the pitfalls of the traditional 2-tier client-server computing? The answer is to separate the UI from the business logic and the business logic from the underlying data store. This results in 3 tiers—*presentation, business logic,* and *data.*

Much of this book will concern itself with 3-tier computing solutions. Java has four major architectures for building 3-tier solutions. One of them is RMI.[17]

5.8.1.2   *RMI Basics*

RMI works by sharing an interface between the client and the server. The interface groups together the methods that a client may call on a server. A class is

---

17. The others are Enterprise JavaBeans, servlets, and JavaServer Pages. The latter two are Web-based, and therefore suffer from the UI deficiencies of Web forms, but Sun calls them part of Enterprise Java, so we will too.

written on the server side that implements the interface, and a special compiler is used to generate *stubs* for the server side and the client side. On the client side, a call to an RMI method looks like any other method call, but it is sent across the network to the server, where the actual instructions are carried out. Any return value is then passed back over the network to the client.

We will walk you through a very simple (and very pointless) example just to show you the tools.

5.8.1.3   *Writing the Interface*

Our interface is pathetically simple. It is a class that sums two integer arguments and returns an integer result. Example 5.10 shows the interface file.

> **NOTE**
>
> The names of the classes in the following examples may seem a bit strange, and they are. It is because we aim to build on this example later.

Example 5.10 The `Session` interface

```
package net.multitool.RMIDemo;

import java.rmi.*;

public interface Session extends Remote {
  public int add(int x, int y) throws RemoteException;
}
```

The two important things to note here are that the interface must extend `java.rmi.Remote` and that any remote method must be defined as throwing `java.rmi.RemoteException`. If anything goes wrong during an RMI call, like someone tripping over a network cable, the call will not complete successfully and an exception of that type will be thrown. It is not possible to have a RMI method that cannot throw this exception.

Beyond those features, you can see that defining remote methods is quite familiar and easy.

5.8.1.4   *Writing the Server Class*

An interface is an "empty vessel." Before any interface can be used, you must
have an actual class that implements the interface. In an RMI application, the
implementing class is the server (Example 5.11).

The class is named `SessionImpl` to emphasize its relationship with the
`Session` interface. There is no requirement to match up such names. Likewise,
the RMI name given, `//penfold/Session`, uses the interface name, but it
could use any name. It is a good idea to develop a naming convention for RMI
interfaces and their implementations. It is *critical* to develop naming conventions for RMI registry names, particularly in production environments. Without a naming convention, it is difficult to avoid confusion and even chaos.
What happens when multiple business units develop RMI code destined for a
single production server, and they have all made an RMI interface named
`Session`, or `Payment`?[18] Bad things happen.

There is no "one size fits all" naming convention that we can offer. Possibilities include using package names in RMI registry names, using some element
of the business area as a component of the name (such as `AccountingSession`,
`ShippingSession`, `ExecutiveSession`). All that matters is that an unambiguous standard be created and followed.

Let's spend some time talking about what this code does.

First, notice that the class extends `UnicastRemoteObject`. This is not
necessary, but using that as a base class saves a lot of server setup. There are
times when you would want to do such setup manually, but for our purpose
here it saves a lot of effort. The class also implements our remote interface.

The first method is a constructor that calls the superclass constructor. At
first glance, this is pointless. Any Java class gets a default constructor that just
calls the superclass constructor, so why is this here? It is here because the superclass constructor throws `RemoteException`. If we didn't define a constructor
like the one here specifying that it throws `RemoteException`, the compiler
would complain that there is an unhandled exception. So we define a constructor identical to a default constructor except that it specifies that it can throw
the exception.

---

18. One solution is to use a more advanced naming system, such as LDAP. See
Section 21.3.2.3.

Example 5.11 The `Session` server implementation

```
package net.multitool.RMIDemo;

import net.multitool.RMIDemo.*;
import java.rmi.*;
import java.rmi.server.*;

/** SessionImpl is the server class for the Session RMI interface.
 */
public class
SessionImpl
  extends UnicastRemoteObject
  implements Session
{
  /** Constructor needed to ensure call to UnicastRemoteObject
   *  constructor and to thus propagate the possible exception.
   */
  public SessionImpl() throws RemoteException {
    super();
  }

  /** A static main() for the server. */
  public static void main(String[] arglist)
  {
    if (System.getSecurityManager() == null) {
      System.setSecurityManager(new RMISecurityManager());
    }

    String rmiName = "//penfold/Session";
    try {
      Session adder = new SessionImpl();
      Naming.rebind(rmiName, adder);
    } catch (Exception e) {
      e.printStackTrace();
    }
  }

  /** Implementation of the RMI method, add. */
  public int add(int x, int y) throws java.rmi.RemoteException
  {
    return x+y;
  }
}
```

Next, we have the server `main()` method. It first sets a security manager. The security manager controls what the VM is allowed to do. A number of default security managers are provided, and here we use one that is designed specifically to give safe and reasonable defaults for RMI applications. You can, of course, write your own security manager. Security managers use "policy specifications" to alter their capabilities. For now, we will explain enough to run a simple example. See Section 5.8.4.2 for more information on policies for our example.

Remember that `main()` is static, so there is no instance of `SessionImpl` yet, and thus also no instance of `Session`. We declare a variable of type `Session`, and set it to a new instance of `SessionImpl`. (There is no need to typecast here because `SessionImpl` implements `Session`, therefore `SessionImpl` is, among other things, a `Session`.) We now have an instance of the server class.

Next, the server must make itself available to the world. It does this by registering itself with the RMI registry (see Section 5.8.3). This is done through a static method of the `java.rmi.Naming` class, `rebind()`. Put simply, this maps a remote object to a string name in the registry. When clients contact the registry looking for a name then, if a remote object is mapped to that name, the communication can take place (yes, we are simplifying at the moment). The call to `rebind()` does not return. The server is up and running.

Finally, we have the implementation of our remote method, `add()`.

This looks like a lot of hassle to go through, and it is, but consider writing an interface that offers, for example, methods like `getDirContents()`, `chDir()`, `downloadFile()`, `uploadFile()`. You've just written something like an FTP server. No matter how many methods you add to your interface, the complexity of the setup code does not increase. Maybe now it looks a little more useful?

5.8.1.5   *Writing the Client Class*

At this point, Example 5.12 should be fairly obvious. Our class has just a single static method, `main()`. It, like our server side `main()`, sets up a security manager. It then contacts a registry on the machine named `penfold` looking for an instance of a remote interface named `Session` (again, `lookup()` is a static method of the `java.rmi.Naming` class). We store that reference in a variable of type `Session` called `sess`. We can then call the `add()` on `sess`. We'll show the server and client running shortly.

Example 5.12 The RMI client program

```
package net.multitool.RMIDemo;

import java.rmi.*;

public class Client {
  public static void main(String[] arglist) {
    if (System.getSecurityManager() == null) {
      System.setSecurityManager(new RMISecurityManager());
    }

    try {
      String name = "//penfold/Session";
      // Obtain reference to the remote object
      Session sess = (Session) Naming.lookup(name);

      System.out.println("Pointless RMI Client. 47 + 13 = " +
                          sess.add(47,13) + ", right?");
    } catch (Exception e) {
      e.printStackTrace();
    }
  }
}
```

5.8.2   The rmic Tool

In order for a remote object to make itself available and in order for a client to be able to call such an object, each method needs a client and server-side *stub* to proxy the method call. Arguments to the method call are converted to streamable data (this process is called *marshaling*) by the client stub, and that data is sent over the network to the server stub, which must convert that stream into object instances on the server side (this is called *unmarshaling*). The server-side stub then calls the actual method implementation. When the method returns, any return values and changes to the state of the arguments must be marshaled by the server stub and sent back to the client stub where they are unmarshaled and stored in the correct locations on the client.

This was the traditionally painful part of writing multitier clients. What **rmic** does is automate the generation of these stubs, so writing a remote method is only slightly more difficult than writing any other method.

To generate RMI stubs for our application, run **rmic**[19] against the class that implements the remote interface:

```
penfold$ rmic net.multitool.RMIDemo.SessionImpl
```

When you are writing "traditional" Java RMI, that is just about all you need to know about **rmic**. The program actually has a large number of options and switches, but most of these are to support alternate protocols and systems, such as CORBA IDL and IIOP. If you know what these are, and make use of these, you will find details on these options in Sun's **rmic** tool documentation.[20]

5.8.3   The rmiregistry Tool

The **rmiregistry** is a naming service that binds RMI server stubs to simple names. Invoking it is incredibly simple. Just type `rmiregistry`. You may want to run it on other than the default port (1099). For that, just specify the port number on the command line:

```
$ rmiregistry 21099 &
```

That example shows us running a registry on port 21099 and running it in the background. You might want to use a nonstandard port in order to run a test version of the service while the production version remains available on the standard port.

That is just about all there is to **rmiregistry**. You can find details in the Sun Java SDK documentation.

5.8.4   Setting Up Servers and Clients

So far, we have written an RMI interface, a server implementation, and a client implementation. We have generated RMI stubs for our RMI object. We are

---

19. Be careful! If you have one or more Java SDKs installed *and* you have the GNU Compiler for Java installed, watch out for your PATH. The Java compiler and the Java runtime from the JDK don't collide with **gcj** because the compiler has a different name and **gcj** compiles to native binaries. But **gcj** does have an **rmic** compiler, and it is usually in /usr/bin, which is usually ahead of your JDK in the executable path. If you run **rmic** and it explodes with errors, make sure you aren't running the **rmic** from **gcj** against .class files from a JDK. (And, yes, this bit me and had me confused for a while!)

20. http://java.sun.com/j2se/1.4.2/docs/tooldocs/solaris/rmic.html

almost ready to fire our system up and give it a try. But first, we'll give you some information about our sample environment and talk very briefly about security.[21]

5.8.4.1 *What RMI Servers and Clients Need to Be Able to Do*

RMI servers and clients need to be able to listen for connections on network ports, and they need to be able to initiate connections on network ports. Back in the Java 1.1 days, there were no limits on what RMI methods could do. The CLASSPATH was assumed to be trusted. With the RMI 1.2 protocol specification, the ability to actually pass bytecodes between VMs over RMI was added. That means that it is possible for clients to pass code to servers. Obviously, this opens a lot of possible security risks. For this reason, RMI got a security management layer. It is the same security manager as the one that applets use. It also provides a default security manager class that has virtually all such capabilities safely turned off. We need to turn on some of these capabilities in order to make our sample work.

The RMI system expects Java classes to be made available through one of two paths.

1. The CLASSPATH, either the environment variable or on the command line.
2. Through a property that points at URL. This URL may be a file: URL, or an http: URL.

We are going to do the simplest case for now. We will have our compiled code installed on both our server system and our client system. The classes will all be referenced relative to the default classpath (in other words, relative to ".", the current directory).

This is not the typical case. The most common case will be for the classes to be available in a JAR file via a Web server, and for the java.rmi.server.codebase property to be set to point to the JAR file via an http: URL.

---

21. We're going to gloss over this subject for now.

Example 5.13 A Java security policy file suitable for the RMI example

```
grant {
  permission java.net.SocketPermission "*:1024-65535", "connect,accept";
  permission java.net.SocketPermission "*:80", "connect,accept";
};
```

5.8.4.2   Our Environment

We have two machines. One, `penfold`, is our server machine. The other, `grovel`, is our client machine. To keep things straight in our samples, the shell prompts will have the host names in them.

If you are using a JDK that supports the 1.2 RMI specification (and we hope you are—it's in all current JDKs), you have to give your server and your client permission to access the network ports needed to run. By default, the Java runtime will look for a security policy file in the home directory of the user running the VM. The default name of the file is `.java.policy`. Example 5.13 shows what we suggest you put in this file, at least to run this example.

> **NOTE**
>
> You will have to put this in your home directory both on the server and on all client machines.

5.8.4.3   Compiling and Running the Server

Our packages here follow Sun's suggested naming convention of your domain name, reversed, followed by your package names. It so happens that Mr. Schwarz's domain is called `multitool.net` (named after his first book, *Multitool Linux*), so we put all of these classes in a package called `net.multitool.RMIDemo`.

For all of the examples in this section, as well as the following section on building and running the client, assume that our current working directory is the directory that contains the `net` directory of our source code.

The output you see in Example 5.14 includes the result of running our client once. Note that the `SessionImpl` class doesn't terminate. It keeps running to service clients indefinitely.

Example 5.14 Compiling and running our server on `penfold`.

```
penfold$ javac net/multitool/RMIDemo/SessionImpl.java
penfold$ rmic net.multitool.RMIDemo.SessionImpl
penfold$ rmiregistry &
 17286
penfold$ java net.multitool.RMIDemo.SessionImpl
Asked to add 47 and 13
```

5.8.4.4 Compiling and Running the Client

Example 5.15 shows the actual steps we ran to build and run the client.

Example 5.15 Compiling and running our client on `grovel`

```
grovel$ javac net/multitool/RMIDemo/Client.java
grovel$ javac net/multitool/RMIDemo/SessionImpl.java
grovel$ /usr/java/jdk/bin/rmic net.multitool.RMIDemo.SessionImpl
grovel$ java net.multitool.RMIDemo.Client
Pointless RMI Client.  47+13=60, right?
grovel$
```

NOTE

We compile the server class, `SessionImpl`, on the client side and run **rmic** against it just to produce the stubs the client requires. You could copy the stub classes from the server machine, or you could put them in a JAR file, put that file on a Web server, and have the `java.rmi.server.codebase` property point to that JAR file. We're taking the simple way here, but in a real implementation, you would not do it this way. We'll cover more realistic cases later.

5.8.5 RMI Summary

RMI greatly simplifies the business of writing multitier client-server applications. It is suitable for many classes of distributed computing problems, but it does lack several features that required in large, mission-critical applications. For one thing, it lacks any sort of transaction support. If a method invocation fails, the client may not know for certain whether the server finished some work, like writing to a database, before the failure. Also, the **rmiregistry** program is a very simplistic naming/lookup system. Clients must know where to find the registry with the resources they need.

RMI is very useful for problems of a certain scale, but it is not, in and of itself, sufficient for high-volume, highly available, mission-critical enterprise systems.[22] But that is what J2EE and EJB are for. We'll deal with those in Part V later in the book.

5.9 THE JAVA DEBUGGER

How can you stand using the SDK? It doesn't even have a debugger!

Wrong. It has a debugger. It just has an extremely basic command-line debugger. Example 5.16 shows the output of its **help**.

Again, we are not going to document everything here. That's what the online Sun Microsystems Java SDK documentation is for. Instead, we will use the debugger to step through the execution of our simple application and show you some of the debugger's basic operations.

There are two ways to invoke **jdb**. One is to attach it to an already running JVM that has been started with remote debugging enabled. See the Java SDK documentation for details on that method. Here we'll show you the simpler case of invoking the program locally by running the application directly under the debugger.

The basic invocation is:

```
$ jdb
```

You may optionally name the class whose main() is to be executed under the debugger, but we usually use the **run** from inside the debugger itself to do this. Remember that if you want to be able to view local variables in the debugger, you must have compiled your class or classes with the -g option of **javac**.

In the rest of this section, we will examine an actual debug session. We will run our single-class application, FetchURL, and use it to retrieve the index.html file from the Web server on the laptop on which this chapter is being written. To refresh your memory, remember that the source code for FetchURL is at Example 3.30. Example 5.17 is what that file looks like.

---

22. If that sentence did not cause you to get "buzzword bingo," then you aren't trying.

Example 5.16 The Java debugger **help** command output

```
$ jdb GetUser
Initializing jdb ...
> help
** command list **
run [class [args]]        -- start execution of application's main class

threads [threadgroup]     -- list threads
thread <thread id>        -- set default thread
suspend [thread id(s)]    -- suspend threads (default: all)
resume [thread id(s)]     -- resume threads (default: all)
where [thread id] | all   -- dump a thread's stack
wherei [thread id] | all  -- dump a thread's stack, with pc info
up [n frames]             -- move up a thread's stack
down [n frames]           -- move down a thread's stack
kill <thread> <expr>      -- kill a thread with the given exception object
interrupt <thread>        -- interrupt a thread

print <expr>              -- print value of expression
dump <expr>               -- print all object information
eval <expr>               -- evaluate expression (same as print)
set <lvalue> = <expr>     -- assign new value to field/variable/array element
locals                    -- print all local variables in current stack frame

classes                   -- list currently known classes
class <class id>          -- show details of named class
methods <class id>        -- list a class's methods
fields <class id>         -- list a class's fields

threadgroups              -- list threadgroups
threadgroup <name>        -- set current threadgroup

stop in <class id>.<method>[(argument_type,...)]
                          -- set a breakpoint in a method
stop at <class id>:<line> -- set a breakpoint at a line
clear <class id>.<method>[(argument_type,...)]
                          -- clear a breakpoint in a method
clear <class id>:<line>   -- clear a breakpoint at a line
clear                     -- list breakpoints
catch [uncaught|caught|all] <exception-class id>
                          -- break when specified exception occurs
ignore [uncaught|caught|all] <exception-class id>
                          -- cancel 'catch' for the specified exception
watch [access|all] <class id>.<field name>
                          -- watch access/modifications to a field
unwatch [access|all] <class id>.<field name>
                          -- discontinue watching access/modifications to a field
trace methods [thread]    -- trace method entry and exit
```

```
untrace methods [thread]  -- stop tracing method entry and exit
step                      -- execute current line
step up                   -- execute until the current method returns to its caller
stepi                     -- execute current instruction
next                      -- step one line (step OVER calls)
cont                      -- continue execution from breakpoint

list [line number|method] -- print source code
use (or sourcepath) [source file path]
                          -- display or change the source path
exclude [class id ... | "none"]
                          -- do not report step or method events for specified classes
classpath                 -- print classpath info from target VM

monitor <command>         -- execute command each time the program stops
monitor                   -- list monitors
unmonitor <monitor#>      -- delete a monitor
read <filename>           -- read and execute a command file

lock <expr>               -- print lock info for an object
threadlocks [thread id]   -- print lock info for a thread

pop                       -- pop the stack through and including the current frame
reenter                   -- same as pop, but current frame is reentered
redefine <class id> <class filename>
                          -- redefine the code for a class

disablegc <expr>          -- prevent garbage collection of an object
enablegc <expr>           -- permit garbage collection of an object

!!                        -- repeat last command
<n> <command>             -- repeat command n times
help (or ?)               -- list commands
version                   -- print version information
exit (or quit)            -- exit debugger

<class id> or <exception-class id>: full class name with package
qualifiers or a pattern with a leading or trailing wildcard ('*')
NOTE: any wildcard pattern will be replaced by at most one full class
name matching the pattern.
<thread id>: thread number as reported in the 'threads' command
<expr>: a Java(tm) Programming Language expression.
Most common syntax is supported.

Startup commands can be placed in either "jdb.ini" or ".jdbrc"
in user.home or user.dir
>
```

Example 5.17 `index.html` used in **jdb** session

```
<HTML>
  <HEAD>
    <TITLE>RedHat Linux Laptop</TITLE>
  </HEAD>
  <BODY>
    <H1>RedHat Linux Laptop</H1>
    <P>You have contacted Michael Schwarz's RedHat Linux Laptop.
    You would probably rather
    <A HREF="http://www.multitool.net/">see his permanent Web
    page</A> since this server goes up and down all the time, what
    with it being on a laptop.</P>
  </BODY>
</HTML>
```

Example 5.18 is an actual transcript of a real **jdb** session. It is annotated with explanatory comments. Our goal here is to get you going. The best way to learn **jdb**, or indeed any of these tools, is to use them.

Obviously, this little session has merely scratched the surface of the Java debugger. You can debug multithreaded applications with commands that can suspend and resume individual threads, list the running threads, switch your "executable view" between threads, and so forth. You can trace method calls. You can monitor variables. You can execute expressions (including assignment expressions, allowing you to force variables to certain values). You can browse classes. You can dump all local variables with a single command. The debugger is quite capable, if a bit limited in user interface.[23] Learn it. Play with it. Step through your favorite Java program with it.

---

23. As you know, we do not automatically like IDEs and GUI development tools (see Section 5.2). A debugger is an exception to that rule. When debugging, a well designed UI with a code pane, a stack pane, a data viewer, a class browser, a thread selection pane, and so on is enormously helpful. You need to be able to see all these elements nearly simultaneously; you need to see the *whole system* as it runs. The command-line debugger makes everything you need available, but with a traditional "glass-teletype" UI that is quite awkward. By all means, learn the CLI debugger, but then find a good Java debugger with a windowed UI of some kind. It is hard to say which compiler UI is the best, but I think we can safely say the command-line debugger UI is the worst! You should know it as a last resort, but use it as a last resort!

Example 5.18 An actual **jdb** session, with commentary

```
$ jdb
Initializing jdb ...
> stop in FetchURL.main (1)
Deferring breakpoint FetchURL.main.
It will be set after the class is loaded.
> run FetchURL http://localhost
run  FetchURL http://localhost
Set uncaught java.lang.Throwable
Set deferred uncaught java.lang.Throwable
>
VM Started: Set deferred breakpoint FetchURL.main

Breakpoint hit: "thread=main", FetchURL.main(), line=48 bci=0
48          for (i = 0; i < args.length; i++)

main[1] list
44       {
45           int i;
46           FetchURL f;
47
48 =>(2)     for (i = 0; i < args.length; i++)
49           {
50               System.out.println(args[i] + ":");
51               System.out.println(new FetchURL(args[i]));
52           }
53       }
main[1] step
>
Step completed: "thread=main", FetchURL.main(), line=50 bci=5
50               System.out.println(args[i] + ":");

main[1] step
> http://localhost:

Step completed: "thread=main", FetchURL.main(), line=51 bci=32
51               System.out.println(new FetchURL(args[i]));

main[1] step
>
Step completed: "thread=main", FetchURL.<init>(), line=8 bci=0
8        {

main[1] list
4     public class FetchURL {
5         private URL requestedURL;
```

```
6
7        public FetchURL(String urlName)
8 =>     {
9            try {
10               requestedURL = new URL(urlName);
11           } catch (Exception e) {
12               e.printStackTrace();
13           }
main[1] step
>
Step completed: "thread=main", FetchURL.<init>(), line=10 bci=4
10               requestedURL = new URL(urlName);

main[1] step (3)
>
Step completed: "thread=main", FetchURL.<init>(), line=11 bci=16
11           } catch (Exception e) {

main[1] step
>
Step completed: "thread=main", FetchURL.<init>(), line=14 bci=27
14       }

main[1] step
>
Step completed: "thread=main", FetchURL.main(), line=51 bci=45
51               System.out.println(new FetchURL(args[i]));

main[1] step
>
Step completed: "thread=main", FetchURL.toString(), line=19 bci=2
19           String rc = "";

main[1] list
15
16
17       public String toString()
18       {
19 =>        String rc = "";
20           String line;
21           BufferedReader rdr;
22
23           try {
24               rdr = new BufferedReader(
main[1] step
>
Step completed: "thread=main", FetchURL.toString(), line=24 bci=3
24               rdr = new BufferedReader(
```

```
main[1] step
>
Step completed: "thread=main", FetchURL.toString(), line=30 bci=28
30              while ((line = rdr.readLine()) != null)

main[1] step
>
Step completed: "thread=main", FetchURL.toString(), line=32 bci=31
32                  rc = rc + line + "\n";

main[1] list
28                  );
29
30              while ((line = rdr.readLine()) != null)
31                  {
32 =>                 rc = rc + line + "\n";
33                  }
34           } catch (Exception e) {
35                 e.printStackTrace();
36                 rc = null;
37              }
main[1] step
>
Step completed: "thread=main", FetchURL.toString(), line=30 bci=55
30              while ((line = rdr.readLine()) != null)

main[1] step
>
Step completed: "thread=main", FetchURL.toString(), line=32 bci=31
32                  rc = rc + line + "\n";

main[1] step
>
Step completed: "thread=main", FetchURL.toString(), line=30 bci=55
30              while ((line = rdr.readLine()) != null)

main[1] step
>
Step completed: "thread=main", FetchURL.toString(), line=32 bci=31
32                  rc = rc + line + "\n";

main[1] dump this   (4)
 this = {
    requestedURL: instance of java.net.URL(id=378)
}
main[1] dump rc     (5)
  rc = "<HTML>
          <HEAD>
```

```
"
main[1] list 36
32                  rc = rc + line + "\n";
33                  }
34              } catch (Exception e) {
35                  e.printStackTrace();
36 =>               rc = null;
37              }
38
39              return rc;
40      }
41
main[1] stop at FetchURL:39        (6)
Set breakpoint FetchURL:39
main[1] cont
>
Breakpoint hit: "thread=main", FetchURL.toString(), line=39 bci=79
39              return rc;

main[1] dump rc
  rc = "<HTML>
          <HEAD>
            <TITLE>RedHat Linux Laptop</TITLE>
          </HEAD>
          <BODY>
            <H1>RedHat Linux Laptop</H1>
            <P>You have contacted Michael Schwarz's RedHat Linux Laptop.
            You would probably rather
            <A HREF="http://www.multitool.net/">see his permanent Web
            page</A> since this server goes up and down all the time, what
            with it being on a laptop.</P>
          </BODY>
        </HTML>
"
main[1] step
> <HTML>
    <HEAD>
      <TITLE>RedHat Linux Laptop</TITLE>
    </HEAD>
    <BODY>
      <H1>RedHat Linux Laptop</H1>
      <P>You have contacted Michael Schwarz's RedHat Linux Laptop.
      You would probably rather
      <A HREF="http://www.multitool.net/">see his permanent Web
      page</A> since this server goes up and down all the time, what
      with it being on a laptop.</P>
    </BODY>
  </HTML>
```

```
Step completed: "thread=main", FetchURL.main(), line=48 bci=48
48              for (i = 0; i < args.length; i++)

main[1] step
>
Step completed: "thread=main", FetchURL.main(), line=53 bci=57
53          }

main[1] step
>
The application exited
$
```

---

1. Here we tell the debugger where to break execution to let us run debugger commands. We do so at the start of the `FetchURL` class' `main()` method. If we did not set a breakpoint, the `run` would have run the program to termination, making it no different from running it with the **java** command (except perhaps a bit slower).

2. The **list** command shows the source line that is about to be executed, along with some more lines to either side. It is a handy way to get a little context. The standard "next line" prompt isn't enough for most of us to get context (unless, of course, we are looking at a line-numbered printout of the source or an editor window at the same time, which we often do).

3. The **step** steps execution one "line" (what a line is can be a bit fuzzy when there's a lot of vertical whitespace in the source, or when multiple method calls occur on one line). Note the information in the status message. The name of the thread is given (our sample is single-threaded, so it is always "main"), as is the line number in the source file and the `bci`. Note that there is a very similar command, **next**, that advances to the next line *in the same stack frame*. In other words, it won't step into method calls, it steps over them.

4, 5. Here we see two uses of the **dump** command. First, we apply it to `this` (which is an implicit argument to any nonstatic method call) to dump the currently executing object. The second instance dumps the `rc` local variable, which is an accumulating string containing the requested Web page. At the moment, it contains only the first few lines.

6. Here we set a breakpoint on a specific source line number. We then use the **cont** command to resume "full speed" code execution.

5.10 RETURN TO THE SOURCE: THE JAVA DECOMPILER

Java includes a decompiler of sorts called **javap**. It is sometimes referred to as the "class file disassembler." We titled this section "Return to the Source," but it is a bit misleading; **javap** simply provides a way to examine the members and methods of a compiled Java class[24] even when you do not have its source code.

The **javap** command takes the same access-modifier command-line arguments as **javadoc** (-public, -protected, -package, -private) to determine which attributes and methods are to be reported. An additional switch, -c, causes the bytecodes of methods to be reported. For details, see Sun's documentation for **javap**.[25]

Example 5.19 shows what you get if you run javap -c on our FetchURL example.

5.11 BUNDLING A JAVA PROGRAM: PUT IT IN A JAR

Distributing a Java application can be a pain. All but the simplest of applications will have many public classes—and since there can only be one public Java class per source file, each Java source file becomes a class file, and the elements of a package name become directory nodes in the path to the class, you end up with a fairly complex collection of directories and files. Wouldn't it be nice to be able to roll the whole mess up into a single binary file for distribution?

Well, you can. The tool to do the job is called **jar**, which stands for Java ARchive.[26] The files produced by this utility are called *JAR files*. The JAR format is the common DOS/Windows ZIP file format, with a few special files to support some special features we will explain as they come up.

---

24. In Chapter 7 we will introduce **gcj**, the GNU Compiler for Java, which compiles Java to native machine code. **javap** is useless with such a file. It deals only with JVM bytecodes as documented in Sun's JVM Specification.

25. http://java.sun.com/j2se/1.4.2/docs/tooldocs/solaris/javap.html

26. An abbreviation made up of syllables from words instead of just initials is called a *portmanteau*. The US Navy is particularly keen on them, using terms like COMSURPAC (Commander, Surface Fleet, Pacific), COMSUBLANT (Commander, Submarine Fleet, Atlantic), and so forth. There. Now you can't claim you didn't learn anything from this book.

Example 5.19 javap output for `FetchURL.class`

```
Compiled from FetchURL.java
public class FetchURL extends java.lang.Object {
  private java.net.URL requestedURL;
  public FetchURL(java.lang.String);
  public java.lang.String toString();
  public static void main(java.lang.String[]);
}

Method FetchURL(java.lang.String)
   0 aload_0
   1 invokespecial #1 <Method java.lang.Object()>
   4 aload_0
   5 new #2 <Class java.net.URL>
   8 dup
   9 aload_1
  10 invokespecial #3 <Method java.net.URL(java.lang.String)>
  13 putfield #4 <Field java.net.URL requestedURL>
  16 goto 27
  19 astore_2
  20 aload_2
  21 invokevirtual #6 <Method null>
  24 goto 27
  27 return
Exception table:
   from   to   target type
     4     16    19    <Class java.lang.Exception>

Method java.lang.String toString()
   0 ldc #7 <String "">
   2 astore_1
   3 new #8 <Class java.io.BufferedReader>
   6 dup
   7 new #9 <Class java.io.InputStreamReader>
  10 dup
  11 aload_0
  12 getfield #4 <Field java.net.URL requestedURL>
  15 invokevirtual #10 <Method java.net.URLConnection openConnection()>
  18 invokevirtual #11 <Method java.io.InputStream getInputStream()>
  21 invokespecial #12 <Method java.io.InputStreamReader(java.io.InputStream)>
  24 invokespecial #13 <Method java.io.BufferedReader(java.io.Reader)>
  27 astore_3
  28 goto 55
  31 new #14 <Class java.lang.StringBuffer>
  34 dup
  35 invokespecial #15 <Method java.lang.StringBuffer()>
  38 aload_1
```

```
 39 invokevirtual #16 <Method java.lang.StringBuffer append(java.lang.String)>
 42 aload_2
 43 invokevirtual #16 <Method java.lang.StringBuffer append(java.lang.String)>
 46 ldc #17 <String "
">
 48 invokevirtual #16 <Method java.lang.StringBuffer append(java.lang.String)>
 51 invokevirtual #18 <Method java.lang.String toString()>
 54 astore_1
 55 aload_3
 56 invokevirtual #19 <Method java.lang.String readLine()>
 59 dup
 60 astore_2
 61 ifnonnull 31
 64 goto 79
 67 astore 4
 69 aload 4
 71 invokevirtual #20 <Method null>
 74 aconst_null
 75 astore_1
 76 goto 79
 79 aload_1
 80 areturn
Exception table:
  from   to  target type
     3   64     67  <Class java.lang.Exception>


Method void main(java.lang.String[])
   0 iconst_0
   1 istore_1
   2 goto 51
   5 getstatic #21 <Field java.io.PrintStream out>
   8 new #14 <Class java.lang.StringBuffer>
  11 dup
  12 invokespecial #15 <Method java.lang.StringBuffer()>
  15 aload_0
  16 iload_1
  17 aaload
  18 invokevirtual #16 <Method java.lang.StringBuffer append(java.lang.String)>
  21 ldc #22 <String ":">
  23 invokevirtual #16 <Method java.lang.StringBuffer append(java.lang.String)>
  26 invokevirtual #18 <Method java.lang.String toString()>
  29 invokevirtual #23 <Method void println(java.lang.String)>
  32 getstatic #21 <Field java.io.PrintStream out>
  35 new #24 <Class FetchURL>
  38 dup
  39 aload_0
  40 iload_1
  41 aaload
  42 invokespecial #25 <Method FetchURL(java.lang.String)>
```

```
45 invokevirtual #26 <Method void println(java.lang.Object)>
48 iinc 1 1
51 iload_1
52 aload_0
53 arraylength
54 if_icmplt 5
57 return
```

A JAR file packages a subdirectory and its descendants into a single file. A Java CLASSPATH specification may contain a JAR filename everywhere it might contain a directory name. Let's say you use the GPL'ed Java personal finance program called **jgnash** and you've compiled it from source, so you have a directory off your home directory called jgnash/bin. Suppose you run the program by directly invoking **java** to run the class jgnashMain and you have $HOME/jgnash/bin on your CLASSPATH. You could clean up the mess on your hard drive by using the **jar** command to squash all the files in jgnash/bin together into a single JAR file, as shown in Example 5.20.

Example 5.20 Making a JAR file

```
$ cd ; mkdir jars
$ jar cvf jars/jgnash.jar jgnash/bin
```

You could then replace the $HOME/jgnash/bin entry in your CLASSPATH with $HOME/jars/jgnash.jar. After that you would still run **jgnash** with exactly the same **java** command you always did, but now you got rid of the cluttered pile of files.

This is only the most basic purpose of **jar**, however. Its uses extend well beyond merely concatenating and compressing collections of .class files.

5.11.1 Deploying Applications

One of the best uses of **jar** is to package applications for distribution. You can put a large Java application into a single file with **jar**, and by using a *manifest* (which we are about to discuss) you can nominate the main class to run in that JAR file. You can then provide a shell script (and a batch file, if you are also deploying to Microsoft Windows) that will set the CLASSPATH to point to the

JAR file and run **java** against it. With this simple setup, users need not even know they are using a Java application—it runs like any other application.

5.11.1.1 *The Manifest File*

The only way in which **jar** really differs from any other ZIP archive utility is in the automatic creation and use of a manifest file, by default named `META-INF/MANIFEST` in the archive. Even if you do not specify a manifest file of your own, the **jar** utility creates one for you. Let's take a moment to look at what goes into the manifest.

A manifest is basically a list of key/value pairs. The key comes at the start of a line and the value comes at the end of the line with a colon separating the two. Example 5.21 shows a sample manifest.

Example 5.21 Manifest from the Payback sample application

```
Manifest-Version: 1.0
Ant-Version: Apache Ant 1.5.3
Created-By: 1.4.1_02-b06 (Sun Microsystems Inc.)
Version: 1.0
Main-Class: net.multitool.Payback.Payback
```

All of these entries were produced automatically by **ant** or the **jar** utility itself, except for `Main-Class`, which we specified (albeit with **ant**, as you will see in Chapter 9). The manifest has certain values that are always filled in by **jar**, but two that you might commonly specify are

- `Main-Class`, which allows users to run a Java application by merely typing `java someJarFile.jar`, without having to know the fully package qualified name of the class that contains the application's `main()`.
- `Class-Path`, which allows you to specify what the classpath should be when the application is run.

There are keys specific to applets, to signed applications, to beans, and so forth. We will address these as it becomes necessary. Full details can, of course, be found in the Sun's documentation for **jar**.[27]

---

27. `http://java.sun.com/j2se/1.4.2/docs/tooldocs/solaris/jar.html`

5.11.1.2 Putting a Compiled Application in a JAR File

Let's assume we are going to manually put a Java application in a JAR file. We will want to specify the name of the class that contains the `main()` method of the application. First off, you want the JAR's directory hierarchy to begin at the folder that contains the first node of each package's name. Our sample application here is in the package `net.multitool.Payback`, so we want our present working directory to be the one which contains the `net` subdirectory. Here's a dump of the directory tree from that point after compilation of our sample application:

```
$ find . -print
.
./net
./net/multitool
./net/multitool/Payback
./net/multitool/Payback/Account.class
./net/multitool/Payback/Purchase.class
./net/multitool/Payback/Cost.class
./net/multitool/Payback/DebtAccount.class
./net/multitool/Payback/Payback.class
./net/multitool/Payback/SavingsAccount.class
./net/multitool/util
./net/multitool/util/SAMoney.class
./net/multitool/util/SAMoneyTest$1.class
./net/multitool/util/SAMoneyTest$2.class
./net/multitool/util/SAMoneyTest.class
$
```

We now want to specify which class contains the application's `main()` method. It happens to be the `Payback` class, so we create a file called `manifest`[28] with the following contents:

```
$ cat manifest
Main-Class: net.multitool.Payback.Payback
```

Next, we use the **jar** utility to create the JAR file:

---

28. It can have any name. The key/value pairs from the file will be placed by the **jar** utility into the standard manifest called `META-INF/MANIFEST.MF` no matter what name you give to *this* file.

```
$ jar cmf manifest payback.jar net
$ ls -la
total 20
drwxrwxr-x    3 mschwarz mschwarz        4096 Aug  4 18:19 .
drwxrwxr-x    7 mschwarz mschwarz        4096 Aug  4 17:57 ..
-rw-rw-r--    1 mschwarz mschwarz          43 Aug  4 18:17 manifest
drwxrwxr-x    3 mschwarz mschwarz        4096 Jul 28 16:16 net
-rw-rw-r--    1 mschwarz mschwarz        7506 Aug  4 18:21 payback.jar
```

The options to **jar** tell it what to do. In our case, -c instructs to create a
JAR file, -m adds the contents of the file named in the next parameter to the
META-INF/MANIFEST file, -f and the next parameter is the filename of the JAR
file being created. If we had not specified -f, the JAR file would have been
written to standard out and an I/O redirect would be needed, but the result
would have been the same:

```
$ jar cvm manifest net > payback.jar
$ ls -la
total 24
drwxrwxr-x    3 mschwarz mschwarz        4096 Aug  4 18:24 .
drwxrwxr-x    7 mschwarz mschwarz        4096 Aug  4 17:57 ..
-rw-rw-r--    1 mschwarz mschwarz          43 Aug  4 18:17 manifest
drwxrwxr-x    3 mschwarz mschwarz        4096 Jul 28 16:16 net
-rw-rw-r--    1 mschwarz mschwarz        7506 Aug  4 18:27 payback.jar
```

Everything that follows parameters required by option letters is considered
to be a file or directory that is to be added to the JAR file. The option syntax
for **jar** is similar to that for **pkzip** in the DOS/Windows world and the **tar**
utility in the UNIX world.

As elsewhere in this chapter, we are just getting you started. See Sun's
documentation for details.

5.11.2 Basic jar Operation

We have already covered the most common case, using **jar** to create a "rolled-
up" Java application. **jar** has many command options besides -c and we'll
document a few of them.

-c

    Create a JAR file.

-u

    Update a JAR file—replace updated files, add missing files.

`-x`

Extract files from a JAR file.

`-t`

List files in a JAR.

`-f`

Specify the JAR filename.

`-v`

Be verbose—display descriptions of what the **jar** utility is doing as it does it.

`-m`

Add the contents of the named file to the manifest.

5.12 THE REST OF THE TOOLKIT

There are additional utilities in the toolkit. Below is a capsule summary of them and their purposes.

extcheck

This utility checks an applet JAR file for any extensions it requires that are in conflict with the current Java runtime environment. (But we don't cover applets in this book.)

jarsigner

This is a utility for digitally signing JAR file. Once a JAR is signed, anyone looking at it can be sure of two things—first, the file was definitely prepared by the owner of the private key that matches the public key used to verify the signature;[29] and second, the JAR file has not been modified in any way since it was signed. In other words, depending upon the care with which the signer treats his/her private key, this certifies the authenticity

---

29. A discussion of public/private keys as an authentication mechanism is beyond our scope here. As a shameless plug, Mr. Schwarz would like to point you to Chapter 10 of his previous book, *Multitool Linux*, which contains a beginner's introduction to public key authentication using GnuPG. Of course, a quick Google search will find you many online descriptions that are free.

and accuracy of the JAR file; you can trust it as much as you trust the signer.

Generally speaking, an applet must be signed by a key that the user trusts in order for the applet to increase its security access to the client machine (open/read/write files, access the printer, and so on). But we don't cover applets in this book.

keytool

This tool is used to create and manage the keys we were talking about in the previous entry. Again, this is used mainly for JAR signing, and JAR signing is used mainly for applet authentication, but we don't cover applets in this book.

rmid

The RMI activation daemon. In the RMI example we showed you in this chapter, you had to start a server manually and leave it running to process requests. *RMI activation* is a system where RMI servers may be started on demand.

serialver

Reports the RMI `serialVersionUID` of a class. This can be useful when trying to track down problems with complex RMI systems, especially when multiple versions of an RMI interface with the same name must be in use at the same time.

native2ascii

As mentioned before, Java uses Unicode for all strings. Most of the time, you and we are working with ASCII-encoded files. This program converts files from one format to the other.

policytool

Remember how we had to set up a security policy file for our RMI demonstration (Example 5.13)? Well, this is a Java GUI application for creating and editing Java policy files.

There are a few more. One group of utilities is related to Kerberos tickets. Another is related to Java IDL and RMI-IIOP, both of which are to allow Java to interoperate with CORBA. If you are in a CORBA environment, you will want to look at those. We've got enough on our plates without trying to jam CORBA in here. You're on your own, buddy. Finally, there are a couple of programs that support the Java plug-in, which is a way to make Java available in browsers.[30]

5.13 Review

For all of its humble command-line interface, the Sun Java 2 SDK provides a complete software development package, with everything you need to write and run a wide gamut of Java applications.

5.14 What You Still Don't Know

Oh dear, where to start? There are all those programs in the kit we glossed over right at the end there. We barely scratched the surface of JNI and RMI. We positively orbited the topics of policy files and JAR manifests.

You now have exposure to the bulk of the Java SDK. It is only the first step up the learning curve. We'll take you up a few more as the book progresses, but mastery comes only with time and experience. So use the tools. Write, compile, and debug a lot of Java code.

5.15 Resources

One of the best sources of information on Java is Sun's Web site for Java, `http://java.sun.com`, where you can find a wide variety of information— tutorials, white papers, API specifications, and more.

---

30. Those browsers that had Java built into them generally used Java 1.0 or 1.1. After Java 1.1 it became clear that it would be a major pain to have to reintegrate each new version of Java into each browser product. It would make browser versions and Java releases dependent on one another and would, in general, be a pain both for Sun and for Microsoft and Netscape (remember Netscape?). Thus, the plug-in architecture was born (okay, plug-ins were for things like RealPlayer and Macromedia Flash too). Since Java 1.2, browser integration has been via plug-ins.

Chapter 6

The IBM Developer Kit for Linux, Java 2 Technology Edition

This chapter introduces the IBM Java Software Development Kit. It does so mainly by pointing out how completely the kit mimics the Sun Java Software Development Kit covered in Chapter 5. Some time is spent on the minor differences and some installation issues.

6.1 WHAT YOU WILL LEARN

- The small number of important differences between the IBM and Sun Java Software Development Kits.
- How to put more than one version of Java on the same development machine and how to switch between them painlessly.

6.2 Use Linux Features to Make Multiple Java SDKs Play Nicely Together

We did not spend much time discussing the installation of Java on your Linux system in previous chapter. In fact, we did not discuss it at all. This is because the installation instructions that come with the SDK are more than adequate if you wish only to install a single Java SDK. But what if you want to install, say, both the Sun Java SDK and the IBM Java SDK? Then things get a bit more interesting.

We're going to review the concept of filesystem links, and how they work on Linux. While it may seem odd to discuss them here, we'll be using links to switch gracefully between different Java installations. Links are a powerful feature in Linux filesystems, and switching SDKs is a good application thereof. If you're already familiar with links, skip ahead to Section 6.2.2.

6.2.1   Links

A link is simply a name attached to a collection of data—that is, to a file. In other words, every file has one set of data and at least one link (a name). But a file may have more than one link. In other words, two different filenames may point to the same data. When you do this, you appear to have two copies of the file, but a change to one also changes the other. Deleting one, however, does not delete the other. It merely deletes the link. The file itself is only deleted when the last link is gone.

6.2.1.1   Hard Links

Links come in two flavors: hard and symbolic. A hard link looks like a file in and of itself. Let's show you a hard link, before and after.

```
$ ls -la
total 12
drwxrwxr-x     2 mschwarz mschwarz      4096 Jul  8 10:11 .
drwx------    50 mschwarz mschwarz      4096 Jul  8 10:11 ..
-rw-rw-r--     1 mschwarz mschwarz        45 Jul  8 10:11 sample
$ cat sample
This is a sample
file to demonstrate
links.

$
```

As you can see, we have a directory with a single file in it, `sample`. Now let's make a hard link to that file.

```
$ ln sample example
$ ls -la
total 16
drwxrwxr-x    2 mschwarz mschwarz     4096 Jul  8 10:13 .
drwx------   50 mschwarz mschwarz     4096 Jul  8 10:11 ..
-rw-rw-r--    2 mschwarz mschwarz       45 Jul  8 10:11 example
-rw-rw-r--    2 mschwarz mschwarz       45 Jul  8 10:11 sample
$ cat example
This is a sample
file to demonstrate
links.

$
```

Notice a few things here. First, other than the size and timestamps being the same, there is nothing obvious to show that these two files are, in fact, the same file. Note also the number just ahead of the owning user and group names. In the first directory listing, `sample` had 1 in that position; now both `sample` and `example` have 2. This number is the *link count*. It tells you how many names are linked to the data associated with this name.

We have a couple more things to point out before we move on to soft links, which are going to be more important for our purposes.

```
$ chgrp wwwdev example
$ ls -la
total 16
drwxrwxr-x    2 mschwarz mschwarz     4096 Jul  8 10:13 .
drwx------   50 mschwarz mschwarz     4096 Jul  8 10:11 ..
-rw-rw-r--    2 mschwarz wwwdev         45 Jul  8 10:11 example
-rw-rw-r--    2 mschwarz wwwdev         45 Jul  8 10:11 sample
$ chmod o-r example
$ ls -la
total 16
drwxrwxr-x    2 mschwarz mschwarz     4096 Jul  8 10:13 .
drwx------   50 mschwarz mschwarz     4096 Jul  8 10:11 ..
-rw-rw----    2 mschwarz wwwdev         45 Jul  8 10:11 example
-rw-rw----    2 mschwarz wwwdev         45 Jul  8 10:11 sample
$ chgrp mschwarz sample
$ ls -la
total 16
```

```
drwxrwxr-x    2 mschwarz mschwarz         4096 Jul  8 10:13 .
drwx------   50 mschwarz mschwarz         4096 Jul  8 10:11 ..
-rw-rw----    2 mschwarz mschwarz           45 Jul  8 10:11 example
-rw-rw----    2 mschwarz mschwarz           45 Jul  8 10:11 sample
$
```

As you can see, a file can have only one set of owners and permissions, no matter how many links are made to it. Changing the owner or permissions of one link changes all hard links at the same time. In other words, the security of a file is like its data: A change to one link is a change to them all.

A link need not be in the same directory as the original name.

```
$ ln example /tmp/sample
$ ls -la
total 16
drwxrwxr-x    2 mschwarz mschwarz         4096 Jul  8 10:13 .
drwx------   50 mschwarz mschwarz         4096 Jul  8 10:11 ..
-rw-rw----    3 mschwarz mschwarz           45 Jul  8 10:11 example
-rw-rw----    3 mschwarz mschwarz           45 Jul  8 10:11 sample
$ ls -la /tmp
total 132
drwxrwxr-x    2 mschwarz mschwarz         4096 Jul  8 10:23 .
drwx------   50 mschwarz mschwarz         4096 Jul  8 10:11 ..
-rw-rw-r--    1 mschwarz mschwarz       118081 Jun  3 18:51 jLin.tar.gz
-rw-rw----    3 mschwarz mschwarz           45 Jul  8 10:11 sample
$
```

Here we made a third link in a different directory; /tmp/sample is a third name for the same data file. Note that we made it from the example link, not the original filename. In fact, as far as the Linux filesystem is concerned, there is no "original" name. None of these names is more significant than any other. When you remove a filename, the link is destroyed and the file's link count is decremented. If the link count goes to zero, the file is removed. That's it. Nothing else.

Hard links have a couple of drawbacks. One of them is a genuine technical limitation and the other is more of a usability problem. The technical limitation is that a hard link cannot be made across mounted filesystems. In the simplest case (we don't want to muddy the waters with LVM[1] or RAID[2] at this point—most Linux distributions do not do LVM or RAID "out-of-the-box"), if you have more than one partition or disk drive, these are "mounted" at different points on the directory tree. For example, Mr. Schwarz's laptop's mount table looks like this:

```
$ mount
/dev/hda2 on / type ext3 (rw)
none on /proc type proc (rw)
usbdevfs on /proc/bus/usb type usbdevfs (rw)
/dev/hda1 on /boot type ext3 (rw)
none on /dev/pts type devpts (rw,gid=5,mode=620)
none on /dev/shm type tmpfs (rw)
$
```

We have one large partition mounted at /, or root, and a small partition mounted at /boot. In all of our hard link examples so far, we have been making links on the root filesystem. Example 6.1 shows what happens when an attempt is made to hardlink between two different mounted devices.

This is what we mean when we say a link cannot cross filesystems.[3]

The other problem is more "touchy-feely." With a hard link, you can see by the link count that other links exist, but you don't know where they are. Symbolic links get you around both of these issues.

6.2.1.2   *Symbolic Links, or Symlinks*

In a sense, symbolic links are much simpler than hard links. A symbolic link is a file that contains the name of another file or directory. Because it is marked as a symbolic link, the system will replace it with the contents of the linked file. Example 6.2 will make this more clear.

---

1. Logical Volume Manager. This is a tool that lets you arbitrarily aggregate disk drives and partitions into a "logical volume" that may be mounted and unmounted as a unit. Such tools are commonly used in serious production servers, but are rare on workstations or simple Linux servers.

2. Redundant Array of Inexpensive Disks. Another heavy server feature that allows multiple disk drives to be linked up as if they were a single disk drive and to act as backup to one another silently and transparently.

3. In a similar vein, there are some networked filesystems that do not support hard links at all because the server or host system doesn't support the concept. Attempts to make links on or to such systems will also fail.

Example 6.1 Attempt to hardlink between mounts

```
$ ln example /boot/sample
ln: creating hard link `/boot/sample' to `example': Invalid cross-device link
$
```

Example 6.2 Symlinking /etc/passwd

```
$ ls -la
total 8
drwxrwxr-x     2 mschwarz mschwarz      4096 Jul  8 15:30 .
drwx------    50 mschwarz mschwarz      4096 Jul  8 15:29 ..
$ ln -sf /etc/passwd passwd
$ ls -la
total 8
drwxrwxr-x     2 mschwarz mschwarz      4096 Jul  8 15:31 .
drwx------    50 mschwarz mschwarz      4096 Jul  8 15:29 ..
lrwxrwxrwx     1 mschwarz mschwarz        11 Jul  8 15:31 passwd -> /etc/passwd
$ cat passwd
root:x:0:0:root:/root:/bin/bash
bin:x:1:1:bin:/bin:/sbin/nologin
daemon:x:2:2:daemon:/sbin:/sbin/nologin
...
etc.
```

What we did here works just like a hard link, but note the attributes on the file: The 1 indicates a symbolic link, and the permissions are read/write/execute for user, group, and other (or for "world" for short). However, these permissions apply to the link, not to the file. Just as with hard links, there is only one set of permissions on the file, and these are on the file that is pointed to, not on the pointer.

One interesting difference between symlinks and hard links is that symlinks do not increment the link count on a file. If we remove /etc/password (a very bad idea, by the way), the symlink would be unaffected, but an attempt to open or read the symlink would not work, because it points at nothing that exists. This is called a *dangling symlink*.

Symlinks may refer to symlinks, and thus you need to be cautious to avoid circular symlink chains. All the shells we have used on Linux report circular symlinks as "too many levels of symbolic links," which sounds like a process exceeding its stack limits but handling it gracefully.

6.2.2   Switching Java Versions by Symlink

Here is the process we went through to install both Sun's Java 2 SDK and IBM's Java 2 SDK on a system at the same time.

1. Download the Sun JDK as a compressed TAR file.

2. Install it to `/usr/java`. The Sun installer named its directory `j2sdk1.4.1_02`, so the full path is `/usr/java/j2sdk1.4.1_02`.

3. Download the IBM JDK and untar it also in `/usr/java`. The base directory in the TAR file was `IBMJava2-141`, so the path is `/usr/java/IBMJava2-141`.

4. Create a symlink called `jdk` in `/usr/java` and make it point at the Sun JDK by default (Example 6.3).

5. Add `/usr/java/jdk/bin` to the system's default `PATH` environment variable.[4] Also add `JAVA_HOME` and `JDK_HOME` environment variables that point to `/usr/java/jdk`.

Now when we run **javac** or any other Java command, we run the version which is pointed to by the `jdk` symlink. If we wish to switch to the IBM JDK, we can just replace the link as show in Example 6.4.

From then on, the machine will be using the IBM Java SDK.

And, of course, by explicitly setting the path and environment variables, you can use whatever you prefer without changing the symlink for all other users on the system. This is an excellent example of how the features of the Linux system can make your life as a Java developer easier—with this general method, you can keep as many Java SDKs from as many vendors as you wish and switch between them at will.

Here, we showed you how to do this on a system-wide basis, but you could, by creating the symlink in your home directory and changing the path for your user account, switch between versions in your own account only, leaving the system-wide default alone. Linux provides endless flexibility for developers.

---

4. Exactly where you do this depends on your distribution. If you aren't sure, you can always do it in the `.bash_profile` file in your user account's home directory.

Example 6.3 Symlinking jdk to the Sun Java SDK

```
# ln -s j2sdk1.4.1_02 jdk
# ls -la
total 16
drwxr-xr-x    4 root      root        4096 Jul  8 15:51 .
drwxr-xr-x   17 root      root        4096 Jun 17 10:18 ..
drwxr-xr-x    8 root      root        4096 May 21 21:09 IBMJava2-141
drwxr-xr-x    8 root      root        4096 Mar  5 14:44 j2sdk1.4.1_02
lrwxrwxrwx    1 root      root          14 Jul  7 22:33 jdk -> j2sdk1.4.1_02
#
```

Example 6.4 Symlinking jdk to the IBM Java SDK

```
# rm jdk
# ln -s IBMJava2-141 jdk
# ls -la
total 16
drwxr-xr-x    4 root      root        4096 Jul  8 15:51 .
drwxr-xr-x   17 root      root        4096 Jun 17 10:18 ..
drwxr-xr-x    8 root      root        4096 May 21 21:09 IBMJava2-141
drwxr-xr-x    8 root      root        4096 Mar  5 14:44 j2sdk1.4.1_02
lrwxrwxrwx    1 root      root          14 Jul  7 22:33 jdk -> IBMJava2-141
#
```

6.3 How the IBM JDK Differs from the Sun JDK

After the last chapter, which was one of the longest in the book, this chapter should come as something of a relief. It is one of the shortest in the book. Why? Because the IBM Java Software Development Kit is practically identical in use to the Sun package. It differs in only a few respects and that is all we will talk about here.

One of the biggest differences is the version of Java available from each vendor. Sun has the newest versions, as they have been defining what those are. IBM is still releasing the 1.3 versions of Java as Sun begins to release 5.0. But you may not want or need the "bleeding edge" of the technology.

6.3.1   Performance

IBM's Java implementation appears to run most code faster than the Sun implementation. Benchmarking something as complex as a Java Virtual Machine is well beyond our scope here (and, in fact, coming up with a benchmark that will actually predict how much faster *your* application will run on one environment versus another is practically impossible). Nonetheless, we have seen some fairly dramatic performance improvements when running Java applications under the IBM JVM—improvements on the order of 50%–100%.

It is interesting to note that it does not matter which Java SDK produced the bytecode files. We see these improvements when the compiled classes are run, no matter which compiler (IBM's or Sun's) was used to produce them. This suggests that it is some combination of a faster virtual machine and/or a better Just-In-Time compiler (JIT) that gives IBM's runtime its apparent performance advantage.

For the most part, we use the Sun development kit and runtime, simply because Sun's is the definition of Java. But if execution speed is proving to be critical for your application, consider the IBM Java runtime. You may see some speed advantages.

6.3.2   Differences in the Commands

You will notice a few differences. For example, there is both a **java** and a **javaw**. Both invoke the Java runtime. The former has the Java console interface, the latter does not. For our purposes, this does not matter. The IBM Java SDK comes with an Object Request Broker Daemon (**orbd**) for CORBA/IIOP while the Sun SDK does not. Again, for our purposes this doesn't matter.

For the bulk of the utilities, the differences are so slight that you can use the Sun documentation for the IBM tools.

6.3.3   IBM Classes

IBM's Eclipse project (which we begin to cover in Chapter 10) provides a large GUI API library called SWT. We won't go into that here; it is covered in Chapter 17. Of more immediate interest is IBM's enhanced `BigDecimal` class (`com.ibm.math.BigDecimal`) which addresses a lot of deficiencies in Sun's implementation of decimal arithmetic. We will be using the standard Java class in our book (as it is the same for all development kits we cover), but you might want to take a look at IBM's FAQ document on their enhanced `BigDecimal` class.[5] It also appears that IBM's class may become the official Sun version in Java 5.0 when it comes out. The primary feature of this class is its ability to deal correctly with rounding and precision, which is of great benefit in financial and scientific applications. Check out IBM's documentation and see if this is something you should use.

Note that Java bytecodes are Java bytecodes. You can download and use the IBM class with the Sun Java Runtime. It is there if you need it.

6.4 WHAT ARE ALL THESE "_G" VERSIONS?

One thing you will notice right away when you unpack the IBM Java SDK is that it has virtually all of the same commands as does the Sun Java SDK, but there is a whole bunch of them duplicated with a mysterious "_g" suffix. What's up with that?

These versions run a Java VM that was compiled with debug information, so that you can report information about bugs and errors that is of use to IBM SDK developers in locating and fixing problems. These versions should not be used for production work, but only to recreate and report bugs.

6.5 REVIEW

Well, we told you this one would be short. With a handful of minor exceptions, the IBM Java SDK is a complete drop-in replacement for the Sun Java SDK. You could go back to the previous chapter and repeat every example and exercise with the IBM Java SDK, and you would get the same results. There is definitely some comfort in knowing that even though you don't have an Open Source Java VM and SDK, at least you have two vendors the produce functionally identical development environments. You are not trapped into a single vendor's offering.

---

5. http://www2.hursley.ibm.com/decimalj/decfaq.html

6.6 WHAT YOU STILL DON'T KNOW

What you still don't know after reading this chapter is similar to what you still didn't know after reading Chapter 5. IBM Java SDK has many things we have not covered, including security policy files, JNI, and RMI.

6.7 RESOURCES

The best source of information about IBM's Java technology is IBM itself. Search the alphaWorks section of their Web site; we used `http://www.alphaworks.ibm.com/nav/java?openc=java+-+Developer+Kits` and found entries for the Java 1.3 Development Kit for Linux, as well as other Java-related downloads, including the Jikes Open Source compiler.

Chapter 7

The GNU Compiler for Java (gcj)

The GNU Compiler for Java provides a native binary compiler for Java code. In this chapter we'll show you how to compile a simple binary application from Java sources.

7.1 WHAT YOU WILL LEARN

You will learn how to compile a binary executable from Java source code using the **gcj** compiler.

7.2 A BRAND GNU WAY

Quite some time ago Richard Stallman started an effort to create a free version of UNIX called GNU[1] (which stands for GNU's Not UNIX—a recursive

---

1. http://www.gnu.org/

acronym). More than that, he tried to convince the world that code should be Free with a capital "F". By this, he meant that it was unreasonable to provide software without both providing the source code and the right to use and modify that code as desired. To ensure this, he and his team created the GPL[2] (the GNU Public License) and founded the Free Software Foundation[3] to foster development and promote the idea.

The story of the founding of GNU/FSF and the motivations behind it[4] makes for a fascinating reading. Even if you are not interested in Free Software, the story prompts you to think in new ways about software, property, and freedom. As interesting as this story is, it is not our topic. The important thing is how the quest to create a Free operating system lead to a native Java compiler and the twists and turns on this way.

7.3 THE GNU COMPILER COLLECTION

If you are going to write a UNIX-like operating system, and one that is "Free" (certainly free of anyone else's intellectual property which might be restricted from the Free Software point of view), the first thing you need is a C compiler. Thus, a great deal of early effort by the FSF went into developing what was originally called the GNU C Compiler, or **gcc**.

Once they had a C compiler, some people began to write hundreds of utilities from **ls** to **grep**, while others began work on HURD, a microkernel for GNU. That work continues to this day. The bulk of the system commands you use on Linux were in fact developed by the FSF as part of the GNU project. This is why Stallman et al. want us all to refer to "GNU/Linux" rather than "Linux".[5] An understandable, if unenforceable, position.

It wasn't long before an effort began to integrate C++ into **gcc**. As time progressed, support for more and more languages and for more and more

---

2. http://www.gnu.org/licenses/gpl.html

3. http://www.fsf.org/

4. http://www.gnu.org/gnu/thegnuproject.html

5. A viewpoint we understand and appreciate, but we do not bow to is that we must *always* say "GNU/Linux." We say it sometimes, but it gets tedious and annoying if used all the time. So we compromise. We tell you about GNU, but we'll usually say just "Linux" in the text.

architectures[6] was being added. At some point, it was decided to rename (reacronym?) **gcc** to mean "GNU Compiler Collection."

Not too surprisingly, as Java emerged and gained popularity, it became one of the languages supported by the GCC using a front end called **gcj**.[7] That is what we'll be talking about here.

7.4 COMPILING OUR SIMPLE APPLICATION WITH GCJ

The basic form of **gcj** is

```
gcj [options...] [codefile...] [@listfile...] [libraryfile...]
```

We'll go over the options in a moment. For now, let's talk about the various kinds of input files the compiler can process.

In the above command-line synopsis, `codefile` refers to a Java source file, a compiled `.class` file (yes, **gcj** can convert already compiled Java byte-codes into native binaries), or even a ZIP or JAR file. A filename prefixed with the at-sign, @, indicates that the file contains a list of filenames to be compiled. That's the `@listfile` entry in the command synopsis. Finally, zero or more library files to link with may be specified on the command line. When you specify them directly (as opposed to using the `-l` command-line option) you must provide the full name of the library.

Like all the other Java compilers we have talked about so far, **gcj** supports the notion of a classpath. It will look in the classpath for unknown classes referenced by the classes you name to the compiler. Since **gcj** can read and compile from `.class` and `.jar` files, you might think you could just make sure that the JAR files from Sun or IBM Java SDK are on the **gcj** classpath and you would be able to compile any Java program using any Java APIs. Alas, you would be wrong. Why? Because the Java APIs are full of native methods, and which methods are implemented in Java and which are native is not documented anywhere.

---

6. A lot of people do not realize this, but **gcc** is a cross-compiler. Precompiled binaries do not always support this, but if you build your compiler from source, you can use **gcc** to compile code for any supported platform. For example, you can compile a program for a PowerPC-based Macintosh on your Intel-based PC.

7. http://gcc.gnu.org/java/index.html

Even if this were not so, it is not permissible under the GPL to distribute binaries without also offering to distribute source code. So, to distribute the Sun or IBM API JAR files would be incompatible with the GPL, and to not distribute them but to depend on them would mean shipping a product that doesn't work out of the box and requires users to obtain some non-Free software in order to work. That is just not acceptable. So the developers of **gcj** have opted to reimplement as much of the Java APIs as possible.

As you can probably guess if you have browsed the Java API Javadoc files, this is a monumental undertaking. The Java APIs are a moving target, and they started huge and grow larger with every new release. There is a parallel project to **gcj** called GNU Classpath[8] which is attempting to implement the entire Java API. Its target for the 1.0 release is to be fully compatible with Java 1.1 and "largely compatible" with Java 1.2. You might want to look at that project for better API support than that provided by **gcj**'s `libgcj`.[9] If you are curious about the present status of `libgcj`'s implementation of the Java APIs, there is a Web page (frequently updated) that compares the status of it against the Java 1.4 packages.[10]

7.4.1   Compiling FetchURL with gcj

We'll discuss **gcj**'s command-line switches in detail in Section 7.5, but we will have to use a couple of them here. First off, be aware that since **gcj** is actually part of **gcc**, all of the non-language-specific switches of that system also work in **gcj**; thus, `-o` specifies the name of the binary output file, and so on. There are many references on **gcc** to which you should refer for details (the manpage on **gcc** is a good place to start). Example 7.1 shows compiling and running `FetchURL` with **gcj**.

---

8. `http://www.gnu.org/software/classpath/`

9. The **gcj** and GNU Classpath projects are in the middle of an effort to merge their libraries into a common library. The GNU Classpath project aims to be a Free Software replacement for the JRE API JAR file. As such, it is meant to be a library of Java bytecodes that may be used as a drop-in replacement in any Java runtime environment. For our discussion, we will assume you are using `libgcj` as shipped with **gcj** itself.

10. `http://gcc.gnu.org/java/jdk14-libgcj.html`

> **TIP**
>
> The source code for `FetchURL` can be found in Example 3.30.

Example 7.1 Compiling and running `FetchURL` with **gcj**

```
$ gcj -o furl --main=FetchURL FetchURL.java
$ ./furl http://www.multitool.net/pubkey.html
http://www.multitool.net/pubkey.html:
<!DOCTYPE HTML PUBLIC "-//W3C//DTD HTML 3.2 Final//EN">
<HTML>
<HEAD>
<TITLE>Michael Schwarz's Public GPG key</TITLE>
</HEAD>
<BODY>
<CENTER>
<H1>Michael Schwarz's Public GPG Key</H1>
</CENTER>
<PRE>
-----BEGIN PGP PUBLIC KEY BLOCK-----
Version: GnuPG v1.0.7 (GNU/Linux)

mQGiBDuv6IQRBACn1TIWUXiEuZtfR+0Lqx6tYBAzIRpljL42O6r5nKHmndsWV71e
FUnhQpQIf+bNGGPMEt0g0vFpD6YWKP4uIEh2o+u1iyIIMs5QH3iqp8kFjbtVZa21
...
...
...
etc.
```

We already explained the `-o` switch which names the resulting binary. The other switch we use here is `--main` which specifies the class containing the `main()` that should be run when the binary is invoked. Remember that every Java class may contain a `main()`. In a multiclass program, the binary needs to know which `main()` to run when the binary is executed.

Remember that `FetchURL` is in the default package,[11] so you simply type the class name as the argument to `--main`. However, if the class is in a nondefault package, the fully qualified name must be used.

---

11. Any class without a `package` declaration is in the default package.

7.4.2   Compiling a Multiclass Program

For contrast, Example 7.2 shows compiling a multiclass program that is contained in a package (it is the Payback debt/savings/purchase calculator).[12]

Example 7.2 Compiling and running a multiclass program

```
$ cd payback/src
$ gcj -o payback -I. --main=net.multitool.Payback.Payback \
net/multitool/Payback/Payback.java
$ ./payback
Payback -- A savings/credit comparison tool
Copyright (C) 2003 by Carl Albing and Michael Schwarz
Released under the GNU/GPL.  Free Software.
. . .
. . .
. . .
etc.
```

The -I switch names a directory that is to be prepended to the classpath. In this case, we added ".", which is the source directory for the Payback program.[13] Notice the package elements expressed with dots for the --main argument, and with slashes for the filename argument.

> **NOTE**
>
> The **gcj** compiler does pick up and use the CLASSPATH environment variable if it is specified. Also, **gcj** has a number of switches besides -I for classpath manipulation. We won't cover those here; -I is the preferred method (according to the **gcj** manpage at any rate).

---

12. Since this chapter was written, XML features were added to Payback that make it no longer work with **gcj**.

13. The Payback code can be found at the book's Web site: http://www.javalinux-book.com/.

7.5 OPTIONS AND SWITCHES

As we have said, **gcj** is part of the **gcc** suite of compilers and therefore supports all of the non-language-specific options and switches of that suite.

As with most reference material in this book, we will only cover the highlights. See the **gcj** manpage or the project's Web site for full details.[14]

`-I`*dirname*

> Add *dirname* to the classpath ahead of its existing contents.

`-D`*name*`[=`*value*`]`

> Add *name* and optional *value* to the system properties list. This is only valid with the `--main` switch.

`--main`

> Specifies which class contains the application's `main()`. This gives the starting point for an application.

`-fno-bounds-check`

> Disable array bounds checking. Like "real" Java, **gcj** checks all array operations to ensure that array bounds are not exceeded. Using this switch disables that check. It speeds up array operations but can introduce subtle and hard-to-find bugs. Use at your own risk.

`-fno-store-check`

> Like `-fno-bounds-check`, this disables a safety feature on arrays. Normally, when you store an object into an array, a check is made to make sure that the object is assignment-compatible with the array type (in other words, that the object is an `instanceof()` of the array type). Using this switch disables this test. It speeds up array operations but can introduce subtle and hard-to-find bugs. Use at your own risk.

There are other switches for native methods, bytecode (as opposed to native) compilation, and some switches related to resources. We leave it as an exercise for the reader to learn and use these where needed.

---

14. `http://gcc.gnu.org/java/`

7.6 REASONS TO USE GCJ

You might think that speed would be the primary reason to use **gcj**, but this is not necessarily the case. Yes, **gcj** is usually used as a native code compiler (it can compile to Java bytecode as well, and thus can be used as a replacement for **javac**), but there is a lot more to Java performance than that. First off, both Sun's and IBM's JVMs have JIT ("Just-In-Time") compilers in them, which convert some or all of a class's bytecode to native code on the fly. In some cases, these compilers may do a better job than the **gcj** compiler, so as a result, initial runs under a JVM are slower than **gcj** but later loops or iterations are comparable or faster. Also performance of both **gcj** and JVM code is highly affected by memory, stack, and garbage-collection parameters which may be modified with command-line options or properties files. So speed is not the determining factor. We have not done sufficient testing or measurement to tell you which environment produces "the fastest code" from a given source file. (We're not even sure exactly what such "sufficient testing" might consist of. All we can suggest is that your try *your* code in all three environments and then make your own choice.)

It is, perhaps, ironic that one of the main reasons why you might wish to use **gcj** is portability. You see, you can only run Sun's and IBM's JVMs on platforms for which they provide a compiled version. Linux runs on several hardware platforms (such as StrongARM) for which Sun and/or IBM do not provide JVMs. Also, if you are running Linux on some architectures, there may be VMs for the "official" OS, but none for Linux on that architecture. This is the case, for example, for SPARC and Alpha. The cross-compilation that **gcj** inherits from the GNU Compiler Collection allows you to compile Java to native code for Linux on those platforms.

Another reason to use **gcj** might be a desire for better integration with code compiled from other languages. **gcj** has JNI support, but also provides its own inter-language integration system called *CNI*, for Compiled Native Interface. We don't have space to cover CNI (and, frankly, we haven't used it enough to be good judges), but its proponents claim that it is both easier to use and more efficient than JNI. You can read up, use it, and judge that for yourself.

Still another reason might be one that we don't like very much. Again, it is ironic that the only Free Software Java compiler is the one best able to produce proprietary binary code. Code compiled with **gcj** is as difficult to reverse engineer as compiled C or C++ code. It is subject to the same sort of binary obfuscation as other native compiled code. If you need to make your code closed and proprietary, **gcj** may be the right tool for you. Naturally, we aren't very fond of this idea, but it is still a reason one might choose the tool.

Finally, we mentioned that speed wasn't a certain factor for choosing **gcj**, but there is an exception. So far,[15] Java is particularly slow at starting and shutting down virtual machines. If you have a Java program that is invoked on demand or in a loop and the VM is started and stopped on each invocation, then **gcj** will give you a huge speed improvement, even if the code executes at the same speed or slightly slower than the JIT JVM code.

7.7 REASONS NOT TO USE GCJ

We can think of three reasons not to use **gcj**. First, the compiled binary will run *only* on the target platform, whereas a Java bytecode binary is portable to any Java runtime without modification or recompilation. Second, **gcj** is not definitive. Sun still "owns" Java and only Sun's implementation can be presumed to be "correct." Third, the **gcj** API classes are not complete. If you visit the API status page we mentioned earlier, you can see what is provided and what is not. If **gcj** lacks an API your application requires, then you can be sure **gcj** is not the tool for you.

7.8 REVIEW

The GNU Compiler for Java is part of the GNU Compiler Collection. It is generally used to compile Java source code into native binaries. It provides many of Sun's API classes, but not all.

7.9 WHAT YOU STILL DON'T KNOW

You do not know how to interface with C/C++ code using **gcj**. You do not know how to use SWT from Eclipse to write GUI apps with **gcj**.

---

15. Sun claims that Java 5.0 will show considerable improvement in VM initialization speed.

7.10 RESOURCES

There are a number of resources for **gcj**, including

- The **gcj** home page.[16]
- The **gcj** FAQ.[17]
- The **gcj** documentation page.[18]
- The JDK1.4 to `libgcj` comparison page.[19] This resource is particularly useful in deciding whether **gcj** is an appropriate tool for compiling your program.
- Many features of **gcj** are, in fact, "inherited" from the parent project, the GNU Compiler Collection. You can find your way to a lot of good information from the GCC home page.[20]

---

16. `http://gcc.gnu.org/java/`

17. `http://gcc.gnu.org/java/faq.html`

18. `http://gcc.gnu.org/java/docs.html`

19. `http://gcc.gnu.org/java/jdk14-libgcj.html`

20. `http://gcc.gnu.org/`

Chapter 8

Know What You Have: CVS

Source control is such a necessary part of good development practice that it ranks right up there with a sound compiler as a critical part of any software project. It may seem like only an administrative overhead to newcomers, but its effect on a project of any size will be felt over time; it's not the first version of a project that needs source control so much as versions 2 and beyond. And it can be a life saver.

One of the Linux tools that is most appreciated on projects around the globe is the Concurrent Versioning System, CVS.[1] It is one of the best, most reliable pieces of software that these authors have ever used. It should be part of your repertoire of software skills, even when you're not running on Linux. But enough praise; back to practicalities.

---

1. As we were writing this chapter, the core developers of CVS released version 1.0 of a new version control system called Subversion. This new system supposedly contains many improvements over CVS. We do not doubt this, and we recommend that you take a look at Subversion before you select a version control tool. Meanwhile, we know CVS, and most Open Source projects are currently managed with CVS. Choosing CVS won't be a bad choice.

8.1 WHAT YOU WILL LEARN

- Why you need CVS—the problem with source code.
- How CVS solves this problem.
- Some basic CVS mechanisms:
  - Importing source
  - Checkout
  - Commit
  - Tagging
  - Branch tagging
  - Status
  - Log
  - Export
- A quick look at a CVS GUI.

8.2 SOURCE CONTROL: WHYS AND HOWS

Consider the following scenario: A customer has called with a problem in the software that your development team released over a month ago. Your developers try to reproduce the problem on their systems without success. What version of software is your team running? Well, there has been a lot of development in the last month, a lot has changed. Some new features have been added—halfway. In other words, it's close but not really the same software. And it's far from being ready to be given to the customer as a fix-release. Well, what's changed since the release was shipped six weeks ago? Can you find or create a set of sources that matches exactly what the customer is running? Can you then provide a modified version that contains only the fix necessary and no other changes?

With such low prices for hard drives these days it is now economically feasible to track your software releases simply by shelving an entire hard drive with each release of your software. It could contain the source code and all the tools in use for that version. But it does make search and comparisons a bit difficult. Still, conceptually, this is almost what you'd like—to be able to access an image of what your source looked like at any given point in time (for example, when released).

Enter **cvs**—the Concurrent Versioning System. It's a *versioning system*, allowing you to retrieve copies of the source based on either date parameters (e.g., last Tuesday) or the labels that you create. It's *concurrent* because it supports multiple simultaneous users.

You may have used a versioning system before that let multiple programmers work with a set of files. Often such systems will "lock" a file while one user is using it, keeping others from modifying it. CVS doesn't work that way—or doesn't have to. Rather it allows users to each modify the same file (truly concurrent), and then reconciles the changes when those changes are made permanent.

To explain all this, it would be best to set down some terminology, as used by CVS.

repository

The master copy of the source.

sandbox

A developer's local copy of the source.

checkout

The process of acquiring a copy of the source (one or more pieces) from the repository.

commit

The process of adding the changes from your sandbox into the repository.

update

The process of revising your sandbox with changes that have occurred in the repository since you last updated or created your sandbox. When you "update" your sandbox, other developers' changes that have been committed to the repository are merged into your source sandbox.

tag

As a noun, is a special label that you create to mark a milestone in your source repository; you can return to that milestone by checking out a copy of the source with that tag.

tag

As a verb, refers to creating a tag in the source repository.

Once a repository has been set up for use by a project, each developer would check out a copy of the source. Thereafter, the typical sequence for a developer would be:

1. Edit.
2. Test.
3. Commit.
4. Go to step 1.

In some organizations, developers will commit and then test. Others will want to only commit changes that have been tested. Which order you choose is a policy decision by your project, not mandated by CVS.

> **TIP**
>
> We recommend that you test before committing because once you have committed your changes, they become available to all others developers. The more people are working together on a project, the more important it is to keep the source base workable, that is, clean compiling at least, so others can keep working.

Sometimes the developer needs to do an update step before a commit. Such a step is used to integrate other developers' changes into this developer's source. Sometimes this goes smoothly; other times it needs some additional work.

A simple scenario might help explain these steps, too.

Two developers, Ti and Kwan, are working on project Doh. They already have a repository set up with all the source for project Doh. Each developer, on his/her own system, checks out a copy of the source (cvs checkout doh). Now let's say that part of the source is a Java class file called Account.java and it has had several changes made already, so Account.java is now at version 1.7 in CVS.

Let's say that Ti finds a bug in Account.java and makes a change to fix that problem. Ti checks in (commits) the changes to Account.java (cvs commit Account.java) so that the repository now contains Ti's changes, which CVS keeps as version 1.8 of Account.java.

All this time Kwan has been busy modifying Account.java (e.g., adding a new method). Remember that Kwan is working from the 1.7 version. When

Kwan goes to commit his modified version of `Account.java` to the repository, he is notified that `Account.java` has been changed since his copy was checked out, and the commit attempt fails. So Kwan does an update which merges the 1.8 version of `Account.java` in with his modified 1.7 version. If all goes well, the resulting file will be a 1.8 version of `Account.java` which includes Kwan's new changes in the right place(s). Kwan just commits this to the repository, and `Account.java` then stands at version 1.9.

Note that cautionary phrase "if all goes well." The merge will work if Ti and Kwan have each modified different parts of the same file. If all Kwan did was add a new method, it would merge just fine. But what if they both make changes in the same region of the source file? It is up to the programmer to resolve such conflicts and commit the source once again.

In such a situation, CVS does what it can to help out. There is an example of a merge conflict later in this chapter. But such conflicts require human intervention.

Merging of conflicts is, undoubtedly, a very manual process, but you will be surprised by how infrequently you need to do this. Most changes will be merged clean with no manual intervention required. That's probably because most often, when two or more programmers are modifying the same file, they are modifying different sections of it.

With merging, you have the ability to incorporate other developer's changes into your version of the source without the fear of losing your changes. No one's changes get lost, no one's files get "stepped on."

8.2.1   Setup

Before you can use CVS to track your sources, you need to initialize a repository. You can use this repository for several different projects, so you only need to do this setup once.

There are two different ways to connect to a repository—directly on a filesystem, or indirectly over a network. We will use the simpler filesystem mechanism for this discussion. The network connections are described in the references at the end of this chapter.

In order for CVS to know where the repository is located and how to connect to it, it looks for an environment variable called CVSROOT. You can assign a value to CVSROOT from the command line each time you create a CVS project, or for more convenience, you can set it in the shell startup script (e.g., `.bashrc`) so that its ready all the time. The CVSROOT value is really only used, though, to set up the project. Once a project is established, the information in CVSROOT is kept, along with other data, in a directory of files (called CVS). From that point on, CVSROOT (the environment variable) no longer needs to be set. The CVS commands will always use what is in the local sandbox to determine where the repository is; the value of the environment variable will be ignored.

It is possible to have different repositories for different projects. One repository might be for your personal work—revisions of memos and documents that you create on your local machine and store in a repository also on your local machine. Another repository might be a shared network-based repository, used for a project at work. Still another might be a network-based project for some Open Source work that you do in your spare time. Since the CVS repository keeps track of whence it comes, you needn't set a value for CVSROOT every time you switch projects. Instead, CVS knows from within the sandbox where to go for its updates, commits, and so on.

So let's get started and create a CVS repository on our local Linux system, in our own home directory. We will call the repository srcbank, as it will be the "bank" where we will deposit our source files.

```
$ mkdir ${HOME}/srcbank
$ export CVSROOOT="${HOME}/srcbank"
$ cvs init
```

The **mkdir** creates the directory named srcbank as a subdirectory of our home directory. The **export** command sets the shell variable CVSROOT to refer to the location of the new directory. The cvs init command initializes the repository with some needed directories and data files.

Before the cvs init command, the srcbank directory is empty. Afterward it contains a directory called CVSROOT (literal name, not the shell variable's value) which contains a variety of administrative files—most of which you need never worry about.

If your are using a remote repository, that is, one that you connect to over a network (typical when you are sharing a repository amongst team members), then you need one additional step—you need to log in to the CVS repository's server:

```
$ cvs login
```

which will prompt you for a password. Having logged in once, you will not need to log in again, even after reboots of your system, as CVS keeps the password (by default; it can be changed) in a file called `.cvspass` in your home directory. This makes using CVS with a remote repository (once you've logged in as simple as if the repository were local). From here on, the commands will all look the same. If your repository is remote, CVS will use the password from your `.cvspass` file, without asking you for it.

8.2.2   Import

Are you wanting to use CVS on an existing project? Have you already got your project at least partly underway? Let's look at how to enter all those files into CVS with a single command.

Not every file that is in a working directory needs to be kept under source control. Some, like `.class` files, are created from the `.java` source files. Others may be just scratch files that you don't want to keep versioned.

To automatically exclude certain files from ever being included in your repository, CVS uses a file called `.cvsignore` that lists filename patterns. Any filename matching a pattern will be ignored by all CVS commands.

Here is a `.cvsignore` file that we recommend for Java developers:

```
*.zip
*.class
```

This will exclude any file whose name ends in `.class` or `.zip`. Note that the comparison is strictly based on a name, not the actual contents. CVS doesn't know what a "class" file is; it is only excluding a file based on its name.

Certain files are not really source files and can't be managed as such, but we would still like to keep versions and a history of changes for them. A good example would be an image file. For example, you may have a corporate logo in a file called `logo.jpg` and at some point you may get a new or revised version of that file. You can use CVS to track such files, but you need to tell CVS that this is a binary file, so that CVS doesn't try to do some special substitutions that it does on check-in and check-out. (More about those substitutions later.)

For now, let's just consider how to tell CVS which files are binary. We can do that on the command line when we create a new file, but for importing a lot of files at once, and to avoid the need to remember doing that each time we add a file, we can put patterns for binary filenames in a CVS file called `.cvswrappers`.

Here is a `.cvswrappers` file that we recommend for Java developers:

```
#
# A recommended .cvswrappers file
#
# jar files - treat as binary:
*.jar -k 'b'
#
# Image file formats - treat as binary:
*.gif -k 'b'
*.jpg -k 'b'
*.png -k 'b'
*.tif -k 'b'
#
# Document file formats - treat as binary
# both MSOffice and OpenOffice.org file formats:
*.doc -k 'b'
*.ppt -k 'b'
*.xls -k 'b'
*.sx? -k 'b'
```

The format of the file is very UNIX-like. A leading # means that the rest of the line is a comment. The asterisk matches any number of any characters. The question mark matches a single character.

Now we're ready to import. The `.cvsignore` file should be placed in the topmost directory of the set of files that you want to import. Then, from that directory, issue the command:

```
$ cvs import Project YourCo import
```

where `Project` is whatever name you want to use for this project (or *module*) in CVS, and `YourCo` is the name of your company or some other designator to differentiate this source from other third-party packages that you may keep in your repository.

Most importantly, execute the `cvs import` command from within the directory, even though the name of the project is likely (but doesn't have to be) the same as the name of the directory in which you sit.

For example, consider a fragment of the filesystem shown in Figure 8.1. You would want to **cd** *into* the directory `coolj` and then issue the **import** command:

```
$ cd coolj
$ cvs import coolj GJSinc import
```

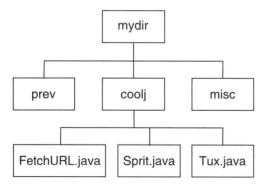

Figure 8.1 A sample directory structure prior to import

This will create a module named `coolj` in the repository, whose contents are all the directories and subdirectories that you see there. But you had to be *in* the `coolj` directory, which may seem counter-intuitive.

Now go to some other directory, one that is *not* part of the `coolj` part of the tree, and check out a copy of the source. For example:

```
$ cd
$ mkdir devsrc
$ cd devsrc
$ cvs checkout coolj
```

> **NOTE**
>
> It is important to check out the source after you've done the import, and *before* you make any changes, because the part of the filesystem that you imported remains untouched. It has no CVS knowledge, so you can't commit changes from that directory, unless you somehow make it CVS-aware. Since these files are your originals, until you've verified that the `cvs import` has gone as planned, it's best not to disturb those files. Create a new directory and check out the module there.

What do you see after the checkout? There should be a single directory, `coolj`, in the directory where you did the checkout (since it was empty when you started). That directory contains a copy of all the files that you checked in, along with a directory named CVS inside that directory and every subdirectory. The CVS directories contain administrative files that help CVS keep track of things for you, which means no CVS tracking information needs to be kept in your source. You should never need to mess with the files in the CVS directory; see the Cederqvist reference in Section 8.6 for more information about these files.

8.2.3   Normal Use

The typical use of CVS occurs after you've made some changes to your source code. At some point, typically after the code compiles cleanly or after the changes have been tested to some extent, you will want to commit your changes to the CVS repository. When you commit one or more files, they become the latest version, the version that others get when they checkout or update the module. To say it another way, when you commit, you make those changes a permanent part of the source repository, available to others.

You can commit a single file at a time, like this:

```
$ cvs commit Account.java
```

Or you can commit several files at a time, like this:

```
$ cvs commit Account.java User.java Xyz.java
```

Or you can commit all the changes from a certain point in the filesystem hierarchy (e.g., the current directory) on down, like this:

```
$ cvs commit
```

(Specifying no files implies the current directory. You can also name a directory explicitly.)

When you commit changes, CVS wants you to provide a bit of commentary to explain what you've changed, to say something about this new version. The comment can be supplied on the command line, with the -m option:

```
$ cvs commit -m "bug fix"
```

If you don't provide the -m parameter and its argument, CVS will invoke your favorite editor (as specified in the environment variable CVSEDITOR or VISUAL or else EDITOR, in that order of precedence). The default, on Linux systems, is to invoke **vi** (see Figure 8.2). In the editor, you can type one or more lines of text; when you exit, the commit will continue to completion.

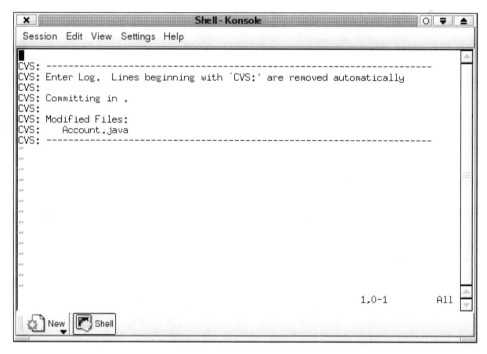

Figure 8.2 CVS asking for commentary as part of a commit

> **NOTE**
>
> If you quit the editor without writing your changes (in **vi**, that would be `:q!`) then CVS will ask if you want to abort the entire commit. If you choose to abort, no changes will be made to the repository. You'll be right back to where you were just before typing the `cvs commit` command.

You will be able to see the comments associated with each version of the file using the `cvs log` command (see Section 8.2.6).

As you will want to provide brief but meaningful descriptions in these comments, it may be helpful to remind yourself what in fact has changed. You can see the differences between the version that you checked out and the file as it stands today by using the `cvs diff` command:

```
$ cvs diff Account.java
```

Here, as in `commit`, you can name one or more files, or even a directory. CVS will display what lines you've added, modified, or removed in each file.

Example 8.1 Sample output from `cvs diff`

```
$ cvs diff Account.java
albing@cvs.multitool.net's password:
Index: Account.java
===================================================================
RCS file: /usr/lib/cvs/cvsroot/JavaAppDevLinux/majorApp/net/multitool/core/
Account.java,v
retrieving revision 1.10
diff -r1.10 Account.java
31d30
<       this.parent = null;
66a66
>     * returns an iterator
93c92
<       children.put(acct, name);
---
>       children.put(name, acct);
$
```

In Example 8.1, CVS has found three differences—one line being re-moved, one line being added, and one line being changed. The < precedes lines from the repository version, and the > precedes lines from the new, that is, changed, version. The `31d30` shows the line numbers from both versions, sep-arated by a single character to indicate what difference action is being described: a for adding lines, d for deleting lines, and c for lines that change.

A typical work sequence might go something like this:

1. Edit some files.
2. `cvs diff` those files.
3. `cvs commit` those files.
4. Go to 1.

The `cvs diff` command is also quite useful for finding out what changed between some previous version of a file and the current version:

```
$ cvs diff -r 1.15 Account.java
```

or between two different previous versions:

```
$ cvs diff -r 1.12 -r 1.15 Account.java
```

or since a certain date:

```
$ cvs diff -D 06-Sep-03 Account.java
```

8.2.4   Update

If there are other people working on this project with you, they will also be making changes. To bring there changes into your sandbox, run the `cvs update` command:

```
$ cvs update
cvs server: Updating .
P Account.java
M User.java
cvs server: Updating subdir
```

Here, `P` indicates CVS has patched in changes to that source file; and `M` indicates you have modified the file. Note that `Xyz.java` is not mentioned. That means there were no updates involved.

The subdirectory `subdir` was also updated, but no changes were made. Had a change been made, you would see the modified files mentioned by name.

You can update a single file at a time by naming that file on the command line, but typically you want to get the changes for all the files in a directory, or even all the changes throughout the project, since a change in one file may be dependent on changes in other files.

Sometimes when you try to commit your changes you will be told that the commit did not succeed because one or more of your files was not up to date. Not to worry; it's easy to bring your files up to date. This leads directly into our next topic. Read on!

8.2.5   Merges

When you commit changes, a new version of each changed file is now part of the repository. If someone else commits changes, that person's changes are now part of the repository as well. But those changes (unlike your own local changes) are yet to appear in your own local copy of the files, that is your sandbox.

The following CVS command will bring your files up to date with all the changes made since you checked out your copy (or last did an update):

```
$ cvs update
```

With that command all the files from the current working directory on down will be updated with the most recent versions of the files from the repository—and not just updated: changes that you have made in your local files will be preserved and *merged* with the new version of the files.

Here's what a successful merge looks like:

```
$ cvs update Account.java
cvs server: Updating Account.java
M Account.java
RCS file: /usr/local/srcbank/JavaAppDevLinux/Account.java,v
retrieving revision 1.17
retrieving revision 1.18
Merging differences between 1.17 and 1.18 into Account.java
M Account.java
$
```

Remember our scenario earlier in the chapter? Our two programmers, Ti and Kwan, have each modified the same file. If all Kwan changed was adding a new method, it would merge just fine. But what if they both made changes in the same region of the source file? Well, the first one to check in his changes will be fine. His commit will succeed. But the second person to try to commit changes to the file will find that CVS will report an error:

```
$ cvs commit Account.java
cvs server: Up-to-date check failed for `Account.java'
cvs [server aborted]: correct above errors first!
cvs commit: saving log message in /tmp/cvsQ9rk01
```

Now, attempting to update will put *both* versions in your local file, marked up by certain character strings to highlight and separate the sections. It is up to the programmer to resolve those conflicts and commit the source once again.

Here's an example of how a conflict might look in a source file:

```
<<<<< ver. 1.7
for (i=0; i<20; i++) {
    myData.callSomething(dollars, time);
}
======
while (i<20) {
    myData.callOtherwise(dollars*(i++), time/60);
}
>>>>>
```

In such a case, the programmer must decide which changes to keep, or how to combine them. After editing the file and removing the dividing lines (i.e., <<<<<, =====, and >>>>>), recompiling and probably a bit of testing, too, the programmer can now do a `cvs commit` to incorporate his changes in the repository.

8.2.6   Log

With each `cvs commit` you are prompted for a comment, to describe the changes that you are committing. What happens to these comments? How can you see them again? Use the `cvs log` command to show the history of a file's revisions and associated comments.

See Example 8.2 for an example of the cvs output command.

Looking down the output of `cvs log`, you can see

- The complete filename—in the repository—of the file whose log we're checking out.
- The local filename in your sandbox.
- Which revision is the "head," that is, the front-most or default revision.
- Which branch, if any.
- What kind of locking mechanism CVS uses. There are some choices, but most users of CVS leave this as is.
- The access limitations. CVS can limit who can modify files (see our reference list if you need to use this).
- A list of all the tags (symbolic names) for this module and to which revision each refers.
- What kind of keyword substitution happens. For binary files this would be `kb`.
- The count of revisions for this file.

Then comes a description of each of the revisions, showing

- The revision number.
- Some stats on the change including the user ID of the user who committed the change.
- How many lines were added and deleted compared to the previous revision.

Example 8.2 An example of running the `cvs log` command

```
$ cvs log Account.java
RCS file: /usr/local/srcbank/JavaAppDevLinux/Account.java,v
Working file: Account.java
head: 1.4
branch:
locks: strict
access list:
symbolic names:
keyword substitution: kv
total revisions: 4; selected revisions: 4
description:
----------------------------
revision 1.4
date: 2003/05/20 11:59:59;  author: albing;  state: Exp;  lines: +80 -5
more comments added
----------------------------
revision 1.3
date: 2003/05/18 15:03:23;  author: albing;  state: Exp;  lines: +3 -2
end case fixed
----------------------------
revision 1.2
date: 2003/05/17 11:05:40;  author: albing;  state: Exp;  lines: +69 -2
actually runs - unit tested
----------------------------
revision 1.1
date: 2003/05/17 10:15:18;  author: albing;  state: Exp;
a rough structure
=====================================================================
```

- The comment that was entered when the user committed the change.

(For a description of state, and why you will almost always see `Exp;`, see the Cederqvist reference in Section 8.6.)

Do you want less output from `cvs log`? You can restrict the information to cover only a certain user's changes (`-w`), to a certain range of revisions (`-r`), and/or between certain dates (`-d`).

For example,

```
cvs -walbing -r1.2:1.4 -d05-Sep03 -d28-Sep-03 Account.java
```

will list only changes committed by user `albing`, only in the revision range of 1.2 through 1.4, and only between the dates of 05 and 28 September of 2003.

Note: do *not* put a space between the -w, -r, or -d and its parameter or CVS will think that the parameter is the name of a source module, and you will see a message like this:

```
$ cvs log -r 1.2:1.4 Account.java
cvs log: nothing known about 1.2:1.4
...
```

which will be followed by output about the `Account.java` module that CVS does know about.

For more variations on the logging output, type:

```
$ cvs log --help
```

8.2.7   cvs status

While the `cvs log` command will tell you about the history of all revisions of a file, you sometimes need to know the status of the current file in your sandbox: Which revision is it? From where did it come? And, most importantly, is it part of the head or part of a branch?

Those questions can be answered with the `cvs status` command. Its output will show the revision number of the file in your sandbox and any "sticky" tags. But to understand what that means, we need to talk about tags first.

8.2.8   cvs tag

We began this chapter asking: "Can you find or create a set of sources that matches exactly what your customer is running? Can you then provide a modified version that contains only the fix necessary and no other changes?" Part of the answers to these questions will depend on your use of the `cvs tag` command. With it, you can set down a label across all your source to mark a particular milestone, so that later you can recall that version of the source. For example,

```
$ cvs tag Rel_2_4
```

will put a tag (that is, a label) called `Rel_2_4` on the head revision of all source files from the directory where this command was executed on down through all its subdirectories. If you run this command from the uppermost directory in your project sandbox, it will label your entire project.

A tag can be applied to a single file or group of files by listing them explicitly on the command line.

> **NOTE**
>
> Certain special characters are not allowed in CVS tags. Specifically, the charac-ters `$`, `.` `:` `;` `@` are not allowed. So you can't use `release_2.4` as a tag. Too bad.

Tags cut across the various revisions of the source. While you *can* specify that a tag goes on the same revision of all sources (e.g., `cvs tag -r 1.3 one_dot_three_tag`), the more typical use is to tag different revisions of each module, the revisions that you've just been working with and testing.

Figure 8.3 shows a tag (QA) that cuts across the various revisions of the different sources. With such a tag, someone can check out a copy of the sources to get the QA release:

```
$ cvs co -r QA project
```

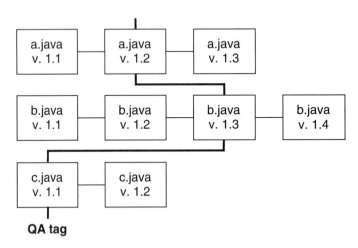

QA tag

Figure 8.3 A tag across three files

Since your project would likely have more than one time in its life that it would be handed off to QA, some people will put date information in the tag, for example, QA_2003_07_15. Others will use a simple tag, such as QA, but such a tag may need to be reused.

If you've put down a tag and decide that you no longer want that tag (for example, your product is preparing for a new QA cycle and you want to reuse last cycle's tag, or maybe you simply misspelled your tag), you can delete it using the -d option.

> **WARNING**
> Once you delete a tag, it's gone forever. It is not available even when you recall earlier versions. If you reuse a deleted tag, it doesn't remember any history from its first use.

Imagine your project has just reached a milestone, like the hand-off to QA, so you have tagged your source accordingly. Now the QA group finds a bug and you fix it. What do you do with the tag? The tag will be on the unfixed version of source. One thing that you can do, *after* you commit your changes, is simply to move the label:

```
$ cvs commit Account.java
...
$ cvs tag -F QA Account.java
```

This will "force" the tag on Account.java to move to the current version.

Such a mechanism works fine for the short term, for quick changes that are put in shortly after the tag has been set down. But what if it takes QA several days to find the bug, and what if, during that time, you've been refactoring Account.java, or adding features for a future release? In those cases, what you really need is a branching tag.

8.2.9 Branching Tags

When you use the -b option with a cvs tag command, then the tag you create is a "branching" tag. That means that you now have two paths in your source repository. You can check out source from, and commit changes to, either of those paths. This allows you to keep moving ahead with new development on the head or tip of the source while providing fixes against a previous version.

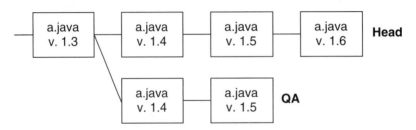

Figure 8.4 A simple branch and merge

Figure 8.4 shows a single source file with a single branch. The tag (QA) may have been applied to multiple files, typically to your entire project. The branched version of each file (for example, 1.3.1.1) is not created until the next change is checked in for that file, so many of the files with the tag may still be on their main source branch.

> **TIP**
>
> When do you want to create a branching tag? You can do it at any time that you lay down a tag. We have found it best to do it right away when you "release" your software, that is, whenever you hand it off to another group (e.g., QA or customers). This provides a label (the tag) to identify what exactly was handed off, but also puts the possibility for branching in place for fixes that may be needed on that branch.

Let's look briefly at the steps you would take to lay down a branching tag named QA, and then apply a fix to that branch.

In the directory where you have your current source, which is what you just released, set down the branching tag:

```
$ cvs tag -b QA
```

> **NOTE**
>
> You have just set down the branching label on the source but you have *not* changed your current set of sources. If you make changes in the current directory (and subdirectories) and check those changes in, you will be making those changes to the head, not the branch, of the source.

Example 8.3 Checking out a tagged revision

```
$ cd
$ mkdir fixes
$ cd fixes
$ cvs co -r QA myproject
cvs checkout: Updating myproject
...
U myproject/Account.java
U myproject/Caltron.java
U myproject/Demo.java
U myproject/Employee.java
U myproject/Person.java
...
$ cd myproject
$ cvs status Account.java
===================================================================
File: Account.java      Status: Up-to-date

   Working revision:    1.2      Sat Oct 26 03:32:17 2002
   Repository revision: 1.2      /usr/local/srctree/myproject/Account.java,v
   Sticky Tag:          QA (branch: 1.2.2)
   Sticky Date:         (none)
   Sticky Options:      (none)

$
```

Now that you have the label set down, you need to check out a copy of *that* version of the source. Since we are checking out a new copy, be sure that your CVSROOT environment variable is set appropriately (see above). Then find some new directory to put your source and check out a copy with the tag, as shown in Example 8.3.

We did a cvs status after the checkout to show you the important difference between this version and the other versions. These files will all show a Sticky Tag in their status. This is the label used to check out or update this version of the source. When you check in changes to these source files, the changes will be against that branch, and not the head.

From there on, everything is the same. Make your changes and just check files in as usual. CVS will remember (via the files in the CVS directory) that you're on the branch, so when you check things in, they'll go to the branch.

The important thing is to create the tag as a *branch* tag so that you can commit changes against that branch. The downside, however, is that you now have two different source versions; bug fixes have to be made in both sources, new features have to be added twice, and so on.

The easiest way to deal with that is to keep your number of active branch tags small; you likely don't want to have to apply a fix to 14 different branches. Also, keep the lifespan of the branches brief—which is, of course, a relative term.

CVS does provide commands to merge a branch back into the source head. But for this, we will refer you to other CVS material. Our job is to give you an overview and a feel for the possibilities. For this sort of task you will want a complete reference manual.

For more variations on `cvs tag`, type:

```
$ cvs tag --help
```

8.2.10 `cvs export`

If you want to produce a copy of your source tree without the `cvs` subdirectories—just the pure source—you can use the `cvs export` command. Like the inverse of import, it will check out a copy of the source, but will not create any of the `cvs` subdirectories that allow CVS to manage the commits, checkouts, logging, status, tags, and so on. In other words, the exported directories are not a CVS sandbox—they're just a copy of the files.

> **NOTE**
>
> Changes made to an exported collection of files cannot be committed back to CVS. Of course you can get the changes back into CVS by creating a sandbox with a `cvs checkout` command, copying all or some of the exported files into that sandbox, and then committing the changes from there. But it's better to think of export as a one-way street.

8.2.11   A Quick Look behind the Scenes

If you are one of those people who worry excessively about efficiency, let us reassure you that CVS is OK. You could think of a CVS repository as saving each revision of a file (for example, versions 1.1, 1.2, and 1.3), but in fact CVS only keeps a single full version of a file—the latest version—and then stores the *deltas*, that is, changes required to revert back to the previous versions. So it keeps a full version of 1.3, but then only the differences between 1.3 and 1.2

and the differences between 1.2 and 1.1. This means that it is always very efficient to get the latest version of any file. (Other systems have tried keeping the
original and the deltas for each revision going forward—but that gets very expensive to retrieve versions with hundreds of modifications. With CVS, the
latest version is always at hand.)

An exception to this are "binary" files, those on which CVS can't do keyword substitutions. The revisions of those files, such as JPEG image files, won't
be stored by deltas, but by complete copies of each revision.

8.3 A GUI: JCVS

If you are a die-hard GUI kind of developer, and aren't yet convinced of the
power and convenience of the command line, then reread Section 1.3.10. If
you are still not convinced, that's OK—you can still use CVS with the help of
a GUI written entirely in Java. This is an implementation of the CVS client,
that is, the portion of the CVS system that communicates with a remote server.
The server does the real work of managing the versions; the client collects the
data, manages the local files, and communicates with the server.

If you're going to use jCVS, you will need to get a CVS server up and
running—or maybe your project administrator has already done that. If so,
read on.

8.3.1   Installing jCVS

jCVS can be downloaded from www.jcvs.org where you can get it as a zipped
archive file. Unzip it into a directory and create a shell script to make it easy to
invoke. Since jCVS is an actual Java program, all the shell script needs to do is
to ensure that its JAR files are on the CLASSPATH and then invoke the jCVS
main class.

Here's a straightforward shell script which will accomplish that:

```
JCVS="/usr/local/jCVS-5.2.2"
CLASSPATH="${CLASSPATH}:${JCVS}/jars/activation.jar"
CLASSPATH="${CLASSPATH}:${JCVS}/jars/jcvsii.jar"
CLASSPATH="${CLASSPATH}:${JCVS}/jars/jh.jar"
CLASSPATH="${CLASSPATH}:${JCVS}/jars/js.jar"
java -jar ${JCVS}/jars/jcvsii.jar
```

You would need to change the definition of JCVS to match the directory where you unpacked the ZIP file, but the rest will work with your location. Of course the classpath could all be set on one longer line, but this way is more readable.

Run jCVS (Figure 8.5) and navigate to the checkout page (Figure 8.6) to fill in the parameters for your CVS server. Then you should be able to contact it for checking out your sources (Figure 8.7).

Figure 8.5 jCVS splash screen

| × | | | | | jCVS II | | | | | ○ ▼ ▲ |

File   Help

| WorkBench | Checkout | Export | Import | Create | Test |

📁 Work Bench

Project Details

Token
Repository
Root Directory
Local Directory
User Name
Host Name
Connect Method
Description

Figure 8.6 jCVS initial screen

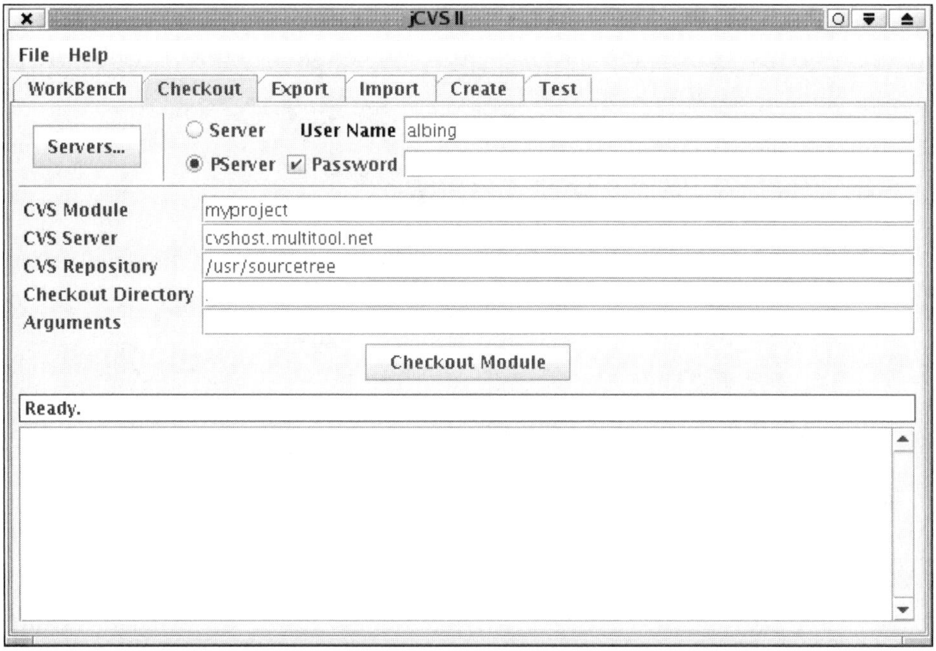

Figure 8.7 jCVS checkout screen

Conspicuous in its absence on the jCVS Web site is a good user manual. Since we're proponents of the command line, don't look for it here, either.

Many, if not most, Java developers these days will be using, at least part of the time, an Integrated Development Environment (IDE). One of the tools that these IDEs integrate is a source code manager, and typically for Open Source tools that means CVS. So while we're not giving you much info on jCVS, you will find a useful GUI for CVS inside most IDEs.

8.4 REVIEW

This chapter has been all about CVS, one of the great jems of the Open Source world. Projects all across the globe depend on CVS to track their source changes, as programmers half a world away collaborate and share source.

We discussed how to import source files into CVS and how to get them back out. We discussed the mechanism for checking in changes and how to sort out collisions for the rare occasions when automatic merges don't succeed. We described how to tag a set of source files for later retrieval, and how to make those tags into branches in your source tree. We also discussed how to show the history of those changes and the status of a source file. Finally, we took a quick look at a GUI for use with CVS, for those so inclined.

8.5 WHAT YOU STILL DON'T KNOW

- The myriad of administrative commands which help you manage and maintain a source library. Most of those commands you won't need, but it's nice to know that they are available, just in case. Refer to the Cederqvist document (Section 8.6) for all the gory details.

- How to set up remote users for sharing a CVS repository on a network, especially the use of the cvs_RSH environment variable.

- How CVS integrates into development tools. We'll see this in the coming chapters; for example, CVS interaction is built into NetBeans, SunONE Studio, and Eclipse.

- How good it feels to have CVS come to the rescue so you can recover a version of something that you thought was lost. May you never have to learn this the hard way.

8.6 RESOURCES

- *Version Management with CVS* by Per Cederqvist et al. is the "official" manual for CVS. It can be viewed as HTML or downloaded as HTML, PDF, or PostScript from `http://www.cvshome.org/docs/manual/`.

- Chapter 6 of *The LINUX Development Platform: Configuring, Using and Maintaining a Complete Programming Environment* by Rafeeq Rehman and Christopher Paul (ISBN 0130826758, Prentice Hall PTR) gives a good introduction to CVS. They give more information, too, on jCVS as well as on how to integrate CVS into Emacs.

Chapter 9

Ant:
An Introduction

Ant[1] is a tool for building and deploying collections of files. It is particularly suited to building and deploying Java applications (in no small part because it is written in Java). Ant is well worth knowing and using for all but the simplest Java applications.

9.1 WHAT YOU WILL LEARN

- How to install and set up Ant.
- Enough about XML to read an Ant buildfile.
- The basic tags used in most buildfiles.
- The extent of our remaining ignorance after completing the chapter.

---

1. I must mention something about the title of this chapter: There was a Monty Python's Flying Circus episode that had this title, and my inner geek couldn't resist.

9.2 THE NEED FOR A DIFFERENT BUILD TOOL

James Duncan Davidson had a problem. Perhaps you've had this problem, too. It has to do with the building of software—compiling, copying, and otherwise modifying files to get all the pieces in all the right places for running a collection of programs.

There are a number of ways to automate the building of software. You can script the compilation using shell scripts or batch jobs. That works fine, but there are two problems with that solution. First, scripts are generally not portable across very different operating systems. That's a serious problem for a language like Java, which is intended to be portable across operating systems. Second, it is difficult if not impossible, using scripting languages, to prevent wasted compiles; the checking and comparing of date stamps on source and object files makes scripts large and difficult to maintain.

Very well, we hear you say. There's **make**. The **make** program has been around for a long time. It is available on many operating systems. It handles the conditional compilation of files very well. It has been around for centuries (it seems). It is well known and widely used. All of this is true, but even this venerable tool falls a bit short in the Java world. First of all, although makefiles are generally far more portable than other scripts, there are still considerable variations in details, and **make** does nothing to mask the differences in file, path, and disk designations that exist across operating systems. Moreover, both **make** and scripts suffer from a more basic problem. Although Java programs can execute reasonably quickly, the overhead of starting a JVM and tearing it down again is considerable. Since **javac** is written in Java, each time it is invoked to compile a source file (one file at a time is the **make** way) this setup and teardown time cost is paid.

But, we once more hear you protest, you can just use **javac** on the entire project! Doesn't it build everything that needs to be built? In the simplest case, yes, it does. But as soon as you share code between projects, or use RMI which requires execution of the **rmic** compiler, or use EJBs, or link in native methods, then **javac**'s dependency resolution just will not work.

Luckily, James Duncan Davidson had this problem. And luckily it really bothered him. And even more luckily for us all, he decided to share his solution.

His solution was Ant, which we will from now on refer to as **ant**. Why **ant**? Well, he suggests that it might be because ants are little things[2] that build big things. He has also suggested (in his preface to the O'Reilly book *Ant: The Definitive Guide*, Jesse Tilly and Eric Burke) that it might stand for "Another Neato Tool." We're inclined to put forth the former, but believe the latter.

James Duncan Davidson wrote **ant** and contributed it to the Apache project, so it is Free Software. And it makes the problems cited above rather piffling. Through the rest of this chapter we will describe how.

9.3 OBTAINING AND INSTALLING ANT

You can obtain **ant** from the Apache Web site.[3] Which version you download will depend on your system and your needs. There are stable releases and daily builds. Unless you have a compelling need for a feature not yet in a stable release, we would suggest you stick with the most recent stable release. As of this writing, that is version 1.5.1.

If you are using RedHat, or another Linux distribution that uses the RedHat Package Manager, **rpm**, then the simplest way to install would be to download the RPMs linked from the Web site and install those:

```
$ rpm -i ant-1.5.1-3jpp.noarch.rpm
```

You have two other options besides the trusty old RPM method. First, you may download a binary *tarball*, a word often used for a compressed file created with the **tar** utility, or you may download and compile the **ant** source code.

Let's take these each in turn.

9.3.1 Installing a Binary Tarball

Binary distributions of **ant** are available in `.zip`, `.tar.gz`, and `.tar.bz2` formats. Utilities are available for all of these formats for Linux, although you

---

2. Not so little anymore. As of this writing, the head of the CVS tree for **ant** weighs in at just shy of 48MB, and there are 5,239 files in there! These totals include a lot of project documentation, but even considering only the `src` subdirectory, we are still looking at 18MB and 1,687 files. It is probably incorrect to call **ant** a "little thing" these days.

3. `http://ant.apache.org/`

will find that generally `.zip` files are intended for Windows machines and `.tar.gz` and `.tar.bz2` for UNIX systems. The `.gz` format is decompressed with the **gzip** utility and `.bz2` files with the **bzip2** utility. The **bzip2** compression algorithm produces better compression, while **gzip** is "more common." If you have a modern Linux distribution, you almost certainly have both installed already.

Once you have the archive file downloaded, you should download one of the files linked next to it. These are cryptographic hashes of the legitimate archive file so you may be (more) assured that the software is the software you think it is. The first, PGP, is an actual digital signature. If you are already familiar with PGP or GnuPG and are comfortable with them, then by all means use this. It is, as you know, a superior form of validation compared to MD5. But explaining how to use digital signatures and GPG keys is beyond our scope here. As for MD5, however, this is fairly easy.

An MD5 hash is a 128-bit value generated in such a way that it is impossible for two different files of the same length to have the same hash value (actually, the term used in the literature is "computationally unfeasible," but for our purposes that is the same thing). If you run the program **md5sum** with the tarball file as an argument and you get the same number as the one you downloaded, you may be certain that the file you have is an exact match with the one that was used to produce the number you downloaded from the Web page. Remember that this is all that is proved by this. If both the file server *and* the Web page have been compromised, then the fact of a match doesn't mean much. A *mismatch* however proves that one of the two has been compromised and you probably shouldn't use the tarball.

You should get in the habit of verifying checksums and digital signatures where they are supported.

If you are still worried about the dual compromise, well, that's where a PGP digital signature can help. It not only proves the integrity of the data; it also proves the identity of the generator. Learn more about PGP (actually, the Free Software version of it, called GnuPG, at the GnuPG Web site.[4]

Once you have downloaded both the md5 file and the tarball, validate and extract the tarball (Example 9.1).

Note that we did this in a regular user's home directory. If you just wish to use **ant** yourself, then this is the way to go. If you wish to make **ant** available

---

4. http://www.gnupg.org/

Example 9.1 Validating and extracting the **ant** tarball

```
$ cat jakarta-ant-1.5.1-bin.tar.gz.md5
2be27d9e09011bf1cc3d1967ee34f7d1

$ md5sum jakarta-ant-1.5.1-bin.tar.gz
2be27d9e09011bf1cc3d1967ee34f7d1  jakarta-ant-1.5.1-bin.tar.gz
$ zcat jakarta-ant-1.5.1-bin.tar.gz | tar xf -
$ cd jakarta-ant-1.5.1
$ ls
bin             docs            etc             KEYS            lib
LICENSE         LICENSE.dom     LICENSE.sax     LICENSE.xerces  README
welcome.html    WHATSNEW
$
```

---

to multiple (or all) users on the system, you will want to untar as `root` and move the resulting directories to locations convenient to other users, such as `/usr/local`.

Whether for one user or for many, there is a handful of remaining tasks to make **ant** usable.

9.3.1.1 *Environment Variables*

The `JAVA_HOME` environment variable should already be set as a result of setting up your JDK. `JAVA_HOME` should point at the base of your JDK installation.

The `ANT_HOME` environment variable should be set to point at the untared installation of **ant**. In our sample here, it would be `~/jakarta-ant-1.5.1`.

Make sure that the `bin` directory of the **ant** installation is added to your `PATH`.

9.3.2 Installing a Source Tarball

We do not encourage you to install **ant** from source, although we do encourage you to download and study the **ant** source. It is an excellent sample Java application.

If you must build from source, the start of the process is the same as above. You download the tarball, verify it with GPG or **md5sum**, then unzip and untar it.

It begins to differ at this point. The **ant** source package comes with a shell script, `build.sh`, that actually builds a minimal version of **ant** and then runs **ant** to complete the install.

Make sure that the JAVA_HOME and ANT_HOME are set as you want them, then execute `build.sh install`. Unless you have installed the optional tasks,[5] you will see several warnings about missing classes. You may safely ignore these.

As with the installation of other packages built from source, you will need to have appropriate permissions for the target directories. This might mean running the install as root, with all appropriate attention and dread.

9.4 A SAMPLE ANT BUILDFILE

Let's go over the basics of creating an Ant buildfile. We'll start with an introduction to XML, and then move on to the specific tags Ant supports and how you might use them to automate a build.

9.4.1   XML for the Uninitiated

The buildfiles of **ant**, usually named `build.xml`, are written in Extensible Markup Language, or XML. Some of the reasons for this are:

- XML is hierarchical.
- XML is standardized.
- XML is widely used and familiar to many programmers.
- Java has many classes for reading, parsing, and using XML.
- XML-based representations of hierarchical data structures are easy to read and parse for both humans and programs.

XML is a successor to SGML, Standard Generalized Markup Language, which is a language for defining markup languages. A markup document may be *validated*. A validated document is one that conforms to a structural specification of the markup tags in the document. Such a specification may be made using a Document Type Definition (DTD), which is a holdover from the way SGML markup languages were specified, or using one of the newer specification

---

5. There is a horde of optional tasks. As the name suggests, they are optional. Include these if you need them. This is the only mention they will receive.

standards, such as W3C's XML Schema. In either case, the DTD or schema specify what tags may be used in the markup, where they may exist with respect to one another, what attributes tags may have, and how many times a given tag may appear in a given place. A document can thus be validated—that is, checked against the corresponding DTD or schema. It's not necessary, however; in many situations, documents can also be used without validation so long as they are *well-formed*—that is, conform to the basic syntax of XML.

HTML, with which even nonprogrammers are familiar, is an instance of a markup language defined in terms of SGML (and XHTML is its reformulation in terms of XML). This book itself was written in Docbook, which is another SGML markup language.

So, if SGML is such a wonder, why is XML all the rage? Well, SGML is one of those standards that attempt to "subsume the world." SGML has very complex and flexible syntax, with many different ways to represent a simple markup construct. Thus, to completely implement an SGML parser is difficult. Recognizing that 90% of the complexity of SGML is needed in only about 1% of cases, the designers of XML realized that they could make a markup specification language only 10% as complicated that would cover 99% of cases (of course, like 85% of statistics, we're making these numbers up, but you get the point).

Implementing an XML parser, while not exactly trivial, is much easier than implementing an SGML parser.

SGML/DSSSL and XML/XSLT are efforts to make the transformation and presentation of hierarchical data easier and more standardized. If what you have read here is all that you know about XML (or SGML), you should certainly consider getting yourself a book on these important standards.

For now, we can say that XML consists of *tags* which are set off from data content by the familiar less-than and greater-than brackets we are used to seeing in HTML:

```
<samplexmltag>
```

Just as in HTML, the tags may have start tag and end tag forms:

```
<samplexmltag>Sample XML tagged data</samplexmltag>
```

The entire construct, including the pair of matching tags and everything inside them, is called an *element*. The start tags may also, like in HTML, carry data inside them in the form of *attributes*:

```
<samplexmltag color="blue">Sample XML tagged data</samplexmltag>
```

If you have an empty element, one that that either does not or cannot have data between its start tag and end tag, you may "combine" the start and end tag by putting the slash at the *end* of the tag:

```
<samplexmltag color="blue"/>
```

Obviously, there is more to it than this, but it is enough to begin with.

XML's uses range from publishing to networked interprocess communications. Our interest here is in using it to represent a model of a piece of software and the various ways that software might be built and deployed. So from here on, we will be discussing not XML in general, but the **ant** document type. Actually, **ant**'s markup language uses unvalidated XML. In other words, there isn't officially a *schema* for **ant**. Thus, the only formal definition for an **ant** XML file is what **ant** accepts and understands. This is more common than it should be. Any XML markup vocabulary really should have a schema, but often XML use starts with "Oh, this is just a quick thing. No one will ever read or write this markup. Just these two programs of mine." These famous last words will one day be right up there with "I only changed one line of code!" As strongly as we feel about this, **ant** really can never have a DTD, at least not a complete one. The custom task feature makes this impossible.

9.4.2   The Buildfile Tags

The buildfile (usually named `build.xml`) begins with a header announcing that this is an XML document and specifying what version of XML is being used in it:

```
<?xml version="1.0"?>
```

The `<?` and `?>` delimiters mark up an XML *statement* (as opposed to an XML tag).[6] In this case, we are declaring that this is an XML document and that it is using XML version 1.0.

---

6. Note that these are the terms we are using to describe XML to a new user. They are not the formal terms for these document elements. For the proper names, consult an XML reference.

9.4.2.1   *The* project *Tag*

Every buildfile must begin with a project tag. A buildfile must contain exactly one project tag.

The project tag contains three attributes:

name
> The name of the project.

default
> The default target (see next section).

basedir
> The base directory of the project. Usually this is "." meaning the directory the buildfile is in.

The project name is just a name. It is not of particular importance to **ant**, although many IDEs that integrate **ant** will make use of the name attribute of the project.

The default attribute names a target tag that will be built by default if a build target is not passed to **ant** (see Section 9.4.2.2).

9.4.2.2   *The* target *Tag*

Every time you run **ant**, you are building a *target*. If you do not specify a target, **ant** will run the target named in the default attribute of the project tag.

A project may contain any number of targets. The target tag has five attributes:

depends
> The name or names of other targets that must be built before this target may be built.

description
> A descriptive name for the target. Displayed when ant -projecthelp is run.

if
> Specifies a property name (see Section 4.4). The target is only built if the named property is set.

`name`

> The name of the target. This is the name entered as an argument to **ant**. This is also the name that may be used in the `default` attribute of the `project` tag.

`unless`

> This is the reverse of the `if` attribute. The target is built unless the property is set.

9.4.2.3   Properties

There is more than one way to set what we might call variables in **ant**. The only one we will concern ourselves with here is *properties*. Properties are like a simple hash, or associative array. They associate value, which is stored as a `String`, with a name, which is also a `String`. They behave very much like the `Properties` class introduced earlier in this book.[7] You can use buildfile properties to associate a single name with a single value that you use in multiple places throughout the buildfile to make configuration changes easier and less error-prone. Some tasks also expect certain properties to be set, as we shall soon see.

You set a property with the `property` tag (Example 9.2).

Example 9.2 A useless `build.xml` example to demonstrate properties

```
<?xml version="1.0"?>

<project name="pointless" default="useless" basedir=".">

  <target name="useless">
    <property name="example.utility" value="nil"/>
      <echo>This example's usefulness:
      ${example.utility}.  OK?</echo>
  </target>
</project>
```

Running **ant** with Example 9.2 gives this output:

---

7. In fact, an examination of the **ant** source code reveals that **ant** properties are stored in a `HashTable`.

```
$ ant
Buildfile: build.xml

useless:
     [echo] This example's usefulness: nil.  OK?

BUILD SUCCESSFUL
Total time: 1 second
```

9.4.2.4   *Tasks*

A *task* is something that must be done to build the target. There is no single "task" tag; instead, each kind of task has its own tag[8] so there are many tags referred to collectively as *task tags*.

There are dozens of standard task tags, but only a few of them are "everyday." We'll introduce a few of them here, and then talk about the tags that don't fall into the project/target/task hierarchy.

Standard task attributes.   All **ant** task tags have at least the three attributes:

`id`
> A unique ID for the task (not required).

`taskname`
> A name for the task, used in logging (not required).

`description`
> A description of the task, used for comments.

The `javac` **task.**   The `javac` task, not surprisingly, runs the Java compiler. Note that since the Java compiler is written in Java and so is **ant**, there is no VM launch overhead to running the compiler. This can make **ant** many times faster than **make** simply for normal compiles.

The `javac` tag is one of the most complex in **ant**.

The `javac` task tag has a very large number of attributes, and may contain quite a number of other tags within it. First off, it is sensitive to a property, `build.compiler`, which may be used to specify that a particular Java compiler version must be used. The use of this will come up later when we build part of

---

8. In fact, task tag names correspond to the names of the Java classes that implement them. This will matter to you only if you wish to write your own **ant** tasks. We will not take you that far in this book.

our application using the GNU Compiler for Java, but for now, and in general, you will not set this property,[9] compiling with the default compiler for the JDK version you are using. This is **ant**'s default behavior.

srcdir
> Location of the Java source files.

destdir
> Location to store the class files.

includes
> Comma- or space-separated list of files (optionally using wildcards) that must be included; all .java files are included when this attribute is not specified.

excludes
> Comma- or space-separated list of files (optionally using wildcards) that must be excluded; no files (except default excludes) are excluded when omitted.

classpath
> The classpath to use.

sourcepath
> The sourcepath to use; defaults to the value of the srcdir attribute or to nested src elements. To suppress the sourcepath switch, use sourcepath="".

classpathref
> The classpath to use, given as a reference to a path defined elsewhere.

extdirs
> Location of installed extensions.

nowarn
> Indicates whether the -nowarn switch should be passed to the compiler; defaults to off (i.e., warnings are shown).

---

9. The one place you are likely to need to set this is when you are using a recent JDK to compile applets that you wish to work in Netscape 4.0 and IE 4.0 and older browsers. But this book doesn't teach you Java applets. We swear.

debug
> Indicates whether the source should be compiled with debug information; defaults to `off`. If set to `off`, `-g:none` will be passed on the command line to compilers that support it (for other compilers, no command-line argument will be used). If set to true, the value of the `debuglevel` attribute determines the command-line argument.

debuglevel
> Keyword list to be appended to the `-g` command-line switch. This will be ignored by all implementations except modern and classic (version 1.2 and more recent). Legal values are `none` or a comma-separated list of the following keywords: `lines`, `vars`, and `source`. If `debuglevel` is not specified (by default) nothing will be appended to `-g`. If `debug` is not turned on, this attribute will be ignored.

optimize
> Indicates whether compilation should include optimization; defaults to `off`.

deprecation
> Indicates whether source should be compiled with deprecation information; defaults to `off`.

verbose
> Asks the compiler for verbose output; defaults to `no`.

depend
> Enables dependency tracking for compilers that support this (Jikes and classic).

The `jar` **task.**   The `jar` task makes a JAR file.

The `javadoc` **task.**   One of the greatest benefits of developing in Java is the nearly automatic generation of thorough and correct documentation. Javadoc is the tool that does the job, and the `javadoc` task is the way to automate document production in **ant**. This tag has a number of attributes that specify where the source to be documented is located, how the documentation is to be produced, and where the documentation is to be placed.

The `copy` **and** `mkdir` **tasks.**   These tasks are used to copy files and make directories.

The `rmic` **task.**   Remote Method Invocation is a distributed computing technology (Section 5.8). RMI requires the generation of server and stub classes that provide the networking support for an RMI-enabled class. This is normally done by the **rmic** compiler, and this is one of the common reasons the Java programmers turn to build automation tools. The `rmic` tag allows **ant** to build RMI classes.

9.4.2.5   Other Tags

So far we have ignored a major component of **ant**. In order to introduce it, we need to give you a (painfully) high-level view of how **ant** works "under the hood."

Task tags actually map directly to Java classes that implement the tasks. Each task class is an instance of the `Task` class (in other words, it is a Java class that either directly or indirectly extends the `Task` class). This is how you can write your own tasks—download the **ant** source code and write your classes that extend the `Task` class.

Tasks are not, however, the only tags that map to Java classes. There is another category of tags that do so. They are called *datatypes*. These are classes that directly or indirectly extend the **ant** `DataType` class.

Generally speaking, a task may require zero to many datatypes to specify the data with which the task works. Some such tags include the `manifest` tag used in our sample `build.xml` file discussed later in this chapter.

We'll mention a couple of the most frequently used datatype tags here and leave looking up the details as an exercise for you.

The `PatternSet, Include,` **and** `Exclude` **datatypes.**   As you may have noticed, the most common tags we have covered allow you to specify the files to be processed using the tag's attributes. Usually, you nominate a base directory and let the task tag process everything in that directory.

There are times, however, when you need finer grained control than that. For example, you might wish to exclude all Java classes whose names end in "`Test`" (Example 9.3).

Other datatypes.   There are many other datatypes used for various purposes. One of them, `FilterSet`, is able to modify files before they are copied or moved. This can be useful, for example, to put build information into a source file for an **About** dialog.

Example 9.3 Using the `PatternSet` datatype

```
<patternset id="nontest.source">
  <include name="**/*.java">
  <exclude name="**/*Test.java">
<patternset>

<target name="build">
  <javac destdir="build">
    <src path="src"/>
    <patternset refid="nontest.source"/>
  </javac>
</target>
```

In general, datatypes give you more sophisticated control than do the attributes of a task. Take a look at the *Ant User's Manual*[10] for full details on **ant**.

9.4.3   A Real, Live Buildfile

Let's take it to the next level and examine a real working buildfile.

9.4.3.1   *Project Organization*

All but the simplest of projects will require multiple classes. Some will require libraries, multiple programs, binary deployment, Web deployment, enterprise deployment, and so on. A project will be most successful if you plan out what goes where in advance. We're going to present a series of suggestions for how to organize the files involved in developing, building, and deploying a Java project with **ant**. By no means is this the only way it might be done, but it has worked well for us.

9.4.3.2   *The* `build.xml` *File for Payback*

Example 9.4 is the actual Ant buildfile for the Payback program in our source code examples. These examples are available on the book's Web site.[11]

---

10. `http://ant.apache.org/manual/`

11. `http://www.javalinuxbook.com/`

Example 9.4 The `build.xml` file for the Payback application

```
<?xml version="1.0"?>

<!--
   $Id: 070_antIntro.sgml,v 1.51 2004/04/13 05:10:45 mschwarz Exp $
   Buildfile for the Payback program.  Payback will calculate
   the length of time and real amount of money it takes to make a
   purchase using various savings or credit accounts. -->

<project name="Payback" default="all" basedir=".">

<!-- The "init" target sets up properties used throughout
   the buildfile. -->
<target name="init" description="Sets build properties">
  <echo>Running INIT</echo>
  <property name="src" value="${basedir}/src"/>
  <property name="build" value="${basedir}/build"/>
  <property name="doc" value="${basedir}/doc"/>
</target>

<!-- The "all" target does nothing but tie together the "jar" and
   "doc" targets. -->
<target name="all" depends="jar,doc"
        description="Pseudo-target that builds JAR and Javadoc">
  <echo>Building ALL</echo>
</target>

<!-- The "build" target compiles the code in the project. -->
<target name="build" depends="init"
        description="Compiles the classes">
  <echo>Running BUILD</echo>
  <mkdir dir="${build}"/>
  <javac destdir="${build}" srcdir="${src}" debug="true"
        deprecation="true"/>
</target>

<!-- The "doc" target generates Javadoc documentation of the
   project.  The "author", "version", and "use" attributes set to
   true cause those Javadoc tags to be used in the final document.
   The "private" attribute set to true causes private methods and
   attributes to be included in the documentation.  We tend to use
   this for projects to provide complete reference documentation.
   You would probably not want to do this for an app or lib
   distributed as a JAR file only. -->
```

```xml
<target name="doc" depends="init"
        description="Generates Javadoc documentation">
  <echo>Running DOC</echo>
  <mkdir dir="${doc}/api"/>
  <javadoc packagenames="net.multitool.Payback.*"
           sourcepath="${src}" destdir="${doc}/api"
           author="true"       version="true"
           use="true"          private="true"/>
</target>

<!-- The "jar" target depends on the "build" target.  It places
  all of the class files in the project into a JAR file, and
  builds a manifest using the "manifest" tag. -->
<target name="jar" depends="build"
        description="Builds an application JAR file">
  <echo>Running JAR</echo>
  <jar basedir="${build}" jarfile="${basedir}/Payback.jar">
    <manifest>
      <attribute name="Version" value="1.0"/>
      <attribute name="Main-Class"
                 value="net.multitool.Payback.Payback"/>
    </manifest>
  </jar>
</target>

<!-- The "run" target depends on the "jar" target.  It executes
  the class named as the "Main-Class" in the JAR's manifest. -->
<target name="run" depends="jar" description="Runs the program">
  <echo>Running RUN</echo>
  <java jar="${basedir}/Payback.jar" fork="true">
    <arg value="${basedir}/accounts.properties"/>
  </java>
</target>

<!-- The "clean" target erases all files and directories that other
  Ant targets might have generated.  It returns a copy of the
  project tree to a "pristine" (some might say "clean") state. -->
<target name="clean" depends="init"
        description="Erase all generated files and dirs">
  <echo>Running CLEAN</echo>
  <delete dir="${build}" verbose="true"/>
  <delete dir="${doc}/api" verbose="true"/>
  <delete file="Payback.jar" verbose="true"/>
</target>

</project>
```

9.5 REVIEW

We've taken a very quick tour through the most popular tool for building and deploying Java applications. We've shown you how to install and set up **ant**. We've given you enough description of XML so that you can read an **ant** buildfile. We've touched briefly on the basic tags used in most buildfiles.

9.6 WHAT YOU STILL DON'T KNOW

What we've covered here will probably explain most of the buildfiles you encounter in the wild. It will probably also give you what you need to know to build most of the buildfiles you will have to build. But we have left out a fair amount.

You can write your own tasks. That's a biggie right there. There are many built-in tasks that we didn't cover. Look those up. They might be just what you need if you find yourself saying, "Boy, **ant** is nice, but I wish it could do X." X might already be a built-in task. And if not, you can write it.

Ant has datatypes that can often be used in place of the simple strings allowed in task attributes. Tasks and datatypes are instances of Java base classes defined in the source code for **ant**. If you download the source, you can write your own classes that extend these base classes and you can thus add your own tags to **ant**.

9.7 RESOURCES

- *The Ant User's Manual*[12] at the Ant project homepage[13] (which itself is part of the Apache Project[14]) is the definitive resource for **ant**.

---

12. http://ant.apache.org/manual/

13. http://ant.apache.org/

14. http://apache.org/

- O'Reilly has also published *Ant: The Definitive Guide* by Jesse Tilly and Eric M. Burke (ISBN 0596001843), which was the first book on **ant** that we read.
- If you are into Extreme Programming you'll want to check out *Extreme Programming with Ant: Building and Deploying Java Applications with JSP, EJB, XSLT, XDoclet, and JUnit* by Glenn Niemeyer and Jeremy Poteet, published by SAMS (ISBN 0672325624).

Chapter 10

Integrated Development Environments

Some people prefer glitz. The shiny sparkle has always attracted the human eye. Sometimes that sparkle is a real gem, a treasure; sometimes it's only a gum wrapper on the sidewalk. Integrated Development Environments (IDEs) add glitz to Java development. At their most basic, they combine (integrate) an editing environment with a compiler. This gives you

- Language-specific formatting of your Java text (different colors, comments in italics, and so on)
- Quick feedback on errors (the ability to click on a compile error message to begin editing at the offending Java statement)
- Automatic word completion, to help you finish typing the names of methods in your Java code
- A point-and-click GUI for that all important "modern" look-and-feel

If those were all they gave you, IDEs would be, in our opinion, leaning toward "gum wrapper." But a good IDE can be more than that. It can be extended to integrate many different tools, including:

- Version control (e.g., CVS, see also Chapter 8)
- One or more Web servers (e.g., Tomcat)
- A build control mechanism (e.g., **ant**, see also Chapter 9)
- Other editors besides the built-in editor
- A specialized editor for building GUIs
- Other languages besides Java

10.1 WHAT YOU WILL LEARN

In this chapter we will examine two major Open Source IDEs, NetBeans and Eclipse. We will show a straightforward installation of each. We will describe the "operating paradigm" of each and show a few major features. It should be enough to get you started using them.

There are several major commercial IDEs, including Idea by IntelliJ, JBuilder from Borland, WebSphere Studio from IBM, SunONE Studio (Enterprise Edition) from Sun, and others. Because they are commercial, and not Open Source, we will not be covering them; their vendors and other experts can provide the documentation and training you need. Be advised, however, that the licenses for such commercial products typically cost anywhere from several hundred to a few thousand dollars per seat. That can make Open Source IDEs look very attractive.

10.2 NETBEANS: THE OPEN SOURCE IDE

NetBeans is an Open Source IDE, freely available, with full source code. It is also the basis for the SunONE Studio (more on that product later).

10.2.1   A Brief History of NetBeans[1]

NetBeans (originally called Xelfi) began in 1996 as a student project in the Czech Republic, with the goal being to write a Delphi-like Java IDE in Java. A company called NetBeans was formed around this project. By May of 1999, after two commercial releases of Developer, the company released a beta of what

---

1. From the `netbeans.org` Web site.

was to be Developer 3.0. In October 1999 NetBeans was acquired by Sun Microsystems. After some additional development, Sun released the Forte for Java Community Edition IDE—the same IDE that had been in beta as NetBeans Developer 3.0. There had always been interest in going Open Source at NetBeans. In June 2000, Sun open-sourced the NetBeans IDE; now it can be found at the `netbeans.org` Web site.

10.2.2 Installing NetBeans

NetBeans can be downloaded from the `netbeans.org` Web site. You will want the NetBeans "IDE" and *not* the NetBeans "platform." The IDE is the fully featured Java development environment. The platform is the underlying core of NetBeans on top of which one can develop other tools—for example, IDEs for other languages. Installation of the IDE consists of only three steps:

1. Download.
2. Install.
3. Execute.

10.2.2.1 Downloading

The first step is to get the software downloaded onto your system. From the `netbeans.org` Web site, navigate your way to a download of the latest IDE. The prepackaged "installers" might work—but if they fail, you have no information as to why, and still less as to what you can do about it. We'll act like "real programmers" and download an archive file. (Here "archive" means a collection of software compressed for easier transmission, not "archive" in the sense of "old documents.") Click on a link to begin the download (you'll need to read, review, and accept the license agreement to proceed). The result should be a file on your system named something like `NetBeansIDE-release35.tar.bz2`.

10.2.2.2 Installing

The installation consists of three steps: untarring the file, adjusting a parameter in a configuration file, then creating a symbolic link for easy startup.[2]

---

2. Thanks to John Zoetebier from New Zealand for his contribution on the NetBeans users mailing list, on which this manual installation procedure is based.

Uncompress the archive:

```
bunzip2 NetBeansIDE-release35.tar.bz2
```

This will leave the file `NetBeansIDE-release35.tar` in place of the `.bz2` file.

You can examine the contents of the TAR file with:

```
tar -tvf NetBeansIDE-release35.tar | more
```

Here the options (`-tvf`) specify to show a table of contents (`-t`) in verbose, that is, long, form (`-v`) from the specified file (`-f`) followed by the TAR filename. The output from **tar** here is piped into **more** so that you can page through it. Type q when you've seen enough, or leave off the | `more` to let it run through without pausing.

Notice that the names of all the files in the TAR archive begin with `netbeans/` which tells us that if we untar the file, it will put all the files into a directory called `netbeans`. Therefore, we don't need to make such a folder beforehand.

Change directory to the directory where you would like to install NetBeans. If you are on a system that may be used by different users, you'll probably want to put it in a more public location like `/usr/local` or `/opt`. If it is for your personal use, you can put it anywhere—just be sure that you have write permissions on the directory where you want to install NetBeans. (Reminder: use `ls -ld .` to see the permissions of the current directory.)

The **tar** command to untar everything in place is simple:

```
tar -xf NetBeansIDE-release35.tar
```

This will extract (`-x`) all the files that are in the TAR file (`-f`) named `NetBeansIDE-release35.tar`. If you'd like to see each file get named as it is extracted, then change the `-xf` to `-xvf` (v for verbose) and you will see a whole long list of filenames displayed on your screen as the file is unpacked.

Next, we need to adjust the startup parameter in the configuration file. The file is in the `netbeans` directory that you just untarred. In there is a directory named `bin`, and in there is a file called `ide.cfg`. Open this file with an editor and change the line that begins `-jdkhome` so that the pathname refers to the location of your Java Development Kit (JDK, see Chapter 5).

Here's an example of the contents of `ide.cfg`:

```
-J-Xms24m  -J-Xmx96m
-J-Xverify:none
-jdkhome /usr/local/java/j2sdk1.4.1_01
```

This specifies that the Java SDK is located in `/usr/local/java/` `j2sdk1.4.1_01`, and in that directory there is a `bin` directory which contains **java**, **javac**, **javadoc**, and so on.

Finally, to make the executable easy to run, we will construct a symbolic link for easy access:

```
$ ln -s /usr/local/netbeans/bin/runide.sh /usr/local/bin/nb
```

This creates a symbolic link from the `runide.sh` file in the current directory to the `/usr/local/bin` directory, as a file named `nb`.

10.2.2.3 Running

Now that you have the symbolic link to the script which runs NetBeans, simply invoke it with `nb` at a shell prompt. NetBeans will start loading (Figure 10.1).

If you get a message like "Command not found," check to see if the shell knows where to look. If you used the same name and location as in the previous example, then make sure that `/usr/local/bin` is part of the search path for the shell. (Reminder: `echo $PATH` will tell you what directories are searched. If you need to, add `/usr/local/bin` to `PATH`, as in:

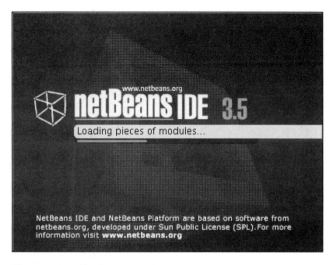

Figure 10.1 NetBeans begins

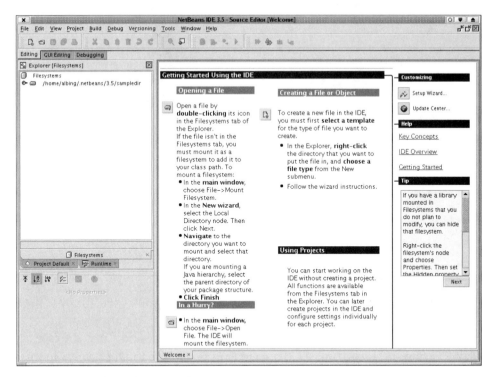

Figure 10.2 NetBeans' main window

```
export PATH="${PATH}:/usr/local/bin"
```

which you can type from the command line for immediate use and then put in the .bashrc file in your home directory to set things this way next time you invoke a shell.)

Also be sure that the script runide.sh has execute permissions on it. (Reminder: check this with ls -l runide.sh and change with chmod a+x runide.sh.)

If all goes well then after the splash screen, you should see the window shown in Figure 10.2.

For more information on installing NetBeans, check out http://www.netbeans.org/kb/articles/install.html#unix.

Now let's take a look at how you might use NetBeans.

10.2.3 Getting Around in NetBeans

Let's take a look, from top down, at NetBeans' main window. First, of course, is the menu bar. There are lots of choices to explore there. Much of what you'll do with NetBeans won't require much use of the menus—there are so many shortcuts elsewhere.

Next comes a row of icons, which are just shortcuts for menu times. This row of icons can be customized, and you can even add your own (see Section 10.2.5).

The three tabs below the icons, labeled **Editing**, **GUI Editing**, and **Debugging**, modify the window to provide three distinct workspaces. Each one customizes the window environment for a specific task, but it is still working on the same files.

Next, on the left, comes the **Explorer**, which is in many ways similar to the tools that you may use for traversing filesystems on a Windows or Linux system.

One oddity of NetBeans is that it doesn't just use the files as it finds them in the directories on your hard drive(s). Rather, is requires you to designate a piece of the filesystem as the part that you want to use. You can designate several such pieces. Each piece is "mounted" as if it were a mountable filesystem. (This is an operating system concept. If you're not familiar with it, don't worry. For the purposes of NetBeans, just think of the IDE as too dumb to know about any files until you tell it about them.)

There are three different types of files that you can mount—local, CVS, or JAR. By specifying the type, NetBeans can treat each one in its special way.

- Local files need no special treatment; they are just the local files on your hard drive.

- If a filesystem is mounted under a version control system (CVS or generic VCS), then its files can have version control operations performed on them (checkin, checkout, and so on), via commands in the IDE. (More on that below.) Also, special directories used by the version control system (e.g., CVS) are hidden from the display, as you almost never want to manipulate these files directly.

- When you mount a JAR file or ZIP archive as a filesystem, NetBeans displays the *contents* of the archive as if they were just files in a directory—which can make them easier to manipulate. More importantly, the JAR is automatically added to the classpath for Java compiling.

Therefore, any third-party JARs that you may need for your project should be mounted.

To mount a local directory as a filesystem, right-click on the little icon labeled **Filesystems** in the **Explorer [Filesystems]** window. Choose **Mount**, then **Local Directory**, and you'll get a filechooser to let you navigate your file structure and choose a directory to mount.

> **IMPORTANT**
>
> To ensure that NetBeans knows how to compile your source, you need to mount the directory that contains the base level of your source as a mountpoint, not just have that directory somewhere in a tree of directories.
>
> For example, let's say that your source is kept in two packages, `com.coolco.projecta` and `com.coolco.util` which implies that you have a directory structure with those names. Let's further assume that you keep them in a directory called `src` which is itself contained in a directory called `brolly`, as shown in Figure 10.3.
>
> The likely thing to do is to mount the `brolly` directory, since it will contain the source and all sorts of other project-related directories. That's fine, as far as it goes. But since the mountpoints in NetBeans are also the CLASSPATH directories, you need to also mount `brolly/src`, so that directories like `com/coolco/util` are found when your Java sources have statements such as `import com.coolco.util.*;`.
>
> It's OK to have the same directory show up in different mountpoints. NetBeans won't get confused, although you may. You'll probably want to edit and compile from the mountpoint of, in this example, `brolly/src`. The `src` folder inside the `brolly` mountpoint would refer to the same files. Just keep the one always open and the other closed, and you should be able to keep them straight.

10.2.3.1 *Filesystem versus Project*

The **Explorer** window has tabs at the bottom which let you look at different aspects of your work. In some instances you'll want the **Project** view. For this, you have to mount file's from the already mounted filesystems in the **Filesystem** view. Seems redundant, no? The **Project** view lets you set properties for the project as a whole or for individual files in the project. These settings apply to that file only for the project. Another project, looking at the same files, might have different settings.

For now, don't worry about the difference. Many people like to work in the **Filesystem** view and never bother with projects. Others, especially those working on multiple products or projects, like **Projects** as a way to switch

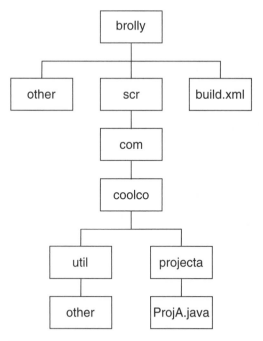

Figure 10.3 A simple source structure

between tasks—you can only have one project active at a time, but when you switch projects, it switches all the mounted filesystems and other settings that you have configured.

10.2.3.2 Editing

Like other IDEs, NetBeans provides its own editing window. It's a GUI point-and-click environment, with syntax highlighting and other helpful features for a programmer.

At the top of the editing window is a toolbar (Figure 10.4). Each icon on the toolbar has a tooltip, a help text that pops up when you rest your mouse pointer over the icon, to explain the somewhat cryptic little icons. Most of the tools are quite handy. With the pulldown menu, you can navigate to any method or class variable within the class. The next four buttons deal with searching: Select any text in your source file, click on the magnifying glass icon, and the search will be performed for the next occurrence of that text. In addition, all occurrences are highlighted. This highlighting can be toggled on or off.

Figure 10.4 NetBeans' **Edit** screen toolbar

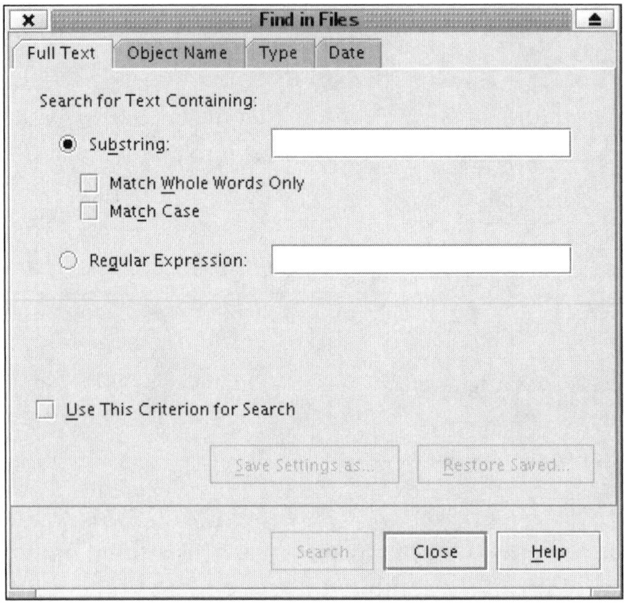

Figure 10.5 NetBeans' **Find** dialog

The toolbar search only works within a single source file. If you want to search across multiple files, go back to the **Explorer** window and right-click on the folder containing the files you wish to search. There is a **Find . . .** command in the pop-up menu. That brings up a dialog box (Figure 10.5) that has multiple tabs for quite extensive filtering of your search. In its simplest use, just type in the text you want to find, and press Enter.

A list of the files which contain the text will appear in a different window, citing filename and linenumber for each file. There you can double-click on any citation to bring up that file in the edit window, at that location.

If you heeded our admonition to learn **vi**, you'll be glad to know that NetBeans can handle the fact that the source files can be modified externally from the IDE. Go ahead and edit any of your source files, even while the IDE is running. When you next touch the file from within the IDE, NetBeans will recognize the fact that the file has been modified and load the new version.

If you haven't yet learned **vi**, you may find yourself quite comfortable using the NetBeans editor. If you dig deeper into NetBeans you can find how to map certain keystrokes to make it even more editor-like. However, mousing and cut-and-paste may suffice for beginners for quite some time.

10.2.4   Integration with CVS

NetBeans comes with a built-in CVS client, which means that you don't need to install any additional features in NetBeans to get it to talk with a CVS server. It has all it needs to check out and commit files from and to a CVS repository. NetBeans can be configured to use external (i.e., outside of NetBeans) CVS commands, but you likely won't need to do that.

What you will need to do, however, is tell NetBeans that the files you are using are under CVS control. You do this by mounting the filesystem not as just a regular filesystem, but as a CVS filesystem. In the **Explorer** window, go to the **Filesystem** tab if you are not already there. On the **Filesystem** icon, right-click your mouse, and from the pulldown menu choose **Mount**, then **Version Control**, then **CVS** (Figure 10.6). What follows will be a wizard-like series of dialogs which you will fill in to describe the type and location of the CVS repository with which you want to work. Those choices and values are specific to your installation, so we'll leave that for you to figure out with your network administrator or whoever has set up your repository.

Once mounted, the CVS filesystem's files will look much like any other filesystem you have mounted—except that the files will show, via their icon, when they have been modified and need to be committed, and will show the version number in parentheses after the filename. The other difference is that there is now a **CVS** command on the pulldown menu (Figure 10.7) that appears when you right-click on one of the filenames (or on its tab in the Edit view).

Move your mouse over the **CVS** command; an additional pulldown menu appears (Figure 10.8). If you've used CVS at all, then you'll recognize the list of commands in the cascaded menu. There are the **Commit**, **Update**, **Diff**, **Log**, **Status**, and **Checkout** commands that you are familiar with. The first item, **Refresh**, is likely unfamiliar, though. Not being a CVS command (it's not part of the command-line syntax), it is a way for you to tell the IDE to

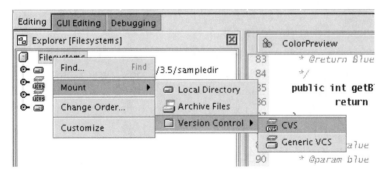

Figure 10.6 Mounting a CVS filesystem

Figure 10.7 Right click on a CVS file

reconsider what it thinks about the CVS-related information displayed in its icons and the parenthetical text.

If you click on a folder instead of a single file, then the **Refresh** command will be followed by **Refresh Recursively** which will do a refresh on each file from there on down the tree.

Figure 10.8 Cascaded menu with CVS commands

Using the integrated CVS is much like using the command line. If you want to see the changes that you've made (before committing), use the **Diff** command. A window will appear showing the two different versions and coloring the lines that have been added, deleted, or changed.

When you need to commit your changes, click the filename, then right-mouse your way to **Commit**. A dialog window will appear for you to type in the comment that you want to be associated with this change. (This comment will appear in the **Log** command display).

To incorporate the changes others on your project may have made on the file, use the **Update** command. A dialog box will display the CVS output showing what was updated and if any merge conflicts occurred. (See Chapter 8 for more on this.)

The CVS commands in the menu, as we've described them so far, don't allow you to add any options to the commands. They just run with the defaults. What if you want to use some of the options available on the CVS command line? Then hold down the Ctrl key just before your make your CVS choices. You should see an ellipsis ("**...**") appear after each CVS command for which you can now select options (Figure 10.9).

Of course one of the great things about knowing the command-line version (see Chapter 8) is that you're not limited to what the GUI tools will do for you. If you can't find the option you want, just go back to a window with a shell prompt, `cd` into the appropriate directory in your source tree, and type the CVS command by hand. As noted earlier, NetBeans is smart enough to

Figure 10.9 Cascaded menu after choosing CVS with Ctrl pressed

catch on to the changes made outside of NetBeans to its files, though you may need to do a **Refresh**, as described above.

10.2.5   Integration with Ant

If you've already discovered **ant**, either by using it on a Java project or by reading this book in chapter order, then you'll know that it's a plus to have **ant** integrated into NetBeans. As of NetBeans version 3.5, **ant** comes bundled with NetBeans and you don't need to install it separately.

NetBeans recognizes a `build.xml` buildfile and gives it a special icon. If you click on the icon for the `build.xml` file in the **Explorer**, it will show each of the properties and then each of the targets (Figure 10.10). Right-click on a target to choose **Execute** to run **ant** with that target. As a shortcut you can either select that target and press the F6 key, or you can just double-click on the target name.

If you are making frequent use of an **ant** build script in your project, you may want to add a shortcut—an icon that you can put on the icon panel—that

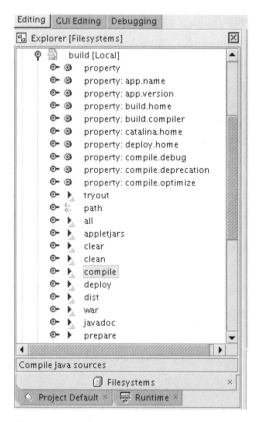

Figure 10.10 Cascaded menu after choosing CVS

will run a specified **ant** target. You can also add a keyboard shortcut, to invoke the target with a keystroke or two. The specific steps for doing that are found in the NetBeans online help. Just look for the section titled Creating a Shortcut to a Target.

There is one other topic worth mentioning about integration with **ant**. Normally in NetBeans, when you compile a Java class, the IDE does the compilation. You can configure the IDE to use different types and versions of Java compiler, but it is the IDE which controls the compile. You can invoke a compile with the F9 key as a shortcut. But if you are building with **ant**, you may want **ant** to do the compiles for you. Fortunately, you can configure NetBeans to do this. Again, we'll refer you to the NetBeans online help, to a section called Indirect Ant Compilation.

10.2.6 Other Add-on Tools

NetBeans is built to allow other tools to be plugged into it. There is a module that you can add to NetBeans to support C/C++ development. But there are various other plug-ins available. The best reference for all of those is the NetBeans Web site.[3] Many of the add-ons are commercial, but one notable tool is available, at least in its simple form, as a free download.

Poseidon for UML Community Edition is a UML modeling tool that integrates with NetBeans. A product of Gentleware AG, it is distributed at their Web site.[4] The Community Edition is offered free of charge, but they have more advanced (professional, enterprise) versions for sale. Their Web site says that Poseidon for UML Community Edition has the following features:

- Fully implemented in Java, platform-independent
- All 9 diagrams of the UML supported
- Compliant to the UML 1.4 standard
- XMI supported as standard saving format
- Runs under Java 1.4
- Diagram export into GIF, PS, EPS, SVG, JPEG, and PNG
- Undo/redo (can be turned on in options)
- Copy/cut/paste within the tool
- Drag and drop within the tool
- Zooming and bird's eye view of the diagrams
- Internationalization and localization for English, German, French, and Spanish
- Code generation for Java
- Sophisticated support of OCL
- Reverse engineering from Java sources
- Auto-layout of reverse engineered diagrams
- Cognitive support, critique mechanism (by default turned off)
- Simple install and update with JavaWebStart

---

3. http://www.netbeans.org/about/third-party.html

4. http://www.gentleware.com/

We won't be discussing its installation or use, but we encourage you to explore this option if you need a UML tool.

10.3 SunONE Studio Community Edition

SunONE Studio (SOS) Community Edition was built on NetBeans and was distributed for free. You would even see the NetBeans logo on startup. As of SOS 5.0 (summer 2003), the Community Edition is no longer available—NetBeans is what Sun recommends for the no-cost download. (The SOS Enterprise Edition is still actively developed and sold by Sun; it is licensed at a cost similar to other commercial packages.)

10.4 Eclipse: The Source of SWT

Eclipse is yet another GUI IDE. The Standard Widget Toolkit (SWT) was invented as part of this project. Since Eclipse uses SWT for its graphics, it has the most familiar GUI look and feel, and it is the fastest performer on lower end hardware.[5] Eclipse is built as an IDE toolkit. Although it was developed in Java/SWT, you can use it to develop AWT/Swing applications. It is build around a plug-in architecture, so it can be an IDE for virtually any language. To use it for Java, you must actually install the Java plug-ins.

10.4.1   Selecting and Installing Eclipse

The main site for obtaining Eclipse is `www.eclipse.org`. Installing Eclipse, particularly for a single user, is incredibly easy. But first, you have a few choices to make as to what to download. As of this writing, the current production release of Eclipse is 2.1.2. If you follow the Downloads link from the main page to the 2.1.2 build, you will see a fairly lengthy list of download choices.

The first major choice you must make is whether or not you plan to write your own plug-ins and extensions to Eclipse. If you do, you will probably wish to download the Eclipse Software Development Kit or the source code and build Eclipse for yourself. We strongly recommend that you choose the Eclipse SDK binary for GTK. The Motif UI is quite dated in comparison. The Eclipse

---

5. It's the fastest performer on high-end hardware too, but the difference is much less perceptible. Really fast and incredibly fast are hard for humans to discern.

SDK contains the Eclipse Platform (which you need), the Java Development Toolkit (which you need), and the Eclipse Platform Development Kit (which you need only if you plan to develop plug-ins for Eclipse). But by downloading the Eclipse SDK package, you get everything you need in one go. You could also download the Eclipse source package and build the whole thing yourself; save that for a spare week. For now, start with a prebuilt binary.

If you scroll down, you will see a collection of files that have "platform" in their names. You will note that there are two choices of Linux binary: one is Motif, the other GTK. If you are not familiar with these, Motif and GTK are two common extensions to the X Window API that provide widgets and other common functions and UI features. One of these, Motif, is rather old and (to brashly add opinion) dated in appearance, but it is very stable and mature. The other, GTK, stands for GIMP Toolkit and was developed to support the remarkable GNU Image Manipulation Program (GIMP). There are other widget/UI libraries that run on top of X Window, notably the Qt library used by KDE.

So, which to use? If you read the documentation on the Eclipse Web site, you will see that the Motif version has been more heavily tested and is available for other platforms than Linux. This is probably because Motif is standard on most commercial UNIX versions, and thus is where emphasis was placed to get the "most bang for the buck" in development and testing.

However, we much prefer the look of the GTK version and, to date, have found no major problems with it, so that is what we use for our examples. There should be no functional difference between the two—merely differences in the look and feel of menus, toolbars, and dialogs. One reason to select Motif might be if you are working in a mixed environment of Linux and other UNIX platforms, where you may be forced to use the Motif version on some platforms, and do not want the "cognitive dissonance" of switching between the two.[6]

So, **step one:** Download `eclipse-SDK-2.1.2-linux-gtk.zip`.

The Eclipse platform is a "generic IDE." You will see the term *perspective* all over Eclipse. A perspective is kind of a collection of tools in the IDE. The package you just downloaded contains a generic perspective called Resource. A

---

6. Please note that the differences are fewer and smaller than the differences involved in switching between any common X Window desktop and Microsoft Windows. If you can handle that (and many of us do every day), switching between Motif and GTK versions of Eclipse will be no problem for you.

perspective is a set of *views*, which are panes within the IDE, each having a specific purpose, such as editing the project contents, editing files, keeping a task list, and so on, as well as menus and toolbars relevant to those views. The Resource perspective has its uses, but it is not the main one you will be using as a Java programmer. As a Java programmer, you will most likely want the Java perspective.[7]

First, you must decide if you are going to install Eclipse in a common location (such as `/usr/local` or `/opt`), or if you are just going to install it in your home directory for your own use. The answer to this question, naturally, depends on whether or not you have root access on the machine and whether or not multiple people actually use the machine.

> **CAUTION**
>
> We are assuming you already have at least one Java SDK installed. If you do not, refer to Chapter 6 for some tips on installing Java SDKs.

We're going to install in the user's home directory. Doing this could hardly be simpler. So, **step two:** From your home directory, type:

```
$ unzip eclipse-SDK-2.1.2-linux-gtk.zip
```

That's it. You're done. Now just `cd` to the newly created `eclipse` directory and type `./eclipse`. The first time you do this, you will see a "Completing the install" banner (Figure 10.11).

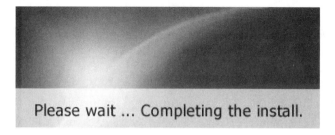

Figure 10.11 Running Eclipse for the first time

---

7. Although you will also often be using the Debug perspective.

Figure 10.12 Eclipse splash screen

During this initial run some workspace directories and data files are set up. These store meta-information about projects and perspectives. After a moment, you will get the standard splash screen (Figure 10.12).

Following this, you will see the initial Eclipse IDE, with a welcome screen in the default Resource perspective (Figure 10.13).

Eclipse works with *projects*. A project is a collection of files that you manage as a group. Usually a project is a single program, although it need not be. Eclipse remembers the state of all projects. If you close Eclipse in the middle of a debug session on a project, the next time you open Eclipse, it will have that same project open in the Debug perspective. If you then switch to another project and switch back, you will come back to the Debug perspective. Eclipse remembers. But we get ahead of ourselves here. You need to create a project.

10.4.2   Using Eclipse for a New Project

Now that you have Eclipse up and running (Figure 10.13), you will want to create a Java project. Eclipse has "wizards" (to use the Microsoft Windows terminology) for creating projects. From the main menu, select **File > New > Project**. You will get the screen shown in Figure 10.14.

Now, you are not an idiot. This is not "Java Applications Programming on Linux for People with Well Below Average Intelligence." We're not going to walk you slowly and painfully through a screenshot of every window Eclipse

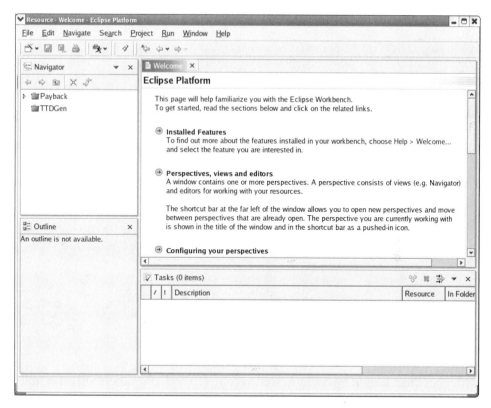

Figure 10.13 The Eclipse Resource perspective

can display and pretend that this is "educational." We like trees too much to do that. So let's pick up the pace a bit. The first screen in Figure 10.14 asks you to select the type of project. The next screen asks for a project name and it automatically chooses a directory to house the project. In Section 10.4.3 we will talk about changing away from this default. For now, trust Eclipse to do it right. Enter a project name and hit the **Next** button.

The next screen shows a tabbed display. The first tab allows you to add folders for source code. If you have already worked out a directory structure for your project, you may build it here. The next tab is the **Projects** tab. Here you specify other projects on which this project depends. The next tab is the **Libraries** tab. Basically, it lets you specify the project's classpath. Eclipse puts its preferred set of JARs on the classpath by default, including those that are standard with whichever Java runtime Eclipse found on startup. The last tab is called **Order and Export**; it allows you to specify the order in which source

Figure 10.14 Step one: New project

folders should be built, as well as to specify which folders are accessible to other projects that name this project on their **Projects** tabs (in other words, this is the "other side" of the **Projects** tab).

That's the final wizard box. Hit the **Finish** button. A dialog box pops up to tell you that the project you just created is associated with the Java perspective. Since you are currently in the Resource perspective, it asks you if it may switch you to the Java perspective. Hit the **Yes** button, and you will be rewarded with the Java perspective display (Figure 10.15).

At this point, your exploration of the Eclipse tools would be more fruitful than anything we could tell you. There is a marvelous book on Eclipse, *The Java Developer's Guide to Eclipse* by Sherry Shavor et al. from Addison-Wesley. We encourage you to seek out that book.

10.4.3   Using Eclipse for an Existing Project

In the previous section, we mentioned that the second wizard screen in setting up a Java project allowed you to override the default path for a project. If you have an existing Java program, point the project path to the directory that is the base for that program's packages. When you create the project (in other

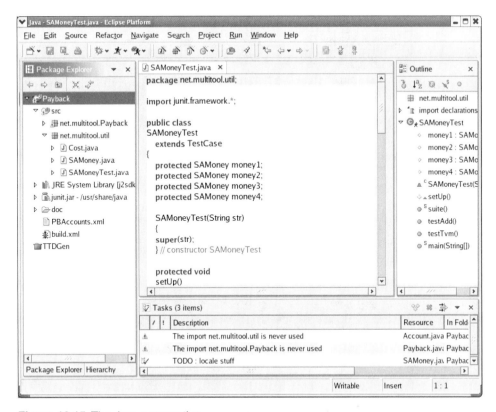

Figure 10.15 The Java perspective

words, when you hit the **Finish** button in the wizard), Eclipse will scan that directory and analyze what it finds there. It does an excellent job of importing a project and "eclipsifying" it, even to the point of recognizing and analyzing an **ant**'s `build.xml` file.

10.4.4   Working with Eclipse

Eclipse is a huge topic. We can't devote enough space to it for this chapter to qualify as a user guide. The best we can do is to offer you a handful of tips.

- The Java perspective consists mainly of the **Package Explorer** on the left, the edit window in the middle, the outline view in the right, and a bottom window that changes based on context. Initially, it is a task list. When you run a Java application, the console output is displayed there, overlaying the task list.

- You can do a lot of what you need to get started on a project by right-clicking in the **Package Explorer**. For example, you can create a package by right-clicking and selecting **New > Package**. When you type a new package name into the resulting dialog box, all required folders are created under the project.

- You can create new classes and interfaces in the same way. If you right-click on a package in the **Package Explorer** and select **New > Class** or **New > Interface**, an appropriate dialog box comes up, and a skeletal file is created in the appropriate place.

You can compile, run, and debug programs by hitting buttons on the toolbar, by selecting from the menu, by right-clicking almost anywhere, and by keyboard shortcuts. To put it plainly: Eclipse is a modern, rich IDE that works like other IDEs you have seen.

Eclipse's real advantages lie in some of the dynamism it offers. As you know, the authors of this book like text mode and command line, but we must admit that Eclipse's refactoring features are a great timesaver. For example, when you use the refactoring tools to change a method, you can be certain that every call to that method, everywhere in the project, is updated. Sure, we staunch CLI guys will tell you that you can use pipes and **sed** to similar effect, but even we must admit that you can miss some. We stand by what we have said: Know all the tools, and you can then choose the right one. But if all you have is a hammer, you'll end up using it to repair a china cup.

10.5 REVIEW

We've given you the choice of two great development environments. With them you can do so much more than just edit and compile. Both are expandable to include other tools, like CVS and JUnit. Each has a slightly different paradigm for how they manage files and projects. It seems the longer we work with one (either one), the more we like it. They kind of grow on you and you get used to some of the shortcuts that they offer. And yet, there are still those times when it's handy to be back at the simple command line.

10.6 WHAT YOU STILL DON'T KNOW

NetBeans comes with a built-in version of Tomcat for serving up Web pages and JSP and Java Servlets. It's very handy for developing and testing on your desktop. We'll look at that more in Part IV of this book.

In the NetBeans help file, you'll find this intriguing note:

> Using Scripting Languages in NetBeans: NetBeans provides you with a scripting feature that lets you use scripts to operate the IDE remotely or from the Scripting Console or by using a scripting file. You can use the scripting languages provided in the Scripting Console, or you can create a scripting class through the New From Template wizard. The following scripting languages are provided with NetBeans: DynamicJava, BeanShell, and JPython. For information on the scripting languages provided, see DynamicJava at `http://www-sop.inria.fr/koala/djava/`, BeanShell at `http://www.beanshell.org/`, JPython at `http://www.jpython.org/`.

We barely got you into Eclipse. Eclipse supports CVS (check out the **Team** submenu). Eclipse provides code refactoring features that allow you to rename classes and methods with automatic update of all affected source. Eclipse provides a feature to "externalize" strings (which takes all string constants out of a module and makes them into properties references, allowing for easy internationalization). It is a powerful Java development platform.

10.7 RESOURCES

NetBeans. NetBeans has some very extensive online help. There are also some very good Web-based documents, including the user guide which can be found at `http://usersguide.netbeans.org/`. Of particular value is the Getting Work Done guide at `http://usersguide.netbeans.org/gwd/` which describes itself as "a more detailed introduction to the IDE than available in the Getting Started tutorial."

Support for NetBeans, as with many other Open Source projects, happens online. There is no toll-free number to call. Instead you subscribe to an e-mail list; all messages sent to the list are then forwarded to everyone on the list. Anyone can respond, and you are encouraged to respond too, to share what you know with others. The NetBeans developers are often the ones who answer the most difficult questions, but lots of times answers come from others who have just made it a little further up the learning curve than you.

To subscribe to the nbusers list, send e-mail to `nbusers-subscribe@ netbeans.org`. You might want to create a special mail folder for the constant stream of messages that you'll get from nbusers. We've seen about 15–20 messages per day, on average, over the past year. You don't need to read them all, but as you scan the subject lines, see if there are ones that you might be able to answer. If you want others to reply to your requests for help, it would only be fair for you to do likewise. For a directory of the many e-mail lists related to NetBeans, go to `http://www.netbeans.org/community/lists/`.

Eclipse.   *The Java Developer's Guide to Eclipse* by Sherry Shavor et al. (ISBN 0321159640, from Addison-Wesley Professional) is an excellent book on the Eclipse platform, particularly from (as the title suggests) the Java developer's point of view. Eclipse is, however, more than just Java. It is designed to be an "IDE Factory," providing a framework for almost any task that involves an edit/compile/deploy kind of lifecycle.

Part II

Developing
Business Logic

Chapter 11

Balancing Acts:
An Imaginary Scenario

In this chapter, the authors wax poetic on practical software development methodologies, and attempt to introduce a simple, or maybe simplistic, example application for use in future chapters.

11.1 WHAT YOU WILL LEARN

We want to share with you some thoughts on practical software development. We are not covering anything specific to Linux or Java in this chapter; there will be no commands to type or syntax to learn here. You may skip ahead to the next chapter—but at your own peril. Those who know and use good software process won't need this chapter, but many programmers don't fall in to that category. In fact, some who think they are using good process may be using too much or too little for their actual situation.

If you are relatively new to the corporate world, or have only worked for one or two companies in your career to date, you may get a taste of how software is done in other corporate cultures. If you are a seasoned programmer with many such experiences, see if this doesn't sound all too familiar.

You will also see the requirements for a simple budget application that will be used in succeeding chapters. It has little to do with real budgets, but lots to do with a simple application that we can use to demonstrate various Java technologies.

11.2 STATEMENT OF THE NEED

Financial planning is something that everyone does. The basic tool of financial planning is the budget. But unlike the home budget, the budget of a large corporation is managed at multiple levels within the organization. Sure, at some level, the board, the CEO, and the CFO decide that "we will spend X million dollars for operations for this quarter," but that is the start of the process, not the end.

From there, the feeding frenzy of middle management begins. And keeping track of things becomes an important aspect of financial control and corporate governance.

Realistically, any large business will already have processes and tools in place that meet this need. We are not expecting that what we develop here will be anything that a business will actually adopt to manage this process. Rather, our goal is to illustrate some methods of software development that actually work to build real Java application. The outline of methods and code could be used to address many classes of enterprise software.

11.3 HOW TO DEVELOP SOFTWARE

There is a science of Software Engineering. The development of software can be made an engineering discipline, with mathematical rules and metrics of success. Every aspect of a complete system can be worked out in detail beforehand so that you know, well before a line of code is written, what the outcome will be.

That's not what we're talking about here.

We are talking about software development not as it happens at NASA, medical device companies, and in factories where nuclear missiles are made. In those contexts, the potential costs of error are extremely high, ranging from the multibillion dollar loss (and public embarrassment) of crashing a spacecraft into Mars, on through having heart pacemakers fire off incorrectly, right to ending life as we know it on this planet. In such cases, no matter how much the correct software costs, you pay it because the consequences of not doing it perfectly are far too high.

> **TIP**
>
> Our discussion is not meant to be scholarship on the topic of software development methodology; instead, it is meant to show simple, basic processes that can bring a reasonable amount of control to a software development project. These steps are, to name a few, requirements gathering, specification, object analysis, database design, development iteration (code, unit test, repeat), and so on.

But most of us who write software do not deal with such consequences. Most of us are keeping track of purchases and payments. We're recording production data. We're tracking manifests and updating inventories. We are the great unwashed mass of MIS software developers. Here we, too, want to do it perfectly right. But every time we go to management and tell them how much it will cost and how long it will take, the little "mass layoff" vein throbs in their foreheads. We are always being told to do it faster and cheaper. And so we find ourselves, again and again, tilting at the windmill of quality.

So where does that leave us? When we go to management with the textbooks of software engineering, they either laugh or scowl. Clearly, the money people are not prepared to support the cost of doing it right. So what do you do? The best that you can. The one thing we can tell you for certain is that the formula for success is not "start writing code and trust to luck."

It is fair to say that even the minimal software development method should include the following steps:

- Requirements gathering
- Use case specification
- Class discovery and problem domain decomposition
- Technical requirements specification (architecturing)
- Testing
- Code and release management
- Production and operations support
- Bug and enhancement tracking

This list, when done in that order, has been referred to as the classic "waterfall" model—each step is done in its entirety (or largely so) before proceeding on to the next step.

Or at least that's the ideal which programmers have often pursued.

The problem is that the process involves people, and people, especially those responsible for the requirements, a) are sometimes unimaginative and 2) keep changing their minds. They start out with some requirements, based on what they think they're going to need. But they just aren't imaginative enough to think of how terrible their system will be for the average user. They also keep changing their minds as to what they want.[1]

The "iterative" approach has been tried as a way to address this problem. Rather than wait for all requirements to be spelled out perfectly, with the iterative approach you jump right in with what you do know, build that, but expect changes to come. The sooner you get a working product or prototype into the hands of the users, the sooner you'll get feedback on what works, what doesn't, and what is really wanted ("what works" is used here not in the testing sense, but in the usability sense).

Note, however, that in the iterative approach, one still gathers requirements, develops designs for the code and the tests, develops them, tests (and fixes) the code, and releases it. It's just that one does that on a much smaller and more rapid basis. You get something runnable sooner, and continue to modify it.

Some people will complain that this makes for more expensive rework, but we (and others) would disagree. You are refining the process. Your reworks are less expensive than if you went to the work of building the entire system only to have some key requirement(s) change—there can be a lot more "wasteage" there.

Be aware, however, that the iterative approach is *not* just "whipping the horses to run faster." It is not just the waterfall model run at high speed. Rather, it is using the early iterations of the product as a sort of a "living" requirements specification, one that you can show to people and that they can try out, in real-world scenarios, and on which they can give feedback. Don't expect to be able to compile complete requirements, but don't give up on talking to your end

---

1. Did you notice that we tried to hint at that ever-enjoyable mid-project shifting of requirements as we went from a) to 2), changing our numbering scheme midway? Minimal humor, admittedly, but if you've lived it, you understand.

users and other stakeholders either. Requirements are still key to delivering a solution.

So with either approach, you'll start with requirements. Let's look at the art of requirements.

11.4 WHAT MAKES A GOOD REQUIREMENT

A good requirement is one that states a need but not a solution. Sounds simple, but it's easier said than done—especially with solution-oriented technical types.

A typical first cut at a requirement might be something like "Our budget application should store its data in the database." While it sounds reasonable, it is really a solution posing as a requirement.

The first step in refining such a requirement is to ask the simple question: "Why?" The answer we're looking for is not "Because we've paid so much for our database software," nor is it "Because we all know SQL." Rather, it should be something dealing with reliability, fault tolerance, the need for transactional integrity, and so on.

Sometimes you may have to ask the "why" question more than once, to refine the requirement(s). "Transactional integrity" is, in a way, a solution. You could ask, "Why do we need that?" For some projects it may be appropriate to ask this, because there may not be a real need for it after all.

But don't overdo it. Push any requirement in a business setting far enough, and you could get something like "To make money." That's not a helpful requirement. You've gone too far. Part of the art of requirements is recognizing when to stop asking why.

A more detailed description of a requirement is that it should be SMART—Specific, Measurable, Attainable, Repeatable, and Testable. Consider the following.

A common concern among users of almost any application is that it be "fast" or "responsive." While we can sympathize with the concern, it will need some refinement before it can be considered a (good) requirement. Applying the "Specific" and the "Measurable" aspects of SMART, we need to specify what constitutes "fast enough."

We can try "No button press in the GUI will delay more than .1 second before providing some evidence of activity to the user, or more than .5 second before completing its operation."

Sounds more formal, and more specific, but is it realistic (i.e., attainable)? If the "button press" is one that updates a database across a network, what effect will network traffic have? What about the size of the operation? If the button press starts an operation that is dependent on the size of some data set, what's the largest it could be and how long will that take?

Depending on how obsessive you or some colleague will be in enforcing these requirements, you would do well to add a few "weasel words" to give you some flexibility in the requirements. Phrases like "on average" or "most" will help. Notice, though, that such words are also the cause of much ambiguity, working against the "Specific" and "Measurable" aspects of good requirements. Use them sparingly, if at all.

We should also consider the "testable" aspect of our requirement for speed. Will we be able to measure this? Can we do so repeatedly? Consider the effect of network traffic on response times. Under what network load will the tests be done and the real usage occur? If you want to test under "normal" network loads, how can you control this (for the sake of repeatability)?

It really is an art to craft good requirements. Moreover, a good requirement for one organization may not work well for another. Some teams, groups, or companies want to be very precise in their use of requirements, viewing them almost like legal contracts for what will be delivered. Such requirements, however, would be greeted with derision in other, more informal, organizations. It's not that the one will produce good software and the other garbage (well, they might). It's more a matter of style. Excessively formal organizations will drown in the details and spend way too much time (and money) arguing over the minutiae of the requirements. Overly informal groups will get sloppy with their requirements and not reap the benefits of building the right thing the first time. As is so often the case in life, the answer lies in striking a balance between two forces, one pushing for exactitude and the other pulling you to get going and do something.

So let's keep going.

11.5 WHOM TO ASK FOR REQUIREMENTS

There are many people to ask about the requirements for a software project or product. Ask yourself the following questions:

- Who is going to use the software that you develop?

- Who is going to use the data that comes from the use of the software (i.e., who will read the reports generated from the data collected either directly or indirectly from the running of the software)?

- Who is going to support the software and who will support the machines on which it will run?

All these people can be considered "stakeholders" in the project.

So where do you start? That's a political more than a technical question. Start with your boss and with whoever is the major backer of the project. Then ask your customers. For in-house IT projects, the "customers" are usually very accessible; for software products, the customer's point of view may need to be represented by marketing and/or customer support people who have had direct contact with the customer base.

11.6 REQUIREMENTS FOR THE BUDGET APPLICATION

Let's take a look at how such requirements might evolve. We'll look at the situation through the eyes of a fictional IT guy named Bob.[2]

11.6.1   Monday Morning, 10 A.M.

Bob gets called in to the office of his manager, Ellen. The conversation goes something like this:

Bob: Yes, Ellen, you wanted to see me?

Ellen: Come in, Bob. Yes. We're just about to enter another budget planning cycle. We've got to propose our next year's budget to the VP by the end of the quarter, and I got to thinking . . .

Bob: Uh-oh.

Ellen: . . . on my way to work today, I got to thinking that we ought to be able to develop a software tool that would help us do a better job of this process.

---

2. We're avoiding giving Bob a title because titles vary so much within our industry. Call someone an analyst and it may mean that they never code. Call someone a programmer and it may mean that they only code and never deal with requirements or even designs. Some use those terms interchangeably. We'll just call him an IT guy.

Bob: We've used a spreadsheet these past few years to do our budgets. You want us to develop another spreadsheet application?

Ellen: No, I want a whole new application.

Bob: You want us to reinvent the spreadsheet?

Ellen: No, I want something simpler and more specific to the budgeting process.

Bob: Tell me more. What are the key features that you see in this application?

Ellen: Well, first of all it needs to be able to work concurrently with all the users. With our spreadsheet, we'd have to take turns with the data entry or we'd risk loosing each other's changes.

Bob: It may just be that we're not using our spreadsheet's advanced features. Shouldn't we investigate that first?

Ellen: No, I'd rather have us invest our time in building the tool we know that we need. At the end of the day your investigation may only show that we still need the tool, and by then it might be too late to build it.

Bob: I hear you saying that the deadline is rapidly approaching.

Ellen: Yes—I want to be able to use it for the budget planning at the end of this quarter. How long do you think it will take you to build it?

Bob: Build what?

Ellen: Haven't you been listening? The budget tool!

Bob: I know that you mean the budget tool—but you haven't really given me enough requirements upon which to base an estimate. Tell me more about how you envision this tool being used.

Ellen: Well, in the past we've taken last year's numbers and just bumped them up by a few percent. Then we look at each category and tweak them. I want a different approach this year. I'm going to take our department's budget, give it a bump, then assign a chunk to each of my reports. I want you to take those discretionary dollars and spell out how you would spend them.

Bob: Shouldn't we be providing you with estimates of what we need for the coming year, rather than you telling us what we have to spend?

Ellen: In theory, perhaps so. But in practice we can only grow the budget by so much. I'd rather skip the charade and jump right to allocating the dollars we will likely be able to spend. Then as the year progresses, I'd like to use this tool to track our spending against this plan.

Bob: But isn't that why we have that big SAP application?

Ellen: Have you ever tried to use it?! Please! The CFO thought it looked great—and on paper it did. But that user interface makes it almost impossible to be productive. And it's as slow as molasses.[3]

Bob: But back to this new application . . . I'm assuming you'll want a GUI on this?

Ellen: Of course. Give it a standard, simple GUI. Something like this. *(She begins to draw on her whiteboard.)*

For any given department there will be a "pool" of money. Those dollars are displayed and can be subdivided into smaller pools of money by creating subaccounts.

But as the money is subdivided those new accounts and associated dollars should become visible by others. And as dollars are spent during the year, we'll want to track those dollars, so those amounts should be visible, too, and subtracted from the overall pool of available dollars.

Bob: Wait . . . back up. What needs to be entered to subdivide an account?

Ellen: The user just picks an account, then chooses to subdivide it, entering the amount to put in each account . . . or even just a percent of the larger pot of money.

Bob: So if he picks one account to subdivide, does it split into two, or three or how many?

Ellen: Let the user choose, but maybe two as a default.

Bob: OK, but we may need to take a harder look at that interaction.

Ellen: So how long will that take? Can you have it ready by the end of this month?

Bob: I'd like to try the "spiral" approach on this project. I can have something for you by the end of this week— from which you can tell me if I'm heading in the right direction. It will just be a beginning, but you'll be able to see something run. By the way, is this tool only for our group?

Ellen: For now it is, but I could see other departments wanting to use it some day. Who knows how far it could go?

---

3. Remember, this is a fictional account. We are providing justification for why they can't use the corporate application. Anyone's use of such a tool can be less than optimal, reflecting more on themselves than on the value and usability of the tool.

11.6.2   Back at His Desk

Bob is now back at his desk pondering the conversation he had with Ellen. "These are not like the requirements we learned about in my software engineering courses," he muses. "I've got that sketch of the UI and a brief description of its functionality. But there seem to be so many unanswered questions."

So what is Bob supposed to do? He could go back and try to get more "face time" with Ellen, and ask lots more questions. Sometimes that's a smart thing to do. Other times such repetition is seen as annoying and a sign of a slow-witted analyst, never mind how obscure the initial discussions were or how many times someone changed their mind about what they want. You will have to judge each situation as you encounter it. At some point, though, you have to deal with whatever information you've been given, and try to make the best of it.

So where do you turn? The next best things to do are to begin to document the requirements as you understand them, to prototype a solution, and to start getting buy-in from other stakeholders. Each of these activities may help bring out more requirements, but that's not a bad side effect.

11.7   Documenting, Prototyping, and Stakeholder Buy-In

Once a project is started, the design must be documented. A prototype may be built to validate and refine the design. Finally, everyone with a stake in the success of the design has to be brought up to speed and needs to agree on what is to be built.

11.7.1   Documenting

After such a conversation, it's smart to try to get your thoughts down on paper as soon as possible. Some of what gets said will fade with time, so work quickly to capture what you can of the requirements that were spoken. Even if you have to leave lots of blanks, keep moving and get as much of the major requirements written down as you can, even if they don't sound very formal or polished. Then go back, revise and edit your statements, filling in the blanks where you can. Sometimes you will need to ask others to get the answers to fill in the blanks. Other times you can use your own judgment and initiative to provide an answer. Out of this process with its subsequent rewrites will come the requirements document.

Some organizations are very formal in their understanding of requirements. They will have company-standard formats which you must follow. But there is no magic format that will make for good requirements. It really all comes down to content.

Here's an informal list of the requirements for the budget application, based on the conversation between Bob and Ellen.

Features:

- Starts with a single lump sum of dollars.
  - How does this first sum get entered?
- Each dollar amount is associated with an "account."
- Any account may be divided into two or more subaccounts.
- The dollar amount associated with a subaccount is specified either in absolute dollars or as a percentage.
  - What if they don't add up?
  - Can the user mix $ and %?
  - Can the user leave the last subaccount's amount blank for "remaining dollars"?
- Tracking of the dollars—not enough info, so not in first prototype.
- Multiple users will have access to the data.
- Concurrent use is allowed and supported.
- Short development time, limited resources.
- Has a graphical user interface; earliest versions may be command-line and terminal interaction.

Not all requirements will be easily forthcoming; not all can be traced back to an exact quote from the previous discussion. Other requirements will need to be inferred from the discussion or from department "culture," or come from your own judgment:

- Platform: "any" PC in Ellen's department—but her developers are all using Linux platforms.
- Future platforms: "any" PC in the company means any Windows, Linux, or Mac OS X.
- Reliability: once entered, data is never lost.
- Maintainability: the application must be easy to maintain.

- Interoperability: there's no requirement to interoperate with any other software but here's an idea for a future version: export/import into CSV format for spreadsheets, and/or XML format for future expansion).

- Response time: "reasonable" interactive speed; subsecond response when entering new accounts and values, so that the user can type quickly and continuously; waiting, if it occurs, should only be at button presses, not between data entries.

11.7.2   Stakeholder Buy-In

Stakeholder buy-in can be another important part of a software project. As we discussed in Section 11.5, stakeholders are any of those people who are touched in some way, direct or indirect, by this software project.

For this simple budgeting program, there will be few stakeholders—it will largely be Ellen and her direct reports. The system will not likely be a large drain on computing resources, so system admins don't need to be brought in at this point. If and when the project expands to include other users across the network and across the enterprise, then the system administrators should definitely be included. There will be few reports from this first cut of the project, and what few there are will only be read by Ellen and her direct reports, so again, there are few others that need to be consulted as stakeholders.

The idea at this stage is to listen to other points of view—those of your stakeholders—to get a different perspective before charging headlong down one avenue of development.

It's not that you will be able to satisfy all points of view—it can be a worthy goal, but it is often unattainable. Rather, you need to hear from all those involved since your software will affect all those people, and understanding something about how it will fit into their roles and daily tasks will help you make better tradeoffs and design better software. It will likely uncover previously unseen requirements. It also has the political benefit of those people knowing that you cared enough to listen to them before sending them a finished solution. It increases the likelihood that your software will be seen as a help, not hinderance.[4]

---

4. As engineering types it is difficult for us to understand and appreciate the importance of this, but in many ways these personal, political, and psychological factors are much more important to the success of a project than are technical choices. It has taken us years to appreciate

11.7.3 Prototyping

Prototyping can be an effective way to carry on the discussion of both requirements and user interface design. Given only a hypothetical or abstract description of some software, it can be very difficult for people to imagine what the implications of its use will be. A simple prototype can immediately bring the discussion down to the concrete; people can point at things and say "I like this" and "I don't like that" and "How would I do so-and-so" and then see whether or not it would work. Sometimes, ideas that sound great on paper turn out to be pretty poor ideas when realized. Prototypes can help you discover that quickly and easily.

One very useful but inexpensive prototyping mechanism can be HTML—that is, creating Web pages. Simple static HTML can be fast and cheap to build, but can begin to approximate what the user interaction will look like—especially for, but not only for, Web-based solutions. It may not be an exact replica of the final product, but for a first step it can really get the discussion moving.

If the UI is too complex for a Web page mock-up, you can still use HTML for prototyping by getting images (screenshots) of what you want your final solution to look like and then making these images clickable on Web pages, to simulate some simple user interaction with hyperlinked image sequences.

The idea is to get something "tangible" in front of people as soon as possible, to further the discussion in a way that written descriptions never can. ("A picture is worth a thousand words.")

Once you've built a prototype, shop it around. Hold informal meetings where you demonstrate the basic functions to stakeholders. We recommend, as much as possible, meeting with one group of stakeholders at a time. That way you can keep your conversations focused. If you have two different stakeholder groups represented and their expertise and interests are wildly different, you'll be boring ½ the participants all the time. Even if their expertise is similar, you may have groups with competing or conflicting requirements. While you need to understand such conflicting requirements and eventually come to some detente, this meeting is not the best venue for settling those issues; it would more likely simply scuttle your meeting and void any value from it.

---

that Dale Carnegie is as important to the software designer as Yourden or Booch. Your users need to be your friends if you want to succeed.

After each meeting, review your requirements and see what more you need to add. Likely at such meetings, you'll begin to get requests for new features.

You have, in fact, begun the iterative process. Even the most bare-bones prototype that may only consist of a sequence of pictures is a first cut of your product. The sooner you can get to a running version, the sooner you will be able to respond to stakeholder suggestions by adding real features.

11.8 REVIEW

A good requirement is one that states a need but not a solution. Your first step is to uncover the needs, while listening to everyone's solutions. These requirements will develop into feature descriptions. These should be documented and then prototyped. The prototype, which is in effect the first release of your product, can then be shown to various groups—stakeholders—as a way to elicit their feedback. This feedback should begin to factor in to what you will build, so now you need to move quickly on to building the real product; do not get stuck enhancing the prototype.

11.9 WHAT YOU STILL DON'T KNOW

Writing good requirements is as much art as it is science, and it involves political science as well. This is not something easily taught in a book, but learned through hard experience.

11.10 RESOURCES

One of the original purposes of the World Wide Web was to allow researchers to share their results. So, you should be able to search the Web for requirements documents from various projects for examples of requirements specification. As with any Web search, remember to consider your source. Just because someone has posted a requirements specification or a template doesn't make it a good example.

Here are three examples that we found on a single simple Google search. They may still be there by now.

- `http://www.progsoc.uts.edu.au/~timj/thesis/web/srs.html`
- `http://www2.ics.hawaii.edu/~johnson/413/lectures/5.2.html`
- `http://www.cc.gatech.edu/people/home/tomoyo/rocky-axel.1.doc`

For those who are serious about their software development process, the Capability Maturity Model for Software from the Software Engineering Institute at Carnegie Mellon University is the standard. Visit their Web site at `http://www.sei.cmu.edu/cmm/`.

If you would like to know more about the spiral approach to software design, you might want to start with the seminal paper on the topic, "A Spiral Model of Software Development and Enhancement," in *Computer* 21, no. 5 (May 1988), pages 61–72.

To see how the director of the Software Engineering Institute views the spiral approach, check out the short and readable introduction at `http://www.dacs.dtic.mil/awareness/newsletteres/technews2-1/disciplined.html`.

Another good look at the spiral, or iterative, approach can be found at `http://www.stickyminds.com/se/S3420.asp` which has a hyperlink for a PDF file of a paper by Philippe Kruchten of Rational Software. The paper covers some pitfalls common to the first uses of the iterative approach; worth the read.

A great survey of key papers on three major approaches—spiral and related topics (including newer work by Boehm), aspect-oriented programming (AOP), and the rational unified process—is at `http://www.rspa.com/reflib/PrescriptiveModels.html`.

11.11 EXERCISES

1. Write requirements for a simple word processor or spreadsheet. Start with some obvious functionality. Add only enough "bells and whistles" for it to be usable for beginners. Show this list to others, especially people familiar with similar applications. What features do they find missing that are important to them? How quickly does your list expand? What might you do to limit the size and the rate of growth of the features list?

2. Discuss the requirements for your application with someone who has no experience with a similar product. How difficult is it to get useful feedback? Now show them (the simple features of) a working spreadsheet or word processor, as if it were your prototype. Does the conversation change? In what ways? Is the feedback now more or less useful than before they saw the prototype?

Chapter 12

Analysis and Design: Seeking the Objects

In this chapter, we will present the barest outline of a software development methodology. For some readers, this will be simplistic and unsuitable. In our experience, however, there are many businesses out there with very small development teams that have very little software engineering experience, even though they have considerable technical and programming skill. Our goal here is to present a bare minimum of analysis and design method, so that we can be sure we have a common basis for discussing the issues of object-oriented analysis and design.

12.1 WHAT YOU WILL LEARN

In this chapter you will learn a very simple method for object discovery and a simple method of documenting this process.

12.2 FACING THE BLANK PAGE

So, you have some requirements. Maybe you even have some UI prototypes. How do you turn that into an object-oriented design for Java classes? How do you confront the paralyzing blank white of your whiteboard, terminal session, or easel?

The simplest way is to start with real-world objects. Stop thinking about everything you have read about object-oriented programming. Instead, ask yourself, "What are the real objects involved in this problem?"

In our case, the more you look at it, the simpler it gets. For the moment, the only real objects we have are people—the users—and accounts, that is, named pools of money. We know that users get accounts from "above," and that they may break those pools down into subaccounts, which they may own or delegate to other users.

At the broadest level, then, we seem to have two "classes" or types of real-world objects: Accounts and Users.

12.3 USING CRC CARDS

So, we need two classes. But what goes into those classes? How do we go about putting the substance into this simplistic framework?

In their now (semi)famous paper presented at the object-oriented programming conference OOPSLA in 1989, Kent Beck and Ward Cunningham introduced a simple, practical design tool for object-oriented design based on a simple, practical 3x5 file card. The CRC cards for our classes are shown in Figures 12.1 and 12.2.

But we are getting a bit ahead of ourselves. These CRC cards are an end product of analysis. They are the starting point for coding. Let's talk a little bit about what is on these cards and how we came to that content.

12.4 FINDING THE OBJECTS

The basic technique for doing OOA[1] with CRC cards is to start with a stack of blank cards. Assemble a design team (this may be one person, or this may

---

1. (object-oriented analysis)

Account	
a pool of dollars	
members	**collaborations**
* name - a String * owner - a User * amount - an SAMoney object * children - an ArrayList (of Accounts) * parent - an Account	* persistence (CRUD) * User

Figure 12.1 Account CRC card

User	
someone who manages budget dollars	
members	**collaborations**
* name - a String * home - an Account	* persistence (CRUD) * Account

Figure 12.2 User CRC card

be dozens).[2] The first step should always be the nomination of the real-world objects. Don't edit or critique at this point. If someone says "computer" as an object, write "Computer" on the top of a card and put it on the table. If someone says "Manager" write it on a card and put it on the table.

---

2. It is fun to gloss over such a complex topic with a single sentence! Obviously, the composition of a design team is a complicated matter. At the very least, a design team must include a representative from the programming team and a future user of the system. On small, simple projects, that may be all you need. On more complex or mission-critical systems, there will have to be additional representatives, such as people from Operations, Support, Training, Quality Assurance, and so on.

To take our example, suppose we have the following list of CRC cards after such an open brainstorming session:

- Database
- Capital Account
- Current Account
- CEO
- Computer
- CFO
- Director
- Keyboard
- Manager

Where do you go from here? Let's articulate a general principle.

The first principle.   If we could teach a programmer only one thing about software design, it would be this idea: less is more. Or, to quote Antoine de Saint-Exupéry: "Perfection is achieved not when nothing can be added, but when nothing can be taken away." Or, to put it yet another way, always use the KISS[3] principle. The best object design is the smallest possible number of classes that model the real objects and meet all the requirements.

You are seeking simplifying abstractions.

First of all, all the objects that represent technologies or implementation details should be removed. In our list, this would include "Database," "Computer," and "Keyboard." While it is likely that all three will be involved in the final product, they are not objects in the problem space. There is no theoretical reason why an OOA session cannot produce a manual, noncomputer solution. It is a common tendency to leap from problem analysis directly to technical solutions. "We can write that in Java," "We can store those in Oracle," "That could be an XML file." Statements like these are to be avoided at this stage. Those are details about the implementation. You haven't got a design to implement yet!

As we said, you are seeking simplifying abstractions. The next step, after culling cards that do not represent real objects in the problem space, is to group together the cards that have any attributes in common. If we look at our

---

3. An acronym for: *Keep It Simple, Stupid!*

remaining cards, we can quickly see that we have two cards that are accounts: "Capital Account" and "Current Account." These are both pools of money. Put them on top of one another on the table. Likewise, it is fairly obvious that "CEO," "CFO," "Director," and "Manager" are all people. Put them together on the table.

Remember that we are looking for simplifying abstractions. The grouped cards should all be obviously variant types of a generic class of objects. In our example, the one is a stack of Accounts, and the other is a stack of People, or, as we will call them, Users. Create new cards for these generic classes. Make a card with "Account" at the top and put it above the first stack. Make another card with "User" at the top and put it above the second stack.

There are two ways that this might simplify your design. For now, all cards below the abstract cards are "on probation." We are going to move on to define the attributes (data) and methods (behavior) of our abstract classes. If the abstract class can handle all use cases without having to treat any of the more specific classes differently, then the specific cards are discarded. If not, then all functionality that is common across the more specific types will be put on the abstract class card, and only those data and behaviors that are different will be put on the more detailed cards.

In the first case, the simplification is a reduction of several potential classes to a single class. This is always a good thing, when it is possible. In the second case, you are identifying potential inheritance relationships.[4]

12.5 FINDING THE METHODS AND ATTRIBUTES

The next step is to start identifying the data and behavior that characterize your classes. Always put such items on the most abstract class first. The only time to add an attribute or method to a more specific class is when it applies to that class and only that class—in other words, only when it represents a difference between the general case and the specific case.[5]

---

4. We'll talk more about that later in the book. As it happens, all of our simplifications in this chapter are examples of the first case.

5. In complex cases, you may find an attribute or method that applies to several, but not all, of the specific cases. In such a case, a new abstract class below the main abstract class, but above all the specific classes that share that attribute or method, may be called for.

12.6 ESSENTIAL AND NONESSENTIAL

So far, we have walked you through a very simple example, and we have made sound choices at every step. In more complex cases, even the best of us will make mistakes. We will head down blind alleys. We will group things together that might belong in separate abstract categories, but should, perhaps, share an interface. These are not so much errors as judgment calls, and skill at recognizing them and making the correct decisions comes only with experience.

For now, the most important questions to ask include:

- **Do I need this class?**

    We are often tempted to create too many inherited classes. When we seek more generic, higher level abstractions, it is often possible to use only the more abstract class. Of course, it is possible to carry that tendency too far. If your methods contain a lot of "if's" to handle various subtypes, that might be a case where you should inherit and overload the method.

- **Should I get functionality by inheritance or composition?**

    Inheritance should be reserved only for cases where a class is a more specific variety of the base class. For example, you might have a Person class, and then you might have Employee and Customer classes inherit common attributes and methods from Person. This is frequently called an "is-a" relationship, as in "A User is a Person." If your proposed inheritance relationship makes sense phrased that way, it might well be a good candidate for inheritance.

    Composition is when you use a class as an attribute. To extend our example, you might have an Address class. You might be tempted to have Person inherit from Address. But a Person is *not* an Address. Try it: "A Person is an Address." Nope. Instead, you should just have an instance of the Address class as an attribute of Person. Such a relationship is often called a "has-a" relationship, as in "A Person has an Address." If the relationship makes sense phrased that way, it is a good candidate for composition. Another way to recognize that you've wrongly used inheritance is if you end up having a radically different class inherit from the same base class. For example, suppose you have a class, Building. Would it make sense for Building and Person to inherit from Address? Are Buildings and Persons more specific instances of the same general type of thing? No, they are not. Building and Person should get Address functionality by composition.

- **Does this attribute or method belong here?**

  If you find yourself specifying nearly identical methods in more than one class, this should make you ask if the classes should have a common base class from which they should inherit, or if there should be a new unrelated class that they all share by composition.

  If the functionality is the same for a set of classes, and the classes are specific instances of a more general type, the method should be on the general class. For example, a `changeName()` method should probably be on Person, not on Employee or Customer, because the functionality is the same for all three classes. By contrast, a `changeEmployeeNumber()` method should be only on Employee. It should not be on Person, because not all Persons are Employees. There may also be methods that are common to both Employee and Customer types, but are radically different in implementation. For example, a `changePassword()` method might change a password in a system-wide LDAP server for an Employee, but might just change a record in a Web site database for a Customer. This is easily done by writing separate methods in each class.

  But should you add a `changePassword()` method on Person? If you want to be able to call the method when treating either a Customer or an Employee as a Person, then you should. But you don't have to implement the method on Person. You can declare `Person.changePassword` as abstract, and then, if you call the method on a Person, it will call the correct method based on what type of Person (Employee or Customer) the Person is. Note that if a class contains any abstract methods, the class itself must be declared abstract and it cannot then be instantiated. Also note that this is often best accomplished not through abstract classes, but through interfaces (see Eckel, pp. 321–322).

These are by no means the only considerations that come to bear on what classes to create and how to arrange and implement them, but they do represent a good start. They are a foundation on which you can build best practices out of your own experience and environment.

Whole books have been written on the topics of object-oriented analysis and object-oriented design. CRC cards are only one part of an array of techniques that can be applied to OOA/OOD. The Unified Modeling Language (UML) is popular in many MIS circles. UML consists of a variety of different diagrams which are used to model parts of an object-oriented design. They are:

Am I Mature? Or Are You My Mommy?

Let us point you at one more business buzzword link. Even though we think this particular site and their work are being ill-applied by many well-intentioned IT managers, there is still a great deal of value in the Carnegie Mellon Capability Maturity Model (`http://www.sei.cmu.edu/cmm/`). At the very least it provides an objective way to assess the level of process sophistication you have in your organization.

The CMM defines five levels of maturity:

1. Initial
2. Repeatable
3. Defined
4. Managed
5. Optimizing

If we may grossly oversimplify (and why should we stop now?), "Initial" means you do things differently every time. You just make your best guess about what the right thing to do is, and you do it. "Repeatable" means that you have hit upon a method that appears to work, and you use it consistently. "Defined" means that somebody has written it down. "Managed" means that the process is actively maintained and supervised in an effort to adapt it to changing circumstances. "Optimizing" means that measurements ("metrics") are made that objectively assess the process, and ensure that continuous improvement takes place and can be so proven.*

What we have shown you in this chapter probably falls in the Repeatable category, a long way from the engineering and management nirvana of Optimizing.

---

* The problem that seems to come up with this system is that very bad processes may be very mature and very good processes may be relatively immature. Obviously, however, an Optimizing process must be steadily moving towards the good.

- Class Diagram
- Sequence Diagram
- Collaboration Diagram
- Use Case Diagram
- Activity Diagram
- Component Diagram
- Deployment Diagram

Using the simple but effective technique of CRC cards can be a good place to start, but you may soon want to move up the OOA/OOD ladder to use tools like Umbrello[6] to make UML diagrams, and perhaps to use the whole UML toolset.[7] Many organizations that we know of will pick and choose various techniques and tools. No matter how far down the road of formal software engineering you go, you must at least make some effort to have a repeatable process that incorporates continuous improvement.

12.7 ANALYSIS PARALYSIS

The catchy phrase "analysis paralysis" has become a cliché. (And how could it not, being so catchy?) What it refers to, of course, is the tendency to become bogged down in details; or the tendency to refuse to start implementation until you are certain that your design is "right."

This is where using a "spiral" development model can pay off. By doing frequent small releases, you can expose subtle design flaws at an earlier stage in development. Often, you can (to trot out another trendy term) "refactor" a small part of your design or implementation. If you have clean object interfaces, this can often be done with minimal disruption because a good object model hides implementation details within classes.

In most cases it is best, once you have the use cases and requirements, to proceed to a prototype object model and learn by doing.

---

6. http://uml.sourceforge.net/index.php

7. http://www.uml.org/

12.8 REAL SOFTWARE ENGINEERING

Let's take a moment here and ask a fundamental question. Is this the best way to make software? And there is another fundamental, but subtly and importantly different question: Is this the right way to make software?

There are techniques and methods of Software Engineering that do approach the ideal of "zero defects." NASA uses such procedures for manned spacecraft. Coders for medical devices do likewise. The outline method we have suggested here doesn't come close to such methods. So, is what we have described the best way to make software? No, it is not. So why don't we all use those zero defect methods? That is easy to answer: cost. It is expensive. Virtually no MIS shop on the planet would be willing to pay the price it takes to get that stability and certainty. The price isn't just dollar cost, either. The Space Shuttle, for example, has computers that still use magnetic core memory, a technology that was old in the 1970s. Why? Because the restrictions imposed by their change control systems would essentially require the entire shuttle to be redesigned and retested if they made such a change.[8]

But this isn't an either-or. You do not have to apply either a full-fledged software engineering methodology, or use nothing at all. Instead, you have to apply some design, development, and maintenance processes that improve the probability of success and reduce the cost of failure. When we recommend version control, requirements gathering, use cases, and CRC cards, we are giving you a bare-bones set of methods that will help to write fairly successful software at reasonable cost in reasonable amounts of time.

To some of you, this will be old news. If you are at level 2 or above on the Capability Maturity Model (see the sidebar in Section 12.6), then you already have some process. But you would be surprised how many business out there do not even have source code control in place. To some of you, what we suggest here will be primitive compared to processes you already have. The point is, no one's level of control and process is "right" (to us, that means "cost-justified") for all cases. But using no method at all is a risk too great for any business.

---

8. An exaggeration to be sure, though maybe not as much as you might think, but you get our point.

12.9 CORE CLASSES

So, let's meet our core Java classes. Here they are, in all their glory (Examples 12.1, 12.2).

12.10 REVIEW

We have discussed a simple approach to object-oriented analysis and design through the use of CRC cards. The ideal outcome is a design with the smallest possible number of classes that model real-world objects while meeting all the requirements.

12.11 WHAT YOU STILL DON'T KNOW

We could list the names of a number of formal software engineering methodologies, but we won't bother. If this chapter has served as your only introduction to object-oriented analysis and software engineering, let's just say you have a lot of reading to do. But beyond that, there is something you need that is much more subtle and difficult to pin down: *experience*. The only way to get good at analysis and design is to do it. It helps to do it in conjunction with experienced people, because they can save you time and pain in acquiring your experience. This chapter is the simplest of foundations. The books give you knowledge. Experience gives you wisdom.

12.12 RESOURCES

Kent Beck and Ward Cunningham, "A Laboratory for Teaching Object-Oriented Thinking", in *OOPSLA'89 Conference Proceedings*, New Orleans, Louisiana, October 1–6, 1989. The special issue of *SIGPLAN Notices* 24, no. 10 (October 1989) is also available online at `http://c2.com/doc/oopsla89/paper.html#cards`.

More on the Capability Maturity Model can be found at `http://www.sei.cmu.edu/cmm/`.

Information on the Unified Modeling Language can be found at `http://www.uml.org/`.

Example 12.1 The `Account` class

```java
package net.multitool.core;

import net.multitool.util.*;
import java.util.*;
import java.sql.*;

public class
Account
{
  private String name;              // A name to identify this account
  private User owner;               // The user assigned to this account
  private SAMoney total;            // Total amt originally allocated to
                                    //   this account
  private SAMoney balance;          // amt remaining unallocated to any
                                    //   subaccounts
  private Account parent;           // The account which contains this
                                    //   account as a child
  private HashMap children;         // The collection of subaccounts,
                                    //   by name
  private static Connection dbConn = null;  // JDBC connection
  private ArrayList payments;        // TODO: unimplemented
  private SAMoney unspent;           // TODO: unimplemented

  /**
   * Create an account, with a pool of dollars to budget.
   * Use this constructor to create the master account.
   * Use createSub to create children of this account.
   */
  public
  Account(String name, User owner, String total)
    throws NumberFormatException
  {
    this.name = name;
    this.owner = owner;
    this.total = new SAMoney(Double.valueOf(total).doubleValue());
    this.balance = new SAMoney(Double.valueOf(total).doubleValue());
                                        // N.B. must not be the same object
    this.parent = null;
    this.children = new HashMap();
  }

  // Static that connects to the DB and either returns the top account,
  // or creates it for us.
  public static Account getTopAccount() throws SQLException {
  Account topAccount = null;

  dbConn = DriverManager.getConnection("jdbc:postgresql:budgetPro?user=mschwarz");
```

```
    if (dbConn != null) {
      // We have a database connection.
    } else {
      // We don't and we must create a top account.
    }

    return topAccount;
    }

    // Simple getter; returns the name.
    public String
    getName() { return name; }

    // Simple getter; returns the total pool of money that this account represents.
    public SAMoney
    getTotal() { return total; }

    // Simple getter; returns the balance.
    public SAMoney
    getBalance() { return balance; }

    // Simple getter; returns the parent account.
    public Account
    getParent() { return parent; }

    // Simple getter; returns the owner of this account, as a User object.
    public User
    getOwner() { return owner; }

    // Census - how many children.
    public int
    size() { return children.size(); }

    /**
     * Get to all the children, via an iterator.
     */
    public Iterator
    getAllSubs()
    {
      return children.values().iterator();
    }

    /**
     * Create a new subaccount (i.e., child)
     * given a name and an amount.
     * The child is connected to the parent, and
     * the parent's balance is reduced by the amount
     * allocated to the child.
     */
```

```
public Account
createSub(String name, String amt)
  throws NumberFormatException
{
  Account acct = new Account(name, owner, amt);

  // Reduce the parent's unallocated funds.
  balance = balance.subtract(acct.getTotal());

  // Connect the accounts to each other.
  acct.parent = this;
  children.put(name, acct);

  return acct;

} // createSub

/**
 * Looks up and returns the account with the given name.
 */
public Account
getSub(String name)
{
  return (Account) children.get(name);

} // getSub

} // class Accoun
```

The Umbrello UML modeller is an Open Source tool for creating the various UML diagrams. You can find it at `http://uml.sourceforge.net/index.php`. We also recommend their online documentation as a good brief introduction to UML and to Umbrello. It can be found from the main Umbrello page, or directly at `http://docs.kde.org/en/HEAD/kdesdk/umbrello/`.

12.13 Exercises

1. Imagine a public library. Carry out the CRC nomination process for a system to track library members and the collection. What list of objects do you come up with? What abstract classes do you find? Which did you discard and why?

2. Extend the purpose of the library program to include generating mailings to members with overdue materials. Did you add classes? Did you add methods and/or members? To which classes did you add them?

Example 12.2 The `User` class

```
package net.multitool.core;

import net.multitool.util.*;
import java.util.*;

public class
User
{
  private String name;
  private Account home;          // TODO: implement

  public
  User(String username)
  {
    name = username;
  }

  public String
  toString()
  {
    return name;
  }

} // class User
```

---

3. A new requirement is added. The system must allow for books, audio recordings, and movies to be checked out for different lengths of time. Did you add classes? Did you add methods and/or members? To which classes did you add them?

Chapter 13

JUnit:
Automating Unit Testing

Testing may not be your favorite task as a programmer; it probably rates just above documentation. Yet here is a tool that has made testing more bearable and more productive for many Java developers—and not just because it has pretty colors and flashing lights.

13.1 WHAT YOU WILL LEARN

- What JUnit is and why it's getting so much attention.
- How some people test before they start coding.
- How to install and invoke JUnit.
- The major JUnit concepts that you need to understand.
- What assertions are available in JUnit.

13.2 JUNIT: WHY ALL THE FUSS?

JUnit is a framework for unit tests. It consists of a handful of classes which you can use to build bunches of test cases for testing your application. JUnit also comes with three test "runners" for running your tests and reporting the test results. So why all the fuss? Why has JUnit been so much in the technical forefront the last year or two?

Start with a straightforward idea, well executed, that can help almost any programmer working on any application. Make it something that can be integrated incrementally into existing projects. Make it robust enough to be used for projects starting "from scratch." Give it a simple but pleasing GUI, and put it to work on a few high-profile projects. Give it some good press coverage. And you've got a winner: You've got JUnit. Besides, it really does help you get useful work done; it makes writing tests a little less work and a little more enjoyable. And working with well-tested code is its own reward—a satisfying experience.

13.3 DESIGN THEN TEST THEN CODE

This is the slogan of the test-oriented crowd, and if it sounds a bit impossible, it is. It's hype—it got your attention, and there is a bit of truth to it, but don't take it too literally.

The approach espoused by the "Testing First" crowd is to start, like all good software development efforts, with design. But once you have pieces designed, move directly into testing. Now you don't have any code that can be tested yet, but you can start *writing* your tests. Then—although the tests will fail, as there is no code to run yet—you can begin keeping score on your progress by running these tests as code gets implemented.

> **NOTE**
>
> Some people like to tout the use of JUnit as an automated tool to track progress, but that's a little hard to do when you can't compile your tests because the classes they need don't yet exist. However, if you document your design of a class by (among other things) creating an empty version of the source, with Javadoc comments for the class and whatever methods you have come up with so far, well, then you've got something that will compile, and thus can be used for tracking progress. It also makes great, tangible documentation. Our point here, though, is that you are doing some coding before you begin testing. It's really more of a back-and-forth between coding and testing.

Let's apply that approach to our previous design discussion. We've described an `Account` class in our design discussion. It needs a name, an owner, and an amount of money when created. It should have a method to create subaccounts, ones that are connected to this account and get allocated some or all of the main account's money.

Example 13.1 is the basic structure of our `Account` class.

That's enough to begin writing a test. We have described the constructor, with the three parameters that it will need. We've also described a method on the `Account` object, one that will create subaccounts. That gives us enough information to write a test that will create an account and then create subaccounts of that account. We can test to see if the accounts are created properly (i.e., are not null) and if the subaccounts use up all the money of the parent account.

When you "test then code," you begin to use the objects that you have designed without getting bogged down in their implementation. You are, in effect, *describing* their external interfaces without implementing them. You are also beginning to use the classes as a user might, though a tester's use is a bit different than the way an application might use them. However, as a user of these classes you are beginning to test the design, by testing the results of the use cases—are these classes really usable?

You may discover that you need some additional functionality. In our example, we can see from the description of our test that we will need a getter method on the account to return the amount of money that remains unallocated to subaccounts. Then we can test to see if it gets used up properly.

There are many more test cases that we could develop for the `Account` class, but let's use just these for now, so that the size of our test case is manageable.

Our next step is to get JUnit installed before we get too deep into developing our test cases. That will give us something to run these tests.

13.4 INSTALLING AND RUNNING JUNIT

It's rather simple to install a standalone version of JUnit. We download a ZIP file from the JUnit Web site, then unzip it into a directory. Adding the JUnit JAR file to your `CLASSPATH` is all that's needed to make JUnit available for you to run it.

Example 13.1 The bare bones of our `Account` class

```java
package net.multitool.core;

import net.multitool.util.*;
import java.util.*;

/**
 * The basic Account class for our budgeting example; this is the
 * first-cut "implementation" where we have just transferred our
 * design into Java code. We can use this much to generate Javadocs
 * and also to begin our JUnit testing (design, test, code).
 */

public class
Account
{
    private String name;      // a name to identify this account
    private User owner;       // the user assigned to this account
    private SAMoney total;    // total amt allocated to this account
    private HashMap children; // the collection of subaccounts,
                              //   by name
    private Account parent;   // it has this account as a child

    /**
     * Create an account, with a pool of dollars to budget.
     * Use this constructor to create the master account.
     * Use "createSub" to create children of this account.
     */
    public
    Account(String name, User owner, String total)
    {
    }

    /**
     * Create a new subaccount (i.e., child), given a name
     * and an amount. The child is connected to the parent.
     */
    public Account
    createSub(String name, String amt)
    {
        return null;        // so it compiles

    } // createChild

} // class Account
```

13.4.1   Downloading and Unzipping

Point your browser at the site `http://www.junit.org/` (Figure 13.1). From the main page, choose the Download heading.

That takes you to a SourceForge site (Figure 13.2); click on one of the sites near you, though any will do. The download is only a few hundred kilobytes, so it shouldn't take long.

You'll be left with a file named `junitX.Y.Z.zip`, where the *X*, *Y*, *Z* characters are the digits that tell you what release of JUnit this is. Our examples show the `3.8.1` release.

> **NOTE**
>
> It's a good idea to inspect the ZIP files that you download before you actually unzip them. We like to know what files and especially what directories are going to get modified or cluttered up by the unzipping. Some ZIP files come with all their files inside of a single folder. Those are fine to unzip in place. Other ZIP files have been built from lots of pieces and unzipping them can make a mess of your current directory, or worse, of other directories that you may not even know about. Instead, play it safe and look before you leap. You can see the list of all the files in the JUnit ZIP file by typing this command:
>
> ```
> $ unzip -l junit3.8.1.zip
> ```
>
> The `-l` option will produce a listing of the contents of the ZIP file. That way you can see what subdirectories it will create, that is, if it is going to unpack into a single directory or make a mess. The JUnit ZIP file is very well behaved in this respect.

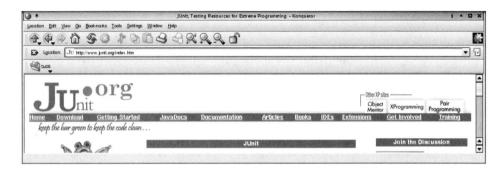

Figure 13.1 The JUnit home page

Figure 13.2 The SourceForge download site

Create a directory and unpack the JUnit ZIP file in there:

```
$ mkdir ~/junit
$ mv junit3.8.1.zip !$
$ cd !$
$ unzip junit3.8.1.zip
```

This warning from the installation instructions is worth noting:

IMPORTANT

Don't install the `junit.jar` into the extention directory of your JDK installation.
If you do so the test class on the filesystem will not be found.

The JDK installation directory has a subdirectory named `jre/lib/ext`. Don't put the JUnit JAR file in there. If you have followed our instructions, you're OK, since we had you create a new directory.

To use JUnit, the `junit.jar` file needs to be in your classpath. For example:

```
$ export CLASSPATH="${CLASSPATH}:${HOME}/junit/junit3.8.1/junit.jar"
```

That's all the installing there is. It doesn't feel like much, because you haven't done much. All it provides is a JAR file that you will use when you want to run tests. That's where it gets interesting.

13.4.2   Using JUnit

To test out your installation, `cd` to the directory where you unpacked JUnit. If it isn't already part of it, add the current directory ("`.`") to your `CLASSPATH`:

```
$ export CLASSPATH="${CLASSPATH}:."
```

Then try:

```
$ java junit.swingui.TestRunner junit.samples.AllTests
```

You should see a Java Swing GUI appear, with a green bar showing the progress of the testing (Figure 13.3).

> **NOTE**
>
> You may see an error message like this in your terminal window:
>
> ```
> (data/time) java.util.prefs.FileSystemPreferences checkLock...
> WARNING: Could not lock System prefs.Unix error code 136742412
> (data/time) java.util.prefs.FileSystemPreferences syncWorld
> WARNING: Couldn't flush system prefs: java.util.prefs.Backi...
> ```
>
> It will keep repeating as long as JUnit's GUI is running. The easiest fix is to make the `jre` directory world-writable while you run the GUI the first time. It will create the files it needs (in a directory, `.systemPrefs`), and thereafter stop pestering you. Remember to change permissions on the directory back to their original value.

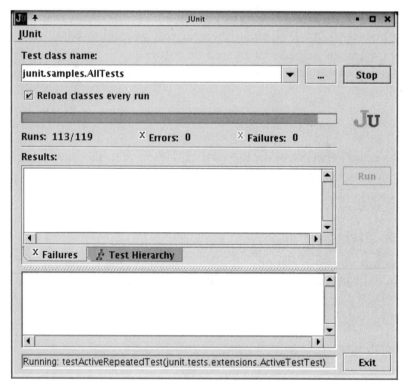

Figure 13.3 JUnit Swing GUI running tests

This is the GUI part of JUnit, part of what has made it so popular. By writing JUnit tests, you get to use their GUI. If you were to develop your own testing mechanism, you would also have to (re)invent a GUI.

There is an AWT GUI for the Swing-averse, but it is less featured. There is also a plain command-line test case runner:

```
$ java junit.textui.TestRunner junit.samples.AllTests
.......................................
.......................................
.....................................
Time: 3.834

OK (119 tests)

$
```

It prints a period for each test that it runs. (Yes, there are 119 periods there. Go ahead; count them if you must.) The command-line version is useful for incorporating JUnit tests into shell scripts (e.g., for testing nightly builds, e-mailing the results) and is used by **ant** when it invokes JUnit.

13.5 WRITING TEST CASES

Writing a test case for your own Java code consists, at its simplest, of writing a new class for each class that you want to test. But this class that you create is built in a special way so that the test harness of JUnit can execute it. That is, the test case class that you create should meet certain naming conventions, so that the JUnit test runners can find what they need in order to run your tests.

More specifically, your test cases will extend the JUnit class `TestCase`. Now, `TestCase` is an abstract class, meaning there are parts that you have to fill in (i.e., methods that you must write) to make it a working class. Moreover, `TestCase` implements (in the Java sense of the word) the `Test` interface. Can you begin to see how the `TestCase` class is a framework? It defines the rough outline of how the test cases will look so that a common test runner can run any test case, no matter who wrote it.

Let's look at a simple example, to see what such a test case looks like. Example 13.2 shows one for testing our `Account` class.

Example 13.2 Simple test case

```
package net.multitool.core;

import java.util.*;            // needed by our class
import net.multitool.util.*;   // needed by our class

import junit.framework.*;      // needed by JUnit

/**
 * for JUnit testing of Account.java
 */
public class
AccountTest
  extends TestCase
{
  // our test instrumentation:
  Account base;
```

```
// run before each test case:
protected void
setUp()
{
  base = new Account("Base", new User("testuser"), "150");
}

// our one test case
public void
testCreateSub()
{
  // Create a subaccount, assigning $50 of our pool of $150.
  Account sub1 = base.createSub("sub1", "50");
  // Make sure that it created something.
  assertNotNull("Couldn't create sub1", sub1);

  // Now a 2nd subaccount.
  Account sub2  = base.createSub("sub2", "75");
  assertNotNull("Couldn't create sub2", sub2);

  // Now a 3rd subaccount, to use up all the $.
  Account sub3  = base.createSub("sub3", "25");
  assertNotNull("Couldn't create sub3", sub3);

  // We should have the same total that we started with.
  assertEquals(150, base.getTotal().getDollars());

  // We should have used up all our $.
  assertEquals(0, base.getBalance().getDollars());

  // Be sure the (sub)account lookup works:
  Account ex2 = base.getSub("sub2");
  assertNotNull("Couldn't find sub2", ex2);
  assertSame(sub2, ex2);

} // testCreateSub

} // class AccountTest
```

Notice how we've named our test case class. We take the name of the class and append `Test` to the end. This is convenient for us—we can easily see which classes have test cases; but more importantly, JUnit can use this and other naming conventions to derive the test case names (more on that later). Notice also that the method in the `Account` class that we want to test, called `createSub()`, gets exercised by a method named `testCreateSub()`—we

Table 13.1 JUnit Naming

	In your original code	In your test case
Class	`MyClass`	`MyClassTest`
Method	`myMethod`	`testMyMethod`

prepend the word "test" to the method name, and capitalize the now-no-longer-first letter. Again, JUnit will use this naming convention, along with introspection, to automatically derive the test names from the actual method names (more on that later, too). The naming conventions we've seen so far are summarized in Table 13.1.

Let's take a quick look at the code. We import the framework for JUnit test cases, so that the compiler can resolve the names that deal with JUnit stuff. The `TestCase` class that we extend is part of that JUnit stuff. It's an abstract class that defines much of what we use for testing. We just fill in what we need.

The `TestCase` class defines a method called `setUp()`. The `setUp()` method is called not just once, but before every test method is called. That way you can initialize variables and get into a known state before each test. Since it's already defined in the `TestCase` class, we can override it (as in our example) to do what we want, or we can not include it in our class and get the default behavior from `TestCase` (which is to do nothing).

There is also a method named `tearDown()` which you can override if you need to close things up at the end of a test case (e.g., close a database connection). As with `setUp()`, its default behavior, as defined in `TestCase`, is to do nothing.

The test case itself—the method where we will exercise our class—is called `testCreateSub` (since we want to test our `createSub()` method). Inside such a method (and we could have more than one) we write code which uses the objects in our application. Then at various junctures in the code we make assertions about the state of things—for example, this variable should be non-null, or this expression should have this particular value.

Those assertions are, to our way of thinking, the tests. We're testing to see if the subaccount was created, or if the main account did, indeed, use up all of its dollars in allocation to the subaccounts. But they are not what is called *tests* by JUnit. Rather, each individual method in a test class is considered a single test. Such test methods are, typically, a collection of assertions surrounding the use of a single (application) method. So in our example, the method `testCreateSub()` is a single JUnit test which asserts various conditions about various invocations of the `createSub()` method. Note that all of the assertions encountered in the execution of the test class must pass for the test to pass.

So what happens if an assertion fails? The assert method will throw an exception, reporting the failure. In JUnit terminology, a *failure* is a test that didn't pass, whereas an *error* is a problem with the running of the test. A missing class or a null pointer exception are errors, whereas an `assertNotNull()` call failing is considered a test failure.

The handy thing about the exceptions that the assert methods throw is that they are, technically speaking, not `java.lang.Exception` throwables but rather belong to the `java.lang.Error` type of throwable. (Don't confuse this technical Java use of the word "error" with our more informal use in the previous discussion of failure versus error.) To quote from the Javadoc page for `java.lang.Error`:

> A method is not required to declare in its `throws` clause any subclasses of `Error` that might be thrown during the execution of the method but not caught, since these errors are abnormal conditions that should never occur.

So the use of `Error` by JUnit's various assert methods is done simply as a convenience for us test developers, so that we don't have to put `throws` ... clauses on all of our method declarations.

13.5.1 JUnit Assertions

These are the various test assertions available with JUnit:

- `assertEquals()`, comparing
  - `boolean` with `boolean`
  - `char` with `char`
  - `short` with `short`
  - `int` with `int`
  - `long` with `long`
  - `float` with `float`
  - `double` with `double`
  - `Object` with `Object`
  - `String` with `String`

- `assertTrue( boolean expression )`
- `assertFalse( boolean expression )`
- `assertNull (Object)`
- `assertNotNull (Object)`
- `assertSame (Object1, Object2)`
- `assertNotSame (Object1, Object2)`
- `fail()`

Each of the assert methods comes in two "flavors," one with a message `String` and one without. For example, there is a method `assertTrue()` which takes a `boolean` as its parameter; typically it would be used with an expression, for example:[1]

```
assertTrue( (sample  actual) );
```

If the condition is not true, an `AssertionFailedError` is thrown. That means, among other things, that if/when your test fails, it will stop executing at that point. The `tearDown()` method, though, will still be executed before proceeding to the next test.

There is also a method of the same name, `assertTrue()`, but with a slightly different signature—it adds a `String` as its first parameter. The string is the message to be included in the error report. Using this variation on `assertTrue()`, our example would become:

```
assertTrue("Sample too small", (sample  actual));
```

In the same way, `assertFalse()` has two versions—`assertFalse(boolean)` and `assertFalse(String, boolean)`—and so on for all other assert methods.

---

1. Yes, the extra parentheses are not needed; they just make the point that this is a boolean expression being passed as the argument to `assertTrue()`. We could also have written it as:

```
boolean result = (sample  actual);
assertTrue(result);
```

Again, the extra parentheses are used just to make it clearer.

The `String` message is very helpful when you get large numbers of comparisons and assertions inside your test cases. It can help you identify which assert in which test failed.

> **TIP**
>
> When writing your assertions, keep in mind the difference between `assertEquals()` and `assertSame()`. The latter will test if the two arguments refer to the very same instance of an object, whereas the former only checks to see that their values are equal. So any two references to objects that are the same will also be equal, but not vice versa. For example:
>
> ```
> String sample = "value";
> String others = "more value".substring(5);
> assertEquals(sample, others);    // will pass
> assertSame(sample, others);      // will fail
> ```

Digging a little deeper into how all this works, it might be worth pointing out that the JUnit `TestCase` class, while an abstract class itself, is also an extension of another class, the `Assert` class. The `Assert` class is the class that defines all these public static methods for asserting the various conditions (see the list above). That is why you don't need any qualifiers on the various assert calls. They are all part of your test case by virtue of it extending `TestCase`. It also means that you could override any of them to get special behavior. This might be useful for `assertEquals(Object, Object)`, to allow you to compare objects of your own kinds, but we don't recommend this. You are better off overriding the `equals()` method of your own object than messing with the JUnit methods. And remember that if you override those behaviors, your tests will only be as good as your implementation of the assert mechanisms.

13.5.2   Running a Test Case

Recall how we ran the JUnit self-tests after installation. We can now use a similar command to execute our own test case. With the `CLASSPATH` still set as above, try compiling and running the test case:

```
$ javac net/multitool/core/AccountTest.java
$ java junit.textui.TestRunner net.multitool.core.AccountTest
```

The `TestRunner` will use introspection and reflection to dig information out of the `AccountTest` class. It will find all the public methods that begin with `test` and have no parameters. It will execute `setUp()`, then one of the test methods, then `tearDown()`; then `setUp()`, then another test method, then `tearDown()`, and so on. Our example has only one test method, `testCreateSub()`, so that will be the one test method it runs.

The result of running the test should look like this:

```
$ java junit.textui.TestRunner net.multitool.core.AccountTest
.
Time: 0.071

OK (1 test)

$
```

13.6 RUNNING TEST SUITES

Quite likely, you'll want to run several tests, exercising the various classes that make up your application. Let's see an example of how to build such a suite of tests (Example 13.3).

While not defined as an interface, the convention is used by JUnit `TestRunner` classes that they will look for a public static method called `suite()` in any class that you ask a `TestRunner` to run. Your class, the one that will define the suite of tests, should return something that implements the `Test` interface. A `TestSuite` object is one such object, and we can fill it with tests gleaned automatically by JUnit from the class names that we supply.

We've also added a `main()` that invokes the text-based user interface for running these tests. That way you can invoke the tests from the command line if you like.

Here are the two commands to compile and execute the `CoreTest` suite, using the Swing GUI:

```
$ javac test/net/multitool/core/CoreTest.java
$ java junit.swingui.TestRunner net.multitool.core.CoreTest
```

When the GUI runs, click on the **Hierarchy** tab and you can see the various tests that make up the suite. Opening the folders will show the tests inside of suites (Figure 13.4).

Example 13.3 A suite of test cases

```java
package net.multitool.core;

import junit.framework.*;

public class
CoreTest
extends TestCase
{
  public
  CoreTest(String str)
  {
    super(str);
  } // constructor CoreTest

  /**
   * Constructs a collection of tests to be run by the TestRunner.
   */
  public static Test
  suite()
  {
    /*
     * Add the results of each separate Test into a big Suite.
     */
    TestSuite suite = new TestSuite("Core Classes");
    suite.addTestSuite(net.multitool.util.SAMoneyTest.class);
    suite.addTestSuite(AccountTest.class);
    suite.addTestSuite(UserTest.class);

    return suite;

  } // suite

  public static void
  main(String [] args)
  {
    junit.textui.TestRunner.run(suite());
  } // main

} // class CoreTest
```

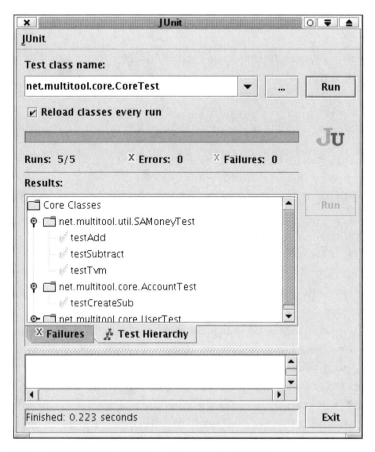

Figure 13.4 The CoreTest running a suite of tests

One last example is the SAMoneyTest.java file that was used in the CoreTest example (Figure 13.4). Did you notice the names displayed in the test hierarchy? They don't match the method names used to run the tests in SAMoneyTest.java because we constructed the suite "by hand" instead of letting the JUnit introspection and reflection find the methods dynamically.

Such manual approach has some advantages. You can restrict the current set of tests being executed to a subset of the entire set of tests. You can also, as this example shows, give other names to the tests. The biggest drawback, though, is the maintenance cost of having to add the test by hand to the suite() method whenever you add another test method.

13.7 REVIEW

We have shown you how to download JUnit and get it running. We have discussed creating a test case and creating a suite of tests. We've looked at the Swing GUI for JUnit but also at the command-line interface. We have shown how our design translates to a minimal code implementation from which we can begin testing. We've discussed the "design, test, then code" approach, and how you can use it to track the progress of your implementation.

13.8 WHAT YOU STILL DON'T KNOW

JUnit can be invoked from **ant**. It is an optional task (not part of the standard **ant** release), but easy to install and get running. Both the `junit.jar` and **ant**'s optional tasks JAR file need to be in your classpath. That's all it takes. See `http://ant.apache.org/manual/OptionalTasks/junit.html` for more details.

JUnit integrates well with Eclipse and other IDEs. It is easy to install and very easy to use when it's part of your IDE. For whichever IDE you choose, get the JUnit plug-in for it and use it.

One area we haven't yet discussed is how to do unit testing for the GUI portion of your application. The basic idea is the same. In order to manipulate your GUI from the test, you may want to investigate the `java.awt.Robot` class. It can be used to generate system input events such as mouse and keyboard actions.

In fact, we've only begun to describe the various ways that JUnit can be used for all kinds of testing. Our focus has been on unit tests during code development, but JUnit can also be applied to integration and release testing. With any large Java application, it is crucial to have a good set of regression tests that can be rerun after features or fixes are added, or after classes have been refactored. JUnit has proven to be very valuable in these situations.

Finally, remember that JUnit is only a tool. The GIGO law[2] tells us not to expect great tests just because we know how to run a tool. Test design, like any good design skill, is art as well as science. Learning the art of testing will pay dividends in better code built faster.

---

2. Garbage In, Garbage Out.

13.9 RESOURCES

Visit `http://www.junit.org/` for all things JUnit-y, including some documentation (though it's not the greatest) and scores of articles which provide tons of useful information.

A very good article on JUnit appeared in the May/June 2003 issue of *Oracle* magazine (online at `http://otn.oracle.com/oraclemagazine`), titled "A JUnit Step-by-Step," by Michel Casabianca.

For more about software testing in general, there is a classic (that is, from early days of computing) book on the subject: Glenford J. Myers, *The Art of Software Testing*, Wiley, New York, 1979.

You may also want to check out *Just Enough Software Test Automation* by Daniel J. Mosley and Bruce A. Posey (ISBN 0-13-008468-9, 2002). Their Web site[3] includes a bibliography of nearly hundred articles and books on client-server and other software testing topics.

13.10 EXERCISES

How many other tests can you think up to add to the `AccountTest` class? Did you include checks for bad behavior—for example, attempting to make too many subaccounts? Add the new asserts and rerun the test.

---

3. `http://www.csst-technologies.com/csstbibl.htm`

Chapter 14

Storing the Data

In this chapter we will very briefly introduce three database products that run on the Linux platform and will support our sample applications. We will also select one of the three and explain how to set up our database tables.

14.1 WHAT YOU WILL LEARN

In this chapter you will learn a little bit about database server products available for Linux, including both commercial and Free or Open Source products. We will briefly discuss some factors that might enter into choosing one over the other. We will then describe how one might design tables to back our application, and how to create and implement those tables in two Open Source databases: MySQL and PostgreSQL.

14.2 FOLLOW THE OBJECTS

One of the consequences of a good object design is a relatively simple database design. For the most part, each class will end up as a database table where each row represents an instance of that class. Beyond that, all that is needed are those tables required to represent relationships between objects.

In this chapter we will show you examples of these relationships, and we will do so in a manner that should easily port to any SQL relational database.

14.3 OF PERSISTENCE

Programs cannot be assured of running forever. Virtually all computer main memory (i.e., RAM) is volatile, meaning that if the power is removed, the data is lost. Since computers are sometimes rebooted, and since the power sometimes goes out, we obviously need some place besides memory to store our class instances. We need persistent (nonvolatile) storage. This can be as simple as streaming our classes out to flat file, or it can be as complex as a clustered multiuser database. We will discuss the selection criteria and how you might choose your persistent storage strategy.

14.4 THINKING OF THE FUTURE, OR PAINTING IN CORNERS

It is important that you try, in your class design, to avoid making the persistence system dependent on a particular storage method or product. If you do this, you can switch storage products or solutions relatively easily.

14.5 ORACLE, POSTGRESQL, MYSQL

One of the first major decisions you must make is what to use as a database server. On Linux systems, you have both Free Software and commercial software options. As we have said before, we will tend to focus on Free Software in this text, but we cannot ignore the most popular database software package out there, which is, of course, Oracle.

Let's take a quick look at each of the "big 3" database choices on Linux platforms.

14.5.1   MySQL

MySQL is a very fast but somewhat limited SQL database system. It is wildly popular mainly because it is simple, fast, and Free. It is everything that you would need to back a dynamic Web site. As of this writing, the stable production version of MySQL is 4.0.16, but most Linux distributions are still shipping something from the 3.23.x series.

At this point, MySQL lacks some key features:

- Stored procedures
- Sub-SELECTs
- Triggers

Version 4.0.x does support some long-awaited features (if you use the InnoDB table type instead of the default MyISAM tables), such as row-level locking, foreign keys, and transactions. But InnoDB tables are not directly available in the 3.23.x versions still shipping with many distributions.

MySQL is an excellent choice for designs that do not require stored procedures, triggers, or transactions. It is widely used as a back end for dynamic Web sites—applications with many reading users and few writing users.

For more information on MySQL, see *Core MySQL* by Leon Atkinson (ISBN 0-13-066190-2).

14.5.2   PostgreSQL

PostgreSQL is a surprisingly complete and full-featured database offering.

Not only does it fully support stored procedures, triggers, views, foreign keys, and transactions, but it also implements an innovative "record versioning" system for multiuser integrity. Unlike many other databases, readers may continue to read consistent data during writing activity (*nonblocking revisions*), and backups may be taken while the database is still available for queries. This is a serious database.

This database has excellent public documentation. Take a look at the PostgreSQL Documentation.[1] Another useful book is *PostgreSQL* by Korry and Susan Douglas (ISBN 0-7357-1257-3).

---

1. http://www.postgresql.org/docs/current/static/index.html

14.5.3 Oracle

What can we say? In the world of databases, this is the top dog. This is the standard against which other database systems are measured. Oracle is the DB that runs the "big applications" out there in the enterprise world. It is also a costly piece of software when it is used for production applications. It is, however, available for free download to use for development. It is emphatically *not* Free Software. You don't have the source code. You don't have the right to modify it, and you don't have the right to pass it on to third parties. That may or may not be an issue for you.

If you need advanced features like high-availability clustering, it is certain that Oracle will work for you. You may download it for evaluation and development from Oracle's OTN (Oracle Technology Network)[2] Web site.

14.5.4 Selection Criteria

For the simple application we are developing, all of these databases are sufficient. But in the real world, there could be many factors that might come to bear upon your selection of a database server product. These factors might include:

- Price
- License terms
- Transaction capacity (speed)
- Integration (does it work with or depend on other software you use?)
- Human resources (do you have operators and developers familiar with the product on your staff, or are they available for hire?)
- Presence (does your organization already use this product?)
- Features (do you have future plans that might require a particular product?)

14.6 Being Self-Contained

One of the common difficulties with software that requires a database is how to get the database structures up and running. Database storage is often not in

---

2. `http://otn.oracle.com/software/products/oracle9i/htdocs/othersoft.html`

files, and even when it is in files on the filesystem, you cannot, when you install a package like BudgetPro, simply put your database files in place, since there are probably other applications that have their tables in those files, and replacing them with yours would destroy that data.

Often, the table creation statements and any initial table rows required are placed in a SQL file and that file is run against the database. Meanwhile, all of the database code that performs application interactions is either in the application code or in stored procedures called by the application code. But there is no fundamental reason to make this distinction. The application can see to it that its database and tables are created.

Of course, you can automate this setup with a shell script, but Java is supposed to be cross-platform. Of course, you can write a batch file for Windows and a shell script for UNIX, but if you just put this setup into your Java code, you don't have to maintain and test separate installation procedures. One of the areas where Java applications tend to lag behind other applications is in installation and setup. You can obviate this somewhat by including database setup in your Java code, thus eliminating the need to write platform-specific scripts.

Consider including your database and table creation statements directly in your Java code, even if it is in a singleton setup class that only runs once.

The basic tables should parallel the objects. So, for our classes, the SQL statements to build the tables might look as shown in Example 14.1.

For the moment, we are confining our table declarations to a form that should work with both Open Source databases.

These are very basic definitions. We will be talking about issues like generating unique IDs for records as we develop the code to back these. Different database products have different "best" solutions, which will make the support for multiple databases more problematic.

14.7 BEYOND THE BASICS

We are going to adopt a very simple strategy for database persistence. We are going to read in the data structures at startup and maintain them as changes are made during execution. That way, any abnormal termination will leave the data in a recoverable state. The application will not require any "save" operation.

Example 14.1 Candidate DB tables for BudgetPro

```
DROP DATABASE budgetPro;

CREATE DATABASE budgetPro;

USE DATABASE budgetPro;

CREATE TABLE Account (
  id INTEGER NOT NULL,
  name VARCHAR(64) NOT NULL,
  user_id INTEGER NOT NULL,
  amount DECIMAL,
  balance DECIMAL,
  parent_account_id INTEGER,
  PRIMARY KEY (id),
  FOREIGN KEY (user_id) REFERENCES User(id)
);

CREATE TABLE User (
  id INTEGER NOT NULL,
  name VARCHAR(64),
  PRIMARY KEY (id)
);
```

We will implement this in the simplest way possible, by directly embedded SQL statements in the application code. But this is far from your only choice.

It is possible to design a "persistence framework," such that all classes that inherit from a persistence base class or implement a persistence interface and follow certain naming conventions for member data can be automatically backed by persistent storage. Java's ability to *introspect*, that is, to look at the names and structures of a class dynamically at runtime, allow one to write such an automatic persistence framework. Several such libraries already exist, including both commercial and Open Source options. This being an Open Source book, we'll call you attention to the Open Source choices:[3]

---

3. Have we tried all of these? Yeah. Sure. Why not? Of course we haven't. Don't read endorsement into this or any of our "here are some choices" lists. These are also not presented in any particular order. We tell you they exist. It is up to you to evaluate their suitability for your purposes.

Hibernate[4]

Hibernate is probably the most widely known Open Source persistence framework. It is released under the LGPL license.

OJB[5]

Billed as "Object Relational Bridge," this one is from Apache. It provides both an ODMG (a persistence API much used in the C++ world) and a JDO (Java Data Objects—Sun's object persistence API specification) API.

Castor[6]

Castor does persistence to both XML and relational databases. They call their RDBMS persistence framework "JDO," but beware: It is *not* compatible with or identical to Sun's JDO. They say it is better.

pBeans[7]

pBeans does fully automated persistence of JavaBeans. You have to follow the rules for writing beans (not EJBs, but the "classic" JavaBeans), but once done, this will automatically persist your instances to any JDBC-compatible database. No XML specification, no SQL scripting, no templates. For the easiest "just save my instance data" type of applications, this can be a good choice.[8] This product even automates the creation of tables, as we advocated above.

Are there others? Heck, yes. Not all of them persist to relational databases. Some persist only to XML. Some to other databases like B-trees or the Berkeley DB system. We didn't concern ourselves with those. We also left off a couple of libraries that appear not to have been developed for more than a couple of years.

---

4. http://www.hibernate.org/

5. http://db.apache.org/ojb/

6. http://castor.exolab.org/

7. http://pbeans.sourceforge.net/

8. But we are not endorsing here.

14.8 PERSISTENCE IS NOT THE WHOLE STORY

In this chapter and throughout this book we take a practical view that a database is there to store an application's data. That's far from the intent. A relational database is designed to create collections of data and to perform logical queries within and between those collections. The relational model is much more than application storage. It facilitates all kinds of data analysis. This is often ignored in enterprises these days.

Don't forget that designing database tables should take into account concerns beyond mere application storage.

14.9 SETTING UP POSTGRESQL FOR BUDGETPRO

Let's turn our attention to installing and starting PostgreSQL to support the BudgetPro application.

14.9.1   Installing PostgreSQL

The simplest way to install PostgreSQL is to use precompiled binary packages. RedHat and Fedora have RPM packages for installing the database and client software (although neither distributes the client libraries for Java due to licensing issues with Java itself). The PostgreSQL project produces RPM packages of their own, including the Java JDBC class library. Those might be your easiest course. Debian packages for PostgreSQL exist, but again, they do not provide the JDBC library.

For our purposes, we are going to assume that you have downloaded and installed the following RPM packages[9] from the PostgreSQL Download page:[10]

- `postgresql-server`
- `postgresql-devel`
- `postgresql-jdbc`
- `postgresql-docs` (optional)

---

9. If you are a user of Debian or another Debian-based Linux distribution, you should be aware that there is a Debian package called `alien`, which can install and manage RPM packages on a Debian system.

10. `http://www.postgresql.org/mirrors-ftp.html`

14.9.2   Creating a `postgres` User

More than likely, installing a PostgreSQL package will create a new Linux user called `postgres` on your system. This is not a login account; it will be used by the database server process daemon[11] (called "postmaster," lest you think that it might be an e-mail server or something). Furthermore, only the `postgres` user is able to create additional database users or any databases.

Obviously, we won't want it to be like this forever. It has the same problem as the `root` user on the OS itself: There's one magic user with all the power. You'll need to create additional users and you'll want to limit what they can do. How to do it?

First off, you can't log in as `postgres`, so you will have to become `root` and then `su` to the `postgres` user:

```
[mschwarz@cassidy mschwarz]$ su -
Password:
[root@cassidy root]# su - postgres
-bash-2.05b$
```

Note that `postgres` didn't have any profile or rc script to set up prompts or anything.

All PostgreSQL databases have owning users, in much the same way that all Linux files have owning users. But PostgreSQL users are not necessarily the same as Linux users.[12] The only PostgreSQL user that exists "out of the box" is `postgres`. You must use the **createuser** command-line utility (or the equivalent SQL) to create a user. Here's an example:

---

11. Historically, daemon processes on UNIX systems used to be run as `root`. But a program error in a daemon would allow a malicious user to execute code as the owner of the process. If that owner is `root`, one programming mistake in a server process could give an attacker total control of the system. Beware of any daemon process that runs as `root`. Nowadays, these run as either a totally nonpriviledged user such as `nobody`, or, if they really need to write files or some such thing, as a catch-all user like `daemon`. The database is an important process and it needs its own security, so it runs as its own user, `postgres`.

12. For most PostgreSQL command-line utilities, if no PostgreSQL username is specified, the current Linux username will be used. This is often a convenient choice, but you might have compelling reasons not to do this.

```
-bash-2.05b$ createuser mschwarz
Shall the new user be allowed to create databases? (y/n) y
Shall the new user be allowed to create more new users? (y/n) y
CREATE USER
-bash-2.05b$
```

Here, we created the PostgreSQL user `mschwarz` and gave him the ability to create databases and new users.

14.9.3 Creating Our Database

Now that our username, `mschwarz`, has been created and is authorized to create databases, we use the **createdb** command to create our database:

```
[mschwarz@cassidy mschwarz]$ createdb budgetPro
CREATE DATABASE
```

Notice that we did this as the Linux user `mschwarz`, so the **createdb** command used that username when it created the `budgetPro` database. What would have happened if we had used a Linux user that did not have a matching PostgreSQL user? Let's see:

```
[albing@cassidy albing]$ createdb budgetPro
createdb: could not connect to database template1: \
FATAL:  user "albing" does not exist
```

> **WARNING**
>
> Note that we have not implemented any security yet. The user `mschwarz` exists, but it does not have a password. Depending on how PostgreSQL security is configured, it may be possible for any user to use the -U option with the PostgreSQL command-line utilities to impersonate `mschwarz`. As packaged for Fedora Core 2, PostgreSQL uses **ident** to check authentication, so when `albing` attempts this, he gets this error:
>
> ```
> [albing@cassidy albing]$ createdb -U mschwarz budgetPro
> createdb: could not connect to database template1: \
> FATAL:  IDENT authentication failed for user "mschwarz"
> ```
>
> Just remember that this behavior is dependent on the local configuration of PostgreSQL. You cannot assume this security is in place just because you are in a PostgreSQL environment. Always be aware of the security configuration of your production environment!

14.9.4   Straight JDBC

Our application is quite simple. We're going to directly integrate database access by simply calling the JDBC interface at startup and making use of that connection again and again for data changes.

Our solution is more than sufficient for the standalone command-line and GUI versions of the application, but it will be left as an exercise for the reader to implement a better solution for the EJB implementation.

What will be lacking? Well, the solution we will implement here will get a single database connection and use it throughout the life of the application. It will be assumed that a single thread is accessing the database. These are all bad assumptions for a multiuser and multithreaded environment such as an application server.

14.9.4.1   Static Account Members

Most of the database code is in the Account class. It consists of a static method, getTopAccount(), which will establish a static connection to the database, create the Account table if need be, and load the top level account (defined as the account record with a null parent) if present or create it if not present.

The username is passed in as an argument. The username must exist in the User table. If it does not, an exception is thrown.

14.9.4.2   Joining the User

Two static methods are added that take a JDBC Connection and a String as arguments. They are getUserIdByName() and getUserByName(). The String is the username to look for. The first method returns the id column for that user. It returns zero (0) if the user doesn't exist. The other returns a User object, or null if the user doesn't exist.

14.10   REVIEW

We briefly examined choices of Open Source SQL database servers. We described how to set up PostgreSQL.

14.11 WHAT YOU STILL DON'T KNOW

This is another chapter that represents a mere gloss of its topic. Visit your local book megamart and just count the number of books on Oracle, MySQL, and PostgreSQL. Database servers and relational database design are very large topics indeed. We have hardly scratched the surface. Our goal here has been merely to give you enough to get started. If you plan to use one of these products, definitely take the time to download and read the official product documentation (for both MySQL and PostgreSQL it is actually quite good), and then take your time looking for after-market books that seem to meet your needs.

14.12 RESOURCES

By no means have we read all the titles available on this topic, but we have read and can recommend:

- Leon Atkinson, *Core MySQL*, ISBN 0-13-066190-2.
- Paul DuBois, *MySQL*, ISBN 0-7357-0921-1.
- Korry Douglas and Susan Douglas, *PostgreSQL*, ISBN 0-7357-1257-3.

14.13 EXERCISES

Is this database fully normalized?[13] If not, what would need to be done to normalize it? What reasons might exist for not fully normalizing a database?

---

13. "Normalization" is a process of eliminating database redundancy and of theoretical optimization of the data model. A decent introduction to the concepts may be found at http://dev.mysql.com/tech-resources/articles/intro-to-normalization.html.

Chapter 15

Accessing the Data:
An Introduction to JDBC

Java provides a back-end-independent interface to databases called Java DataBase Connectivity classes, or JDBC. We introduce the basics of the system here, and illustrate portability that makes it possible for our application to switch between two different database back ends.

15.1 WHAT YOU WILL LEARN

We will cover the basics of interaction with a database in Java. This involves

- Establishing and tearing down connections to a database
- Querying data in the database and reading the results
- Performing other database operations that modify data, but do not return data results

We assume that you are familiar with simple SQL constructs.

15.2 INTRODUCING JDBC

For many real-world applications, there are copious amounts of data associated with them. Programmers first learn to store data into files, but serious applications require a database. Java programs can connect to and query a database with the help of several Java classes which together make up the Java DataBase Connectivity API, or JDBC.

With JDBC, your Java programs will be able to connect to databases anywhere on the network and to query data from the database with the simple syntax that database programmers have been using for years—SQL.

JDBC provides an *abstraction*, a way to talk about the various aspects of working with a database which is largely vendor-independent. Implementations of JDBC can be, and are, built for many different databases and even other data sources, such as flat files and spreadsheets.

The Linux environment offers several choices of databases, the two most popular being MySQL and PostgreSQL. Both are Open Source projects available with most major Linux distributions, as well as online for downloading. For many Java and Linux developers, however, the use of Java and Linux will include their development environment and the servers to which they deploy their applications, but the database to which they connect will still be the corporate database. For most commercial applications this is an Oracle database, the industry leader, and due to its major presence in the marketplace we will use Oracle in our examples as well.

> **NOTE**
>
> JDBC interfaces are available for almost any commercial database with any significant marketshare. See Section 15.9 for a URL that has a list of such choices. Most of what you will learn in this chapter will apply regardless of the database you connect to.

To make even the most basic use of JDBC, you must understand three basic operations:

- First, establishing and tearing down connections to your database server
- Second, querying data
- Finally, reading up the results of that query

These three operations correspond to JDBC objects for doing these very things, namely the classes `Connection`, `PreparedStatement`, and `ResultSet`.

Let's jump right in and look at some code. Example 15.1 will make a connection to a MySQL database, prepare a query statement, execute the query, then read up the results.

Let's also look at a similar example, but this time for an Oracle database (Example 15.2). Notice how much is the same between the two examples, and which parts are different.

The only real difference between the two programs has to do with the connections. Once the connection to the database is established, the rest of the code is exactly the same—which is what you'd hope for in an abstraction. This is a good news for developers: "Learn once, use anywhere."

15.3 MAKING CONNECTIONS

The most complicated part of JDBC is establishing the connection. There are several ways to make a connection, depending on how much information about the connection driver you want hard-coded into your application. We are going to keep it simple and describe one straightforward way to connect.

The `DriverManager` class is where our application goes to get its connection to the database, as shown in our example. Many different JDBC drivers can register with the `DriverManager`, and it can make the connection to the kind of driver that you want based on the URL that you provide in the call to `getConnection()`. So where did our example register anything with the `DriverManager`? Well, it happened indirectly, via the `Class.forName(...).newInstance();` call. That loaded the class and created an instance of it. The JDBC specification says that when a `Driver` class initializes it must register with the `DriverManager`. So it happened "under the covers," in loading the driver class.

Another difference between the two examples deals with how the username and password are supplied to the database. Both are supplied in the URL, though in different syntax. That syntax is at the discretion of those who implemented the JDBC driver for that particular flavor of database. If we were to construct the URL at runtime, so that the user could supply a username and password dynamically, we'd want to remove the difference in how the URL is constructed. To do that we could use a call to `getConnection()` with a signature that includes the username and password as separate `String` parameters:

Example 15.1 Simple sample program using JDBC for MySQL

```java
import java.sql.*;

public class
MyCon
{
  public static void
  main(String [] args)
  {
    try {
      // A simple connection example looks like this:

      Class.forName("com.mysql.jdbc.Driver").newInstance();

      String url = "jdbc:mysql://host.domain.com/test"+
                   "?user=blah&password=blah";

      Connection conn = DriverManager.getConnection(url);

      // query
      String mySQL = "SELECT id, pw FROM Users WHERE name = ?";

      PreparedStatement stmt = conn.prepareStatement(mySQL);
      stmt.setString(1, args[0]);

      // execute the query
      ResultSet rs = stmt.executeQuery();

      // read the results
      while(rs.next()) {
          int id = rs.getInt("id");
          String pw = rs.getString("pw");

          System.out.println("id="+id);
      }
    } catch (Exception e) {
        System.out.println("Exception: "+e);
        e.printStackTrace();
    }

  } // main

} // class MyCon
```

Example 15.2 Simple sample program using JDBC for Oracle

```
// import oracle.jdbc.driver.*;
import java.sql.*;

public class
MyCon
{
 public static void
 main(String [] args)
 {
   try {
     // A simple connection example looks like this:

     Class.forName("oracle.jdbc.driver.OracleDriver").newInstance();

     String url = "jdbc:oracle:thin:mydbusername/mydbpasswd"+
                  "@host.domain.com:1521:dbname";

     Connection conn = DriverManager.getConnection(url);

     // query
     String mySQL = "SELECT id, pw FROM Users WHERE name = ?";

     PreparedStatement stmt = conn.prepareStatement(mySQL);
     stmt.setString(1, args[0]);

     // execute the query
     ResultSet rs = stmt.executeQuery();

     // read the results
     while(rs.next()) {
       int id = rs.getInt("id");
       String pw = rs.getString("pw");

       System.out.println("id="+id);
     }
   } catch (Exception e) {
       System.out.println("Exception: "+e);
       e.printStackTrace();
   }

 } // main

} // class MyCon
```

```
Connection conn = DriverManager.getConnection(url, username, password);
```

Getting this to compile and run requires you to have the appropriate JDBC JAR files available. For Oracle, see your Oracle DBA, or see pages 228–229 of *Java Oracle Database Development* by David Gallardo. For MySQL, it's an easy download you can install from the Internet.

15.3.1 Downloading JDBC for MySQL

The JDBC implementation for MySQL is available for free from `http://www.mysql.com/downloads/api-jdbc.html`.

The current version at the time of writing was `mysql-connector-java-3.0.9-stable.tar.gz` which you can unpack as follows:

```
$ gunzip mysql-connector-java-3.0.9-stable.tar.gz
$ tar xvf mysql-connector-java-3.0.9-stable.tar
```

That leaves you with a directory named `mysql-connector-java-3.0.9-stable` which contains a JAR file named `mysql-connector-java-3.0.9-stable-bin.jar` along with some directories (which are the contents of the JAR, unpacked) and a few miscellaneous files.

From the readme file:

Once you have unarchived the distribution archive, you can install the driver in one of two ways:

- Either copy the `com` and `org` subdirectories and all of their contents to anywhere you like, and put the directory holding the `com` and `org` subdirectories in your classpath, or
- Put `mysql-connector-java-3.0.9-stable-bin.jar` in your classpath, either by adding the *full* path to it to your CLASSPATH environment variable, or putting it in `$JAVA_HOME/jre/lib/ext`.

Unlike JUnit, it is OK to put this JAR in the `ext` directory.

15.4 QUERYING DATA

Back to our example. Do you remember the portion that built the query? Here it is again:

```
// query
String mySQL = "SELECT id, pw FROM Users WHERE name = ?";

PreparedStatement stmt = conn.prepareStatement(mySQL);
stmt.setString(1, args[0]);
```

If you're at all familiar with SQL then you'll recognize the SQL syntax within the `String mySQL`. Whatever you want your query to be, just build it as literal text. The query is "parameterized" by using the "?" character. Wherever a "?" appears in the query string, you can substitute a value with the `setString()` method on the `PreparedStatement` class.

There are a variety of set*XXXX*() methods where *XXXX* stands for different data types. Besides `setString()`, the most common ones are `setInt()`, `setBigDecimal()`, `setDouble()`, and `setTimestamp()` which set the parameter from an `int`, `BigDecimal`, `Double`, and `Timestamp` classes, respectively. The `java.sql.Timestamp` class is basically a `java.util.Date` augmented for compatibility with SQL's notion of `TIMESTAMP`. Read more about it on the Javadoc page for `java.sql.Timestamp`, or read the `java.sql.PreparedStatement` page for more on the other `set` methods available.

The two arguments to each of these `set` methods are the index and the value that you want to substitute. The index is simply the count of which question mark gets substituted, starting with 1 for the first one. Caution: The parameters start at one, even though most other things in Java, such as `Arrays`, `ArrayLists`, and so on, are zero-based. So it's not uncommon in code that uses JDBC to see something like this:

```
setInt(i+1, args[i]);
```

> **NOTE**
> Building SQL queries out of `String` literals is made easier in Java by a convenient mismatch between the two languages. In Java, `Strings` are delimited by double quotes (") whereas in SQL literals are bounded by single quotes ('). Thus in Java, you can construct SQL queries that contain literal string references without much trouble, as in:
>
> ```
> String clause = "WHERE name != 'Admin'"
> ```

If this all seems rather simplistic, well, it is. It may not be a very sophisticated way of blending SQL with Java, but it is very effective. Notice that you don't get any syntax checking on the SQL query when you write your program, though it will throw an exception at runtime if you try to execute ungrammatical SQL. For this reason it is not uncommon to try out all your SQL beforehand, cutting and pasting the queries out of the SQL program that you use for directly talking with your database. Some developers even like to keep their queries in files, to be read at runtime. This has the added flexibility (and risk) of being able to change the query without recompiling the code. Since the recompile doesn't provide any syntax checking on your query string anyway, it seems a reasonable way to go, provided that you properly write-protect the files containing the queries.

15.5 GETTING RESULTS

Returning to our example, we see that we can execute the query on the `Statement` object and then get out the results:

```
ResultSet rs = stmt.executeQuery();

// read the results
while(rs.next()) {
  int id = rs.getInt("id");
  String pw = rs.getString("pw");

  System.out.println("id="+id);
}
```

The results of a query are returned in a `ResultSet` object. The easiest way to think of it is to consider it an iterator over the rows that result from the query. In its simple form it is, like an iterator, a one-pass, once-through traversal of the data. Since the result set is iterating over rows, we need to get at the individual columns of results with a further method call on the `ResultSet`. You can see that inside the `while` loop of the example.

The query was built to retrieve the columns `id` and `pw` from our table. The `getInt()` and `getString()` methods use those column names to retrieve the data from the `ResultSet`.

> **TIP**
>
> The case (UPPER or lower) of the column name strings is ignored, so you could write ID and pW and it would work fine. Some developers prefer, for example, to use all-uppercase names of columns. We recommend using a consistent case throughout to avoid confusing those who later have to read your code.

There is another form for each of those get*XXXX*() calls that takes as its argument the column number rather than name. Since our query selected "id, pw", the id is column one and pw is column two, so we could have written:

```
int id = rs.getInt(1);
String pw = rs.getString(2);
```

In addition to the get methods, ResultSet also has some boolean methods that will help your application figure out how far in the result set the iterator has reached: isBeforeFirst(), isFirst(), isLast(), and isAfterLast(). There is, however, no way to tell how big the result set is directly from this simple result set.

More complex manipulation of the ResultSet object is possible if we create the PreparedStatement with a different method call, one that lets us provide additional parameters to specify this more complex behavior. We could use:

```
conn.prepareStatement(mySQL,
                ResultSet.TYPE_SCROLL_INSENSITIVE,
                ResultSet.CONCUR_READ_ONLY);
```

which lets us specify a type of scrollable behavior and whether (CONCUR_UPDATEABLE) or not (CONCUR_READ_ONLY) the results set can be updated.

Once we've built the prepared statement this way, we can move the iterator forward or backward, to absolute (e.g., row 7) or relative (e.g., 3 rows back) positions. For a good discussion of this topic, see page 257 and the following pages in the Gallardo book.

If you're still hung up on the fact that you can't get the size, in rows, of the result set from our first example, notice that you can now do that with this more flexible, "scrollable" result set. To find its size before reading any data, position it `afterLast()`, then `getRow()` to get the size, then position it back to `beforeFirst()` to be ready to read.

15.6 UPDATES, INSERTS, DELETES

Not every action on a database returns a `ResultSet`. Operations that create the tables in a database, or those that modify, insert, or delete rows of data don't return rows of values. For those sorts of SQL statements, we don't call `executeQuery()`—we call `executeUpdate()` instead. It returns an `int` giving the number of rows affected by the execution. In the case of a CREATE TABLE operation, it simply returns 0.

15.7 REVIEW

Connecting a Java application to a database is a key step in real applications. The mechanisms for doing that are varied and can be complicated. We've picked a single approach for connecting, to keep it simple and to highlight the similarities and differences between two different database implementations.

The rest of the conversation with a database depends as much on your SQL skills as on Java skills. Java will take strings of SQL, which can be parameterized, and, via JDBC calls, send them to be executed by the database. The results are like iterators; they can be retrieved, row after row, for further processing. Updates, inserts, and deletes are also easily done, with a few simple calls to process the SQL.

15.8 WHAT YOU STILL DON'T KNOW

We've skipped over lots of topics to keep this simple. There are a variety of ways to connect to a database that we haven't covered; the most important one may be the use of a `DataSource` instead of a `DriverManager`. As of Java 1.4.1, the `DataSource` is the preferred means of making connections to your database. While it makes the code more portable (e.g., if you're planning on moving around, changing databases and/or database servers), it is more complicated to set up—there are more "moving parts" to get right. If you already have a Java Naming and Directory Interface (JNDI) service running, thought, it's very straightforward (see page 254 and the following pages of Gallardo).

We haven't covered the basic `Statement` class suitable for fixed queries with no parameters (instead we used `PreparedStatement` which will work with or without parameters), nor have we discussed the `CallableStatement` class for calling stored procedures in the database. With what you know now, though, you should be able to glean enough information from the Javadoc pages on these classes to do what you need, as they are similar to the `PreparedStatment` class.

`RowSets` extend `ResultSet` to include mechanisms for listening for data changes and for JavaBeans functionality. But again, Javadoc information or a comprehensive book on the subject would be a good next step, now that you have the basics in hand.

We haven't covered the `ResultSetMetaData` class, which provides a way for you to get the names of the columns that come back from the query. Again, check the Javadoc for details on its use.

We also haven't said anything about transactions, a key element in many database applications. We'll say more about that as we get into the enterprise-scale applications.

What we have covered should enable you to connect to a database, make real queries, and process the results. There are more advanced techniques to learn for special cases, but what we've covered here, accompanied by the Javadoc pages for `java.sql.*` classes, should be enough to create useful, real applications.

And of course there is always that other good teacher, experience. So go try some of what you now know.

15.9 RESOURCES

If you are going to use an Oracle database, we highly recommend *Java Oracle Database Development* by David Gallardo (ISBN 0130462187, Prentice Hall PTR), part of their Oracle Series. It includes several introductory chapters on database design, SQL, and even PL/SQL. It then has a much more thorough coverage of JDBC topics, with examples specific to Oracle, than we can cover in our limited space.

A JDBC implementation for MySQL is available at `http://www.mysql.com/downloads/api-jdbc.html`.

JDBC tutorial information, as well as lots of other JDBC information, is available from Sun at `http://www.java.sun.com/products/jdbc/`.

If you are working with a database other than mySQL or Oracle, you might want to check out `http://servlet.java.sun.com/products/jdbc/drivers` for a list of approximately two hundred JDBC implementations for various databases.

15.10 EXERCISES

1. Write a program that connects to a database and, for each of the tables specified on the command line, prints out the table name and the number of rows in that table.

2. Using what has been covered in this chapter, write a simple non-GUI SQL program, allowing the user to enter SQL statements, executing them, and showing the results (like a simplified SQL/Plus program). Can you provide some simple editing of the SQL? Or can you implement escaping to an external editor, for example, **vi**?

3. Make it possible for the user of your SQL program to set and change the connection URL—via an environment variable, command-line parameter, or even from within the program. Your SQL program will then be able to query a variety of databases from various vendors.

Part III

Developing
Graphical User Interfaces

Chapter 16

Getting in the Swing of Things: Designing a GUI for BudgetPro

Sometimes you gotta have a GUI; even we will admit that command lines only go so far. When it comes to simple interactions with casual users, a Graphical User Interface is a great step forward ... if it's done well. The toolkit for building such an interface with Java is called Swing. The original Java toolkit is AWT (A Windowing Toolkit), and is still in use, but much less attractive. We'll take a quick look at some major pieces of Swing, and show a complete example—a GUI for our budget application. After this example, you will have the tools you need to construct some real GUIs on your own.

16.1 WHAT YOU WILL LEARN

- The Swing GUI paradigm.
- A simple standalone Swing application.
- Some basic Swing objects—buttons and labels.
- A bit about layout managers.
- A more complex object—the `JTable`.

16.2 A Simple Swing Program

Let's take a look at a very simple (in its function, not in its composition) Swing program—a simple "Hello, world" that will appear in a window (Example 16.1).

Example 16.1 A simple Swing application

```
import java.awt.*;
import javax.swing.*;

public class
hw
{
  public static void
  main(String[] args)
  {
    //Create the top-level container
    JFrame frame = new JFrame();
    JLabel hi = new JLabel("Hello, world.");
    frame.getContentPane().add(hi, BorderLayout.CENTER);
    frame.setDefaultCloseOperation(JFrame.EXIT_ON_CLOSE);
    frame.pack(); // kicks the UI into action
    frame.setVisible(true);

  } // main
} // class hw
```

Now compile this program and run it from the command line like this:

```
$ javac hw.java
$ java hw
```

You should then see a small window appear, looking as in Figure 16.1.

Figure 16.1 "Hello, world" in a Swing window

While this may look like a lot of extra junk just to say "Hello, world," remember that a GUI is not just providing output in fancy windows, but also monitoring and responding to a wide variety of user inputs—a capability of which we make little or no use in this example. But you can see some of this extra capability—grab the lower left corner of the window frame and expand and resize the window.

16.3 STOMPIN' AT THE SAVOY, OR THE SWING PARADIGM

When we say "Swing," we generally mean the set of classes in the `javax.swing` package and its subpackages (such as `javax.swing.table`). The packages are libraries of code that give you predefined classes from which you can construct a GUI for your application. The programs you write will be written in Java, the syntax will look like Java, but there will be a lot of creation of classes, uses of interfaces, implementations of abstract classes, and a variety of method calls that all deal with these Swing classes.

So what's going on with all this stuff? What can we expect to do, see, write? In most applications that a programmer writes, it is the job of the programmer to design and write the code for the main execution path of the program. "Yes, every program has a beginning, middle, and an end" (with apologies to "Seymour and his frozen yoghurt stand," from Sesame Street). But it's not quite the same with Swing. While it does have to have a beginning, middle, and end (these are, after all, basic Von Neumann architecture machines), the big difference is that you do not have to write most of the control logic; it comes as part of the Swing set.

Look at it this way. With Swing, as with other GUI toolkits, you don't have to write code to deal with the mouse, keyboard shortcuts, or painting characters onto a graphical screen. You don't have to write all the code associated with a button press, because, while it seems simple enough, a button press is really a quite complex user interaction, involving repainting of the button's border, possibly its shading or changing its icon, coordinating that with the mouse presses and releases, and deciding whether the releases happen within or without the boundaries of the button—all this and more, just for a simple button press. All this has been done for you, and packaged up into Swing classes.

So what is left for you to do? You have to:

- Construct the various items that will appear on the screen (in one or more windows).
- Specify the location of these objects in the windows (layout).
- Provide snippets of code that are the *actions* associated with various *events* (events happen, for example, when a button is pressed or a mouse is clicked). These actions are the guts of the code that make your application behave how you want.

Remember, some behaviors are enforced by the GUI as part of standard "look and feel." Some things, like layout, are up to you to do well so long as you keep within the standard UI guidelines. And some is just specific to your application.

With that in mind, let's walk through the "Hello, world" example for a brief description of what each line does.

We begin with some `import` statements, to resolve references to both Swing and AWT classes. Swing is built on top of AWT, so some of the classes that you use will actually be AWT classes. The biggest difference this makes to you is in the `import` statements.

We then begin our class declaration, followed by the definition of the only method in this class, `main()`. Swing applications will typically have other methods, but for our simple example we only need this one.

Now comes some real Swing. The creation of a `JFrame` object is very important. In Swing we need to have containers to hold the objects that we want to display. The `JFrame` is a top-level container, one specifically meant to hold other objects, but also meant to be the first one of a containment hierarchy. (There are only three such top-level containers in Swing: `JFrame`, `JDialog`, and `JApplet`.)

Next we create a `JLabel`. It's a Swing object meant to hold small amounts of text. The text can be either constant or changing, but it's not user-editable (that would be a different kind of Swing object).

We add the label to the frame, so that when the window (the `JFrame`) appears, it will show our text inside.

The `setDefaultCloseAction()` does what you think. When you press the X in the upper right of the window frame (or wherever your window manager puts it), then not only will the window go away, but the program will stop running. (This is not the standard default value since `JFrame`s can contain other JFrames, and for most frames you wouldn't want closing the frame to quit the program.)

When we "pack" the frame, that's when the real magic happens. It kicks off the GUI activity on a separate thread, but also packs the various pieces that we've added to the frame, sizing them as best it can to fit into the frame, and sizing the frame to hold all the pieces. We see little of that with our example, which has only one label.

As an aside, pack() is inherited from awt.Window, which describes the "magic" thus:

> A component is displayable when it is connected to a native screen resource. A component is made displayable either when it is added to a displayable containment hierarchy or when its containment hierarchy is made displayable. A containment hierarchy is made displayable when its ancestor window is either packed or made visible.

So pack()-ing the frame connects it to a "native screen resource," which effectively gets the whole GUI thing going.

And now back to the business at hand.

Finally, the setVisible() call makes the window appear. Then the main() is done. In case you're wondering, go ahead and put a System.out.println() message after the setVisible(). It will be printed right away. The main() has ended; the GUI activity is happening on another thread.

16.4 SLOW, SLOW, QUICK-QUICK, SLOW: THE BASIC SWING OBJECTS

Let's take a quick look at a variety of Swing objects that you can use to build a GUI. Like any job of craftsmanship, it helps to be familiar with your tools. What you can build will be aided (and limited) by the tools with which you build, and by how familiar you are with them. Here are some pieces which can be put together to make Swing GUIs:

button
    A push button to trigger actions; can contain text and/or an icon.

radio button
    A group of buttons where only one value can be chosen at a time.

check box

A choice of one or many of a small set of options.

combo box

A pull-down list of choices.

menu

A special case of a pull-down choice, a part of the border of a main window.

label

A small amount of text, typically used to label other controls.

text field

A simple display and/or entry of one line of text; think "fill-in-the-blank" kinds of forms, password entry, and the like.

text area

A multiline display and/or entry of text, all in a single font format.

text pane

Same as text area, plus multifont support, image display, and more; really more like a word processor in a window.

list

Selection from a list.

table

A two-dimensional display—rows and columns of data.

tree

A display of hierarchically-structured data.

slider

A graphical control for selecting a value.

tool tip

A bit of text that appears over objects when the mouse hovers.

progress bar

A graphical display of progress.

color chooser

A control for selecting colors from a palette.

file chooser

A window for interacting with the filesystem—selecting a directory or a filename.

In addition to all these, there are various kinds of containers—objects whose job is to hold and display the other objects:

panel

A simple container.

split pane

A container divided into 2 separate parts.

scroll pane

A complex control with scrollbars, used to hold objects larger than the displayable area.

tabbed pane

A complex control with tab buttons to select different panels.

toolbar

A container for holding objects (usually buttons) which can attach to different sides of a window, or separate from a window and stand alone.

16.5 LAYOUT MANAGERS

Once you decided on all the graphical objects that you want to pack into your GUI, there is still one major hurdle—where to place all the objects. This can be one of the more challenging parts of GUI design because so many different screen sizes are available to the end user. How do you make your GUI look good to all (or most) of them?

Beginners often want to fix their components to absolute locations—for example, by sketching the GUI out on a piece of graph paper and then using those coordinates to fix the location. But with a windowing display, the user can grab a corner of the window and resize it. So, consider that piece of graph paper—what if it just got stretched to twice the size? Do you want all the controls to just get bigger? Buttons need not grow larger, but it would be nice to have additional space contributed to text areas. Consider a word processor: When you resize its window you only want the text area to expand, not the menus and icons.

Layout managers are meant to address the issues of component placement and sizing. Some are very simple, others are much more complex. All have their advantages and disadvantages. We'll use a few in our example to give you a taste of how they work.

16.6 BEYOND ARTHUR MURRAY: ACTIONS, LISTENERS, EVENTS

With any serious GUI comes a lot of advanced Java, especially constructs like anonymous inner classes. These are useful when we implement actions for our buttons and listeners for user selections.

Keep in mind that there are three different time frames that we're considering—compile time, construction time, and event time. Compile time is obvious, and the compiler will complain if it cannot access what it needs due to scoping problems. Construction time is when the program constructs the GUI objects for display in a window using the new and add() calls as well as layout managers. Event time is when the user presses a button or edits text in a field, or when other external events change data.

16.7 GETTING DOWN TO CASES: DESIGNING A GUI FOR BUDGETPRO

Our goal is a GUI for the BudgetPro application. We've already built a command-line version, so we want to have the same general functions but with the convenience and glamour of a GUI. The GUI will need to:

- Display the current account (name and dollars)
- Display the list of subaccounts that are part of this account
- Provide a way to create a new (sub)account
- Provide a way to move down into a subaccount
- Provide a way to move up to the parent account

From this brief list we devise a simple display with a heading that contains the current account and its dollar status, a table which lists the subaccounts, and, at the bottom of the window, some buttons—one for creating new accounts and one for viewing subaccounts. Of course, we'll also need a button to close or exit the application. In order to move back up from a subaccount, we'll add a button up in the header, an up-arrow, which will take us back to the parent account.

Now we could show you a hand-drawn sketch of what this UI might look like, from our rough description, but we'll cut to the chase and show you the finished product. This is the GUI for the BudgetPro application, in three stages. First comes the GUI when we first start up, with no subaccounts (Figure 16.2).

When the **New Subaccount** button is pressed, a dialog will appear to collect the information need to create the subaccount, namely the new account's name and the dollar amount to allocate to that account (Figure 16.3).

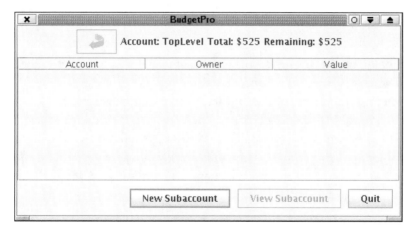

Figure 16.2 BudgetPro GUI: top account window

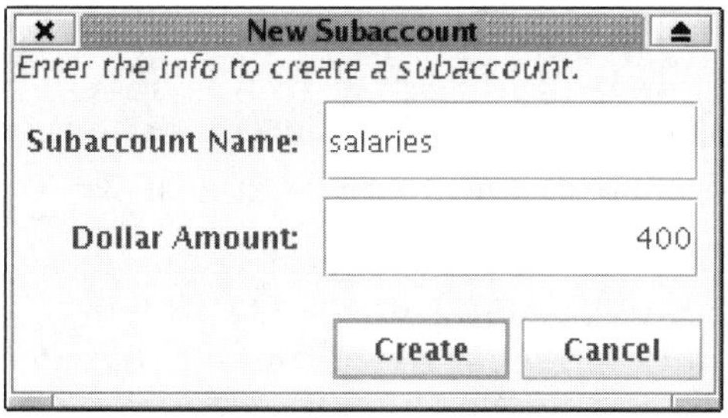

Figure 16.3 BudgetPro GUI: creating a (sub)account

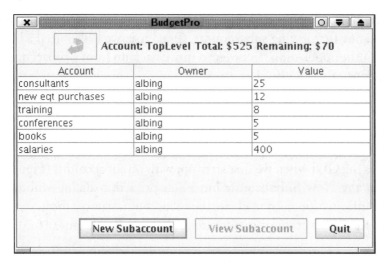

Figure 16.4 BudgetPro GUI: viewing subaccounts

Finally, Figure 16.4 is a look at the main GUI window for BudgetPro once several accounts have been constructed.

There is more to describe, but let's walk through the code that builds this GUI and explain the parts as we go. The complete listing is available online at http://www.javalinuxbook.com. We'll make reference to the line numbers of the listing in Appendix B, but sometimes we'll show excerpts of the code as we go. You might find it handy to have a listing of the code (on paper or in your browser) as you read the next several sections.

16.7.1 Overview

We divide the work between two GUI classes: one for the main window and the other for the dialog that will appear when we want to create a new subaccount. All of the other GUI elements will be either existing Swing classes or their extensions as anonymous inner classes in our code. (More on those later.)

So that means that we have four of our own classes that we're working with: two from the core of our application, Account and User, and two from the GUI side of things, BudgetPro and AcctDialog. This will be reflected in the package structure; we'll put BudgetPro and AcctDialog into the net.multitool.gui package. This will effect both the location of the source

(to be put into `net/multitool/gui`) and the `package` statement on line 1 of
`BudgetPro.java`:

```
1 package net.multitool.gui;
```

16.7.1.1 Instance Variables

Take a look at the picture of the BudgetPro GUI. Count the GUI objects that
we need: four buttons, three labels, and let's not forget the (empty at first) table
of subaccounts. These are declared in lines 23–31. (Ignore lines 22 and 32
for now, we'll cover them later. Line 34 declares our dialog—more on that
later, too.)

```
21   // gui components
22   private JFrame frame;    // needed by dialogs to root themselves
23   private JLabel nam;
24   private JLabel tot;
25   private JLabel val;
26   private JButton upton = new JButton(
                        new ImageIcon("net/multitool/gui/back.gif"));
27   private JButton creat = new JButton("new subaccount");
28   private JButton view  = new JButton("view subaccount");
29   private JButton clos  = new JButton("quit");
30
31   private JTable list;
32   private AbstractTableModel model;
33
34   private AcctDialog askem;   // make once, use often
```

16.7.1.2 Main

Skip all the way to the last method of the class, line 289 and following. It's the
`main()` which gets run when we run this class. If we focus on the major piece
involved in getting our GUI together, it's these lines:

```
JFrame frame = new JFrame("BudgetPro");
frame.getContentPane().add(status, ...);
frame.getContentPane().add(list, ...);
frame.getContentPane().add(buttons, ...);
```

We're leaving out lots of intermediate text to emphasize the "real" work.
We create a `JFrame`, the outermost window object. We add into it all the other

GUI pieces—the status line, the table list of accounts, and the buttons. The JFrame is a bit odd here, in that you have to add objects to its content pane; other container objects you can just add to directly. (We could have done the getContentPane() once, store the result in an intermediate variable, and do the adds to it, but the efficiency gain is unimportant here because we only need to do this once, to get the GUI started.)

When we've got it built, we pack the frame, and make it visible:

```
frame.pack();
frame.setVisible(true);
```

That's the basic core of what you need to do with any GUI: construct its pieces, add them to the frame, pack the frame, and make it visible. Now you're off and running. The rest is just details.

16.7.2 Creating Pieces

The three pieces that we create—the status, the list, and the buttons—will each package up their objects into an intermediate container, a JPanel, and return that container to main(). This not only serves to chunk the problem into fewer pieces (just three parts, not eight or more), but also helps with the formatting. Each piece can format its objects relative to each other. Then main() only has to lay out the three big pieces. So watch for each of the create...() methods to return a JPanel—a good approach when you build your GUIs, too.

The JPanels returned to main() are just Swing objects. They, like the buttons or labels (that we will see here shortly), just get added into other containers. For main(), that container is the JFrame, the main window. Any container will have a layout manager, the mechanism by which objects are placed in that container. For JFrame, the default is the BorderLayout manager. When you call the add() method on a container using a BorderLayout, you can specify (as a second parameter to the add() method) where the object being added will get placed. The constants defined for placing objects are NORTH, SOUTH, EAST, WEST, or CENTER—hence the "Border" of BorderLayout. There are also relative position values: PAGE_START, PAGE_END, LINE_START, and LINE_END which are just like north, south, west, and east, respectively, provided that the ComponentOrientation is set to LEFT_TO_RIGHT. (If you really want to know, check the Javadoc page for java.awt.BorderLayout.)

With a `BorderLayout`, if you put something in the NORTH section, it will appear across the top area of that container. If you resize the container (e.g., drag the window edges), it will take extra space and use it for horizontal, but not vertical, stretching. That is, the objects won't get bigger than they need to vertically, though they will stretch wider. The same is true for SOUTH, but the objects are at the bottom rather than top of the container. Putting something in EAST or WEST will move them to the left or right of the container. For these two areas, though, space when resizing a window is added to the objects vertically, but not horizontally. Putting an object in EAST or WEST will let it get taller, but not wider.

The CENTER area, the default location if you use the `add()` method with no second parameter, will use extra space both vertically and horizontally.

Adding more than one object into a region (e.g., NORTH) will result in only the last item added being displayed. For this reason, too, one often builds intermediate containers to hold several objects. Then the single container object is added to one of `BorderLayout`'s regions.

16.7.2.1 *Simple* `JLabels`

Let's look at the simplest of the three pieces that we create for our GUI—the top line of information indicating the status of the account. In lines 88–107 we create this portion of the GUI.

```
 88    private Component
 89    createStatus()
 90    {
 91      JPanel retval = new JPanel();    // default: flow layout
 92
 93      upton.addActionListener(upAction);
 94
 95      nam = new JLabel("Account: Name");
 96      tot = new JLabel("Total: $");
 97      val = new JLabel("Remaining: $");
 98
 99      retval.add(upton);
100      retval.add(nam);
101      retval.add(tot);
102      retval.add(val);
103
104      setStatus();
105
106      return retval;
107    } // createStatus
```

It consists of three parts, one for the account name, one for the total value of the account, and one for the remaining value. Each part will be represented by its own label, using a JLabel object. (We could have done the entire line in one label, but this gives us a few more objects to manipulate.) Since we want to group the labels together, we create a JPanel, which is a Swing container, to hold all these objects. We'll also add the JButton object (the variable named upton).

A JLabel is a simple Swing object. You can construct an empty one with new JLabel(); but you can also construct a label with a String as its initial value, which is more useful. You can later change a label's value with a call to its setText() method, as you see here from line 117:

```
117     tot.setText("Total: $"+current.getTotal());
```

16.7.2.2 FlowLayout

The JLabels are added to their JPanel, but with no position argument, unlike the JFrame and BorderLayout used in main(). JPanel has a different default layout manager: It uses FlowLayout. With it, added objects are placed side by side according to the window size. If the window is narrowed, they will simply flow onto the next line. (You won't see this behavior if you narrow the Budget-Pro window, but that's because the JPanel has been added to the JFrame's NORTH region, which means it's no longer just a FlowLayout that determines sizes.) FlowLayout is a layout that's easy to use, but doesn't give you much control; it was just fine for our purposes here.

16.7.2.3 BoxLayout

Another simple layout mechanism is the BoxLayout. It allows you to place the objects like stacking boxes—though they can be stacked horizontally as well as vertically. Look at line 224:

```
224     retval.setLayout(new BoxLayout(retval, BoxLayout.X_AXIS));
```

Here we are creating a BoxLayout object and associating it with our JFrame to manage its objects. When we create a BoxLayout we can tell it that we want to stack our objects horizontally (using either X_AXIS or LINE_AXIS) or vertically (using either Y_AXIS or PAGE_AXIS). Note that the BoxLayout object needs to be told about (i.e., given a reference to) the container (here, `retval`, a `JPanel`) whose objects it will manage, but that the container also needs to be told (via `setLayout()`) about the `BoxLayout` object. A bit confusing, perhaps.

Another handy part of `BoxLayout` is the uses of *rigid areas*, invisible objects that do nothing except putting some space between objects. These rigid areas are defined in pixels; for our GUI we create them with no height and a width of ten pixels. They are held together using "horizontal glue" (see line 226)

```
226        retval.add(Box.createHorizontalGlue());
```

so that if the window is stretched, the extra space doesn't get added between the buttons, but only to the "glue" component, which absorbs all extra space. This keeps all the buttons to the right hand side of the window.

16.7.2.4 JButton*s*

The method named `createButtons()` actually packs up the buttons into a `JPanel` to return to the caller. It begins like this:

```
218    private Component
219    createButtons(JRootPane root)
220    {
221      JPanel retval = new JPanel();    // default: flow layout
222
223      //Lay out the buttons from left to right.
224      retval.setLayout(new BoxLayout(retval, BoxLayout.X_AXIS));
225      retval.setBorder
                   (BorderFactory.createEmptyBorder(10, 10, 10, 10));
226      retval.add(Box.createHorizontalGlue());
227      retval.add(creat);
228      retval.add(Box.createRigidArea(new Dimension(10, 0)));
229      retval.add(view);
230      retval.add(Box.createRigidArea(new Dimension(10, 0)));
231      retval.add(clos);
```

The buttons themselves were created at the beginning of this class, in lines 27–29, thus:

```
27    private JButton creat = new JButton("New Subaccount");
28    private JButton view  = new JButton("View Subaccount");
29    private JButton clos  = new JButton("Quit");
```

Note that the constructor takes a `String` argument—that's the text that will appear in the button. A button may also have an icon (image) in it (more on that in just a bit). These buttons, as created, don't do anything. When clicked on by the user, they will behave as real buttons (depress, then release), but no action will occur. Yet.

16.7.2.5 Actions for Buttons

We need to attach an action to each button, which is little more than a special class to hold the code that you want to be run when the button is pressed. We can define the action as an anonymous inner class, so that the code is right there, inline with the rest of our code. Then we just attach that code to the button. Here is an example of that for our close button (the one labeled **Quit**):

```
234     ActionListener closAction = new ActionListener()
235     {
236       public void
237       actionPerformed(ActionEvent e)
238       {
239           System.exit(0);
240       }
241     } ;
```

`ActionListener` is an interface—a very simple interface that defines just one method, `actionPerformed()`. You can take any class, have it extend `ActionListener`, and then define an `actionPerformed()` method for it. That class can then serve as the action for a button. Here we just create an in-line class that does nothing but the `actionPerformed()` method, and a pretty simple one at that. It simply exits.

We could define the action elsewhere, and then just use the reference to the action. If we had put the declaration of `closAction` at a higher lexical scope (out at the beginning of the class definition, for example) then other UI elements could also use this action. Of course, if you're going to share your action between GUI elements, be sure that you write the code to be reentrant.

Lines 244–267 (still within the `createButtons()` method) define the action for the button labeled **New Subaccount**. Line 268 connects it to the button. Don't pay attention to the specifics of this action just yet. We'll discuss it in detail below, once we know more about the other objects. Here is how that action is built:

```
244     ActionListener creatAction = new ActionListener()
245     {
246       public void
247       actionPerformed(ActionEvent e)
248       {
249         Account child;
250         // get the info via a Dialog (of sorts)
251         if (askem == null) {
252             askem = new AcctDialog(frame, "New Subaccount");
253         } else {
254             askem.clear();
255             askem.setVisible(true);
256         }
257         String subName = askem.getName();
258         String subAmnt = askem.getAmnt();
259
260         // if empty, assume the operation was cancelled, else:
261         if ((subName != null) && (subName.length() > 0)) {
262             child = current.createSub(subName, subAmnt);
263             setStatus();
264             model.fireTableDataChanged(); // notify the table
265         }
266       }
267     };
268     creat.addActionListener(creatAction);
```

We defined the action for the **View Subaccount** button (as we said you could) elsewhere in the program. Its action is defined in lines 54–75. Then on line 271 we connect the action to the button. (We'll get back to this button's action, too, once we've discussed the JTable.) But after we've attached the action, we also disable the button (line 273).

```
270     // function is to get selection from table and cd there
271     view.addActionListener(cdAction);
272     // but it starts off disabled, since there is no data yet
273     view.setEnabled(false);
```

In Swing, a button is either enabled or disabled. Enabled buttons are the active ones on which you can click. Disabled buttons are grayed out and not responsive to clicks. We can make a button either active or inactive with a method on the button called setEnabled() whose argument is a boolean—true to enable the button, false to disable it. For example:

```
203            if (lsm.isSelectionEmpty()) {
204                view.setEnabled(false);
205            } else {
206                view.setEnabled(true);
207            }
```

However, we start with the **View Subaccount** button disabled until the user has created and selected some subaccounts worth viewing.

16.7.2.6 *The* createStatus() *Revisited*

There is one other button on the BudgetPro application, one that is not located in this bottom panel of buttons. It's the one on the status line. It, too, starts up disabled or grayed out—but it has an image in it. Any JButton can contain either text or an image, or both, but we've chosen to do just one or the other in our application. We declare it like any other button:

```
private JButton upton;
```

but for its initialization we use a variation of the JButton constructor, one that takes an ImageIcon object as its parameter:

```
upton = new JButton(new ImageIcon("net/multitool/gui/back.gif"));
```

Why do we do that all in one line? When you read it, you can certainly think of it as two steps:

```
ImageIcon backup = new ImageIcon("net/multitool/gui/back.gif");
upton = new JButton(backup);
```

but we have no other need for the image, so we don't need to keep a reference for it in a variable. Some programmers prefer to write it out in two simple steps, as it is easier to read and perhaps to maintain. We've chosen to put it all in the JButton's constructor to show that we're making no other use of the image. Which style do you prefer?

And what about a button that needs to contain both text and an image? There is a constructor that takes both a String and an ImageIcon. Then you can set certain attributes of the JButton to position the text relative to the image. Look in the Javadoc of JButton for the methods setVerticalTextPosition() and setHorizontalTextPosition().

16.7.2.7 `JTable`*: The Workhorse of Data Display*

Look again at our GUI application. In its center you see the table object:

Account	Owner	Value
consultants	albing	25
new eqt purchases	albing	12
training	albing	8
conferences	albing	5
books	albing	5
salaries	albing	400

This is a `JTable`. A simple way to create a `JTable` is by passing in two arrays to the constructor—first, a two-dimensional array of data objects, and second, a one-dimensional array of column names. Notice that we said data objects; you need to use `Integer` objects, not simple `int` types, and `Doubles` instead of `doubles`. This allows the constructor to take any `Object` type and display it in the table via the object's `toString()` method.

While this form of a table is simple to use, it usually isn't enough for all the various things you'll want to do with a table. Let's look at the "industrial strength" table initialization. For that, we need to talk about a table model.

16.7.2.8 Table Model

If you've ever taken an object-oriented design class, they've probably talked about the Model/View/Controller design pattern. (If you haven't taken such a class, at least read a good book or two on the subject; it will improve your Java programming skills.) A simpler version of this pattern is the View/Model pattern. What it describes is separating the core of the data from the frill of its presentation—*what* you want to display versus *how* you want to display it. The Model is the underlying data; the View is one particular way to show that data.

This View versus Model distinction is used to great effect with `JTable` and `TableModel` objects in Swing. What you need to do is create a `TableModel`, then give that `TableModel` to the `JTable` via the `JTable`'s constructor. The `TableModel` will give you all sorts of control over your data—how, where, and when to get or update it. The `JTable` will display it and let you rearrange or resize the columns.

Rather than implement a complete `TableModel` from scratch, Swing gives us a helping hand with its `AbstractTableModel` class. `AbstractTableModel` is a partially implemented class which handles most of the grundy details—it has most of the `Table` interface implemented. You only need to implement three methods:

```
public int getRowCount();
public int getColumnCount();
public Object getValueAt(int row, int column);
```

Together, these three methods give a pretty good definition of a table: how many rows it has, how many columns it has, and how to access the value at any (row, column) location. Notice, too, that the `getValueAt()` returns an `Object`, so you can't return an `int` or `float` or `double`. You can only return an `Integer`, `Double`, and so on. Another option is to return a `String` value of the number that you want to display.

Let's take a look at how the `AbstractTableModel` was implemented in the BudgetPro application. We begin at line 135, inside the `createList()` method. The `createList()` method is going to build the central portion of our GUI, the table display. In order to do that, it creates an `AbstractTableModel` to give to the `JTable` it creates on line 193. The `AbstractTableModel` is defined inline as an anonymous inner class that implicitly extends `AbstractTableModel`. This section of code is listed in Example 16.2; follow along as we discuss it further.

(An aside: We could also have defined this inner class elsewhere in the class file, as a class which explicitly extends `AbstractTableModel`. However, as with the icon we used in the `JButton` example, we have no further need of the object other than this single use, so we didn't bother to create it as a standalone entity. Both ways work, and are more a matter of preference or of how familiar you are with the inline syntax.

In our implementation of the `AbstractTableModel`, we are going to include column headings, so we begin with a definition of `Strings` for our column headings (line 137). Then the `getColumnCount()` method, one of the three methods that we need to implement in this class, is simply a matter of returning the size of this array (line 159). Lines 139–142 override the `getColumnName()` method, which isn't one of the three that we *must* implement. But if we don't, the default behavior from `AbstractTableModel` will return nulls, so we'd get no column headings. Instead, we use the column number as an index to our array of column names.

The `getRowCount()` method is almost as simple (lines 144–155). The number of rows that this table should display for any account is the

Example 16.2 Defining our `AbstractTableModel`

```
130    private Component
131    createList()
132    {
133      JScrollPane retval;
134
135      model = new AbstractTableModel()
136        {
137          private String [] columnNames = {"Account", "Owner", "Value"};
138
139          public String
140          getColumnName(int col) {
141            return columnNames[col];
142          } // getColumnName
143
144          public int
145          getRowCount()
146          {
147            int retval;
148
149            if (current != null) {
150                retval = current.size();
151            } else {
152                retval = 1;      // testing only
153            }
154
155            return retval;
156
157          } // getRowCount
158
159          public int getColumnCount() { return columnNames.length; }
160
161          public Object
162          getValueAt(int row, int col) {
163            Object retval = null;
164            Account aa = null;
165            // return "---";   // rowData[row][col];
166            int count = 0;
167            for (Iterator itr=current.getAllSubs(); itr.hasNext(); )
168            {
169              count++;
170              aa = (Account) itr.next();
171              if (count > row) { break; }
172            } // next
```

```
173            switch (col) {
174            case 0:
175                    retval = aa.getName();
176                    break;
177            case 1:
178                    retval = aa.getOwner();
179                    break;
180            case 2:
181                    retval = aa.getTotal();
182                    break;
183            } // endswitch
184            return retval;
185          } // getValueAt
186
187        public boolean
188        isCellEditable(int row, int col)
189        {
190          return false;
191        } // isCellEditable
192      };
193    list = new JTable(model);
194    list.setSelectionMode(ListSelectionModel.SINGLE_SELECTION);
195
196    list.getSelectionModel().addListSelectionListener(
197        new ListSelectionListener()
198        {
199          public void
200          valueChanged(ListSelectionEvent e)
201          {
202            ListSelectionModel lsm = (ListSelectionModel)e.getSource();
203            if (lsm.isSelectionEmpty()) {
204                view.setEnabled(false);
205            } else {
206                view.setEnabled(true);
207            }
208          } // valueChanged
209        }
210    );
211
212    retval = new JScrollPane(list);
213
214    return retval;
215
216  } // createList
```

number of subaccounts defined for the account. Since we're defining our `AbstractTableModel` as an inner class, we have access to the data in the outer (`BudgetPro`) class. We use the instance variable `current`, which refers to whichever account we're currently working with. A quick check of the `Account` class shows that an `Account` object can return the number of subaccounts (or "children") via its `size()` method. So for our `getRowCount()` method we return `current.size()`—provided that `current` is not `null`. If it is `null`, we return `1` rather than `0`, so that the table itself shows up and the headings appear. (But it also means that `getValueAt()` has to deal with requests for data from the first row when data may not exist.)

The core of what makes our data appear is the `getValueAt()` method, lines 161–185. Since each row represents a subaccount of the current account, we'll just iterate through `current`'s list of subaccounts until we reach the row-th subaccount; for example, to get the third row we iterate over this list of subaccounts until we get to the third one returned by the iterator's `next()` method. This is a bit "brute force," to keep marching over the list of accounts, but for our small data size it's not bad. (Another approach would be to change the `Account` class to provide a method to return the *n*-th subaccount. Then it can use its internal knowledge of the way it stores subaccounts to provide a more efficient access. Alternately, our extended `AbstractTableModel` could iterate over the list once and store the subaccounts in an array, for quicker access later; the trick here is that the array needs to be refreshed every time the account changes—so we took the simple approach.)

Once we have a row selected, we use the `switch/case` construct to choose the correct data for the requested column. (See the listing in Example 16.2, lines 173–183.)

The return value for `getValueAt()` is an `Object`. Here's one situation where that is very useful. Refer to the definition of the `Account` object and you'll see that `getName()` returns a `String`, but `getOwner()` returns a `User` and `getTotal()` returns an `SAMoney` object. Since `retval` is the most generic type, `Object`, it can handle all three results.

But how does `JTable` deal with these odd types? How can it display an `SAMoney` object when it doesn't know what one is? There is both a simple and a complicated answer to that question; we'll try to give you both.

16.7.2.9 *Renderers*

The simple answer is that `JTable`, to display the data returned by `getValueAt()`, will call the `toString()` method on the object. As long as we return an object which has a `toString()`, we're fine. Both `User` and `SAMoney` do have such a method, so they fit fine here.

The more complex answer has to do with why `JTable` calls the `toString()` method at all. The `JTable` uses, behind the scenes, a complex table cell display mechanism, called a *table cell renderer*. A renderer is an object that displays data in a certain way. Each table cell renderer returns a GUI component, and if you don't want to use the default renderer, you can define your own table cell renderer for your table. This allows you to display almost anything you can imagine inside a table's cell. The renderer acts as a template for those cells and will be called upon with the result of the `getValueAt()`, along with a few more parameters, so that it can build and display the resulting cell.

Let's revisit our simple explanation above, in light of the concept of a renderer. The default cell renderer for a `JTable` uses just a `JLabel`. When called upon, the default cell renderer is given the object returned by `getValueAt()` and the renderer fills its `JLabel` by calling its `setText()` method, passing in the result of `toString()` on the given object. That's how `toString()` got called on all our results. You can explicitly set a different renderer using the `setDefaultRenderer()` method on `JTable`.

In the Javadoc for Swing table objects we find this interface:

```
public Component
getTableCellRendererComponent(JTable table,
                              Object value,
                              boolean isSelected,
                              boolean hasFocus,
                              int row,
                              int column)
```

This tells us that if we want to write a class which can act as a renderer, it needs to implement this method. The method will be called with the value returned by `getValueAt()`, but the `row` and `column` (and `table`) will be repeated here in case your renderer cares. For example, having the `row` and `column` would allow you to create a table with the third column of the table in green—your method could check the column number, and if it is 2 (columns are numbered 0, 1, 2, . . .) set the background color to green for the `Component` that you would return.

```
JLabel retval = new JLabel();
// ...
if (row == 2) {
    retval.setBackground(Color.GREEN);
} else {
    retval.setBackground(Color.WHITE);
}
return retval;
```

The full implementation of a renderer can also take into account whether or not the cell is selected and/or has focus. This has to do with enabling mouse clicks to select either that particular cell or the row or column containing that cell. You will likely want to render the cell differently (with a darker color, perhaps) to show that it has been selected. Whatever the renderer, you set up and then return a GUI component whose attributes (font, color, size, and so on) are used to display that cell.

We hope you get the idea—there is a lot more to renderers than we will cover here. The Java Tutorial covers them more, and the Javadoc pages have some introduction, too.

Similar to renderers are editors. When a user clicks in a table cell, the table may allow him or her to edit its contents. A cell editor is needed to do that, and then your program needs to do something with the value that was entered. For our BudgetPro example we avoid this complexity by disallowing the user to enter anything into the table—our table is for display only. We do this on lines 187–191 by overriding the method `isCellEditable()` to always return `false`:

```
187        public boolean
188        isCellEditable(int row, int col)
189        {
190          return false;
191        } // is CellEditable
```

Notice that the method is passed the `row` and `column` means that you could make some cells editable and some not.

16.7.2.10 *Selection Listeners*

Let's look at the last part of the table that we implement for BudgetPro:

```
194    list.setSelectionMode(ListSelectionModel.SINGLE_SELECTION);
```

This call tells our table (list) that we want to allow the user to select only a single row or column at a time. Valid options are:

```
ListSelectionModel.SINGLE_SELECTION
ListSelectionModel.SINGLE_INTERVAL_SELECTION
ListSelectionModel.MULTIPLE_INTERVAL_SELECTION
```

The latter two allow the user to select more than one row at a time; multiple intervals mean that the selected rows can be discontinuous. (Think "Shift+click" versus "Control+click" as the user action that selects these.)

So what will our program do, once the user has made a selection? The selected row is a subaccount of the current account and we will allow the user to display that account and its subaccount, if any. Think of it as "changing directory" into that account, to look at or change its status.

For a table to take an action when a selection is made you need another listener called a *selection listener*. We wrote:

```
196    list.getSelectionModel().addListSelectionListener(
197      new ListSelectionListener()
198      {
199        public void
200        valueChanged(ListSelectionEvent e)
201        {
202          ListSelectionModel lsm =
                              (ListSelectionModel)e.getSource();
203          if (lsm.isSelectionEmpty()) {
204              view.setEnabled(false);
205          } else {
206              view.setEnabled(true);
207          }
208        } // valueChanged
209      }
210    );
```

Similar to how a table has a table model behind it, it also has a selection model behind it. We don't need to reimplement an entire selection model; we just retrieve the default one from our table (list.getSelectionModel()) and add a listener to it so that it will notify us when something has changed.

The javax.swing.event.ListSelectionListener is an interface with only one method, so it's easy to extend and override it in place, as we do, beginning at line 197. When called, it will be handed an event (e) and we take the source of that event and coerce it to a ListSelectionModel. That's safe to

do here because it can't be any other type of event—or we wouldn't have been
called. All we're doing with it is checking to see if the user just selected or dese-
lected something. The only action we take is to enable or disable the view
button.

Deep inside the cdaction object is a line that does the real action that
we're after with our selection. It says:

```
61        int row = list.getSelectedRow();
```

This shows that a JTable (list) has a method, getSelectedRow(), which
will return the row number of the row that the user has selected (that is,
clicked on). This is all part of the action listener (defined on lines 54–75 of
BudgetPro) for the **View Subaccount** button.

```
54   private ActionListener cdAction = new ActionListener()
55   {
56     public void
57     actionPerformed(ActionEvent e)
58     {
59       // this is the action for VIEW subdirectory;
60       // a "cd" into the subaccount.
61       int row = list.getSelectedRow();
62       // System.out.println("Row="+row); // DEBUG; TODO: REMOVE
63       if (row > -1) {                // only if a row was selected
64         String subname = (String) model.getValueAt(row, 0);
                                                     // name column
65         Account next = current.getSub(subname);
66         if (next != null) {
67           current = next;
68           // System.out.println("cd to:"+current.getName());
69           setStatus();
70           // notify the table, too
71           model.fireTableDataChanged();
72         } // TODO: else infodialog or Beep.
73       }
74     }
75   } ;
```

With the row number in hand, the actionPerformed() method can
then use the row number to look up the account name. Since the account name
is in the first column (numbered 0) of our table, we call getValueAt(row, 0)
to get that name. Then we give the name to the current account to look up the
subaccount (line 65).

As long as this returned `Account` is not null (line 66), we can make it the current account (line 67). At that point the display needs to be updated, so we: 1) call our own `setStatus()` method, to update the upper portion of our GUI, and 2) tell the table that its data has changed (line 71).

16.7.2.11 *Ready, aim, fire!*

A word about the `fire...()` methods. They are not part of the `TableModel` interface definition. Rather, they are part of the `AbstractTableModel` class. When a Java class is declared abstract it means that some methods need to be implemented by those classes that use (extend) this class. An abstract class can still have lots of intact, completely implemented methods, and that is the case with `AbstractTableModel`.

The `TableModel` interface defines methods for adding and removing listeners. Any implementation of the `TableModel` interface needs to support these, and to notify any listeners when a change occurs. Such listeners will receive a call to their `tableChanged()` method when such a change occurs. But it doesn't tell us how such notification is triggered. Moreover, the change event, when received by the listener, needs to define the extent of the change—just a single cell? a whole row? a column? all columns? and so on.

The `AbstractTableModel` provides some methods for us to call when a change in the data has occurred, methods that will then notify all the registered listeners (Table 16.1). Moreover, it has different methods depending on the extent of the change, so that the `TableModelEvent`, sent to all `TableModelListeners`, can be constructed with the appropriate definition of what has changed.

We used (line 71) the `fireTableDataChanged()` since the content of the table will change with a change of accounts, but the structure remains the same. It is also a handy all-purpose method for you to use if you'd rather not add the complexity of determining which rows have changed to your code.

Finally, remember that anyone who uses (extends) `AbstractTableModel`, including the `DefaultTableModel` class, gets these methods for their use.

There are several other interactions that are supported by `JTables`, ones that don't require you to do anything to provide them to your application's end user. When running the BudgetPro GUI, did you try to drag the column headings? You can also rearrange and resize columns. This is the default behavior for `JTables`. You can turn it off, however, if you want your columns to be fixed:

Table 16.1 `AbstractTableModel` methods for data change notification

Method	When to use
`fireTableCellUpdated(int row, int col)`	Use when only a single cell has changed.
`fireTableRowsUpdated(int first, int last)`	Use when the given range of rows (inclusive) have changed.
`fireTableRowsDeleted(int first, int last)`	Use when the given range of rows (inclusive) have been deleted.
`fireTableRowsInserted(int first, int last)`	Use when the given range of rows (inclusive) have been inserted.
`fireTableDataChanged()`	Use when any/all of the row data have changed, including the number of rows; columns have not changed.
`fireTableStructureChanged()`	Use when the columns have changed—that is, when the names, number, or types of columns have changed.
`fireTableChanged(TableModelEvent e)`	An all purpose method, where you have to define the change in the `TableModelEvent` object.

```
table.getTableHeader().setResizingAllowed(false);
table.getTableHeader().setReorderingAllowed(false);
```

The call is not made on the table directly, but rather on its header. We get the `JTableHeader` object with the call to `getTableHeader()`. There is much more that could be said about `JTableHeader` objects, but we will leave that "as an exercise for the reader"; we've got to draw the line somewhere.

16.7.2.12 Scrolling

One last thing to mention about the `createList()` method is how we deal with tables that are larger than the viewing area. This is typically done with a *scroll pane*, a GUI element familiar to anyone who has used a word processing program. Such scrolling is accomplished in Swing by putting the potentially big object, such as our table, into a `JScrollPane` container.

Don't think of it as adding scrollbars to the table. Rather, we're putting the table into a container that has scrollbars, and this container is smart enough to retrieve and display the table's header separately from the table (thus, the table's data scrolls but the header stays put).

Here, in one step, we create the `JScrollPane` object and initialize it with the `JTable` that we want to be scrolled over.

```
212       retval = new JScrollPane(list);
```

Think of the `JScrollPane` as a window with scrollbars through which we can view the `JTable`. It has the convenient side effect of taking care of the table's heading for us. Without the scroll pane (e.g., if we just put the `JTable` in a `JPanel`) we'd get only the data and no heading, unless we also did a lot of extra work using other objects and method calls.

It is possible to set the `JScrollPane` to show horizontal as well as vertical scrollbars. Those scrollbars can be made to be always or never visible, or visible only as needed. Setting a scrollbar to "never visible" effectively turns off any scrolling in that direction. Use the `setHorizontalScrollBarPolicy()` and `setVerticalScrollBarPolicy()` methods to set the value to one of:

```
JScrollPane.HORIZONTAL_SCROLLBAR_AS_NEEDED
JScrollPane.HORIZONTAL_SCROLLBAR_NEVER
JScrollPane.HORIZONTAL_SCROLLBAR_ALWAYS
```

Scroll panes can scroll over any GUI element—that is, any `Component` object, not just tables. For more information on scroll panes, be sure to refer to the Javadoc pages.

16.7.2.13 *Dialogs*

We have covered most of the code in the main GUI functionality—the way it initially creates its parts and lays them out for display. We have examined the `JTable` in some considerable detail and looked at a few actions associated with buttons. Now we need to get to the user interaction that allows us to create a new account.

Lines 244–268 of BudgetPro are the action that gets attached to the button for creating a new subaccount.

```
244        ActionListener creatAction = new ActionListener()
245        {
246          public void
247          actionPerformed(ActionEvent e)
248          {
249            Account child;
250            // get the info via a Dialog (of sorts)
251            if (askem == null) {
252                askem = new AcctDialog(frame, "New Subaccount");
253            } else {
254                askem.clear();
255                askem.setVisible(true);
256            }
257            String subName = askem.getName();
258            String subAmnt = askem.getAmnt();
259
260            // if empty, assume the operation was cancelled, else:
261            if ((subName != null) && (subName.length() > 0)) {
262                child = current.createSub(subName, subAmnt);
263                setStatus();
264                model.fireTableDataChanged(); // notify the table
265            }
266          }
267        };
268        creat.addActionListener(creatAction);
```

Looking at the constructor for an `Account`, we see that we need three things: a `User` object (who will own the subaccount), a name for the new subaccount, and the dollars to be allocated to this subaccount. To keep our example simpler, we will always use the current user as the `User` for creating the new `Account`. That means we only need some way to get the name and dollar amount.

In the GUI world, this sort of information is typically provided in a dialog box, a window that has blanks to be filled in (Figure 16.5). Then, when the dialog is closed, we can ask that dialog for the values that the user provided.

Swing has some ready-to-use dialogs for warnings or for simple single value inputs. Since we want to get two pieces of data, we need to create our own dialog and display it.

What may seem strange about the `createAction()` is that we only create the dialog once (line 252), when the reference to it (`askem`) is null (line 251). Thereafter, we simply clear out the previous values (line 254) and make the dialog visible again (line 255). That is all that it takes to use the dialog more

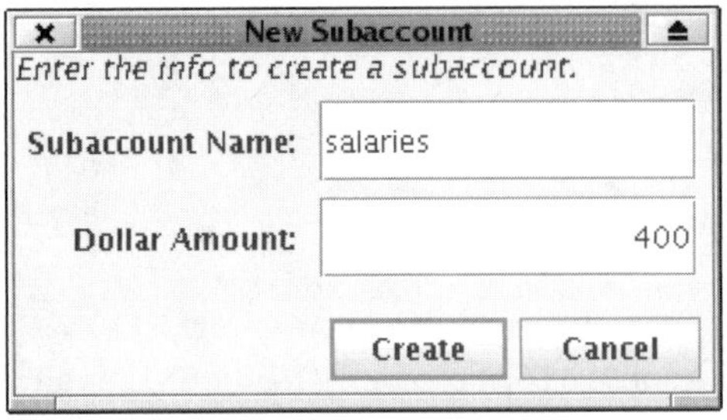

Figure 16.5 Dialog for creating a new subaccount

than once. We could throw away the dialog (or let it get garbage-collected) by declaring it internal to the `actionPerformed()` method. Then on each button press the dialog would need to be recreated. Well, it's slower to do it that way, and for a button click we want quick response—so we keep it around from one use to the next. When the user closes the dialog, all that really does is makes it invisible; to reuse it, we make it visible again.

Notice, too, that in either case—creating the dialog or making it visible—control does not return to our method until the user has dismissed the dialog. That's because it's a *modal* dialog, one that allows no other interaction with the application until the user has responded to this dialog.

The dialog is dismissed (finished, ended, put away) simply by making it no longer visible. For example:

```
73          dialog.setVisible(false);   // go away
```

New to our application, in `AcctDialog`, is the `JTextField`. On lines 22 and 23 we declare two of them, one for the account name and the other for the amount.

```
22    nameField = new JTextField(25);
23    amntField = new JTextField(9);
```

The size that we pass in to the constructor is the number of characters; it sets a maximum for that field, but also gives a clue to some layout managers as to how big the field needs to be.

Speaking of layout managers, we use a few here, including a `BoxLayout`, to format the buttons relative to each other; a `BorderLayout`, to hold the overall dialog; and a newer layout manager, the `SpringLayout`, which is new as of Java 1.4. The Swing Tutorial provides a handy utility class for dealing with `SpringLayouts`, and we make use of it to format the labels and text fields relative to each other.

Similar to a `JTextField` is a `JPasswordField`. It behaves just like a `JTextField` but instead of showing the characters that the user types it shows, by default, an asterisk for each character typed, thereby hiding the password from passers-by. The character that is displayed can be changed to other than the asterisk—see the Javadoc page.

We do something new with our `JLabel` in `AcctDialog`, too. We mess with its font:

```
44      Font font = label.getFont();
45      label.setFont(label.getFont().deriveFont(font.PLAIN, 14.0f));
```

This gets the font from the label, however it might have been set, then creates a new value for the font, keeping whatever font family it might have been, but making it 14 pt plain (not italic, not bold).

We also put HTML text in the `JLabel`:

```
40      JLabel label = new JLabel("<html><p align=left><i>"
41                  + "Enter the info to create a subaccount.<br>"
42                  + "</i>");
```

All but the oldest versions of Swing will display the HTML text as it would be formatted by a browser. Here, we make the text *italic* by means of the (now deprecated) `<i>` tag, thereby undoing the effort to make it plain in lines 44 and 45.

One of the arguments to the dialog's constructor is the `JFrame` inside which the dialog will appear. Lines 102 and 103 round out this picture, setting the size of the dialog and anchoring its position relative to the parent frame. The last step for the constructor is to make the dialog visible, thereby passing control to it.

16.8 REVIEW

When programming in Swing, we create the GUI objects and then let Swing do the work of managing all the interactions. We created:

- Containers to hold GUI objects, such as `JFrame` for our outermost window, `JPanel` for an assortment of objects, and `JScrollPane` for viewing larger objects through a scrollable window.

- Labels (`JLabel` class) to hold either a short bit of text, or an image, or both; it can even take snippets of HTML, for fancier formatting and coloring of text.

- Buttons (`JButton` class) to which we attached actions—the code fragments that get called when the buttons get pushed; a button could have text and/or an image displayed in it.

- Actions—whether for buttons or selections (or other triggers yet to be discussed), an action is the code that runs when the event (e.g., button press) occurs.

- Text fields (`JTextField` class) to take small amounts of user input; our application didn't need the other types of text fields (`JTextArea` and `JTextPane`) useful for much more extensive user input.

- A `JTable` instance and its associated `TableModel`, `SelectionModel`, and `TableCellRenderer` which provide tremendous flexibility and control over table behavior and contents.

- A `JDialog` instance with custom content, to allow for multiple user inputs; the dialog comes and goes with its visibility; since it's a modal dialog, when it is visible, it "hogs" all the user interactions; it is possible to make nonmodal dialogs, but our application didn't need to.

- `LayoutManagers` for our `JFrame` and `JPanels`, used to place objects within a container with various algorithms for placement and expansion.

16.9 WHAT YOU STILL DON'T KNOW

One could spend a career learning the vagaries of layout managers, especially the way they interact (e.g., a `BoxLayout` inside the various regions of a `BorderLayout`). There is still an art to getting all the interactions right; it's often quickest to prototype the layout before you get too committed to a particular layout. Also, putting objects into containers can help you subdivide the layout problem into more manageable pieces. You can even go so far as to write your own `LayoutManager`, a topic we do not cover in this book.

The information that we display in the `JTable` in our example is hierarchical. Swing provides a `JTree` object for displaying such information. Like a filesystem tree familiar to many PC users, the JTree allows you to view multiple levels at once and to open and close nodes, exposing or hiding their subtrees. It would make more sense to use the JTree in our example, but then we wouldn't have been able to describe all the ins and outs of the JTable, a class that is so useful in so many applications.

There are many more Swing classes that we haven't discussed, though many will behave similarly to those you have seen here. There are topics that we have avoided—for example, we haven't talked about sorting JTables by clicking on the column headings, or about TableColumnModels which add another layer to JTables. Some of what you would need to know in order to use these Swing classes you can glean from the Javadoc pages. The information there should make more sense now, based on your experience with the various Swing mechanisms that you've seen in these pages. For some other Swing topics you will have to search farther, and there are plenty of books on the topic—the classic one, the *The JFC Swing Tutorial* from Sun, being over 900 pages long. Is it any wonder that we didn't cover it all in this chapter?

16.10   RESOURCES

- *The JFC Swing Tutorial: A Guide to Constructing GUIs* by Kathy Walrath and Mary Campione, Addison-Wesley, also available online at `http://java.sun.com/docs/books/tutorial/uiswing/index.html`.

- Our favorite bookmark within the Swing tutorial, the visual index of the various Swing components, is at `http://java.sun.com/docs/books/tutorial/uiswing/components/components.html`.

- If you want a better understanding of layout managers, we recommend this tutorial by Jan Newmarch at Monash University in Australia: `http://pandonia.canberra.edu.au/java/xadvisor/geometry/geometry.html`. Don't let the mention of AWT scare you away. Almost all of the layout managers (except BoxLayout and SpringLayout) are actually from AWT, and they all apply to Swing.

16.11   EXERCISES

1. Use different layout managers to create of the status area of the BudgetPro main window, laying out the status information differently. Make the

button and account name information left-justified, and stack the **Total** and **Remaining** labels vertically on top of each other. Do you always need to create new intermediate containers? Can you do it just with `GridBagLayout`?

2. Modify the BudgetPro program so that it displays a pop-up dialog when you try to create a subaccount with more money than is available to that account.

3. Modify the dialog used for creating subaccounts, so that it also prompts for the owner's name. This can get more complicated if you want to allow only valid user names. Instead, let any name be entered and create a `User` object for it.

4. Modify the BudgetPro program and associated classes to allow for editing of the values in the accounts, so that the user can change dollar allocations. Start with the ability to edit the value in the table (custom editor).

5. Replace the `JTable` (and the **View Subaccount** button) with a `JTree` object.

Chapter 17

Other Ways:
Alternatives to Swing

In which we discover that Swing is not the only GUI game in town. In so doing we learn the rudiments of the Standard Widget Toolkit and we describe some of the key limitations of this alternative toolkit.

17.1 WHAT YOU WILL LEARN

This chapter will introduce the basic classes of SWT, the Standard Widget Toolkit, which is an alternative GUI library developed mainly for the Eclipse Java IDE.[1] Development of Eclipse has been led primarily by IBM.[2]

---

1. http://www.eclipse.org/

2. http://www.ibm.com/

17.2 THE IBM SWT TOOLKIT

The Standard Widget Toolkit is a complete GUI library for Java, completely independent of Swing and AWT. It is implemented as a library of native methods, so it cannot be ported to any Java runtime unless that platform has the native part of the SWT library implemented for it.

17.2.1   Another GUI Toolkit. Why?

The first question one should ask, perhaps, is why create an alternative GUI? Good question. The answer, according to the SWT FAQ,[3] primarily has to do with execution speed and look-and-feel similarity to native GUI applications on each platform.

If we may editorialize, we find neither reason particularly compelling, although the execution speed argument made some sense when the Eclipse project started. Swing is unlikely to win any performance awards, even though each version brings some improvements in speed.[4] Still, these reasons do not seem particularly compelling for such a large duplication of effort and functionality.

Whatever the reason, SWT exists. SWT works by providing a thin abstraction layer over native GUI features. It is a small GUI library. It is implemented using the Java Native Interface, so it requires that a native binary library be implemented for your platform. Fortunately, such implementations exist for all platforms Eclipse runs on. So if you can run Eclipse, you can write and run SWT applications.

---

3. `http://dev.eclipse.org/viewcvs/index.cgi/~checkout~/platform-swt-home/faq.html`

4. The question of speed in Java is a rather tired argument. If maximum speed is a primary concern, Java is probably not your first choice of a development language. In our experience, speed is something everybody says they need, but more often than not other considerations such as development time and error rate are much more important. Java is fast enough for virtually all MIS applications, and that is the market Java is squarely aimed at. Our computers keep getting faster, disk drives and memory keep getting cheaper. The "resource" and "performance" arguments only apply to applications where experienced designers would already have chosen C or assembly language. Besides, with the JIT compilers in both Sun's and IBM's JDKs, a well-written Java application is often as fast or faster than some other compiled languages, at least on the second run of the code.

17.2.2   Duplicated Effort. Why Cover It?

The next logical question is, "If you think SWT is unnecessary with Swing already there, why cover it in your book?" Also a sensible question. The answer is that there is very little published literature on this library (a notable exception being Chapter 10 of *The Java Developer's Guide to Eclipse* by Shaver et al., from Addison-Wesley). Also, SWT provides the only fully functional GUI library that will work with the GNU Compiler for Java. As such, it is a major required component if you wish to write native compiled GUI applications on Linux systems.

Of course, there is another reason. Anyone heavily into Linux is well aware of the political and philosophical debate about Free Software and Open Source. If the core values of Free Software are critical for you, you should be aware that the IBM Common Public License[5] under which Eclipse (and thus SWT) are published is a Free Software license. You get the source code, you may use it in your own products, and it imposes obligations similar to the GNU GPL,[6] but goes even further by requiring you to grant royalty-free licenses for any patents you hold in derivative works.

So you might choose SWT (or not) for political or philosophical reasons. Both authors still suggest Swing first because it is the official Java GUI library. When an employer wants to know if you can write a Java GUI application, he or she almost certainly means a Swing application. Philosophy is great, but it may not put the food on your table. You need to know that Swing is not Free Software (and neither is either of the major Java SDKs), and SWT is Free Software, but it is up to you to decide what best serves your interests.[7]

---

5. http://www.eclipse.org/legal/cpl-v10.html

6. http://www.gnu.org/licenses/gpl.html

7. A lot of people couldn't care less about the Free versus non-Free issue, but I must say that many of my most interesting workplace discussions have arisen from this issue. It is the first issue in my career that has had programmers talking about the balance between their personal interests, their employers' interests, and the public interest. Wherever you stand philosophically, I think it is good that programmers are thinking about the consequences of their work at all of these levels. I wish there were more pressure at all levels of business to consider and balance all of these interests.

17.2.3   Portability: Better *and* Worse

How about portability? Well, it depends on what "portability" means to you. If portability means "looks and runs the same on all platforms," then Swing offers better portability. If portability means "runs on all platforms for which there is a Java runtime," then Swing offers better portability. If portability means "looks like a native application on all supported platforms," then SWT is your choice. Make your selection accordingly.

> **TIP**
> The bottom line: If you only learn one Java GUI, make it Swing.

17.2.4   The Rest of the Chapter

The rest of this chapter will be devoted to describing the basic classes of SWT by converting one of the application classes from the previous chapter from Swing to SWT. We will not attempt to explain the operating principles of GUIs. For an introduction to GUI programming, see the previous chapter on Swing. It introduces the concepts and programming principles for GUI programming in Java. SWT is functionally similar, although quite spartan, providing only basic windows, controls, and events.

Eclipse also contains a family of higher level user interface classes, known collectively as JFace, that provide UI features such as dialogs, wizards, font handlers, and images. We will not cover JFace in this book.

17.2.5   SWT: Close to the Metal

SWT breaks some of the Java contract. For example, you cannot rely on garbage collection to clean up SWT objects. Any SWT object you create with new must be explicitly destroyed with a call to the dispose() method. Why? Since SWT is implemented with native methods, the low-level implementation allocates native OS data structures and objects that must be explicitly freed. Since the Java garbage collector cannot be relied upon to collect objects at a certain time (or ever, for that matter), these allocations can result in memory leaks and address space conflicts. As we shall see, however, SWT is well designed to minimize the amount of this that you need to worry about.

SWT is also close to the metal in the sense that it does not abstract the underlying message-based event system that drives both X Window and

Microsoft Windows. If you have ever written an X Window or Microsoft Windows application in straight C (without a GUI framework library or class library), you have written a `main()` function that contains an *event loop*. SWT actually puts simple method calls around this core message queue event loop. We'll cover the details of this in the next section where we introduce the `Display` and `Shell` classes.

17.2.6   "Hello, world" SWT Style

SWT consists mainly of classes that represent controls—such as buttons, text areas, scrollbars, and so on—and layout managers which are much like layout managers in Swing. But there are two other classes: `Display`, which models the interface between your Java application and the underlying windowing system, and `Shell`, which effectively represents a single window.

The application in Example 17.1 is a parallel to the simple Swing program in the last chapter (Example 16.1).

This simple program, like its parallel in the Swing chapter, is deceptive. Sure, this is a lot of code to say "Hello, world" but it is because what we are setting up here is an event-driven program that must respond to any valid user input.

17.2.6.1   Setting Up to Run an SWT Application

One advantage of Swing that we haven't pointed out up to now is that it is part of every Java runtime (well, not **gcj**; more on that later), so you have all the classes on your classpath without any special setup. Not so with SWT. The exact procedure for setting up to run an SWT application depends on what development environment you are using.

There is an excellent set of directions for running an SWT application under Eclipse in the SWT FAQ.[8] No matter what your environment is, there is a basic series of steps:

1. Download the Eclipse SDK.
2. Install it.

---

8. `http://dev.eclipse.org/viewcvs/index.cgi/~checkout~/platform-swt-home/` `faq.html?rev=1.83content-type=text/html#standalone`. Note that this link is to the current revision in CVS as of this writing. You should take a look at the parent page to see if there is a newer revision.

Example 17.1 A simple SWT application

```java
import org.eclipse.swt.*;
import org.eclipse.swt.layout.*;
import org.eclipse.swt.widgets.*;

/**
 * @author mschwarz
 *
 * Sample SWT "Hello, world" application
 */
public class SWTHelloWorld {

  public static void main(String[] args) {
    Display disp = new Display();
    Shell window = new Shell(disp);
    window.setLayout(new RowLayout());
    Label label = new Label(window, SWT.NONE);
    label.setText("Hello, world.");
    window.setSize(320,160);
    window.open();

    while (!window.isDisposed()) {
      if (!disp.readAndDispatch()) {
        disp.sleep();
      }
    }

    disp.dispose();
  }
}
```

3. Extract the SWT JAR files.

4. Extract the SWT JNI files.

5. Configure your development environment.

Let's go over these in a bit more detail.

SWT was developed as a GUI library for the Eclipse project. It is distributed as part of Eclipse. There is no official standalone SWT package. The right way to obtain SWT is to download and (at least temporarily) install the Eclipse SDK. See Section 10.4 for details.

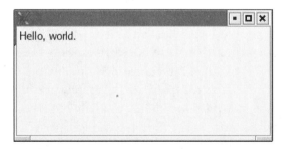

Figure 17.1 Running the SWT version of "Hello, world"

If you have followed our sage advice and downloaded the GTK version of the Eclipse SDK, then you need to copy out the SWT JAR files. There are two files in the GTK version, and just one in the Motif version. The GTK version's files are `swt.jar` and `swt-pi.jar`. They are both in the `eclipse/plugins/org.eclipse.swt.gtk_2.1.2/ws/gtk` directory. You will need to have both of these JAR files on the classpath of any SWT application you are compiling or running.

Remember that SWT is a JNI library. You must also have the native Linux shared libraries. These need to be made available to the Java native loader. The files you need are located in the `eclipse/plugins/org.eclipse.swt.gtk_2.1.2/os/linux/x86` directory. The `.so` files there must be available to any running SWT application. There are a couple of ways to do this. First, as described in Section 5.7, you can set the `LD_LIBRARY_PATH` environment variable. You also can use the `-D` parameter for the runtime VM to set the `java.library.path` property.

If you want to, you can copy these files out of the `eclipse` directory to some other location and then erase the `eclipse` directory with the lovable old standby, `rm -rf eclipse`.

Oh, by the way, once you have compiled the sample code above and set your classpath and Java library path correctly, running the application produces the window shown in Figure 17.1.

17.2.6.2 Anatomy of an SWT Application

Before we launch into this discussion, we should point out that the Javadoc documentation for all SWT packages is available as part of the Eclipse Platform documentation.[9] You might want to use that resource along with this lightweight tutorial to fill in the gaps and shortcuts.

It should not be too surprising that there are similarities between SWT, AWT, and Swing. They all take different approaches to solving the same problem, namely how to control the complexity of a graphical event-driven application. Because the problem is the same, there can't help but be similarities between different solutions. By now you may have deduced that the `Shell` class is an analog to the `JFrame` class, and that SWT uses a system of layout managers not too different from Swing. If so, you are on the right track and well on your way to using SWT.

If we had to summarize the difference in approaches between SWT and Swing, it would be that SWT tries to provide a small number of complex classes, and Swing tries to provide a large number of simpler classes. Obviously, this is a generalization, but everybody generalizes. Sorry.

The `Display` is a class that provides the link to the underlying GUI system. Think of it as an abstraction of the interface to the windowing system. In almost all cases, an SWT application will have exactly one instance of `Display`.

The `Shell` class represents a window. This class descends from a series of abstract parent classes, so if you look at the Javadoc for `Shell` and think it is simple, be sure to drill down into those parent classes! We'll discuss `Shell` quite a bit more as we go along.

17.3 PORTING BUDGETPRO TO SWT

The conversion of an existing application is a complex process. Always consider rewriting from scratch. Still, it is worthwhile to show an application converted from Swing to SWT, because it will emphasize the relationship between the two.

We begin with the reobjecting. Starting with the `BudgetPro` class, we need to add an instance of the `Display` class. Then the `JFrame` becomes a `Shell`. Likewise, the `JLabels` become `Labels`. Then . . . Wait a minute. You don't need a blow-by-blow account. Maybe it would be simpler to show you what SWT classes roughly correspond to the equivalent Swing classes (Table 17.1).

---

9. `http://download.eclipse.org/downloads/documentation/2.0/html/plugins/`
`org.eclipse.platform.doc.isv/reference/api/`

Table 17.1 Major SWT widgets and their Swing equivalents

SWT widget	Analogous Swing component	Description
Button	JButton	Display widget that sends notification when pressed and/or released.
Canvas	java.awt.Canvas, but see also java.awt.Graphics2D	Composite widget that provides a surface for drawing arbitrary graphics. May be used to create custom widgets.
Caret	javax.swing.text.Caret	A cursor used as the insertion point for text.
Combo	JComboBox	Widget that permits the user to choose a string from a list of strings, or to enter a new value into a text field.
Composite	JPanel	Widget that is capable of containing other widgets.
Group	JPanel	Composite widget that groups other widgets and surrounds them with an etched border and/or label.
Label	JLabel	Nonselectable widget that displays an image or a string.
List	JList	Selectable widget to choose a string or strings from a list of strings.
Menu	JMenu	User interface widget that contains menu items.
MenuItem	JMenuItemA, JCheckboxMenuitem, JRadioButtonMenuitem	Selectable widget that represents an item in a menu.
ProgressBar	JProgressBar	Nonelectable widget that displays progress to the user.
Scale	JSpinner	Widget that represents a range of numeric values.
ScrollBar	JScrollPane	Widget that represents a range of positive numeric values. Used in a Composite that has V_SCROLL and/or H_SCROLL styles. The mapping to Swing is not very tight here, since JScrollPane is like a combination of Composite and ScrollBar.

Table 17.1 *(Continued)*

SWT widget	Analogous Swing component	Description
Shell	JPanel	Window that is managed by the OS window manager. A Shell may be a child of a Display or another shell.
Slider	JSlider	Widget that represents a range of numeric values. Differs from a Scale by having a "thumb" to change the value along the range.
TabFolder	JTabPane	Composite widget that groups pages that can be selected by the user using labeled tabs.
TabItem	Any JComponent	Selectable user interface object corresponding to a tab for a page in a tab folder.
Table	JTable	A selectable widget that displays a list of table items that can be selected by the user. Rows are items, columns are attributes of items.
TableColumn	JTableColumn or instance of TableColumnModel	Selectable widget that represents a column in a table.
TableItem	TableCellRenderer or TableCellEditor	Selectable widget that represents an item in a table.
Text	JTextField, JPasswordField, JFormattedTextField, JTextArea, JEditorPane, JTextPane	Editable widget that allows the user to type text into it.
ToolBar		Composite widget that supports the layout of selectable toolbar items.
ToolItem	JButton	Selectable widget that represents an item in a toolbar.
Tree	JTree	A selectable widget that displays a hierarchical list of user-selectable tree items.
TreeItem	MutableTreeNode	Selectable user interface object that represents a hierarchy of items in a tree.

We are going to walk you through converting only one of the GUI source files for the BudgetPro application. We will leave converting the rest as an exercise for you. We'll talk about some of the entertaining differences between the models. As you shall see, there is no clear "winner" here between SWT and Swing. Almost all technical choices—SWT versus Swing, Java versus C++, Emacs versus **vi**, or for that matter UNIX versus Windows—are tradeoffs. This is no exception. There are things we like about SWT. For simple GUI applications, we think it is easier to set up and use. We think it is easier to learn in its entirety than Swing. Swing, on the other hand, is more complete, offering classes that will do more than SWT. So the best solution depends (as always) on your requirements.

17.3.1   Step 1: Convert the Class Members

We are going to tackle converting `BudgetPro.java` from Swing to SWT. In real life, this is an exercise you are unlikely to have to carry out. You will more likely write your GUI applications from scratch. But going through the conversion provides a useful roadmap for talking about the architecture of SWT; it teaches you SWT in terms of a class library with which you are already familiar.

First off, we change the packages imported at the start of the file. Remove all of the `awt` and `swing` packages. If you are using an IDE, this should flag every single line of code that touches the GUI as an error. This can be a big help when you are doing a mass conversion like this. When you have killed all the compile errors, you know you are well on your way to completing the conversion.

Replace the `import` statements with the imports you are likely to need for your SWT application. These are:

```
import org.eclipse.swt.*;
// The static SWT class, which contains a number of constants.

import org.eclipse.swt.widgets.*;
// The widgets library.  Almost all your display elements are here.

import org.eclipse.swt.events.*;  // Event handlers

import org.eclipse.swt.layout.*;  // Layout managers
```

We will go into these families of classes in more detail as we convert the members and methods of `BudgetPro.java`.

The next step is to convert the GUI members of the class from the Swing classes to their SWT counterparts. Of course, SWT requires the `Display` class, which has no analog in SWT, so we add a `Display` type member named `disp` just ahead of the `frame` member.

Next, we change the type of `frame` from `JFrame` to `Shell`. We could rename the member,[10] but why add to our typing burden? The name is still clear and meaningful, even if it doesn't match the SWT name.[11] There's more to it than just changing the type, however. The constructor call for the `JFrame` doesn't match any constructor for `Shell`. In fact, the `Shell` constructor requires a `Display` object argument, and all subsequent constructors for widgets and controls require a `Composite` as an argument.

This is a key difference between Swing and SWT. Swing allows you to build GUI components in arbitrary order at arbitrary times and then join them up to the GUI with an `add()` method call. SWT instead requires that you link your components up to the GUI element they belong to *when they are constructed*. There are good reasons for this difference. Remember that SWT allocates native objects and memory that Java's garbage collector cannot recover. Because of this, SWT makes the promise that if you call the `dispose()` method on any SWT object, it will dispose of it and everything it contains. That allows you to clean up all resources from an SWT program by calling `dispose()` on the top level `Display` object. If SWT allowed you to build GUI structures independently and then graft them onto the hierarchy, it could not keep this promise. For this reason (amongst others) SWT objects are always built in a fairly rigid top-down manner.[12]

The most direct consequence of this is that we have to get rid of the constructors on these declarations. We'll start construction in the `main()`. So, away with the constructors for the GUI elements. We now need to change the `JButtons` to `Buttons` and the `JLabels` to `Labels`. Again, if you are using a dynamic IDE, you should see your error count skyrocket with these changes

---

10. If you are using Eclipse, this is easily done throughout your code with the Refactoring feature.

11. All right, I'm being lazy. Write your own book if you don't like it.

12. In some ways, this greatly simplifies SWT programs, but at the cost of some reusability. With Swing, you could construct a panel or other GUI element and reuse it in many places. You can achieve the same thing in SWT by encapsulating such a construct in its own class and passing in a parent to the constructor, but this is a bit more bulky and complex than the Swing way.

Key SWT Abstractions

`Composite` is one of the key abstractions in SWT. Any control that may contain other controls is a `Composite`.

Here's a quick rundown of the key abstract classes and interfaces in SWT, along with the basics of the functionality they embody:

- A `Widget` is the abstract superclass of all user interface objects in SWT. At this level the methods exist that create, dispose, and dispatch events to listeners. Every single class we use in this chapter, with the exception of event handlers and layout managers, is a `Widget`.

- A `Control` is the abstract superclass of all windowed user interface classes. This is almost all of the UI classes, either by direct descent or through classes such as `Sash` or `Scrollable`. All constructors for `Control` classes require a `Composite` parent class as a constructor argument.

- A `Composite` is a `Control` which is capable of containing other `Control`s. One direct descendant of `Control` which is very similar to the Swing `JPanel` is `Group`.

The relationships and the power of these abstractions will become clear as you work with real-life examples.

(well, maybe not really skyrocket, since the `import` changes have already produced a lot of errors right off the bat).

Finally, we remove the `AbstractTableModel` member. SWT has a simpler (and more limited) table functionality that we will discuss later.

17.3.2 Step 2: Converting the `main()` Method

The main (pun unintended) changes that need to be made here include allocating the SWT `Display`, changing from instantiating a `JFrame` to a `Shell`, doing away with the Swing "look and feel" stuff (an SWT application always looks like a platform-native application, that's SWT's main selling point), and reworking the construction of the GUI. We'll explain that a little bit later.

For now, we take care of the simple changes. Remember that `main()` is a static method, so we do not have any nonstatic class members available right now. The original `BudgetPro` constructor took a `JFrame` argument, now it will have to get a `Display` and a `Shell`. So we have to allocate a local `Display` and a local `Shell`. We also need to add the `Display` argument to the `BudgetPro` constructor.

After this is done, we modify the call to the constructor to pass the local `Display` and `Shell` to our class instance.

Next, we have to set a layout manager. The original application used the Swing `BorderLayout` layout manager. SWT doesn't have such a critter. Fortunately, the original used only the north, center, and south positions of the `BorderLayout`. SWT has a simple layout manager called a `FillLayout` that puts its contained controls in a single row or column, equally sized. Putting the three controls in a column will end up looking much like using the north, center, and south of a `BorderLayout`. So we change the call to the `frame.setLayout()` to pass in a new `FillLayout` and add the `SWT.VERTICAL` attribute.

The `SWT` **Class**

The `SWT` class is pretty bare-bones. Its primary use is a library of named constants used for attributes to `Widget` (and other) constructors. You'll see such `SWT.xxxx` constants all over your typical SWT application. There are a handful of methods that the `SWT` class provides, all of them static, including `error()`, which throws an `SWTException`, `getPlatform()`, which returns a string with the name of the platform on which SWT is running, and `getVersion()`, which returns an `int` version number.

It also has a subclass, called `OLE`, which is a Windows-only class that provides ActiveX support for SWT. Obviously, such use is nonportable and non-Linux, so we won't talk any more about it.

The next block of code in `main()` sets the Swing look and feel. SWT has nothing like this. All SWT applications look like native applications (we seem to be saying that a lot), so all of this code may be removed.

The next block of code calls methods on the application object (`app`) that, in the original, construct the three "chunks" of UI and add them to the frame using the `BorderLayout` attributes. Since, as we explained earlier, all SWT controls must be explicitly joined to a parent control when they are constructed, the separate create-then-add semantics used in the original will not apply. In the next section, we will walk through converting one of these three create methods. For now, it is enough to know that they will be changed to be methods that return `void` (no return value) and the calls to `add()` may be deleted.

That completes the conversion of `main()`.

17.3.3   Step 3: Converting the GUI `build()` and `init()` Methods

Lest you believe that this means the application is ready to run, just try compiling what you have. Got a few errors yet, don't we?

Let's walk through converting the `createStatus()` method and its related methods. We'll then briefly discuss converting the `createList()` and `createButtons()` concentrating on the details of the unique UI widgets used in each.

17.3.3.1   *Converting the GUI* `build()` *Method*

In BudgetPro, the top part of the UI is the status pane. It consists, basically, of three labels. In the original application, this pane is constructed by the `createStatus()` method. In the original, it returns a Swing `Component`, which is then placed by calling `add()` on a container managed by the caller.

In SWT, `Widgets` must be joined to their containers *at construction*, so we must restructure this code a little bit. We create a `Group` to hold our classes together as a unit. We attach the group directly to the parent `Shell` by using the member variable `frame`. We set the layout manager to be `RowLayout`.

We then populate the `Group`. First, we add the **Up** button, which is only enabled when in a subaccount. While SWT does support image buttons, we take the shortcut of using the `SWT.ARROW` style, bitwise-or'ed with the `SWT.UP` style. Next, we populate the group with our `Labels`.

Note a change we will talk about some more below: The listener for the `Button` object called `upton` is changed. The method is renamed from `addActionListener()` to `addSelectionListener()`. Event handling in SWT is similar to Swing/AWT, but not identical, as we will see when we go over the rewrite of the actual event handler code a little later on.

These are the only changes we make to this method.

CAUTION

If a `Composite` has no layout manager, each `Widget` in the `Composite` must have its size and position explicitly set, or else their sizes will default to zero, and they will all be invisible! Tremendous details on SWT layout manager classes can be found in the article "Understanding Layouts in SWT" by Carolyn MacLeod and Shantha Ramachandran on the Eclipse Web site.[13]

17.3.3.2   *Converting the GUI* `init()` *Method*

The `setStatus()` method is called whenever the data in the core model changes. Its job is to update the UI to reflect those changes. More specifically, it updates the status pane at the top of the UI. There are corresponding methods for the list pane and the button pane.

Oddly, there are no changes in this particular method. The purpose of this method is unchanged. It updates the `Label`s with the new numbers and checks to see if the current `Account` is the top level `Account`. If it is, the **Up** button is disabled, otherwise it is enabled.

It turns out that all of the methods called on the UI classes in this method have the same names and purposes in Swing and SWT. Don't assume this will be true in the other cases.

17.3.3.3   *Reworking Event Handlers*

Finally, in the litany of conversion, we have to modify the event handlers. In this case, the only event of interest is when the **Up** button is pressed. Pressing a `Button` produces a `Selection` event.

In SWT, there are several types of events. Generally, you specify a class that will handle the event by calling one of the `add...Listener()` methods on the `Widget` that you wish to process the event for. Examples of these method calls include:

- `addSelectionListener()`
- `addControlListener()`
- `addFocusListener()`
- `addHelpListener()`

---

13. `http://www.eclipse.org/articles/Understanding%20Layouts/Understanding%20`
`Layouts.htm`

- `addKeyListener()`

- `addMouseListener()`

- `addMouseMoveListener()`

- `addMouseTrackListener()`

- `addPaintListener()`

- `addTraverseListener()`

There are others. SWT naming conventions define an interface for which each `add...Listener()` method is named. For example, there is a `SelectionListener` interface. Many such interfaces have multiple methods, each to handle a distinct kind of event; for example, the `MouseListener` interface defines separate methods to handle a button down event, a button release event, and a double-click event. As in Swing, it is common to implement event listeners as anonymous inner classes that implement the listener interface. However, since it is common to be interested only in some (or even only one) listener event, it is annoying to have to implement the full interface, since you have to provide method implementations for every event. For this reason, SWT also provides classes called *adapters* that implement "do-nothing" methods for every listener event. These also follow a naming convention. For example, the adapter for the `MouseListener` interface is a class named `MouseAdapter`; the `SelectionListener` interface has an adapter named `SelectionAdapter`, and so on.

For us, this means that we are going to create a reference to an anonymous inner class that implements the `SelectionListener` interface by extending the `SelectionAdapter` class. This is probably the weirdest common code construct in Java. Let's take a direct look at that method (Example 17.2).

If you can correctly answer the following question, then you can be reasonably assured that you do, in fact, understand what is going on here. Would the program compile and run correctly if the type of the `upAction` variable were changed to `SelectionAdapter`? The answer is in the footnote.[14]

---

14. Yes, it would. The reason is that the `addSelectionListener()` method takes an argument of type `SelectionListener`. Both `SelectionListener` and `SelectionAdapter` are of that base type. Aren't `Objects` wonderful?

Example 17.2 The upton Button event listener class reference declaration

```
private SelectionListener upAction = new SelectionAdapter()
{
  public void widgetSelected(SelectionEvent e)
  {
    // this is the action for UP arrow icon;
    Account next;
    next = current.getParent();
    if (next != null) {
      current = next;
      setStatus();
    }
  }
} ;
```

17.3.4   Completing the Conversion of the BudgetPro Class

To keep this book to a reasonable size, we are always trying to avoid covering the same ground more than once. We won't walk you through the details of converting the createList() and createButtons() methods as we did with the createStatus() method, but we will talk about the details of converting to SWT of some of the classes used in those methods.

17.3.4.1 The Table, TableColumn, and TableItem Classes

Without a doubt, the biggest change the BudgetPro class requires in order to convert from Swing to SWT lies in the table pane of the UI. The Table class is the root of tables in SWT. The TableColumn class defines the names and headers of the columns. TableColumn constructors must have a Table as their first argument, followed, as usual, by a numeric style specification. The TableItem class defines a row in the Table. As with TableColumn, the TableItem constructor must have a Table as its first argument, followed by a numeric style.

If you think about it, this is an extension of the same design philosophy that requires that all constructors name their parent Composite. While Swing's abstract table model permits a nice separation between the data and the presentation, implementing a similar system in SWT would violate its strict container semantics.

You will need to follow the basic rewrite process outlined above and you will have to squish the Swing abstract table model into the simpler SWT table model. This will be your biggest challenge. Go to it. It is a great way to learn. Of course, you can also just download the complete SWT application from the book Web site.[15]

17.3.5 Completing the Conversion of the Application

Completing the conversion of the `BudgetPro` class does not complete the conversion of the entire application. The `AcctDialog` class must also be converted. Use the same techniques we described here to convert that class as well. (Or, again, just download the complete SWT application.)

17.3.6 Closing Thoughts

Our overall impression is that SWT is more easily comprehended in its entirety than Swing. It may be easier to learn SWT first, since Swing's core model is more complex but more powerful. But SWT and Swing weren't developed in that order and Swing is still much more widely used.[16]

For many GUI applications, our feeling is that it may be faster to write in the SWT idiom. The problem lies in that SWT's model has limitations that Swing's does not. Notably, SWT GUI elements are in a single rigid tree structure. It is not possible to have a factory class that constructs a GUI element such as a dialog box which is passed up to the caller to be grafted into place on a GUI. Instead, the parent element must be passed in, so all GUI elements belong to the single tree from the moment they are created. Also, by introducing objects that cannot be garbage-collected, SWT brings into your application the possibility of a class of bugs that Java otherwise eliminates.

Moreover, while converting a Swing application helped give this chapter shape, we would, in general, prefer that an application be designed with its GUI toolkit in mind. You would likely make slightly different design decisions depending on which style of the GUI you choose.

---

15. http://www.javalinuxbook.com/

16. A gut feel—not based on any real statistics.

17.4 SWT AND GCJ

Up to now, we have told you again and again that SWT will work with **gcj**. But no Linux distribution with which we are familiar provides SWT with **gcj** out of the box. So how do you get SWT to play nice with **gcj**? Unfortunately, you have a bit of work to do. Fortunately, the work is not particularly difficult.

Before we proceed, we must acknowledge those who have been there before. We, too, had heard about SWT's usability with **gcj** but we had never bothered to try it because there was no documentation on how to do it. We first made the attempt thanks to a great IBM developerWorks article by Kirk Vogen entitled "Create Native, Cross-Platform GUI Applications." Follow the URL[17] to the information that enabled us to write this chapter.[18]

SWT source code is included in the Eclipse SDK download. See Section 10.4 for details on where and how to download and install Eclipse. Once you have Eclipse, you need to get your mits on the SWT source code. What we will do is compile the SWT source into a shared object file that we can link to any **gcj** application.

We're assuming that you've got **gcj** installed. We're assuming that you've unzipped the Eclipse SDK. We're assuming you're still reading the book. We have to make that assumption. The first thing you need to do is to unzip the SWT source code. It is found in `ECLIPSE_INSTALL/plugins/org.eclipse.platform.linux.gtk.source_2.1.2/src/org.eclipse.swt.gtk_2.1.2/ws/gtk`. If you are using (as we recommend) the GTK version of Eclipse,[19] there are two files in there: `swtsrc.zip` and `swt-pisrc.zip`.

Once you have these unzipped, you have to compile the code with **gcj**. There are two different patterns these files follow. Files that do not contain native methods are compiled with a command line that looks like this:

---

17. `http://www-106.ibm.com/developerworks/library/j-nativegui/`

18. Please note that Kirk's article provides links to additional documentation and to an **ant** buildfile that automates the steps we are going to teach you manually here. We certainly didn't want to steal anything from Mr. Vogen (or from IBM—scary!), so we will instead direct you to the (copyrighted) IBM Web resources. The article is worth checking out. It can save you some time over our version of the process. It is up to you.

19. Be aware: As helpful as Kirk Vogen's article and files are, they are written to an old version of **gcj** and they assume you are using the Motif version of Eclipse. His scripts work only with the Motif version.

```
$ gcj -c SomeClass.java -o SomeClass.o
```

Files that do contain native methods are compiled with a command line that looks like this:

```
$ gcj -fjni -c SomeClass.java -o SomeClass.o
```

That said, it does no harm to compile a source file that has no native methods with the -fjni flag. This gives us a quick and dirty way to make our library file.

```
$ find . -name "*.java" -exec gcj -fjni -c {} \; -print
```

Remember, you are in UNIX-land. Leverage your tools! In this case, the advantage of using **find** is that, should the SWT source change (classes added or removed), our "compile process" will handle it. Obviously, you can take this in more sophisticated directions with **make** or **ant**. But this will get the job done for us for now.

That will compile all of the SWT source.[20] Next, we want to assemble all of the object files produced into a shared object.

```
$ gcj -shared -o swt.so $(find . -name "*.o" -print)
```

Once again, we leverage our tools. This time, we use **bash** execution quotes around our **find** command to get all of the .o filenames added to our **gcj** command that builds the shared library. For our final trick, we will compile our HelloWorld class from the start of this chapter with **gcj** and our new SWT shared library:

---

20. When we did this with Eclipse 2.1 GTK and **gcj** version 3.2.2, we had one compile error where the return type of the org.eclipse.swt.custom.TableCursor.traverse() method was void, whereas the Control.traverse() method (from which TableCursor inherits) was boolean. So we hacked it. We changed the return type of TableCursor.traverse() to boolean and had it return true. We didn't test to see if this was right! Use at your own peril!

```
$ gcj -classpath=~/eclipse/plugins/org.eclipse.swt/swt.jar:\
~/eclipse/plugins/org.eclipse.swt/swt-pi.jar -c HelloWorld.java
$ gcj -main=HelloWorld -o HelloWorld Hello.o swt.so
$ export LD_LIBRARY_PATH=.:~/eclipse:\
~/eclipse/plugins/org.eclipse.swt/ws/gtk
$ ./HelloWorld
```

Et voilà! You have the HelloWorld application! Again. But now it is an executable binary. Enjoy.

17.5 REVIEW

Compared to Swing, SWT is a somewhat simpler GUI library. Unlike Swing, it is Free Software and Open Source. It provides a full GUI library for use with **gcj**. It is part of the Eclipse project. It uses native methods that require calls to dispose of allocated objects. It has a rigid hierarchy that requires that lower level GUI components be linked to their parents when they are constructed. This means there are some limitations on how applications may be constructed. SWT is much less commonly used than Swing. Swing is the lingua franca of Java GUIs. SWT is definitely worth knowing, but if you want your skills to be marketable, it is probably best to start with Swing.

17.6 WHAT YOU STILL DON'T KNOW

We just scratched the surface of SWT `Widgets`. There are a bunch we haven't covered.

17.7 RESOURCES

- SWT was written to support the Eclipse IDE. Eclipse is at `http://www.eclipse.org/`.

- An introduction to SWT can be found at the same site: `http://www.eclipse.org/articles/Article-SWT-Design-1/SWT-Design-1.html`.

- Part 2 of the same article is at `http://www.eclipse.org/articles/swt-design-2/swt-design-2.html`.

- The full list of Eclipse technical articles (including those on SWT) may be found at `http://www.eclipse.org/articles/index.html`.

- A good introductory article can be found on the `Developer.com` Web site: `http://www.developer.com/java/other/article.php/3330861`.

- As always, consider using `Google.com` to find additional information.

- In dead-tree form, Chapter 10 of the book *The Java Developer's Guide to Eclipse* by Sherry Shavor et al. (Addison-Wesley, ISBN 0-321-15964-0), also provides an introduction to SWT.

17.8 EXERCISES

1. Complete the conversion of the `BudgetPro` class.

2. Complete the conversion of the entire BudgetPro GUI application.

3. While you have Eclipse installed, follow the instructions to unpack the SWT examples. In particular, run the `ControlExample`. This is an application that demos all the major `Widgets`, while giving you the ability to apply most (if not all) of the style values to them dynamically. It is like a `Widget` browser that can get you familiar with the look and feel of SWT `Widgets` quickly. Run it. Play with it. Become friends with it. Also, remember you have the source code for this application. Want to know how to code a given `Widget`? Look!

Part IV

Developing
Web Interfaces

Chapter 18

Servlets:
Java Pressed into Service

Java was first seen by many programmers as a way to enhance Web pages by adding some actual code to them, to be run in the browser. But the real power of Java was unleashed at the other end of the client-server connection, when Java was pressed into service on the Web server—to help serve up pages, sometimes of its own making, to Web clients all across an enterprise.

18.1 WHAT YOU WILL LEARN

- What servlets are.
- How to write a simple servlet.
- More complex servlet matters (servlet state).
- An example—our BudgetPro application as a servlet.

18.2 SERVLETS: PROGRAM-CENTRIC SERVER-SIDE DOCUMENTS

Servlets are Java programs that are run by a Web server. At its simplest, a servlet is a Java class that is invoked by a Web server (referred to in some contexts as the servlet's *container*). A servlet is run not from the command line as a regular Java program, but by visiting its URL. Point a Web browser at a servlet's address and the Web server (the one which serves up that address) will run the servlet and send its output back to the browser (see Figure 18.1). So you can see that typical output for a servlet is HTML—what better thing to send to a browser?

Now, more and more servlets are using XML as their output and then converting it to HTML via XSLT stylesheets, but we're trying to keep things simple here.

In their most generic form, servlets are classes which implement the `Servlet` interface. That means that they provide three methods:

- `init(ServletConfig config)`
- `service(ServletRequest request, ServletResponse response)`
- `destroy()`

The `init()` method gets called when the Web server starts up the class. (Think of the `init()` method as a constructor; Java doesn't allow constructors to be defined for interfaces, so `init()` plays that role.)

The `destroy()` method gets called whenever the Web server takes the servlet out of service. This might happen when a system administrator wants to shut down the system, or shut down just that particular Web service.

Naturally, the `service()` method is the method that gets called whenever requests for this servlet arrive at the Web server. The server knows that the requested service is provided by this servlet, so it packages up certain data and sends it along as a request to the servlet. Thus, servlets can provide data in this generic request/response kind of protocol. Simple, but vague, right now.

Servlets get a bit more interesting when we look at the `HttpServlet` class. This class extends `Servlet` and adds two more methods that must be implemented:

- `doGet(HttpServletRequest   request,   HttpServletResponse response)`

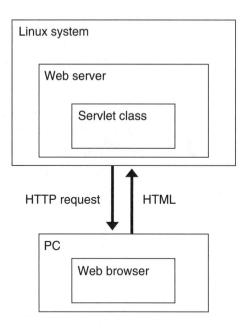

Figure 18.1 Servlet diagram

- doPost(HttpServletRequest request, HttpServletResponse response)

We hope that you've noticed the similarity between doGet(), doPost(), and the previously mentioned service() method. More on that in a minute.

18.3 PERSPECTIVE

To better understand the interaction with servlets, let's consider the requests that come to a Web server. Web servers serve up Web pages. At first (in the early days of the Web) that just meant simple flat HTML files, along with a few image types. A Web browser would send a request to a Web server in the form of a URL, such as http://www.dom.com/file.html, which would be sent to the Web server named www at the dom.com domain. It would look up the file named file.html in its directory and send it back to the browser.

That approach worked fine, and still does today. But this only covers *static* Web pages, ones whose content doesn't change. Users want to get at lots more information today, not all of which has been embodied in static Web pages.

Rather than require fancier browsers with more dynamic querying or other capabilities, Web servers became smarter and were able to talk to other programs that would generate HTML on the fly and send it back as the response to an incoming request. In the Java environment, this mechanism includes the `Servlet` and related classes.

As for requests coming from a browser, they come in two flavors—GET and POST. The GET request is a request via a URL. Simple URLs that appear as hyperlinks on a Web page are sent as GET requests. Any additional parameters appear at the end of the URL as `name=value` pairs separated by "&". The parameters are separated from the URL with a "?" character:

```
http://www.google.com/search?hl=en&ie=ISO-8859-1&q=java
```

The example URL includes three parameters:

- `hl=en`
- `ie=ISO-8859-1`
- `q=java`

The POST is virtually the same, except that the name=value pairs don't appear on the URL but are sent in a less visible way. The net result is the same, and the same methods can be used in the servlet to retrieve the parameters. The POST requests typically come from HTML `form` elements, as when you fill in the fields of a form and press a submit button (though forms can specify that the browser use GET as the submission mechanism for a particular form). The biggest advantage to posting the form is that the parameters don't appear in the URL, which is both more aesthetically pleasing and avoids problems from accidentally revisited pages or user-altered parameters.

One further twist: URLs are not necessarily literal paths to files anymore. The Web server can interpret parts of the URL as an alias for some other program. So `http://www.google.com/search` may not actually refer to a directory named `search` on the Google site, but more likely tells the Web server to use its search program. We'll discuss this more in Chapter 19.

So servlets are given requests which have come from browsers (and other Web clients), and then they respond with output. In our examples, we'll be sending HTML back. There are lots of other choices, too. Since browsers understand other formats, a servlet might also send back plain text or even image data. Another choice gaining popularity is having the servlet generate XML and then using a conversion via stylesheets to produce HTML. This allows for the formatting to be changed (e.g., to apply a new corporate look to the pages) without changing the content or the programs that generate the content.

Since a Web server (e.g., Apache Tomcat) is typically configured to run constantly, that is, to always be around, then a servlet is also always around. (The Web server keeps a reference to the class, so the class is not garbage collected—hence its persistence.) Well, "always" here means "as long as the Web server and the operating system are up and running."

An aside: Not all servlets are for Web browsing. Sometimes servlets can be used as daemons that hang around in the background doing other tasks (e.g., background processing of some database records). The browser interface, if any, may only be for the purpose of providing an administrative interface to the daemon. The administrator would then have a Web page to which to go, in order to see how many records have been processed. This page may also have buttons to reset, restart, or shut down the process. While we typically think of servlets being for the production of dynamic Web pages, here the Web pages would only be an aside to the real purpose, that of processing database records.

18.4 HOW TO WRITE A SERVLET

So how do you write a servlet? You may already have figured it out, from what we've described so far. You need to:

- Write a Java class that extends `HttpServlet`
- In that class, write the following methods:
    - `init()`
    - `destroy()`
    - `doGet()` and/or `doPost()`

That's the basic idea. There are lots of details about what arguments are supplied, what other resources are available, what methods can be used to get at parameters, and so on. We'll discuss some of those in our example servlet.

Let's start with a simplistic servlet, one that will dynamically generate the "Hello, world" string as a Web page (Example 18.1).

Example 18.1 A "Hello, world" servlet

```
/*
 * HiServlet.java
 */

package net.multitool.servlet;

import javax.servlet.*;
import javax.servlet.http.*;

/**
 * Simple Servlet that generates a page of HTML
 */
public class
HiServlet
  extends HttpServlet
{
  /**
   * Think of this as the constructor for the servlet.
   * We need do nothing for our example,
   * but we should call our parent object.
   */
  public void
  init(ServletConfig config)
    throws ServletException
  {
    super.init(config);
  } // init

  /**
   * Called when the Web server is shutting down
   * or wants to shut down this particular servlet.
   * We need do nothing.
   */
  public void
  destroy()
  {
  } // destroy

  /**
   * Handles the HTTP GET method.
   * @param request servlet request
   * @param response servlet response
   */
```

```
protected void
doGet(HttpServletRequest request, HttpServletResponse response)
  throws ServletException, java.io.IOException
{
  doBoth(request, response);
} // doGet

/**
 * Handles the HTTP POST method.
 * @param request servlet request
 * @param response servlet response
 */
protected void
doPost(HttpServletRequest request, HttpServletResponse response)
  throws ServletException, java.io.IOException
{
  doBoth(request, response);
} // doPost

/**
 * Requests for both HTTP GET and POST methods come here,
 * because we're not doing anything different
 * between the two request types.  This way we need only one
 * version of the code that does the real work.
 * @param request servlet request
 * @param response servlet response
 */
protected void
doBoth(HttpServletRequest request, HttpServletResponse response)
  throws ServletException, java.io.IOException
{
  java.io.PrintWriter out = response.getWriter();
  response.setContentType("text/html");
  /* output our page of html */
  out.println("<html>");
  out.println("<head>");
  out.println("<title>A Java Servlet</title>");
  out.println("</head>");
  out.println("<body>");
  out.println("Hello, world.");
  out.println("</body>");
  out.println("</html>");

  out.close();
} // doBoth
```

```
/**
 * Returns a short description of the servlet.
 */
public String
getServletInfo()
{
  return "Very Simple Servlet";
} // getServletInfo()

} // class HiServlet
```

Whew! That is a lot of code for only a simple "Hello, world," but remember that this is not just a run-on-your-desktop application. This is a network-based servlet that can respond to concurrent requests from across the network and talk to Web browsers. There's a lot of plumbing that needs to be connected to a Web server for the servlet to run, and that's what most of this code is—just the connections. The other verbose part is all of the HTML that we spit out around our message. You can make it even more elaborate, with background colors and other HTML decorations if you want to try it yourself.

Once you've written a servlet, though, you can't just run it from the command line like any Java class.[1] Much of the work of a servlet is done behind the scenes by the Web server (e.g., Tomcat). The tougher question is, "How do you run a servlet?" That involves issues of configuring the Web server, setting up directory locations, and so forth. It's the subject of the next chapter.

Once you've deployed this servlet (by reading the next chapter and/or with help from your IDE), you can run the servlet and talk to it via your browser. We've pointed a browser window at one such deployment to get a highly uninteresting Web page (Figure 18.2) whose HTML source (in your browser menu, select **View > Page Source**) is shown in Figure 18.3.

---

1. Well, actually, you could if it had a `main()` method defined. Our example doesn't, but a servlet class is still a Java class, and you might define a `public static void main()` method that would allow you to run it from the command line as a way to drive the rest of the class for simple testing. Of course, such a simple test harness wouldn't be driving a Web browser, and so on but technically it is possible. We didn't want to lie to you.

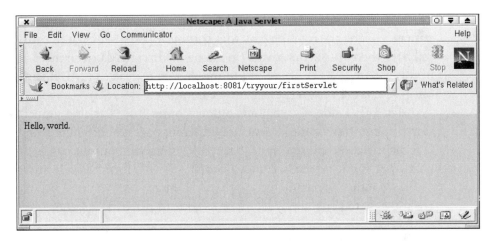

Figure 18.2 A very simple page from our servlet

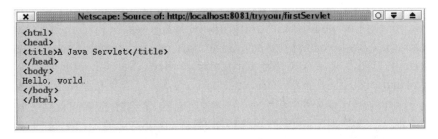

Figure 18.3 The servlet-generated source of our simple page

18.5 INPUT, OUTPUT

OK, so we've dynamically created a Web page—but the contents of that page don't change. The real use for servlets comes from having them produce dynamic content, not just from dynamically producing content.

One way for the content to be dynamic is to extract it from a database. Using what we described in Chapter 15, you can add code to pull values from tables in a database. Consider a query that will return multiple rows of results. Each row could be displayed as a row in an HTML table for display on a Web page.

Using a loop, we can generate lots of HTML with little code. This is handy for generating HTML tables. We would likely generate the `<table>` tag outside a `for` loop, but the `<tr>` and `<td>` tags would be output from within the loop, one for each iteration of the loop. (If you're not picturing that, be patient. There are examples of this coming up. If you're not conversant in HTML, then you better check out some of the HTML references at the end of this chapter. We're going to assume that you speak HTML fluently. Come on—we can't cover everything in one book.)

The other side of dynamic content comes from variable input. Google's search engine, for example, generates different pages for different search strings. It is the variation in user input that results in varying output pages. On a Web page, user input typically comes from an HTML form. The form values can be passed either as parameters on the URL or as POST values. URL parameters are also easy to generate by hand, or to code in place in <a> tags. For example,

```
<a href="/servlet/doSuch?cmd=find&value=joe">
```

is an HTML tag for a hyperlink which will invoke the doSuch servlet and pass in the parameters cmd and value. (It's a servlet not because the pathname is /servlet, but we use that for illustrative purposes. In fact, the servlet invoked may not even be called doSuch; it all part of servlet mapping that recognizes certain URLs as aliases for particular servlets. See Chapter 19 for a fuller explanation.)

The point is, we can invoke the same servlet repeatedly (even simultaneously) but with different values for our parameters, so we can program it for different behaviors and different output.

These parameters are available to the servlet via the request argument of the doGet() and doPost() methods. You can get an enumerator over all of the arguments (using getParameterNames()), or if you know it's name (and you likely would, since you're writing the program) you can ask for a particular argument.

The previous example used an argument called cmd, whose value we could retrieve thus:

```
String act = request.getParameter("cmd");
```

The parameters all come as Strings. If your arguments are numeric, you'll have to parse them (and error-check them—HTML forms are, understandably, weak on validating their input; tons of JavaScript have been written to deal with this, but this is beyond the scope of this book.)

Some parameters may have embedded spaces and other special characters that would disrupt a URL. To deal with that, browsers encode the characters in form fields before sending them to a Web server. You can see that in some URLs—space gets replaced with a "+" character, and special characters (such as the plus sign) get replaced with a character sequence for hexadecimal values (for example, "+" becomes %2B). The getParameter() method will automatically decode those. But we need to remember this if we want to generate any literal URLs in the HTML that we produce. (See the URLEncoder class in the Javadoc documentation for servlets.)

One more annoyance that must be dealt with: What if the URL contains the same argument twice—for example, www.google.com/search?cmd=search&cmd=bogus?

If you make the call to getParameter() you will get the first value (search). If you want to handle such a situation differently, you can call getParameterValues() which will return an array of Strings for all the different values. In our example,

```
String [] allofem = getParameterValues("cmd");
```

will return an array such that:

```
allofem[0] = "search"
allofem[1] = "bogus"
```

If there was only one value, then you get an array of one element. If the parameter wasn't used in the URL, getParameterValues() returns null.

18.6 MATTERS OF STATE: COOKIES, HIDDEN VARIABLES, AND THE DREADED "BACK" BUTTON

The toughest part about working with HTML is, perhaps, its *statelessness*. HTML and browsers were not designed to keep a connection going. It's not a phone call type of connection, where the line is kept open between the browser and the Web server. Rather, it's a one-shot, send-me-what-you've-got mechanism more like postal mail (but without the stamp). Here's the rub: Just because you mail a letter, you can't assume that you'll get an answer back. There is no on-going connection between browser and server, except for the duration of the data transfer. Once you've got your complete page displayed, the connection is gone.[2] About the best one can hope for is that you'll use what, in our postal analogy, would be like a supplied reply envelope. This allows the servlet engine of the Web server to track requests from the same user and provide a session capability across requests. It will use your browsers *cookie* mechanism to store this session's ID used to track your session. If you don't have sessions on, it will need to use URL rewriting, whereby the URLs generated will have an added parameter, the session ID.

Unlike the early days in the life of the Web, nowadays virtually everyone has cookies enabled in their browsers—anyone who shops at amazon.com, at least. This makes session tracking so much easier for the servlet developer. The Web server handles all that automatically, and you only need to make a few calls to the session-related methods of the HttpRequest.

To get a session for a user, ask for one from the HttpRequest:

```
HttpSession session = request.getSession(true);
```

The boolean parameter says whether (true) or not to create a session if one does not yet exist for this user. Once you have a session, you can store objects associated with that session:

```
session.setAttribute("cart", shopCart);
```

where shopCart is any serializable Object and "cart" could be any String that you want to use to later identify and retrieve this object, for example:

```
Basket myCart = (Basket) session.getAttribute("cart");
```

Notice that we need to explicitly cast the object type returned by getAttribute(), because it returns a generic Object.

18.6.1 Cookies

For any information that you want to save for longer than the duration of a session, you may want to investigate cookies—little bits of data (4K max; typically only a few bytes) sent to the browser for it to store and send back at a later time. You make a cookie thus:

---

2. You can go to another page, just be staring at the page for a long long time, or you might have shut down your browser completely—and the server-side servlet will never know.

```
Cookie snack = new Cookie("name", "value");
snack.setMaxAge(36000); // lifetime in seconds (10 hours)
```

Setting the maximum age of the cookie to a positive value is needed to let the browser know that it needs to store the cookie on disk. After that many seconds the cookie will be discarded by the browser as no longer relevant. Notice, too, that you must send the data inside the cookie as a string, and when you retrieve it, you'll have to parse that string.

Then you can send the cookie as part of a response, along with your other output:

```
response.addCookie(snack);
```

Getting data back via cookies involves requesting data from the `HttpServletRequest` object. All the cookies associated with your URL are sent with the HTTP header to this address. You make the call:

```
Cookies [] allSuch = request.getCookies();
```

and then you have to look through the list looking for the cookie you want:

```
if (allSuch != null) {
    for(i=0; i  allSuch.length; i++) {
        Cookie c1 = allSuch[i];
        if ("DesiredCookieName".equals(c1.getName())) {
            String result = c1.getValue();
            // ... now do something with it
        } // endif
    } // next cookie
} // endif
```

While cookies have gotten a lot of press, especially in the early days of Web technology, we've found much less use for them than for session objects. Session objects stay on the server, cannot be modified or deleted by the user, and are easier to look up and use. The drawback, or course, is their limited lifespan. But if you really want to leave data around for the next time some user visits your servlet, you may be better off putting the data in your own database and identifying that user by means of a cookie or by some login mechanism.

Let's take a look at a complete servlet example.

18.7 DESIGNING A BUDGETPRO SERVLET

When designing a servlet, there are many different patterns to follow. We can't hope to cover all the approaches that can be used for effective servlet programming. What we hope to do is show you our previous BudgetPro GUI application rewritten as a servlet, so that you can see the mechanics of a working servlet application. From this, you can become accustomed to the mechanics of a servlet so that you'll feel comfortable with other approaches, too. All servlets need to use these basic mechanisms.

Our BudgetPro GUI application was started from the command line, with a name for the budget and a total dollar amount. We'll use a static HTML page with a form for supplying that information. That will invoke our servlet. The servlet will use HTML pages analogous to the windows we used in our GUI—there will be a main screen that shows the current account listing its subaccounts, and there will also be a screen for creating new subaccounts.

One nice feature of HTML-based Web applications is that you can use hyperlinks as a way to both select something and take an action on it. We'll use that feature in lieu of a **View Subaccount** button. Instead of selecting a subaccount and then pressing **View Subaccount**, the user will only have to click on the name of the subaccount. As a hyperlink, it will make the request to the servlet to view that subaccount.

We will still use a button to send us to the screen for creating the subaccounts. We could have used a hyperlink, but this makes the browser page look a bit more like the GUI version.

18.7.1   Prototype

When designing servlets, it's handy to use static HTML pages as a prototype for the work to be done. You can mock up the various screens using HTML, simulate interactions by using hyperlinks to move between the screens, and get a feel for what the screens and interactions will look like.

Such a prototype also serves as a "runnable" specification. It can sometimes be easier to show the action than to describe it with words. And if you take care when you are building these static HTML pages, most of the HTML can be reused directly in the final product. (This will be even more true when we get to JSP.)

18.7.2 Design

Let's review what we need our servlet application to do for us. Given an account name and the initial dollar amount, we need to:

- Create a top-level account with that amount of dollars
- Display the current account and its total and remaining dollars, along with a list of its subaccounts, if any
- Create subaccounts, specifying a name and dollar amount
- Make a selected subaccount be the current one, displayed as above

After each or any of these actions, the servlet has to spit out the HTML page for the user to view. If the user wants to create a subaccount, then the servlet produces a form page for entering the name and dollar amount for the subaccount. When the user presses a **Create** button on that page, the browser tells the servlet (via the form data) that the servlet should create the subaccount and redisplay the current account with this new subaccount added to its list.

> **TIP**
>
> It may help to think of the servlet as a two-step process, with a current and future perspective. The first step is the action that the servlet must perform based on the supplied parameters (e.g., create a new account). The second step is the creation of the page allowing the user to take the next (future) action. That page reflects the state of things after the parameter-driven action has occurred. In our example, that means showing the list of subaccounts including the one that we just created.

Let's spell out in more detail what our interactions with the servlet will be, and describe what output we expect for each of those inputs. We will create a keyword to tell the servlet what function we want it to perform; we'll call the parameter `func`. We will sometimes need two other parameters: `name` and `dollars`.

Table 18.1 shows our design as a compact reference.

The code for our servlet is at `http://www.javalinuxbook.com/`. Let's look at some of the key parts of the servlet in more detail. We'll look at: 1) reading the parameters, 2) the core business logic of the servlet, as described in Table 18.1, and 3) how we create and output the HTML.

Table 18.1 BudgetPro servlet actions

func **parameter**	**Other params**	**Action**	**Next screen**
begin	name, dollars	Create a top-level account, save in the session.	main
mkacct	none	none	subacct
cancel	none	Get account from session.	main
create	name, dollars	Get account from session; create subaccount.	main
cd	name	Get account from session, look up subaccount by name, save as current in session.	main
back	none	Get account from session, get parent from account, save as current in session.	main

The parsing of the parameters is very straightforward. The `request` parameter, part of the signature of the `doGet()` and `doPost()` methods, can be used to retrieve the parameters we need:

```
String act = request.getParameter("func");
String name = request.getParameter("name");
String dollars = request.getParameter("dollars");
```

Notice that we always ask for all three parameters, even though we will often use only one (`act`). Once we have the requested function in `act`, it's just a matter of if-then-else-ing our way through the possible values and taking the appropriate actions. We store, or retrieve, the current account in the session manager, thereby providing continuity between browser requests (Example 18.2).

The output is the page to send back to the browser. We create that page as an object, either an `AccountView` or a `SubPage`. The `HttpServletResponse` provides us with an output channel on which to write.

```
java.io.PrintWriter out = response.getWriter();
if (nextPage != null) {
    response.setContentType("text/html");
    out.println(nextPage.toString());
}
```

Example 18.2 Implementing the BudgetPro servlet actions

```
if ("begin".equals(act)) {
    Account top = new Account(name, theUser, dollars);
    session.setAttribute("top", top);
    session.setAttribute("current", top);
    nextPage = new AccountView(top);
} else if ("mkacct".equals(act)) {
    // show the subaccount creation page
    nextPage = new SubPage(null);
} else if ("cancel".equals(act)) {
    Account current = (Account) session.getAttribute("current");
    nextPage = new AccountView(current);
} else if ("create".equals(act)) {
    Account current = (Account) session.getAttribute("current");
    try {
        current.createSub(name, dollars);
        nextPage = new AccountView(current);
    } catch (NumberFormatException nfe) {
        // show the subaccount creation page (with error message)
        nextPage = new SubPage("Bad number format");
    }
} else if ("cd".equals(act)) {
    Account current = (Account) session.getAttribute("current");
    Account nextAcct = current.getSub(name);
    session.setAttribute("current", nextAcct);
    nextPage = new AccountView(nextAcct);
} else if ("back".equals(act)) {
    Account current = (Account) session.getAttribute("current");
    Account nextAcct = current.getParent();
    session.setAttribute("current", nextAcct);
    nextPage = new AccountView(nextAcct);
} else {
    log("Unknown func=["+act+"]");
    response.sendError(HttpServletResponse.SC_NOT_IMPLEMENTED);
}
```

The way that we construct the output, it will all get sent back to the user
in one fell swoop. That's fine for relatively short pages with rapid response time.
If response time is a major concern and you are sending large quantities of data,
you may want to change things a bit. Instead of building up the output in a
`StringBuffer` and then getting it all back with a `toString()` call, you could
take each of our `append()` calls and make them individual `out.println()`

calls, to send each snippet of HTML separately. The output can be flushed explicitly, too, using

```
response.flushBuffer();
```

You might do such a call just before beginning a database operation, or place such calls at strategic points through your output.

18.8 REVIEW

We have seen that servlets are Java programs that are run by a Web server. They typically, but not necessarily, produce output intended for a browser. By implementing the `HttpServlet` interface, your Java class will have all the methods needed for it to be run by a Web server. We looked at a simple example and saw its output to a Web browser, then we looked at another example using our BudgetPro application.

18.9 WHAT YOU STILL DON'T KNOW

There is more that we haven't discussed, so if you're going to do some serious work with servlets, be sure to do some additional reading, especially on these topics:

- The servlet lifecycle and the need for thread safety.
- How to keep the servlet output from being cached.
- Dealing with failures.
- Initialization parameters.
- Other kinds of output.
- Sharing between servlets.
- How to configure and deploy servlets (this is coming up in the next chapter).

18.10 RESOURCES

The definitive place for all the details is the Java Web site at Sun,[3] particularly the pages dealing with `javax.servlet.http` classes.

Some of the best material on servlets comes from:

- *Core Servlets and JavaServer Pages* by Marty Hall and Larry Brown, ISBN 0-13-009229-0, a Prentice Hall PTR book.
- Its sequel, *More Servlets and JavaServer Pages* by Marty Hall, ISBN 0-13-067614-1, also by Prentice Hall PTR.
- *Java Servlet Programming, Second Edition* by Jason Hunter and William Crawford, ISBN 0596000405, from O'Reilly.

18.11 EXERCISES

1. Modify the BudgetPro servlet so that it responds differently for the `doGet()` and `doPost()` methods. Have `doPost()` continue to work as is, but have `doGet()` report the number of different users and the number of accounts that they have created. (You may need to "instrument" the code—that is, add additional statements—to start counting such things.)

2. Change BudgetPro to do its output on the fly instead of building the entire page before output. Can you notice any difference in the display time?

3. Design error handling for BudgetPro to prevent the user from allocating more than is available in the (sub)account. Will you use Java exceptions? If so, which object will throw them and which will catch them? How will you inform the user of the error? Implement your design.

---

3. `http://java.sun.com/j2ee/1.4/docs/api/`

Chapter 19

JSP:
Servlets Turned Inside Out

In our last chapter, the BudgetPro servlet example spent a lot of code generating the HTML output for the servlet to send back to the browser. If you want to change the HTML for any page (for example, add a background color), you would have to modify the Java code (obviously)—but you're not really wanting to modify the logic of the servlet, you only want to tweak its output. The HTML that a servlet generates can be scattered among output statements, string concatenations, classes, and method calls. Servlets, we might say, bury the HTML deep inside the code. We're now going to take a look at JavaServer Pages (JSP) which do the opposite—they expose the HTML and hide the code down inside.

This technique has been given the fancy description, *document-centric server-side programs*. They are "document-centric" because the HTML code is so visible—JSP content looks like (and is) HTML with some additions. They are "server-side" because all the work is done on the server and all the additions and special features of JSP are boiled down to a simple stream of HTML by the time it gets to the browser.

19.1 WHAT YOU WILL LEARN

- Theory of operation: how JSP can be thought of as servlets "inside out."
- Three simple JSP directives: `scriptlet`, `declaration`, `expression`.
- Servlet variables made available: `request`, `response`, `out`, `session`.
- Server-side includes.
- A tiny bit about tags.
- `jsp:useBean`.
- A look at our BudgetPro using JSP.
- The correct spelling of JavaServer Pages.

19.2 SERVLETS TURNED INSIDE OUT: JSP

Take a look at the `AccountView.java` class in the BudgetPro servlet example. It consists almost entirely of

```
sb.append("</a></td>");
```

method calls which build up a string of HTML. Instead, this could have been calls to do the output right then and there:

```
out.println("</a></td>");
```

Either way, if we want to modify the HTML, we have to modify the Java code. While that's not difficult, it can be error-prone. It would be nice to *not* have the Java syntax in the way when we want to modify the HTML. (That's especially true when you want to put quotation marks in your HTML:

```
out.println("<input name=\"name\" size=\"20\">");
```

It's not that it can't be done; the `\"` just gets hard to read and hard to get right the first time.)

One way to externalize all the HTML is to put it into a file. Then our Java application could read the file at runtime and send its contents to the browser. Not bad, but what about the dynamic parts? Remember how we generated the table from the `for` loop in `AccountView.java`:

```
for (Iterator actit = acct.getAllSubs(); actit.hasNext(); ) {
    Account suba = (Account) actit.next();
    sb.append("<tr>");
    sb.append("<td><a href=\"BudgetPro?name="+suba.getName());
    sb.append("&func=cd\">");
    sb.append(suba.getName());
    sb.append("</a></td>");
    sb.append("<td>albing</td>");
    sb.append("<td>");
    sb.append(suba.getTotal().toString());
    sb.append("</td>");
    sb.append("</tr>\n");
} // next acct
```

That would be hard to do with file-based HTML.

Another approach, the one used by JavaServer Pages, would be to use the HTML file as input to a converter program—one which would take each line of HTML, for example

```
<input name="name" size="20">
```

and produce a line of Java code:

```
out.println("<input name=\"name\" size=\"20\">");
```

Notice how the converter would be the one to handle the escape sequence for the quotation marks; we get to write straight HTML—it has to deal with the backslashes.

This is the basic idea behind JavaServer Pages. JSP files are nothing more than HTML (with some additions that we'll discuss shortly) which are compiled into Java programs—servlets, to be exact—that are then run to produce the Web page. The conversion happens no later than the first time the Web server tries to serve up that JSP. If it hasn't yet been converted, it will convert it into Java code and start the servlet. Thereafter, other requests to that page go directly to the servlet. If you modify the JSP file, then the Web server recognizes that the file has been modified and reconverts it.

But why go to all this trouble? It's not for the static HTML that we need JSP, but rather for the dynamic bits. Remember that `for` loop, above, used to make the HTML table of subaccounts? Let's look at part of a JSP that does the same thing:

```
<table border=1 width=50%>
<tr>
<th>Account</th>
<th>Owner</th>
<th>Value</th>
</tr>
<% // for each subaccount:
  for (Iterator actit = acct.getAllSubs(); actit.hasNext(); ) {
    Account suba = (Account) actit.next();
%>
    <tr>
    <td><a href="BPControl?name=<%= suba.getName() %>&func=cd">
    <%= suba.getName() %>
    </a></td>
    <td>albing</td>
    <td>
    <%= suba.getTotal().toString() %>
    </td>
    </tr>
<%
 } // next acct
%>
</table>
```

Notice how it starts off as simply the HTML building the table opening. Then we encounter some Java source code, enclosed in delimiters (`<% ... %>`), then back to plain HTML. There's even a line which intermixes HTML and Java:

```
<td><a href="BPControl?name=<%= suba.getName() %>&func=cd">
```

To understand what's going on here, let's take a look at four pieces of syntax that are the keys to JSP.

19.3 How to Write a JSP Application

Writing a JSP application consists, syntax-wise, of writing your desired output page in HTML and, where you need the dynamic bits, putting Java code and/or other special syntax inside special delimiters that begin with `<%`.

There are four special delimiters that we should describe if you're going to work with JSP. The bulk of your JSP will likely be HTML. But interspersed among the HTML will be Java source or JSP directives, inside of these four kinds of delimiters:

- `<% code %>`
- `<%= expression %>`
- `<%! code %>`
- `<%@ directive %>`

Let's look at them one at a time.

19.3.1 Scriptlet

The code that appears between the `<%` and `%>` delimiters is called a *scriptlet*. By the way, we really hate the term "scriptlet." It seems to imply (falsely) a completeness that isn't there. It is too parallel to the term "applet," which is a complete Java program that runs inside a browser. A scriptlet isn't necessarily a complete anything. It's a snippet of code that gets dropped inside the code of the servlet generated from the JSP source.

Recall that servlets may have a `doPost()` and a `doGet()` methods, which we collapsed in our example by having them both call the `doBoth()` method. Same sort of thing is happening here with the JSP, and the `doBoth()` ends up doing all the output of the HTML. Any snippets of Java code from within the `<%` and `%>` delimiters get dropped right in place between those output calls, becoming just a part of a method.

It can be useful to keep this in mind when writing JSP. It helps you answer the questions of scope—who has access to what, where are variables getting declared and how long will they be around? (Can you answer that last question? Since any variable declared inside the `<%` and `%>` will be in the JSP equivalent of our `doBoth()` method, then that variable will only be around for the duration of that one call to the `doBoth()`, which is the result of one GET (or POST) from the browser.)

The source code snippets can be just pieces of Java, so long as it makes a complete construct when all is converted. For example, we can write:

```
<% if (acct != null) { // acct.getParent() %>
    <a href="BudgetPro?func=back">
    <img src="/back.gif">
    </a>
<% } else { %>
    <img src="/back.gif">
<% } %>
```

Notice how the `if-else` construct is broken up into three separate scriptlets—that is, snippets of code. Between them, in the body of the `if` and the `else`, is plain HTML. Here is what that will get translated into after the JSP conversion:

```
if (acct != null) { // acct.getParent()
    out.println("<a href=\"BudgetPro?func=back\">");
    out.println("<img src=\"/back.gif\">");
    out.println("</a>");
} else {
    out.println("<img src=\"/back.gif\">");
}
```

Do you also see why we describe it as being "turned inside out"? What was delimited becomes undelimited; what was straight HTML becomes delimited strings in output statements.

As long as we're on the topic of conversion, let's consider comments. There are two ways to write comments in JSP, either in HTML or in Java. In HTML we would write:

```
<!-- HTML comment format -->
```

but since we can put Java inside of delimiters, we can use Java comments, too:

```
<% // Java comment format %>
```

or even:

```
<% /*
    * Larger comments, too.
    */
%>
```

If you've been following what we've been saying about translation of JSP into Java code, you may have figured out the difference. The Java comments, when compiled, will be removed, as all comments are, from the final executable.

The HTML-based comments, however, will be part of the final HTML output. This means that you'll see the HTML comments in the HTML that reaches the browser. (Use the **View Source** command in your browser to see them. As HTML comments, they aren't displayed on the page, but they are sent to the browser.) This is especially something to be aware of when writing a loop. Remember our loop for generating the table?

```
<% // for each subaccount:
   for (Iterator actit = acct.getAllSubs(); actit.hasNext(); ) {
     Account suba = (Account) actit.next();
 %>
     <!-- Next Row -->
     <tr>
     <td><a href="BPControl?name=<%= suba.getName() %>&func=cd">
...
<% } // next acct %>
```

We've put a comment just prior to the `<tr>` tag. What will happen is that the comment will be part of the generated HTML, and since this is a loop, the comment, just like the `<tr>` and other tags, will be repeated for each iteration of the loop. Now we're not saying this is undesirable—in fact it makes the resultant HTML more readable. But be aware that these comments will be visible to the end user. Be careful in what you say in them. The additional transmission time required for these few extra bytes is probably imperceptible, unless your comments are large and repeated many times.

19.3.2 Declaration

The other place that code can be placed is outside the `doGet()` and `doPost()`. It is still inside the class definition for the servlet class that gets generated from the JSP, but it is not inside any method. Such code is delimited like this:

```
<%! code %>
```

The exclamation mark makes all the difference. Since it's outside any method, such code typically includes things like variable declarations and complete method declarations. For example:

```
<%! public static MyType varbl;

public long
countEm()
{
    long retval = 0L;
    retval *= varbl.toLong();
    return retval;
}
%>
```

If you tried to do something like this inside of a scriptlet, you would get errors when the server tries to compile your JSP. Such syntax belongs at the outer lexical level. The use of the `<%! ... %>` syntax puts it there.

19.3.3 Expression

This delimiter is a shorthand for getting output from a very small bit of Java into the output stream. It's not a complete Java statement, only an expression that evaluates into a `String`. Here's an example:

```
<h4>As of <%= new java.util.Date() %></h4>
```

which will create a Java `Date` object (initialized, by default, with the current date/time) and then call the `toString()` method on that object. This yields a date/time stamp as part of an `<h4>` heading.

Any methods and variables defined inside the previously described delimiters are OK to use with this expression shorthand.

There are also a few predefined servlet variables.

We've described how the JSP is converted into a servlet—the HTML statements become `println()` calls. This all happens inside of an `HttpServlet`-like class, just like our `BudgetProServlet` extends `HttpServlet` in the previous chapter. In such a class, the method called when a request arrives from a browser looks very much like our `doBoth()` method:

```
doBoth(HttpServletRequest request, HttpServletResponse response)
```

> **TIP**
>
> If you want to see the source for the servlet that gets generated when a JSP is converted, and if you're using NetBeans, right-click on the filename (in the **Explorer** view) and, from this menu, choose **Compile**. Then do it again and you'll notice that the second choice on the menu is **View Servlet** (Figure 19.1).
>
> If you are using Apache Tomcat as your Web server, just look in the `work` subdirectory in the directory where Tomcat is installed. In the appropriate subdirectory you will find both the `.java` and `.class` files for your converted JSP with the `.jsp` suffix converted to `$jsp.java` and `$jsp.class` respectively. For example, `BPAcct.jsp` becomes `BPAcct$jsp.java` and is compiled into `BPAcct$jsp.class`.

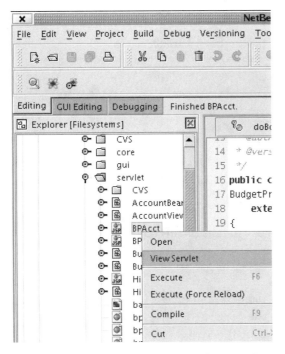

Figure 19.1 Viewing the converted JSP in NetBeans

The point here is that a request object and a response object are defined by the way the servlet is generated. They are called, oddly enough, `request` and `response`. In addition to these, a `session` is defined and initialized, just like we did in our servlet example. (What were we thinking?)

There are a few other variables that the converted servlet has created that we can use. We'll summarize them in Table 19.1. To read more about how to use them, look up the Javadoc page for their class definition.

Remember that these can be used not only by the `<%= %>` expressions, but also by the `<% %>` snippets of code.

19.3.4 Directive

The last of the special delimiters that we will discuss is the one that doesn't directly involve Java code. The `<%@ ... %>` delimiter encompasses a wide variety of directives to the JSP converter. We don't have the space or the patience to cover them all, so we'll cover the few that you are most likely to need early on

Table 19.1 JSP predefined variables

Type	Variable name
PageContext	pageContext
HttpSession	session
ServletContext	application
ServletConfig	config
JspWriter	out

in your use of JSP. We have some good JSP references at the end of this chapter for those who want all the gory details of this feature.

```
<%@page import="package.name.*" %>
```

is the way to provide Java `import` statements for your JSP. We bet you can guess what that happens in the generated servlet.

Here's another useful page directive:

```
<%@page contentType="text/html" %>
```

You'll see this as the opening line of our JSP, to identify the output MIME type for our servlet.

JSP also has an `include` directive:

```
<%@include file="relative path" %>
```

This directive is, for some applications, worth the price of admission alone. That is, it is such a useful feature that even if they use nothing else, they could use JSP just for this feature. It will include the named file when converting the JSP—that is, at compile time.

It can be used for common header and footer files for a family of Web pages. (If you're a C programmer, think `#include`.) By defining one header file and then using this directive in each JSP, you could give all your JSP the same look—say, a corporate logo and title at the top of page and a standard copyright statement and hyperlink to your webmaster's e-mail address at the bottom.

Be aware that this inclusion happens at compile time and is a source-level inclusion. That is, you are inserting additional source into the JSP, so if your included file contains snippets of Java code, they will be part of the resulting program. For example, you could define a variable in the included file and reference in the including file.

Also, since this inclusion happens at compile time, if you later change the included file, the change will not become visible until the JSP files that do the including are recompiled. (On Linux, this is simply a matter of **touch**ing all the JSP, as in:

```
$ touch *.jsp
```

assuming all your JSP files are in that directory. Touching them updates their time of last modification, so the Web server thinks they've been modified so the next access will cause them to be reconverted and their generated servlets reloaded. You get the idea.

There is another way to do an include in JSP—one that happens not at compile time, but at runtime. The syntax is different than the directives we've seen so far, but more on that in minute. First, an example of this kind of include:

```
<jsp:include page="URL" flush="true" />
```

In this format, the page specified by the URL (relative to this Web application's root) is visited and its output is included in place amongst the output of this JSP, the one doing the include.

A few quick notes:

- Be sure to include the ending "/" in the directive; it's part of the XML syntax which is a shorthand for ending the element in the same tag as you begin—that is, `<p />` instead of `<p> </p>`.

- When all is working, `flush` being `true` or `false` doesn't matter; when the included page has an error, then `flush="true"` causes the output to the browser to end at the point of the include; with `flush="false"`, the rest of the page will come out despite the error in the include.

- The page that is being included is turned into its own servlet. That is, it is its own JSP. You don't have to just include static HTML, you can include a JSP.

- Since this is a runtime include, all you are including is the output of that other page. You can't, with this mechanism, include Java snippets or declarations, but only HTML output.

Table 19.2 New XML syntax for JSP constructs

Standard format	New HTML format
`<% code %>`	`<jsp:scriptlet> code </jsp:scriptlet>`
`<%! code %>`	`<jsp:declaration> code </jsp:declaration>`
`<%= expr %>`	`<jsp:expression> expr </jsp:expression>`

19.3.5   New Syntax

But what about that new syntax? It's an XML-conformant syntax, and it's the syntax for all the newer features added to JSP. In fact, even the old JSP syntax, the statements that we've discussed, have an alternative new syntax (Table 19.2). Prior to JSP 2.0, that syntax was reserved for JSP that produce XML rather than HTML. (That's a whole other can of worms that we won't open now.) Now, as of JSP 2.0, both forms can be used, if your Web server is JSP 2.0 compliant.

You can see that the old syntax is more compact and less distracting than the large tags. We suspect that means the old syntax is likely to continue to be used for a long time yet.[1]

This new syntax is also used for the last two parts of JSP that we will cover, `useBean` and tag libraries.

19.3.6   JavaBeans in JSP

For those who really want to avoid doing any Java coding inside of a JSP, there is additional syntax that will provide for a lot of capability but without having to explicitly write any Java statements. Instead, you write a lot of arcane JSP directives, as we'll show you in just a bit. Is this any better? In some ways yes, but in other ways, no, it's just different syntax.

What we'll be able to do with this additional syntax is:

1. Instantiate a Java class and specify how long it should be kept around
2. Get values from this class
3. Set values in this class

---

1. The newer XML-style syntax would be useful if your JSP are generated by an XSLT stylesheet or are validated against a DTD, both topics being beyond the scope of our discussion.

The syntax looks like this:

```
<jsp:useBean id="myvar" class="net.multitool.servlet.AccountBean" />
```

which will create a variable called `myvar` as an instance of the `AccountBean` class found in the `net.multitool.servlet` package. Think of this as:

```
<%! import net.multitool.servlet.AccountBean; %>

<% AccountBean myval = new AccountBean(); %>
```

So can `AccountBean` be any class? Well, sort of. It can be any class that you want, as long as it is a bean. It doesn't have to end in "`Bean`", but it does have to be a class which has:

- A null constructor (you may have noticed there is no syntax to support arguments to the constructor on the `useBean` statement).
- No public instance variables.
- Getters and setters for instance variables.
- Getters and setters named according to a standard: `getTotal()` or `isTotal()` and `setTotal()` for a variable called `total` (`isTotal()` would be used if we had a boolean getter, that is, if the getter returned a `boolean`; otherwise it would expect `getTotal()` as the getter's name).

Otherwise, its a normal class. These restrictions mean that you can call the class a "JavaBean" or just "bean," and there is additional JSP syntax to manipulate the class. Specifically:

```
<jsp:getProperty name="myvar" property="total" />
```

will do, in effect, the following:

```
<%= myvar.getTotal() %>
```

or

```
<% out.print(myvar.getTotal()); %>
```

Similarly, we can set a value in the JSP with this syntax:

```
<jsp:setProperty name="myvar" property="total" value="1234" />
```

which will do, in effect, the following:

```
<% myvar.setTotal("1234"); %>
```

So this would hardly seem worth it, but there are other syntax constructs that make this much more powerful. Remember that we're working with Web-based stuff, with a JSP that will be invoked via a URL. That URL may have parameters on it, and we can map those parameters onto a bean's properties—that is, connect the parameters to setters for a given bean. We replace the `value` attribute with a `parameter` attribute, for example:

```
<jsp:setProperty name="myvar" property="total" parameter="newtot" />
```

which works the same as:

```
<% myvar.setTotal ( request.getParameter("newtot") ); %>
```

We can take that one step further and map all the parameters that arrive in the URL to setters in one step:

```
<jsp:setProperty name="myvar" parameter="*" />
```

So if you design your JSP and your HTML well, you can get a lot done automatically for you. One other thing going on behind the scenes that we've glossed over is the type of the argument to the setter. The parameters all come in as `Strings`. However, if your setter's type is a Java primitive, it will automatically convert to that type for you, instead of just passing you `Strings`.

One final twist on using beans is the duration of the bean and its values. If you don't specify otherwise (and we have yet to show you syntax to do otherwise) your bean will be around for the duration of the request, at which time it will be available to be garbage-collected. Any values in the bean will not be there on the next visit to that URL (i.e., the next call to that servlet).

Here is the syntax to make that bean last longer:

```
<jsp:useBean id="myvar" class="net.multitool.servlet.AccountBean"
             scope="session" />
```

which will make it stay for the duration of the session. You may remember (or you can flip back and look up) how we created and used session variables in the servlet. The same mechanism is at work here, but behind the scenes. You only use the specific syntax in the useBean tag, and it does the rest (getting and storing) for you.

19.3.7   Tag Libraries

Well, we're almost done with JSP, but the one topic that we have yet to cover is huge. It's the trap door, or the way back out, through which JSP can get to lots of other code without the JSP author having to write it. Tag libraries are specially packaged libraries of Java code that can be invoked from within the JSP. Just like the useBean, they can do a lot of work behind the scenes and just return the results.

There are lots of available libraries, which is one reason for this topic to be so huge. We could spend chapters just describing all the various database access routines, HTML generating routines, and so on available to you. Perhaps the leading tag library is the JSP Standard Tag Library (JSTL).

Here are two of the most common directives used with tag libraries. First is the directive that declares a library to be used:

```
<%@ taglib prefix="my" uri="http://java.sun.com/jstl/core" %>
```

You then use the prefix as part of the tag name on subsequent tags that refer to this library. For example, if we had an out directive in our library, we could use my as the prefix, separated by a colon: <my:out ...>.

The second directive we will show is a for loop. The for loop mechanism provided by this library is in some ways simpler than using Java scriptlets. It comes in many forms, including one for explicit numeric values:

```
<my:forEach var="i" begin="0" end="10" step="2">
```

This example will loop six times with i taking on the values 0, then 2, then 4, and so on. Another variation of the forEach loop can also make it easy to set up the looping values:

```
<my:forEach var="stripe" items="red,white,blue">
```

In this example it will parse the items string into three values: red, white, and blue, assigning each, in turn, to the variable stripe. In fact the items attribute can also store an array, or collection, or iterator from the Java code that you may have declared (or that is implicit from the underlying servlet). The `forEach` will iterate over those values without you having to code the explicit `next()` calls or index your way through an array.

The bottom of the loop is delimited by the closing tag:

```
</my:forEach>
```

For more information on these and other tags, check out

- `http://java.sun.com/products/jsp/jstl`
- `http://jakarta.apache.org/products/jsp/jstl`
- The references at the end of this chapter

Beyond the standard library of tags, there are other third-party collections of tags; you can also create your own libraries, called *custom tag libraries*. While a useful and powerful thing to do if you have a large JSP-based application, such details would expand this book well beyond its scope. If you're interested in this topic, please follow up with some of the excellent references at the end of this chapter.

19.4 USING JSP WITH BUDGETPRO

We could have taken the BudgetPro example from the previous chapter and simply translated it all into JSP files. The reason we didn't is that it's not how you are likely to find JSP used "in the wild." Since JSP files become servlets, it is not uncommon to find JSP and servlets mixed together—not arbitrarily, but in a sensible way. Remember the Model/View/Controller (MVC) pattern from your readings on object-oriented programming and design patterns?[2] Well, JSP makes for a reasonable View, and a plain servlet can act as the Controller. The Model is typically the database behind all this. That's what we've done with the BudgetPro example.

We've taken the two main chunks of output code—that for the main account display and the form used for creating subaccounts—and turned those

---

2. If not, then a) you should do some more reading, and b) the MVC pattern is a "classic" way to divide the work of a GUI into three distinct parts: Model—the data behind what you are doing or displaying; View—a particular way to display that data; and Controller—an object that acts as the "traffic cop" to various inputs and events, sending messages to either the View, or Model, or both.

into JSP files. The main servlet class (`BudgetProServlet.java`) is thus "gutted" of its output, and the new version (`BudgetProController.java`) acts as the controller. Requests come to it via HTTP requests, but for output, it redirects the browser making that request over to the appropriate JSP.

This introduces a new bit of servlet syntax—redirecting a request to another URL. The action is taken by means of a method call on the HTTP response object:

```
response.sendRedirect("BPAcct");
```

Whereas in the previous, servlet version of BudgetPro, we would create an object that was the next page of output:

```
nextPage = new AccountView(current);
```

In this version, we instead redirect the response to a JSP that produces the output for that page.

So how does the JSP know for which account it should display information? That is shared between the JSP and the controller servlet via the session information. As with the previous, servlet-base BudgetPro, the session is used to store the current account. It can be retrieved from the session information, as seen in line 11 of `BPAcct.jsp`:

```
11:    <% Account acct = (Account) session.getAttribute("current");
```

That variable (`acct`) is then used throughout the JSP to get the appropriate data for display, as in:

```
21:    Account: <%= acct.getName() %>
```

We could also have used a session JavaBean. Such a mechanism requires more setup on both sides, the controller and the JSP, but has the advantage of removing more literal Java code from the JSP. ("We leave this as an exercise for the reader!")

19.5 REVIEW

We've looked at server-side Java processing with JavaServer Pages which can be thought of as servlets turned inside out. From that simple concept we looked at our servlet example and converted it to use JSP. We also looked briefly at the syntax for JSP tags and the JSTL, but encouraged you to do more reading on this topic.

19.6 WHAT YOU STILL DON'T KNOW

We didn't yet discuss the spelling of JavaServer Pages. If you've read through this chapter, you may have noticed that there is no space between Java and Server but there is a space between Server and Pages. If you've read this chapter, you may also have some idea of why it's spelled this way: It's the JavaServer that's doing the work—serving up the Pages. OK, it's not a huge deal, but it is worth knowing how to spell something kerectly, rite?

There are volumes that we could have written about tag libraries. Large scale projects, and any project with a database connection behind it, will find tag libraries invaluable at providing standard mechanisms for database access. Check out the resources, below, for more information on tag libraries.

19.7 RESOURCES

Some of the best material on JavaServer Pages comes from two of the books we mentioned in the previous chapter. You now understand how interrelated the two topics of servlets and JSP are, and these two books cover both topics very well:

- *Core Servlets and JavaServer Pages* by Marty Hall and Larry Brown, ISBN 0-13-009229-0, a Prentice Hall PTR book.
- Its sequel, *More Servlets and JavaServer Pages* by Marty Hall, ISBN 0-13-067614-1, also by Prentice Hall PTR.

As we said, the topic of tag libraries is huge, and just writing about JSTL could fill it's own volume. It has. We recommend:

- *Core JSTL: Mastering the JSP Standard Tag Library* by David Geary, ISBN 0-13-100153-1, Sun Microsystems Press.

To get it straight from the horse's mouth, there is the official Sun specifications for JSP, available at

- `http://java.sun.com/products/jsp/ download.html#specs`

19.8 EXERCISES

1. Convert the controller and the JSP to share their data via JavaBeans.
2. Add a control button to each page (`BPAcct.jsp`) to return not just one level upwards, but back to the top level account. (Hint: The controller can store a reference to the top level account in a session variable named `top`.)

Chapter 20

Open Source
Web Application Servers

Servlets and JSP need to be served up by something; that something is a Web application server. What started as simple Web servers serving up little more than HTML pages developed into Java application servers—the backbone of the enterprise IT environment.

20.1 WHAT YOU WILL LEARN

In this chapter, we will describe the installation of both the JBoss and Geronimo Java application servers on a Linux platform. These servers not only run servlets and JSP, but they are also, as we shall see in later chapters, J2EE EJB containers, so the installation part of this chapter is important for using the technologies and examples covered in the remaining chapters. We will review the System V init system and explain how to add JBoss to the regular system of services on your Linux box. We will show you how to use groups and permissions to enable a number of nonroot users to do the basic application server administration.

20.2 DOWNLOADING JBOSS

JBoss[1] is a complete *application server*. It provides a full, production-ready, J2EE environment. Be aware that as of this writing JBoss 4.0 has just passed the Sun J2EE certification tests, but even prior to the certification JBoss has been one of the most widely used J2EE application servers.

A great deal of JBoss information can be found on the JBoss Web site.[2] Visit the site's download page[3] to download the product.

> **NOTE**
>
> Version 4.0 of JBoss has only just become available, so you will see us using the prior production stable version, 3.2.3. By the time you read this, however, version 4.0 will be the better choice. What we describe should apply equally well to both.

First off, you must choose what form of the product to download. The choice is really between a binary and source distribution. Within that choice, you can choose between a number of compression methods. We will download and install a binary. Just click on `jboss-3.2.3.tgz` and save the file. Before we install, we need to consider some issues of management.

20.3 BE AN ENABLER, OR "LET'S BE CODEPENDENT!"

People often give inadequate consideration to the issues of management of software systems. This is especially true of Java systems, which are, by their nature, cross-platform. We have the luxury of dealing only with Linux systems here, so we can make some practical suggestions most books ignore.

---

1. JBoss is actually a combination of two distinct projects: JBoss, the EJB container and JMS server, and Tomcat, the servlet and JSP server. You can install and use Tomcat alone. We won't bother to do that in this book. We'll install JBoss and use JBoss for everything. We are also lazy typists who do not like to keep typing JBoss/Tomcat, so we'll refer to it merely as JBoss from now on. If you are deploying only servlets and JSP, then, by all means, download and install Tomcat only. It is part of the Apache Jakarta project.

2. `http://www.jboss.org/index.html`

3. `http://www.jboss.org/downloads/`

Up to this point, we have largely been considering a situation where the Java developer is working on an individual workstation where he or she has `root` access. Now that we are talking about application servers, we are dealing with systems where, as the software progresses from development through rounds of testing to production, we will want to limit the people who are able to change certain elements of the system. Often, the "quick and dirty" strategy is to share out the `root` password to a number of users. This is a serious security risk, even when all parties are trusted. Why? Because `root` isn't a person. When someone logs in as `root`, we do not know who that person is. We only know that it is someone who knows the `root` password. In some businesses, this is an unacceptable ambiguity in audit.

A common alternative is to restrict `root` login to the console only, and to require the use of the **su** ("set user") command to promote an already logged-in user to `root` status. This provides a link back to the individual, so actions can be traced to single person. That improves auditability.

This strategy is better, but since `root` is an all-or-nothing proposition, it is a fairly blunt instrument. Once someone can **su** to `root`, that someone can do *anything*. That's a lot of power to give to someone who just needs to be able to install WAR files.

Yet another strategy is to set up the **sudo** system.[4] Using **sudo**, you can specify what people can execute which commands as `root`, and where they may do it from. In other words, you might let user `alice` start and stop the Web server and mount and unmount filesystems when she is logged in to a local machine, but only to start the Web server when she is logged in on a machine outside your network. Check out the manpage for **sudo** to learn more. Even this isn't the best solution for the present issue.

The best solution is not to require `root` power at all if you can avoid it. Remember that permissions on files in Linux are assigned to *users*, *groups*, and *others*. Most people do not think about the middle tier, groups. But groups are the best way to give control over parts of the filesystem to a collection of users without requiring them to share an account and password.

20.3.1   Nonroot-Installed Software

The problem with all of the power-sharing strategies we outlined earlier is that once the user escalates to `root`, there is no way to limit what he or she can do

---

4. Some folks pronounce this "ess-you doo," and some "pseudo." Whatever floats your boat.

(well, **sudo** lets you limit it, but a mistake can be fatal—consider what happens if you let them run a program that lets them escape to a shell). So, for example, if you want to let the Web services group install and maintain JBoss, but you don't want them to mess with any standard software on the system, then create a separate place for nonsystem software.

Two common places for such software on Linux systems are `/opt` and `/usr/local`. We tend to use `/usr/local` mainly because this is the default path on an awful lot of software that uses **autoconf** to handle cross-platform compilation (it is used by the majority of Free Software programs, but exceptions include what are arguably the four most widely used Free Software packages: the Linux kernel, the Apache Web server, the Perl language, and XFree86). So we are going to install JBoss under `/usr/local` and we are going to give a number of users the power to install and manage software in `/usr/local`.

You will need to be `root` to carry out this procedure. Here are the steps—but don't worry, we'll pad them out with a lot of ponderous explanation:

1. **Create the group.**

    Groups are defined in the file `/etc/group`. Each line in that file defines a group. Each line is of the form:

    ```
    GroupName:x:GroupID:GroupMembers
    ```

    `GroupName` is the name of the group. It is the group name that shows up in long form **ls** output. The second field is for the group's password. If we may confess, we don't know if this feature works anymore. You used to be able to specify a group password, but this defeats the whole purpose of not sharing passwords. Sharing passwords is a security risk. Don't do it. The third field is the group ID number. Remember that files have owning users and owning groups. These are both stored as numbers. User numbers are known as `uids` and group numbers as `gids`. These numbers should be unique. If you reuse a number for more than one group, the effect could be indeterminate, since it would depend on how a given program was written. Don't reuse numbers. The final column is a comma-delimited list of user names. Those named users are said to belong to the group. We'll talk some more about what that means as we go on.

Imagine that user names `bob`, `ted`, `carol`, and `alice` are part of `carl` and `michael`'s Web development team and each has an account on the box on which we intend to install JBoss.

So, we create a group entry in the `/etc/group` file:

```
local:x:100:carl,michael,bob,carol,ted,alice
```

If Bob later leaves to join the custodial staff, simply remove his name from the group and he loses his access.

TIP

The user's default group is specified in the `/etc/passwd` file. Here's a sample:

```
mschwarz:x:500:500:Michael Schwarz:/home/mschwarz:/bin/bash
```

The fields of this are:

```
username:passwd:uid:gid:userinfo:homedir:loginprog
```

where:

- `username` is the login name of the user.
- `passwd` is the user's encrypted password. Or rather it used to be. Now, this is usually `x` and the encrypted password is stored in the `/etc/shadow` file. This is because `/etc/passwd` must be world-readable. The shadow file is not. This prevents someone reading the encrypted passwords to do an offline dictionary attack.
- `uid` is the numeric user ID associated with this username.
- `gid` is the numeric group ID of this user's default group. Look for this number in `/etc/group` to find the name of the default group.
- `userinfo` is additional information about this user. Sometimes called the gecos field for obscure historical reasons,[5] this field usually stores the user's real name and possibly other information like office location and phone number.
- `homedir` is the user's home directory.
- `loginprog` is the name of the program that will be executed when the user logs in. This is usually a shell, but it may be any program.

---

5. See `http://www.hyperdictionary.com/dictionary/GCOS` if you are dying to know why.

NOTE

There are two strategies that Linux distributions follow for assigning a default group to a new user. One is to put all users into a group called `staff` or some such. This is widely considered a security risk since it often leads to making files accidentally readable or writable by all users on the system. The more common method is to create a group for each user when the user is created.

TIP

If you get in the habit of creating groups, you might want to assign the numbers systematically: 500–599 groups for programs, 600–699 groups for program installation, 700–799 groups for company departments to allow them to control their own Web content, and so on.

2. **Change group ownership of** `/usr/local`.

Odds are, `/usr/local` already exists on your system. It may even have several programs installed in it. You must give the group ownership over everything in `/usr/local` and below. The **chgrp** command changes the group owner of files, and the `-R` argument says to do so recursively:

```
# cd /usr/local
# chgrp -R local .
```

At this point, everything in `/usr/local` and below is group-owned by the `local` group.

3. **Set group permissions on** `/usr/local`.

Basically, you want the group to be able to read and write everything in `/usr/local`. To do this, you need to change the permissions on all the files with the **chmod**. As with **chgrp**, this command takes a `-R` argument that recursively walks the directory tree. We need to give everyone in the group read and write permission on all the files:

```
# chmod -R g+rw .
```

> **NOTE**
>
> We are assuming you are carrying out these steps in sequence and thus your current working directory is still `/usr/local`.

4. **Set directory permissions on** `/usr/local`.

   You want slightly different permissions on directories. First, you want the group to have execute permission on directories. This allows each member of the group to make each directory his or her current working directory. See Eric Raymond's *Unix and Internet Fundamentals*[6] for a good basic introduction to file permissions on UNIX.

   Also, on Linux systems, when a user creates a file, that file is, by default, group-owned by the user's primary group,[7] which is not what we want here. We want files created by a user in this directory to be group-owned by the `local` group. To do this, we have to set the *setgid bit* on all the directories in `/usr/local` and below. When a user creates a file in a directory that has the setgid bit set, that file will be group-owned by the group-owner of the directory *if the user is a member of that group*. If the user is not, it will be group-owned by the user's default group as usual. So we need to set execute and setgid permissions on all the directories in `/usr/local` and below:

```
# find /usr/local -type d -exec chmod g+xs {} \; -print
/usr/local
/usr/local/share
/usr/local/share/bochs
/usr/local/share/bochs/keymaps
/usr/local/share/bochs/keymaps/CVS
/usr/local/share/doc
...
...
etc.
```

---

6. `http://en.tldp.org/HOWTO/Unix-and-Internet-Fundamentals-HOWTO/disk-layout.html#permissions`

7. Which is the group ID specified for the user in the `/etc/passwd` file.

With this setup, members of the `local` group can manage files and programs in `/usr/local` and below as they wish. They have full power over the files and they need nothing but their own login credentials to do it. The `root` password can remain private.

20.3.2 Finer Grained Control

This pattern can be repeated. We can give ownership of different branches under `/usr/local` to other groups to allow control to be doled out in small sets.

20.4 INSTALLING JBOSS

Using a platform-neutral system like Java has both advantages and disadvantages. A disadvantage is that, generally, Java products don't use the traditional installation mechanisms of your native platform. You don't install an RPM or a DEB. But this is somewhat offset by the fact that all a Java application needs is for its classes to be arranged in a particular pattern on the filesystem. In other words, all you need to do to install JBoss is to unpack the tarball.

You did the hard part already. Since you have created the group and made yourself a member of that group,[8] any member of the group can install the product:

```
$ cd /usr/local
$ tar xzvf jboss-3.2.3.tgz
jboss-3.2.3/lib/
jboss-3.2.3/client/
jboss-3.2.3/docs/
jboss-3.2.3/docs/dtd/
jboss-3.2.3/docs/dtd/html-svg/
...
...
etc.
```

---

8. Group membership is established at login. It may be necessary to log out and log back in to take advantage of a newly created group. There are other obscure ways, such as running a subshell with the `login` argument or running `su -`, but the simplest is to log out and log back in.

> **TIP**
>
> At this point we suggest using one more Linux filesystem trick. The tarball un-packs into a directory whose name includes the product version—in this case, `jboss-3.2.3`. In many cases, you will want to be able to have more than one version of JBoss installed on a box simultaneously, either because you need to port projects from one version to another, or perhaps because you need to de-velop applications that will run on different versions on different target servers. To make your life easier, create a symbolic link to a generically named directory, such as `jboss`, and have that symlink point to `jboss-3.2.3`. Then you can write your startup and shutdown scripts to use the `jboss` pathname. You can then switch to another version by changing where the symlink points:
>
> ```
> $ cd /usr/local
> $ ln -s jboss-3.2.3 jboss
> ```
>
> This process is discussed in detail in Section 6.2 in the context of switching between Java SDK versions.

20.5 THINGS THAT MAKE IT GO

In order to explain how to integrate an Open Source application server into your system, we have to do a little Linux Sysadmin training. We need to show you how server processes are generally managed on Linux systems.

20.5.1 System V Init System

Virtually all Linux distributions use some variant of the System V init system to create and customize programs and services that run at the startup of the box. Now, we don't want to write a Linux system administration manual, but we do need to tell you enough to decide how to make JBoss available when needed on your server.

The core of the System V init system is the `/etc/inittab` file. Everything else devolves from this configuration file. In the days before network services, the primary startup tasks were to get **getty** programs running and then run a single startup shell script. The `/etc/inittab` file handles these tasks beautiful-ly. Since then, the world of UNIX and Linux has become a complex mixture of client-server programs and protocols, so a complex set of conventions has been developed to turn the primitive `/etc/inittab` into a much richer set of controls. Let's take a very brief look at `/etc/inittab` and how it works; then we'll move on to the extended scripts that manage server processes. That is where we will integrate JBoss.

A key concept in the System V init system is the *runlevel*. The idea is that a system can have a number of "standard" configurations, numbered from 0 to 6, where 0 is shutdown, 1 is single-user, 2 to 5 are up to the system administrator, and 6 is reboot. The **init**[9] command can be used (by the `root` user) to change the system from its current runlevel to another:

```
# init 1
```

What happens when you issue such a command is determined by the `/etc/inittab` file. Let's take a look at the out-of-the-box `/etc/inittab` file from a Fedora Core 1[10] system (Example 20.1).

This is a pretty complex file, and we don't want to bog down in it too much, since most of what interests us occurs outside this file.

The basic format of a line in `/etc/inittab` is:

```
id:runlevels:action:process
```

The `id` is a unique 1–4 character identifier. The `runlevels` is a list of the runlevel numbers to which the record applies. The `action` specifies what action is to be taken. The `process` is the program to run. The `respawn` action, for example, tells **init** that when the process exits, it should be run again. The `once` action says it should be run once on transition to the runlevel. We won't go into too much more here. See the `man inittab` page for details.

The part that concerns us are the `10` through `16` entries. Note that these cause the `/etc/rc.d/rc` script to be run once, with the runlevel passed as an argument. This is the key to System V init system.

---

9. **telinit** is a common alias from other UNIX implementations. Linux symlinks this to **init**.

10. During the writing of this book, RedHat decided to put their completely Free Software OS out to a public-controlled project and to stop calling it "RedHat." The name RedHat is reserved for Fedora-based Linux systems that must be purchased with support contracts. It is still the same system with a different name maintained by basically the same people. The key difference is that you *cannot* purchase support for Fedora (at least from RedHat, we expect some enterprising folks to offer Fedora support for a fee at some point).

Example 20.1 Fedora Core 1 default /etc/inittab file

```
#
# inittab        This file describes how the INIT process should set up
#                the system in a certain runlevel.
#
# Author:        Miquel van Smoorenburg, miquels@drinkel.nl.mugnet.org>
#                Modified for RHS Linux by Marc Ewing and Donnie Barnes
#

# Default runlevel. The runlevels used by RHS are:
#   0 - halt (Do NOT set initdefault to this)
#   1 - Single user mode
#   2 - Multiuser, without NFS
#       (The same as 3, if you do not have networking)
#   3 - Full multiuser mode
#   4 - unused
#   5 - X11
#   6 - reboot (Do NOT set initdefault to this)
#
id:5:initdefault:

# System initialization.
si::sysinit:/etc/rc.d/rc.sysinit

l0:0:wait:/etc/rc.d/rc 0
l1:1:wait:/etc/rc.d/rc 1
l2:2:wait:/etc/rc.d/rc 2
l3:3:wait:/etc/rc.d/rc 3
l4:4:wait:/etc/rc.d/rc 4
l5:5:wait:/etc/rc.d/rc 5
l6:6:wait:/etc/rc.d/rc 6

# Trap CTRL-ALT-DELETE
ca::ctrlaltdel:/sbin/shutdown -t3 -r now

# When our UPS tells us power has failed, assume we have a few minutes
# of power left.  Schedule a shutdown for 2 minutes from now.
# This does, of course, assume you have powered installed and your
# UPS connected and working correctly.
pf::powerfail:/sbin/shutdown -f -h +2 "Power Failure; System Shutting Down"

# If power was restored before the shutdown kicked in, cancel it.
pr:12345:powerokwait:/sbin/shutdown -c "Power Restored; Shutdown Cancelled"
```

```
# Run gettys in standard runlevels
1:2345:respawn:/sbin/mingetty tty1
2:2345:respawn:/sbin/mingetty tty2
3:2345:respawn:/sbin/mingetty tty3
4:2345:respawn:/sbin/mingetty tty4
5:2345:respawn:/sbin/mingetty tty5
6:2345:respawn:/sbin/mingetty tty6

# Run xdm in runlevel 5
x:5:respawn:/etc/X11/prefdm -nodaemon
```

NOTE

Some Linux distributions run different scripts for each runlevel instead of passing the runlevel as an argument to a single script. The details are not important. The net effect is that a script is run for each runlevel.

Sure, you could put the code to run JBoss directly in that script if you want. But these scripts have been designed to handle arbitrary sets of services without you having to modify those scripts directly. How? By doing what Linux (and its UNIX antecedents) does so well: making complex systems out of simple parts.

Each service you might wish to start and stop gets a shell script that controls it. This shell script must take a command argument. The minimum set of commands that must be supported are start and stop. Other options such as restart and status are often supported, but start and stop are the important ones.

The script for **atd**, the one-shot job scheduler, is a fine example. Let's take a look at it (Example 20.2).

Example 20.2 The **atd** init shell script

```
#!/bin/bash
#
# /etc/rc.d/init.d/atd
#
# Starts the at daemon
#
# chkconfig: 345 95 5
```

```
# description: Runs commands scheduled by the at command at the \
#    time specified when at was run, and runs batch commands when \
#    the load average is low enough.
# processname: atd

# Source function library.
. /etc/init.d/functions

test -x /usr/sbin/atd || exit 0

RETVAL=0

#
# See how we were called.
#

prog="atd"

start() {
  # Check if atd is already running
  if [ ! -f /var/lock/subsys/atd ]; then
    echo -n $"Starting $prog: "
    daemon /usr/sbin/atd
    RETVAL=$?
    [ $RETVAL -eq 0 ]  touch /var/lock/subsys/atd
    echo
  fi
  return $RETVAL
}

stop() {
  echo -n $"Stopping $prog: "
  killproc /usr/sbin/atd
  RETVAL=$?
  [ $RETVAL -eq 0 ] && rm -f /var/lock/subsys/atd
  echo
    return $RETVAL
}

restart() {
  stop
  start
}

reload() {
  restart
}
```

```
status_at() {
  status /usr/sbin/atd
}

case "$1" in
start)
  start
  ;;
stop)
  stop
  ;;
reload|restart)
  restart
  ;;
condrestart)
  if [ -f /var/lock/subsys/atd ]; then
    restart
  fi
  ;;
status)
  status_at
  ;;
*)
  echo $"Usage: $0 {start|stop|restart|condrestart|status}"
  exit 1
esac

exit $?
exit $RETVAL
```

This script is from a RedHat Linux system. Those comments at the top are a magic incantation for the **chkconfig** program that ships with that distribution[11] (and with Fedora Core). We'll talk more about **chkconfig** in the next section.

As you can see, the basic premise is that when a daemon is started, the process ID is saved into a file. If the "stop" option is passed, the PID is looked up and the process is killed. That's the basic idea. But wait! There's more!

Each runlevel has a directory of scripts. Let's look at the contents of such a directory (Example 20.3).

---

11. The RedHat **chkconfig** program is conceptually similar to the one in the IRIX operating system.

Example 20.3 A directory of scripts

```
[mschwarz@host238 mschwarz]$ cd /etc/rc5.d
[mschwarz@host238 rc5.d]$ ls
K01yum            K73ypbind           S18rpcgssd        S58ntpd
K05saslauthd      K74nscd             S19rpcidmapd      S80sendmail
K11jboss          K89netplugd         S19rpcsvcgssd     S80spamassassin
K12mysqld         S00microcode_ctl    S20random         S85gpm
K15httpd          S04readahead_early  S24pcmcia         S90crond
K15postgresql     S05kudzu            S25netfs          S90vmware
K20nfs            S06cpuspeed         S26apmd           S90xfs
K24irda           S08iptables         S28autofs         S95anacron
K35smb            S09isdn             S40smartd         S95atd
K35vncserver      S10network          S44acpid          S96readahead
K35winbind        S12syslog           S55cups           S97messagebus
K36lisa           S13irqbalance       S55sshd           S97rhnsd
K50snmpd          S13portmap          S56rawdevices     S99local
K50snmptrapd      S14nfslock          S56xinetd
```

Notice the file `S95atd`? Let's look at the long form **ls** output for that file:

```
[mschwarz@host238 rc5.d]$ ls -la S95atd
lrwxrwxrwx  1 root    root    13 Feb  2 02:08 S95atd -> ../init.d/atd
```

The file is a symbolic link to the file in the `init.d` directory! If you take a look at the actual script run by the `/etc/inittab` file on a runlevel change, you will notice that what it does is to pick up all the files in the `rcX.d` directory (where X is the runlevel being changed to[12]) that begin with the letter K, run through them in numerical order, and execute the linked scripts with `stop` as the argument. It then picks up all the files that begin with S, runs through them in numerical order, and executes the linked scripts with `start` as the argument.

This sounds like a mess, but it is actually a very nice way to automate the starting and stopping of services by runlevel. Adding or removing a new service is simply a matter of creating the `/etc/init.d` script, and then adding the

---

12. That phrase actually caused my high school grammar teacher to materialize in my office and scold me. I invite anyone who can come up with an elegant and grammatical way to phrase that to contact me at `mschwarz@multitool.net`. I'm perfectly serious.

appropriate symlinks to the `rcX.d` directories.[13] So, first we have to take an init script and modify it to run JBoss.

20.5.2   RedHat/Fedora chkconfig

RedHat and its stepchild, Fedora, use a program called **chkconfig** to automate the setup and integration of init scripts.

The **chkconfig** program has four basic functions. Two involve adding and removing services from management. That's our main interest here, but we'll get to that in a moment. The other two involve querying and setting the runlevels in which services run. That is the more common use, so we'll look at those first.

```
[root@host238 root]# chkconfig --list ntpd
ntpd            0:off   1:off   2:off   3:on    4:off   5:on    6:off
```

> **TIP**
>
> `chkconfig --list` without specifying a service name will list all the services managed by **chkconfig**, including those that are provided by **xinetd**, which we will not cover here.

As you can see, `ntpd` runs at runlevels 3 and 5, and does not run at any others. The `--list` argument lets you query the runlevels.

```
[root@host238 root]# chkconfig --levels 2345 ntpd on
[root@host238 root]# chkconfig --list ntpd
ntpd            0:off   1:off   2:on    3:on    4:on    5:on    6:off
```

The `--levels` argument lets you specify a list of runlevels that will apply to the named service. The last argument may be `on` or `off` to specify which setting to apply to those runlevels. The current value (`on` or `off`) for a specified

---

13. Just a quick reminder that not all Linux distributions name their directories or scripts in precisely the same way, but they all use something similar. By examining the `/etc/inittab` file and the contents of the `/etc` directory, you should be able to figure out the details of any given distribution. Over time, more and more distributions have come to exactly match the naming scheme described here. RedHat, Fedora, and Debian, for example, all follow this naming scheme.

runlevel is overwritten by whatever you specify. There is more to this; see the manpage for **chkconfig** for details.

Now, before we put JBoss under management, we need to make a script for it. Or rather, we need to modify the one provided by JBoss. In the `bin` subdirectory of JBoss, you will find a script called `jboss_init_redhat.sh`. You will notice that it has the "**chkconfig** mojo" in it—that is, the "`chkconfig:`" comment line. We mentioned this in passing when we looked at the **atd** init script, but we didn't tell you what those three numbers after the colon actually mean. The first is the list of runlevels in which you want the program to run. The second is the start priority, which is the number that will follow the `S` in the `rcX.d` runlevel symlink directory. The third number is the stop priority, which is the number that will follow the `K` in the `rcX.d` runlevel symlink directory.

These start and stop priority numbers can be very important indeed. Some services (like NFS) depend upon others (like portmap). Your JBoss server might depend on a service like mysqld or postgresql. Don't toy with these orders lightly. You can seriously mess up your services if you don't know what you are doing. Still, you will probably have to tweak things to get them completely right. Just be cautious and think about every change.

Example 20.4 is the script as it comes with JBoss 3.2.3.

There are three things we have to change here. The first are the runlevels in the "`chkconfig:`" line (we'll show you the changed lines with a couple of lines of context):

```
#
# chkconfig: 345 80 20
# description: JBoss EJB Container
#
```

Next, we may need to change the paths to JBoss and to the Java runtime. In our case, if you installed into `/usr/local` and created the symbolic link as we suggested, you don't need to change the JBOSS_HOME, but you have to change the JAVAPTH variable:[14]

---

14. We are assuming you have set up your Java SDK as described in Chapter 6. If your **java*** commands are located somewhere else, change this path to point at them.

Example 20.4 Out-of-the-box JBoss init script for RedHat

```sh
#!/bin/sh
#
# JBoss Control Script
#
# chkconfig: 3 80 20
# description: JBoss EJB Container
#
# To use this script,
# run it as root - it will switch to the specified user.
# It loses all console output - use the log.
#
# Here is a little (and extremely primitive)
# startup/shutdown script for RedHat systems. It assumes
# that JBoss lives in /usr/local/jboss, it's run by user
# 'jboss' and JDK binaries are in /usr/local/jdk/bin. All
# this can be changed in the script itself.
# Bojan
#
# Either amend this script for your requirements
# or just ensure that the following variables are set correctly
# before calling the script.

# [ #420297 ] JBoss startup/shutdown for RedHat

# define where jboss is - this is the directory
# containing directories log, bin, conf, etc.
JBOSS_HOME=${JBOSS_HOME:-"/usr/local/jboss"}

# make sure Java is on your path
JAVAPTH=${JAVAPTH:-"/usr/local/jdk/bin"}

# define the classpath for the shutdown class
JBOSSCP=${JBOSSCP:-"$JBOSS_HOME/bin/shutdown.jar:$JBOSS_HOME/client/jnet.jar"}

# define the script to use to start jboss
JBOSSSH=${JBOSSSH:-"$JBOSS_HOME/bin/run.sh -c all"}

if [ -n "$JBOSS_CONSOLE" -a ! -d "$JBOSS_CONSOLE" ]; then
  # ensure the file exists
  touch $JBOSS_CONSOLE
fi
```

```
if [ -n "$JBOSS_CONSOLE" -a ! -f "$JBOSS_CONSOLE" ]; then
  echo "WARNING: location for saving console log invalid: $JBOSS_CONSOLE"
  echo "WARNING: ignoring it and using /dev/null"
  JBOSS_CONSOLE="/dev/null"
fi

# define what will be done with the console log
JBOSS_CONSOLE=${JBOSS_CONSOLE:-"/dev/null"}

# define the user under which JBoss will run,
# or use RUNASIS to run as the current user
JBOSSUS=${JBOSSUS:-"jboss"}

CMD_START="cd $JBOSS_HOME/bin; $JBOSSSH"
CMD_STOP="java -classpath $JBOSSCP org.jboss.Shutdown --shutdown"

if [ "$JBOSSUS" = "RUNASIS" ]; then
  SUBIT=""
else
  SUBIT="su - $JBOSSUS -c "
fi

if [ -z "`echo $PATH | grep $JAVAPTH`" ]; then
  export PATH=$PATH:$JAVAPTH
fi

if [ ! -d "$JBOSS_HOME" ]; then
  echo JBOSS_HOME does not exist as a valid directory : $JBOSS_HOME
  exit 1
fi

echo CMD_START = $CMD_START

case "$1" in
start)
    cd $JBOSS_HOME/bin
    if [ -z "$SUBIT" ]; then
        eval $CMD_START ${JBOSS_CONSOLE} 2>1
    else
        $SUBIT "$CMD_START ${JBOSS_CONSOLE} 2>1 "
    fi
    ;;
stop)
    if [ -z "$SUBIT" ]; then
        $CMD_STOP
    else
        $SUBIT "$CMD_STOP"
    fi
    ;;
```

```
restart)
    $0 stop
    $0 start
    ;;
*)
    echo "usage: $0 (start|stop|restart|help)"
esac
```

```
# define where JBoss is - this is the directory
# containing directories log, bin, conf, etc.
JBOSS_HOME=${JBOSS_HOME:-"/usr/local/jboss"}
```

```
# make sure Java is on your path
JAVAPTH=${JAVAPTH:-"/usr/java/jdk/bin"}
```

Finally, we don't need to run the "all" configuration, we only need the default configuration at the moment, so we change the argument to the run.sh invocation:

```
# define the script to use to start JBoss
JBOSSSH=${JBOSSSH:-"$JBOSS_HOME/bin/run.sh -c default"}
```

JBoss Configurations

When you unpacked JBoss, it contained three predefined server configurations located in jboss/server. The three configurations are named all (which runs every single service JBoss supports, including RMI/IIOP and clustering features), default (which runs only the set needed to run servlets, JSP, and EJBs), and minimal (which runs just JNDI, the logger, and a URL deployment service; no Web container, no JMS, no EJBs).

In effect, the selected configuration *is* the server. You can, of course, customize any configuration, and you may create additional configurations.

Now, this script allows you to run JBoss as any user. It defaults to user jboss if none is specified. You have to decide what to do here. Without specifying a user, it will run as root. That is a major security risk. On an out-of-the-box RedHat or Fedora system, there is no user called jboss. We will have to create one. There are a lot of security concerns to creating a special "nonlogin" user. The most important involve changing the user entries in /etc/passwd

---

Example 20.5 Using **chkconfig** to include JBoss start script

```
[root@cvs root]# cd /usr/local/jboss/bin
[root@cvs bin]# cp jboss_init_redhat.sh /etc/init.d/jboss
[root@cvs bin]# chkconfig --add jboss
[root@cvs bin]# chkconfig --list jboss
jboss           0:off  1:off  2:off  3:on   4:on   5:on   6:off
[root@cvs bin]# /etc/init.d/jboss start
CMD_START = cd /usr/local/jboss/bin; /usr/local/jboss/bin/run.sh -c default
```

---

and /etc/shadow after you create the user. Unfortunately, the JBoss program needs to run a shell script, so you cannot set the shell to /sbin/nologin as is usual. Set the password for the user in /etc/shadow to x, which is completely invalid and will forbid login to the account by password.

Finally, you will need to add the user jboss to any groups you created for JBoss management (such as local in our case). Truth be told, it would be a good idea to use the jboss user to install JBoss. It will avoid having to deal with some file ownership and permission issues. If you do not do this, the simplest way to get this init script working (you will get permission errors) is to run

```
chmod -R g+w /usr/local/jboss
```

That will make the script work with the jboss user, provided jboss belongs to the group owner of the JBoss installation.

The final step is to copy your modified script to its final destination and run **chkconfig** to install it in all the runlevels (Example 20.5).

You now have JBoss running. You can start and stop it with the script, and it will come up and shut down automatically depending on the runlevel you switch to. Beauty, eh?

20.5.3   Other Distributions

You don't need **chkconfig** to set up equivalent scripts. In fact, the same script provided by JBoss for RedHat will work with most distributions that use System V init system. You will have to copy the init script and then create the appropriate symlinks manually, or locate the automated setup tools for your particular distribution (Debian, for example, has many such tools which you select with their package management system).

20.5.4   IDE Integration

Another piece of software you might want to look at is JBoss-IDE,[15] an Eclipse plug-in for JBoss. The software is not downloadable from the footnoted Web site, it is available only from the Eclipse Install/Update manager, so run your copy of Eclipse and install it. We will not cover JBoss-IDE here, but if you use Eclipse as your development platform, JBoss-IDE is very useful for managing and deploying EJB's, servlets, and JSP.

20.6 DISPOSITION OF FORCES

Not to go all Sun-Tzu on you or anything, but if you want to win the war, you must control the initiative. In other words, move only when you are ready. Deploying software into JBoss could not be easier *if* you get everything ready before you begin.

You see, the key is to create a correctly configured WAR file, as a `build.xml` file from our project does (Example 20.6).

If you look at the `deploy` task, you will see that it simply copies the WAR file to a particular directory under the Web server[16] and, it turns out, that is all you need to do to deploy to JBoss. JBoss will notice the new WAR file, stop any existing version, and start the new one. It all depends on getting the WAR file right.

20.7 APACHE GERONIMO

An up-and-coming alternative to JBoss is Apache Geronimo. Part of the Apache Software Foundation's set of projects, Geronimo is an Open Source, Apache-licensed[17] implementation of the J2EE specification. Furthermore, Geronimo aims to be an Open Source J2EE implementation that is J2EE-certified by

---

15. `http://www.jboss.org/developers/projects/jboss/jbosside`

16. Note that that's normal for development. For integration and production, either someone authorized will run the same build on the target, or (more likely) the WAR file will be "formally" built, tagged, and copied to the test or production server. We'll talk more about that when we get to application maintenance issues.

17. Most notably, it doesn't require anyone to open the source of their changes or customizations if they improve on an Apache software project, unlike the GPL which does.

Example 20.6 Ant `build.xml` for the BudgetPro servlet and JSP examples

```
<!-- =============== File and Directory Names ================ -->
<!-- ...
  app.name     The name of our application, used for file/dir names.
  build.home   The name of the directory into which the
               "compile" target will generate its output.
  server.home  The name of the directory where the Web server
               is installed.
  deploy.home  The name of the directory into which the WAR file
               will be copied.
-->

  <property name="server.home" value="/usr/local/jboss" />
  <property name="deploy.home"
          value="${server.home}/server/default/deploy"/>


<!-- ... -->

<!-- =============== Deploy Target ============================ -->
<!--
  The "deploy" target copies the WAR file into a location required
  (i.e., defined) by the servlet container. For some servlet
  containers, you must restart them before they will recognize our
  new/modified Web application.  Others may reload automatically.
-->

  <target name="deploy" depends="compile"
        description="Deploy application to servlet container">

    <!-- Copy the contents of the build directory -->
    <mkdir   dir="${deploy.home}"/>
    <copy  todir="${deploy.home}" file="${app.name}.war"/>

  </target>

<!-- ... -->

<!-- =============== Product WAR file ========================= -->

  <target name="war" depends="compile"
        description="Create WAR file to be deployed">
    <war destfile="${app.name}.war" webxml="web/WEB-INF/web.xml">
      <fileset dir="${build.home}"/>
    </war>
  </target>
```

Sun.[18] We will take a quick walk through the installation of the Apache Geronimo Java application server. Geronimo not only runs servlets and JSP, but it is also, as we shall see in later chapters, a J2EE EJB container, so the installation part of this chapter is important for using the examples and technologies covered in the remaining chapters.

Geronimo is a complete application server. It provides a full, production-ready, J2EE environment. It is the stated goal of the Geronimo project to pass the Sun J2EE certification tests. Such certification will, in all probability, quickly make Geronimo one of the most widely used J2EE application servers.

A great deal of Geronimo information can be found on the Geronimo Web site.[19]

> **NOTE**
>
> As of this writing, the project was just nearing the certification process. Only the milestone releases were available for downloading. By the time you read this, however, a fully certified version will likely be production-ready. There may be slight differences in the download and installation procedures. Be sure to follow the instructions from the Web site and any readme files for the most up-to-date information.

First off, you must choose what form of the product to download. The choice is really between a binary and source distribution. Within that choice, you can choose between two compression methods, **zip** or **tar/gzip**. While the first is typical for Windows distributions and the second for Linux, you can choose either, as Linux has utilities for decompressing both. More importantly, the binaries are Java JAR files so they are not tied to a particular operating system. We will download and install a binary. Just click on the `tar.gz` filename and save the file.

If you haven't read the previous sections because you were going to skip JBoss and just use Geronimo, please go back and read Section 20.3. It deals with administration and privileges for setting up your installation, and you'll want to know that for this chapter's installation discussion, too.

---

18. As of this writing, there was still a legal hurdle to overcome, since Sun requires derivative works to be branded and compatible, whereas the Apache license places no such requirements on its derivative works. This may be resolved by the time you are reading this.

19. `http://geronimo.apache.org/`

20.8 INSTALLING GERONIMO

Using a platform-neutral system like Java has both advantages and disadvantages. A disadvantage is that, generally, Java products don't use the traditional installation mechanisms of your native platform. For Linux users that means that with Java you don't install using an RPM or a DEB. But this is somewhat offset by the fact that all a Java application needs is for its classes (in JARs) to be arranged in a particular pattern on the filesystem. In other words, all you need to do to install Geronimo is to unpack the tarball.

You did the hard part already. Since you have created the group and made yourself a member of that group (see Section 20.3), any member of the group can install the product:

```
$ cd /usr/local
$ tar xzvf geronimo.tar.gz
...
$
```

> **TIP**
>
> At this point we suggest using one more Linux filesystem trick. The tarball unpacks into a directory whose name includes the product version—in this case, `geronimo-1.0-M1`. In many cases, you will want to be able to have more than one version of Geronimo installed on a box simultaneously, either because you need to port projects from one version to another, or perhaps because you need to develop applications that will run on different versions on different target servers. To make your life easier, create a symbolic link to a generically named directory, such as `geronimo` and have that symlink point to `geronimo-1.0-M1`. Then you can write your startup and shutdown scripts to use the `geronimo` pathname. You can then switch to another version by changing where the symlink points:
>
> ```
> $ cd /usr/local
> $ ln -s geronimo-1.0-M1/ geronimo
> ```
>
> This process is discussed in detail in Section 6.2 in the context of switching between Java SDK versions.

20.9 RUNNING THE GERONIMO SERVER

Getting the Geronimo server up and running is simply a matter of running a
Java application contained in the `server.jar` file in the `bin` directory.

```
$ cd /usr/local/geronimo
$ java -jar bin/server.jar org/apache/geronimo/Server
```

That last parameter looks like a pathname, but it isn't. It is a *configuration
ID* which just uses the pathname-like syntax as a namespace, to be unique to
Geronimo (by virtue of the `/org/apache/geronimo` prefix). That name tells
the server which of the several possible configurations you want to use. For
more information on the other configurations, refer to the Geronimo Wiki.[20]

Having once invoked a particular configuration, you need not repeat that
configuration choice on subsequent invocations. That means that the next time
you run Geronimo, you can just use:

```
$ java -jar bin/server.jar
```

If you want to put this in a startup script you'll want to use the full
specification, so as to be absolutely sure what you are getting.

To stop the server invoked from a command line, simply type Control-C.
If the server was invoked from a startup script, you will need to find its process
ID (e.g., with the **ps** command) and use the Linux **kill** command to send it
a signal.

20.10 REVIEW

In this chapter we have looked at the installation of both the JBoss and
Geronimo Java application servers on a Linux platform. For both of these Open
Source servers installation was little more than getting the JAR files in a usable
location. We reviewed the System V init system and explained how to add JBoss
to the regular system of services on your Linux box. We showed you how to
use groups and permissions to enable a number of nonroot users to do the basic
application server administration.

---

20. `http://wiki.apache.org/geronimo/`

20.11 WHAT YOU STILL DON'T KNOW

There is configuration information about your Web applications that must be provided to the Web servers in XML files. A small bit of this will be discussed in Chapter 23, but much of this you will need to find elsewhere. Since this information is in XML and specific to each application server, there is little of it that is specific to the deployment on a Linux system.

20.12 RESOURCES

Documentation on JBoss is available from `JBoss.org`. They have an interesting business model in that they open-source their code but charge for the documentation. Expect to see more third-party books on JBoss, or you may see a move toward Geronimo instead.

Geronimo is, as of this writing, a bit sparse on documentation, too. There is a Wiki site with the beginnings of documentation. Try and hunt down what you need starting from `http://wiki.apache.org/geronimo/` and at the `http://geronimo.apache.org/` home page.

Part V

Developing Enterprise Scale Software

Chapter 21

Introduction to Enterprise JavaBeans

This chapter will serve as an almost criminally brief introduction to Enterprise JavaBeans, their varieties, and their uses.

21.1 WHAT YOU WILL LEARN

You will learn the basics of Enterprise JavaBeans and the Java Naming and Directory Interface, which is how applications and EJB's meet up with one another.

21.2 EXPANDING TO EJBS

All right, we'll admit it. It is a bit of a stretch to expand our sample application to the J2EE Enterprise JavaBean component model. The truth is, given the small data requirements and simplicity of our application, the Web front end that we put on our application in the previous chapters is probably sufficient to scale our application to even very large organizations.

That confessed, we still think our example is the best way to address our topic. Why? Because EJBs are a large topic, worthy of several books (and we encourage you to read some of them, such as *Enterprise JavaBeans Component Architecture* by Gail Anderson and Paul Anderson (ISBN 0-13-035571-2). We simply cannot teach you all about EJBs in our book. Our goal here is to introduce the concepts, provide a working example, and explain how to deploy and maintain an EJB system on Linux using JBoss. Believe us, we'll have enough to cover to achieve that modest goal.

21.2.1 EJB Concepts

In a way, the use of the term *Enterprise JavaBean*, with its echo of the older term *JavaBean*, is unfortunate. Apart from the similar intention of creating reusable components, the two technologies have little in common.

21.2.1.1 *The Life Cycle of an Enterprise JavaBean*

Most of the books on EJBs that we have seen start with the simplest type of bean and work their way up in complexity. We're going to dare to be different, because the most complex case isn't that hard, and once you understand it, the functions of all the other types of EJBs become obvious. They simply don't implement what they do not need.

For the moment, assume that an EJB is a simple class that provides a set of methods to clients. The methods represent business functions that clients want the server to carry out.

Implementing an Enterprise JavaBean requires implementing three Java source files:

- An object that represents the bean implementation
- An interface called the *home interface* that represents the interface between the bean and the EJB container
- An interface called the *remote interface* which represents the methods that a client may call on the bean

We'll get into the details of these interfaces (and the sometimes obtuse reasons behind) a little later on. For now, we will concentrate on the implementation.

The implementation class contains methods that are there only to allow the container to control the bean and to inform the bean of impending changes to its status. Those methods are defined in the bean class that the implementation class extends. The classes one extends to implement a bean are:

- `SessionBean`
- `EntityBean`
- `MessageBean`

Please forgive us right now for admitting that we will not cover message beans in this book beyond a brief description in the next section. For details on message beans, take a look at Chapter 8 of *Enterprise JavaBeans Component Architecture* by Gail Anderson and Paul Anderson (ISBN 0-13-035571-2).

Not all of the control methods need to be implemented in all cases, but the full set is not that large or difficult to understand. They correspond to important "life events" in lifetime of the bean. The primary events are: creation, destruction, passivation, activation, persist to DB, restore from DB, and context switching.

Creation. A bean is created when its constructor is called. As we shall learn, the calling of the constructor has absolutely no connection with a client request. For session beans, the container maintains a pool of instances to handle client requests. For entity beans, a bean (most commonly) represents a database table, and the `setEntityContext()` method is used to move that bean from row (instance) to row as needed.

In practice, this usually means that a number of instances of the bean are created when the application server is started. Additional instances are created as the demand for this bean (number of clients, number of calls per unit time) increases.

Destruction. As you know, Java objects do not have explicit destructors, but when a bean instance is destroyed, an explicit method in the `Bean` class is called to permit shutdown operations to take place.

This is quite distinct from activation and passivation. Activation and passivation are operations carried out when the application server needs to shove aside some `Bean` instances that may still be needed by clients in order to make room for an active request that requires more than the available system resources.

Passivation and activation. As we said above, passivation involves the container asking the beans that are still potentially needed to step aside to allow more urgent tasks (probably beans that are being actively called) to use resources tied up by otherwise idle beans. Think of this as like memory swap in an operating system. The bean will save any data and context information into some sort of persistent storage, which may be a database, flat files, XML files, whatever, when it is passivated.

Context switching. Since both session and entity beans may be called upon to service requests from multiple clients, it is necessary to provide a method whereby the container can notify the bean which "context" (which may be loosely said to be a client) is active at the moment. In stateless session beans this is not necessarily implemented, but in stateful session beans and in entity beans this activity must be supported.

How is this distinct from passivation and activation? Passivation is the temporary "swapping out" of a bean to make room for something else. Context switching is the move of a Bean instance from client to client. Or, to put it another way, passivation makes room for some other bean to become active and serve a client.[1] Context switching switches a given bean from client to client.[2]

21.2.1.2 The EJB Container

A J2EE application server has two *containers*: a Web container and an EJB container. You can also think of these as "servers" in the more classic sense. J2EE calls them containers because it emphasizes the idea that you place Java objects (applets, servlets, and Enterprise JavaBeans) into the container that can run them (a browser, a Web container, an EJB container). The J2EE specification specifies the exact relationship between these application objects and their container. For EJB's, the container provides lifecycle control, network management, load management, perhaps clustering services, CMP (container-managed persistence) services, and so on. We'll talk a lot more about container services

---

1. This is a simplification. A container can passivate a bean to make resources available for any purpose, not just for another EJB. Beans might be passivated because some process on the server outside the application server needs resources. It is entirely dependent on how the application server is written. What is said here is conceptually true, if not actually true ;-)

2. Again, saying "client-to-client" is a simplification. A single client may have multiple threads interacting with multiple beans, and a context switch might be performed to serve different requests from a single client. Again: conceptually true, if not actually true.

as we go along. For now, be aware that the container will start, stop, instantiate, destroy, and provide network services to the EJBs it contains.

21.2.2 Bean Types

Enterprise JavaBeans come in more than one variety. Let's take a look at those.

21.2.2.1 Session Beans

A *session bean* is a reusable component that represents a collection of server methods. The intention is that each such method represents some business process, such as `addCustomer()`, `createShoppingCart()`, and so on.

Session beans are thus organized around business processes. Actually, a session bean is not much more than a facade that collects a business process API into a single class. But remember what EJBs give you—networked server-based functionality, load balancing, clustering features, reliability, failover, and the ability to handle increased demand by merely adding more `Bean` instances and server hardware. The power comes not from how EJBs extend the language, but from how they automate and hide infrastructure.

Session beans come in two major varieties: stateless and stateful. Let's take a look at what they offer and the differences between the two.

Stateless Session Beans

What they are.   A stateless session bean is one where each method call is completely independent of any other method call, whether by one or many clients.

An EJB application designed this way has certain advantages. Since a single `Bean` instance can be switched from client to client on demand (because no state information is kept between method invocations), a small number of `Bean` instances can handle a large number of clients. Compare this with stateful session beans described below.

Why you would use them.   In a sense, this is the optimum bean. If you can design your application to use nothing but stateless session beans (perhaps backed by entity beans), then you have a maximally flexible, extensible, and adaptable enterprise application—one that can be easily scaled from a single application server to a very large cluster. Why? Because the lack of state information means that any single `Bean` instance can serve any given client at any time that it is free without requiring any distribution of client information between `Bean` instances.

From the client's perspective, the client can connect to any instance of the `Bean` on any server at any time to get the same work done.

Stateful Session Beans

What they are.   A stateful session bean is one that remembers its client between method invocations. It maintains some information between calls from a client. Because of this, a given `Bean` instance can only handle one client at a time, and if an instance is to be switched between clients, the information about the previous client must be saved so that the client's session may be restored later.

An application that is designed around stateful session beans will generally require more resources than one designed around stateless session beans (described above) because each active client requires a dedicated instance of the `Bean`.

Why you would use them.   We think we've beaten the issue of the advantages of stateless beans into the ground. But what are the advantages of a stateful bean?

Many types of client interaction require the bean to "remember" something about the client. The classic (and, by now, almost cliché) example is a Web-based shopping cart application. The remote interface for a stateful `ShoppingCart` EJB might look something like this:

`createCart`
> Creates a new shopping cart for the customer.

`addItem`
> Adds an item to the shopping cart.

`delItem`
> Removes an item from the shopping cart.

`purchaseCart`
> Processes the cart; charges the credit card; generates pick list, shipping list, and invoice; discards cart.

`abandonCart`
> Discards the cart.

Here, items like the identity of the customer and the list of items in the cart must be preserved between method invocations. Obviously, it is possible to present such an interface through a stateless bean by creating some sort of a session identifier token and passing that in to every method, thus allowing the stateless session bean to save this data to a database and then load it back, but the primary advantage of a stateful session bean is that this work is done for you through the setting of the bean's *context*.

So, the primary advantage of stateful session beans is that the server side can keep track of client data for you. The primary disadvantage is that the container will try its best to keep an instance of the `Bean` around for every client, so it must sometimes swap an idle instance out to make room for an active instance, which is an expensive operation. But—and this is important to keep in mind—it is much less expensive than reading and writing this data on every call to a stateless bean! You have to understand what is happening under the hood if you want to produce an optimal design. If you need state between method calls, a stateful bean is likely to be the most effective way to go.

21.2.2.2 Entity Beans

What they are. An entity bean is often described as an object that represents a row in a database table. This is the most typical case, but it isn't always so. We have worked on a J2EE application where the entity bean represented an XML document in the filesystem.

The general idea is that enterprise applications tend to work on lists of similar things: customers, employees, locations, accounts, servers, inventory items, and so on. An entity bean is an object that represents a single item in such a list. In other words, it is an interface to a data item. And, yes, in practice there is one entity bean class for a table and one instance of the class for each row.

Obviously, a J2EE container doesn't maintain an in-memory instance for every row of every table. In fact, you can think of both entity beans and session beans as ways to automate keeping the optimal balance between in-memory instances for speed and data storage for memory utilization.

Entity beans can be written to manage the persistent storage itself, using code added to the bean implementation by the bean author (this is known as *bean-managed persistence*, or BMP), or they may be written to allow the container to automatically manage the data in the underlying database for you (this is known as *container-managed persistence*, or CMP). Which you use may depend many factors, including the databases your container supports, the complexity of your database, the quantity of non-Java clients, or the amount of legacy code.

Entity beans can be a hard sell in many development environments. We can see three strong reasons to resist the use of entity beans.

1. **Heterogenous environments.** In many enterprises, rich and diverse sets of development environments exist—Windows.NET and ASP clients, mainframe clients, C and C++ applications, third-party applications, and Java. The solution many database environments adopt is to use stored procedures that are shared across all of these platforms to concentrate database access into a common set of code. Stored procedures do not tend to be written with the kind of strict row-to-object mapping that entity beans model so well; instead, they are often designed to support specific business processes. That fits so well with the session bean model that you may be tempted to implement a session bean facade in front of such stored procedures and leave it at that.

2. **Legacy code.** A variation on the above argument exists when there is already a considerable body of code, perhaps even Java code written directly using JDBC, that accesses the database and performs the common operations. Here again, the simplest solution is to put a session bean facade on the already existing code.

3. **Mobile cheese.** One of the trendy business books published recently is titled *Who Moved My Cheese?* and it is about the negative ways in which people react to change. You might very well meet resistance simply because the technology is new and unfamiliar, and represents a change in thinking about data persistence from what the development staff is used to doing.

So, where is it suitable? Entity beans are particularly well suited to environments that are homogenous by being based either mostly on Java or on CORBA/IIOP. Further, they are well suited to environments where the bulk of the work is the editing and manipulation of small numbers of entities per session, as opposed to large reports or statistical queries where a session might want to use many or all rows in a table.

Please note that using entity beans in such appropriate cases in no way precludes other types of use! You just won't likely use entity beans for them. In other words, you don't have to use it just because it is there.

One further word. This is by no means an established doctrine, but it seems to be common practice to keep entity beans hidden behind session beans. In other words, it seems to be commonplace to not allow clients (Web applications, Java applications) to communicate directly with entity beans, but rather to have session beans perform all entity bean operations. This is probably because the idea of session beans is to decouple business process from implementation details, and entity beans, no matter how much they hide the underlying database, are still rather tightly coupled to the implementation of the data storage.

Why you would use them.   Essentially, they allow you to write your data access layer exactly once, and then reuse it any number times without worrying about capacity and management. Also, by trying to keep the most often used data in fast memory, they can, when running on a powerful container or cluster of containers, keep many client operations running much faster than a strict write-read update back end.

21.2.2.3 *Message Beans*

What they are.   We're going to gloss over message beans in our book, but you should know what they are. A message bean represents an interface to a message queue. An entity bean represents a transaction where completion of the call tells you the operation has fully completed. A message queue, on the other hand, is an interface where you are given the firm promise that system will get to this when it can. The client doesn't know where or when the message will be handled. It doesn't know if it was successful or not. But it does know that it is the problem of the queue reader.

There are many such operations in large enterprises. And there are many products that implement such functionality. Microsoft offers Message Queue Server (MSMQ). IBM has MQSeries. Message queues are common with operations that take time, or need to be batched, or require human intervention.

Why you would use them.   Let's go back to our shopping cart idea. Management might want a daily sales report. You could send each and every item purchased to a message bean. Then a process to read that queue might be kicked off once a day and the report produced without hitting the database that supports all the current Web users. That's a good example of how a message queue (and thus a message bean) might be used. Again, we're not going to work with message beans here.

21.2.3   Under the Hood

We're not going to take apart the source code for JBoss here, but we do want to spend some time talking about what is going on in an EJB container. It isn't magic. The whole system is built on some familiar technologies that you can learn all about if you want to. First of all, the default protocol for EJB session and entity beans is RMI. That's right. A major part of an EJB container is the code to set up RMI connections between beans and clients. RMI is an application protocol that defines how to encode the state of a Java class, transfer it over a network (using TCP/IP sockets), and restore the coded data to a local implementation of the class (the encoding/decoding process is called *marshaling/unmarshaling*). That's part one. Knowing where to find the appropriate bean is the next part.

21.3 WHAT'S IN A NAME? AN INTRODUCTION TO JNDI

JNDI abstracts a type of service known generically as a directory service. We need to introduce that concept and then describe a few common examples of such systems. Then we can explain how JNDI abstracts these various services.

21.3.1   Naming and Directory System Concepts

Directory services are one of the dark mysteries of modern computing. Why? Because if the people who developed these systems ever let on how simple they actually are, everyone would understand and be able to use them well. Then where would we be?

In practice, a naming system is what we programmers call an associative array, or, when we are feeling less verbose, a simple hash of name/value pairs. That's it. The core concept isn't any more complicated than that. The most familiar naming service out there (one that we are sure you use every day) is the Internet Domain Name Service, or DNS. This is a system that maps domain names (like `www.somedumbnetwork.net`) to IP addresses (like `205.117.29.1`). In the world of directory services, such a name/value pair is called a *binding*.

Of course, the devil is in the details. DNS is implemented by a complex network of name servers that pass requests up and down a distributed hierarchy of name servers. That part can get quite complex, but the core idea is that you have a name (the domain name) and a value (an IP address) that you join together. DNS can actually bind other information, such multiple alias names for a single canonical name/IP pair, a mail handler name for a domain, and other general purpose data which the DNS administrator can choose to share.

So, naming services are a way to join names and values together.

Before we move on, let's make sure we understand how general and universal this concept is. A filesystem can be thought of as a naming service. A UNIX filename (like, say, `/etc/inittab`) can be thought of as a way of linking that name with the data it contains. So the key is the name (`/etc/inittab`) and the value could be either the data it contains, or perhaps a file handle that, when read, returns the data contained in the file.[3]

There are some other common features of naming systems that we should point out. They are frequently hierarchical. A domain name such as `www.multitool.net` actually indicates the host `www` in the `multitool` domain within the `net` domain. The name `www.multitool.com` is not related in any way with the name `www.multitool.net`. They are contained in different top-level domains. They do not intersect. Likewise, the name `/etc/inittab` would be completely unrelated to, say, `/tmp/inittab`—because `inittab` is a file in the `etc` directory, and `inittab` is a file in the `tmp` directory. So, most naming systems are hierarchical. They differ in how the levels of the hierarchy are indicated, and in how absolute names are constructed from components of the hierarchy, but they share this common concept.

So, that's naming. Next come directory concepts.

A naming service is good, but what happens if you don't have the key and you need to go looking? That's what directories are for. Consider the **ls** command. Why do you need it? Have you ever run it? Of course you have. Why? Because you often don't know the exact name of something or where exactly it is in a naming system. You need to be able to look for what you want. That is the "directory" part of naming and directory services. You want something that lets you query and browse the naming system to find what you want.

The **ls** command will give you the complete contents of a directory, or it will allow you to query a directory by specifying wildcard names. These are examples of *browse* and *query* features. We'll talk more about these concepts in relation to naming and directory systems in general and to JNDI in particular.

---

3. The first case would be a name/value pair, the second case would be a name/reference pair. The distinction is often not important, but it does exist.

Key to directory services is the concept of a *context*. A context is a set of bindings with a common name, expressed in a common way. In our filesystem example, `/etc` is a context. A context may contain other contexts that follow the same naming convention. For example, `/etc/sysconfig` is a context that is a *subcontext* of `/etc`. Likewise, `multitool.net` is a subcontext of the `net` context.

A context is distinguished by having a naming convention for itself and its subcontexts, and it must have means of creating bindings, removing bindings, and querying or listing bindings.

Since JNDI is designed to operate across multiple naming and directory systems, it is necessary to talk about *naming systems* and *namespaces*. A naming system is a connected set of contexts that use the same naming convention. Thus, Internet domain names are a naming system, UNIX filenames are a naming system, and so on. A namespace is a set of names in a naming system. These terms will have significance later when we'll talk about JNDI.

A naming system binds a name to a value. Directory services bind a directory object to one or more *attributes*. A naming service could be thought of as a simple case of a directory where "name" and "value" are the attributes of the directory object. A directory can store many more attributes (bindings) for a given name than can a naming service. Directory services also (in general) support the notion of searches and queries.

A *directory object* represents an object in the computing environment. This might be a server, a printer, a user, a router, whatever. Each object would have a set of attributes that describe the object. A *directory* is a connected set of directory objects.

In the directories we know about (see Sections 21.3.2.4 and 21.3.2.5 for the limits of our knowledge), directory objects are arranged in a hierarchy, so that they serve as naming contexts as well as directory objects.

21.3.2 Common Directory Services

Now that you have seen the concepts, we can cover a few common implementations of naming and directory services.

21.3.2.1 Domain Name Service (DNS)

This is probably the most familiar naming and directory system. It is used all the time to resolve Internet host names to IP addresses, and it is commonly used to obtain the names of mail servers for domains. It also has less often used features to look up arbitrary data for domains. These features are not used often because standard DNS has no authentication and authorization controls. Information in DNS is, inherently, public information.

21.3.2.2 Filesystems

The UNIX filesystems, NTFS, FAT, and other filesystems provide name-to-data mappings that are compatible with JNDI. When they are combined with networked filesystems, such as SMB, CIFS, NFS, and even **rsync** and FTP, files can be made available over the network through JNDI.

21.3.2.3 LDAP

LDAP is the "Lightweight Directory Access Protocol." There is an old joke that a platypus is a swan put together by a committee. If that is so, then it often seems that LDAP is the platypus of name and directory services.

To be fair, LDAP has the heavy burden that goes with any standards that are produced by a large committee-driven process. It has to try to be all things to all people. LDAP is a query and transport protocol specification of the ISO X.500 naming and directory service standard.[4] Like other ISO and ANSI standards, the specification is robust to the point of uselessness. LDAP is designed to allow every possible name system in the Universe to be subsumed into a single, uniquely addressable Directory Information Tree. Every entry in LDAP has a *distinguished name*, which is an unambiguous specification of the name from the root of the tree. So far, this is like the other naming systems. There is a root, there are nodes at each layer, and then, at the bottom, there is data. What makes X.500 and LDAP different is that each node consists of not just a name, but of a *type/name pair*. An example of an LDAP name might be:

```
url=http://www.multitool.net/,cn=M. Schwarz,o=MAS Consulting,st=MN,c=us
```

---

4. If you are dying to know, X.500 is a naming and directory services standard from the International Standards Organization (ISO), an international technical standards body. X.500 has a transport and query protocol specification of its own, but it uses the ISO OSI (Open Systems Interconnection) network protocol standard. OSI is rarely used because TCP/IP took off first and has been hacked and hacked again to keep it alive and well. At one time, it looked like IP address space limitations would push the world to OSI protocols, but hacks like CIDR, private subnets, and now the (less hackish) IPv6 make it look like TCP/IP will be here for quite a while. In a sense, then, LDAP is X.500 over TCP/IP. Or, to put it another way, LDAP is a TCP/IP implementation of ISO X.500.

At each node there is a type (`c`, `cn`, `url`, and so on) and a name (or value) for that type. The definitions of these types and the lists of types permitted at a particular level depend on a *schema* which is controlled by whoever controls the server that serves the given level of the hierarchy. In other words, as with DNS, if you want to be part of the public, global namespace, you have to play by the rules of the ancestor nodes. You can do what you want with your point of control and below, but you must obey the naming schema of all of your ancestors.[5]

This explains why so few organizations actually use LDAP globally (i.e., integrating directly with all other public LDAP servers in the world). Instead, they tend to use LDAP by setting up schema and servers that are completely internal and private so that they do not have to use the many required parent nodes it would take to hook up to the global LDAP namespace.[6]

LDAP can (and does) fill books of its own. The type/name pairs are bulky to type and hard to remember, but they allow you to easily map in entire other naming systems, by simply assigning a type to a naming system and allowing that system's names to be values at that level. Remember that these names are hierarchical, so everything under `cn` (normally used for "common name") applies to (in this case) Michael Schwarz. If I defined the schema for my space, I could put anything I wanted under that name.

A common use of LDAP is for centralizing authentication and authorization data for users. Users authenticate to LDAP and all systems in an organization can validate a single credential to authenticate the user—the holy grail of single sign-in. Alas, doing this right is nontrivial because LDAP doesn't specify any mandatory authentication and encryption scheme. (Thus it is often the hacker's holy grail of single sniff-in and 0wn3d systems.)

---

5. We want to be clear: You only have to do this if you wish to give those ancestors and outside users access to your directories. You are free to create entirely private directory structures that need not conform to anyone else's schema. It all depends on the purpose and audience of your directory.

6. Another reason is that LDAP itself has no cryptographically secure authentication or transport mechanisms. That means that hooking up all your directory data to the global Internet gives hackers a one-stop opportunity to steal your data. Not good. Of course, as with other protocols, there are several add-on security mechanisms for LDAP.

21.3.2.4 Novell Directory Service (NDS)

Novell, the folks behind Netware, came up with NDS, which provides full directory services like LDAP/X.500, but (according to the computer press—let us confess right now that we have never directly used NDS or Microsoft's Active Directory) with a simpler API and easier administration. We don't know enough about it to comment on it. But we do know that JNDI can access it.

21.3.2.5 Microsoft's Active Directory

We have to do the same hand-waving here. Active Directory provides similar functionality to NDS and LDAP. We don't know enough about it to comment on it. But, again, JNDI can talk to it.

21.3.3 Putting a Face to a Name: JNDI

The Java Naming and Directory Interface package is designed to provide a common way to access all of these disparate naming and directory services.

The JNDI architecture consists of the JNDI API, which provides a consistent API, and a Service Provider Interface (SPI), which requires an instance to connect to each naming service (such as DNS, LDAP, the RMI registry, and so on).

Basic naming system functionality is obtained through the `javax.naming` package. Directory services are provided by the `javax.naming.directory` package.

Since JNDI can span multiple naming and directory systems, there are no absolute root contexts, so the `InitialContext` class exists to provide a base from which all other names and directories may be looked up.

21.3.3.1 A Sample JNDI Program

The next couple of sections describe a very simple JNDI application that uses the DNS Service Provider Interface to do directory operations on a DNS domain. The source code for the class is shown in Example 21.1.

Example 21.1 A sample JNDI application

```
     import java.util.*;
     import javax.naming.*;
     import javax.naming.directory.*;

 5
    public class GetDomain {
      private Hashtable env = new Hashtable();
      private DirContext dctx;
      private String domainQuery;
10
      public GetDomain(String dom2Query) throws NamingException {
        domainQuery = dom2Query;
        env.put(Context.INITIAL_CONTEXT_FACTORY, "com.sun.jndi.dns.DnsContextFactory");
        dctx = new InitialDirContext(env);
15    }

      public NamingEnumeration getDomainMembers() throws NamingException {
        return dctx.list(domainQuery);
      }
20
      public static void main(String[] args) {
        GetDomain gd = null;
        NamingEnumeration ne = null;

25      try {
          gd = new GetDomain(args[0]);
          ne = gd.getDomainMembers();

          while (ne.hasMore()) {
30          Object o = ne.next();

            System.out.println("Object ["+o+"]");
          }
        } catch (Exception e) {
35        e.printStackTrace();
        }
      }
    }

40
```

Example 21.2 is what we get when we run this program against one of the author's DNS domains.[7]

Example 21.2 Running `GetDomain` against the `multitool.net` domain

```
[mschwarz@cassidy simpleApp]$ java GetDomain multitool.net
Object [baroni: java.lang.Object]
Object [erik: java.lang.Object]
Object [www: java.lang.Object]
Object [class: java.lang.Object]
Object [jboss: java.lang.Object]
Object [penguin: java.lang.Object]
Object [mail: java.lang.Object]
Object [cvs: java.lang.Object]
Object [stiletto: java.lang.Object]
Object [penfold: java.lang.Object]
Object [ns2: java.lang.Object]
Object [ns1: java.lang.Object]
Object [irc: java.lang.Object]
[mschwarz@cassidy simpleApp]$
```

The `GetDomain main()` **method.**   This is another "single class" program example. In this case, the `main()` method creates an instance of the class, passing the first command-line argument to the constructor. We'll cover the constructor in the next section. By now, you will recognize that this is one of the purely pedagogical examples. Note the complete lack of input validation and error checking on the number and content of the command-line arguments.

Establishing an initial context.   For both naming and directory services, it is necessary to establish an *initial context*. A context is a collected set of names. A directory system is a connected set of contexts. Our example is for DNS. We must set an initial context for DNS. The class constructor (lines 11–15) does that.

---

7. Note that directory operations in the JNDI DNS Service Provider Interface are done with DNS zone transfers. Many domains, especially large domains, disable zone transfers either for security reasons, or because they generate a lot of network traffic and are a popular tool for Denial of Service (DoS) attacks on name servers. To put it simply: This program won't work on a lot of domains, especially from outside.

So what is going on here? This constructor is a bit unusual, isn't it? The `InitialDirContext` is a "context factory." It takes an "environment," which is a `Hashtable`, that provides the information needed to make the context. And what is that information? At a minimum, the constant value associated with `Context.INITIAL_CONTEXT_FACTORY` must be associated with the class name of the real context factory for the directory system—in this case, `com.sun.jndi.dns.DnsContextFactory`. If you are from a C/C++ background, think of this as a function pointer.[8]

We now have an initial directory context, which we can use to search.

Going from the initial context to a DNS entry.   Let's now consider a use case for this little program. The program begins at `main()`, line 21. We create an instance of our class and an instance of `NamingEnumeration` (which we will discuss in a moment). We do some very lazy error handling by enclosing the entire process in a simple `try`/`catch` block[9] and treating all exceptions the same. The first thing we do is construct an instance of our class, passing in the first command-line argument[10] as the domain name to use for setting the initial context.

Next, we get an enumeration of all the names in that context. This is done through a method in our class that simply wraps the actual JNDI call that obtains this enumeration. The real event is on line 18. The `list()` method of the directory context returns a `NamingEnumeration`, which is an extension of the classic `Enumeration` Java class. With it, you can iterate over the contents of the context—which we do in lines 29–33. We rely on our old `Object` method, `toString()`, to make these names readable for us. Of course, each

---

8. Of course, it is not. What really happens here is that the code in `InitialDirContext` uses the `Class` class to load the specified class by name. All JNDI context factory classes implement the `Context` interface, so `InitialDirContext` uses the ability of `Class` to load the class by its name as an instance of `Context`.

9. JNDI has a particularly rich collection of exceptions. When a naming or directory operation fails, it is usually possible to determine exactly how and why it failed from the type of `Exception` thrown. All JNDI `Exceptions` extend `NamingException`, so they also make it quite easy to handle them in a lazy manner. In a real production application, you should at least make some effort to differentiate between failures where the network is not working and failures where the network is working fine, but the named resource does not exist. Believe us, if you have to support your application in production you will care about the difference.

10. Again, very bad production coding. Note that no attempt is made to check the number of arguments passed or their contents.

entry in the enumeration is actually a binding that binds the name to either a name object or to a context object.

If, when you encounter a context, you save the current context, set the current context to the new context, and make the method recursive, you would walk from the present context on down. In theory, you could set your initial context to "." (which is the root of DNS) and this program would dump the whole domain name system to you.[11]

21.3.3.2 *Learning More about JNDI*

As with so much in this book, we have had time and space to cover only the basics. There is so much more to JNDI. For now we want to point you at Sun's excellent JNDI Tutorial.[12] JNDI is covered in more depth in many books, including *JNDI API Tutorial and Reference: Building Directory-Enabled Java Applications* by Rosanna Lee and Scott Seligman, ISBN 0201705028.

21.3.4 Using JNDI with JBoss

For our purposes, it is important to know that JBoss uses JNDI to provide much of the EJB container infrastructure. The primary use is to look up the EJBs, as we shall see in the code examples in the following chapters.

21.4 REVIEW

We covered the basic concepts behind the various types of EJBs. We talked about the events in the life of a bean. From here we will go on to describe actual implementations and discuss how a bean is written and deployed to a J2EE container.

---

11. If you are a relatively unschooled net hooligan, let us assure you that this is only "in theory." Before you go off and attempt a DoS attack on the entire Internet with a simple Java class like this, we have to tell you that JNDI DNS enumerations depend on a DNS protocol feature called *zone transfers*. Most high-level DNS servers will not do zone transfers at all, and many will only accept zone transfer requests from internal addresses. Sorry.

12. `http://java.sun.com/products/jndi/tutorial`

21.5 WHAT YOU STILL DON'T KNOW

Where to begin? Your humble authors themselves are still learning the intricacies of J2EE. We have more or less ignored message beans. We have not described the local and local home interfaces, concentrating instead on the remote access of beans. This is because remote access is what client applications will most often use. But entity beans, for example, can only call one another through the local interface, and, in practice, a session bean will likely provide remote access but call any other beans through a local interface.

A quick examination of your local bookstore's computer books section will reveal that J2EE is a vast topic, just by the number of books on the topic and their thickness. Our goal here is to give you enough to make a quick start in using EJBs on a Linux-hosted application server. From there—well, those thick books are probably your next stop.

21.6 RESOURCES

- `http://java.sun.com/products/jndi/tutorial/trailmap.html` is Sun's JNDI tutorial.
- Sun has a J2EE tutorial (`http://java.sun.com/j2ee/1.4/docs/tutorial/doc/index.html`) that is a great place to start.

Chapter 22

Building an EJB

In this chapter we write a very simple EJB and compile it.

22.1 What You Will Learn

- What a simple EJB example looks like.
- What are the several pieces that you need to make an EJB.
- How to compile the pieces of an EJB.

You'll find the full text of our example on the book's Web site at http://www.javalinuxbook.com/. We will only use code excerpts in this chapter.

22.2 EJBs: You Don't Know Beans?

Enough theory about EJBs and naming services and the like. It's time to put together an actual EJB so you can see one run. First we need to write our EJB classes, then compile them. Then, in the next chapter, we'll package them, along with other supporting information, into an EAR file. But let's begin by writing some Java classes.

It's not that we just write a single EJB class, say a session bean, and we're done. Keep in mind that we're going to be using these beans in a distributed environment, so we need a way to have an application running on one system find, create, look up, or otherwise access the bean running on another machine somewhere in our enterprise network. The job of EJBs is to simplify (up to a point) the efforts of the application programmer doing all this, and make it seem as if the bean is quite local or at least independent of location.

Here's how it works. Any application that wants to use the functions provided by an EJB must first locate the bean. It uses a naming service (Chapter 21) for this. What it gets from the lookup is something called a *home interface*. The home interface object is in effect a factory for producing *remote interfaces*, which are the proxies for the actual service(s) that our application wants to use. A remote interface has the method signatures that give the functionality that the application is after, but it doesn't do the actual work of the bean. Rather, it is a proxy for the bean. The remote interface's job is to do all the work behind the scenes to marshal the arguments and send them off to the bean, and to unmarshal the results returned from the bean.

So it's a three step process:

1. Do the lookup.
2. Use the home interface to produce a remote interface.
3. Use the remote interface to call the methods on the bean.

What's all this talk about interfaces? They provide a way to define the methods you want to use, but without having to write all the code to do it. For example, with the remote interface you may define a method to do something with several arguments, say `Blah(a, b, c)`. Now the remote object doesn't really do the `Blah` work; its job is to marshal the arguments (serialized a, b, and c) and send them off to the EJB to do whatever `Blah` is, and then unmarshal the results. So you as an application programmer will write the guts of `Blah` in the EJB object, but for the remote object, its proxy, you only need to declare the method signature. Then the job of the EJB container (e.g., JBoss or Geronimo) is to provide the smarts of the proxy—that is, to generate a Java class that implements your interface, along with the code that knows how to contact your EJB and marshal and unmarshal the arguments and results. That's right, the EJB container (server) makes code that uses your interfaces, along with its own code, to do the infrastructure work of EJBs.

Talking about all these pieces of an EJB can be confusing, too. Sometimes it is helpful to think of an EJB as a single class; sometimes it's better to think of it as a family of classes that act together pretending to be a single bean that is distributed across several hosts. This can make it a bit confusing when talking about an EJB—do we mean the family of interacting classes or do we mean the single class that provides the application functionality that we want?

The names of EJB classes and EJB interfaces (which we will extend and implement) don't help much either—they can be confusing, too. For example, we will extend EJBObject, but not to write an EJB session bean; no, we extend SessionBean for that, but EJBObject is the name for the remote interface. Go figure.

A bit of perspective may help here. The names Remote, Local, and Home are used as modifiers on these classes. Local means "on the same host as the bean." But Home and Remote don't offer much of a clue. The home interface is what we get from a lookup; it produces remote objects (objects which implement the remote interface). A remote object is what our application uses as if it were a Java object doing what we need, even though its application-specific activity will happen on a bean somewhere else on the network.

Let's look at a very very simple example, to see the pieces in action.

22.2.1 SessionBean

Let's write a stateless session bean that will compute the time value of money. Why that? Well, two reasons. First, we already have an SAMoney class with a save() method for computing some values; and second, we need some simple, stateless, but somewhat computationally intensive task to make for a halfway reasonable example.

The real guts of an EJB, the core of the application functionality—in our example, the computation of the time value of money—is the session (or entity) bean. For our session bean we begin by implementing the SessionBean interface, which means that we need to define these methods:

```
public void setSessionContext(SessionContext context) { }
public void ejbCreate() { }
public void ejbRemove() { }
public void ejbActivate() { }
public void ejbPassivate() { }
```

which, for our example, we can implement as empty methods. A stateless session bean never needs an activation or passivation method to do anything—it is pointless to passivate a stateless session bean. Why? Since it's stateless, any instance of it is as good as any other, so the instances are interchangeable and there's no need to passivate one to get to another—just use the one available. It follows that if a bean is never passivated, it will never have to be activated.

But why no body to the `ejbCreate()` method? Well, our bean isn't doing anything extra. This would only be used if our example were more complicated and we needed to do application-specific initializations. For example, if the bean had to connect to a database (and did not use entity beans), it might establish the JDBC connection in `ejbCreate` and close it in `ejbRemove()`. Similarly, we can have an empty `ejbRemove()` method.

Next we add our own methods, the ones that provide the application functionality. For our MoneyBean application, we'll add `save()` and `debt()` methods which will use an `SAMoney` class by calling its `save()` and `debt()` methods. Example 22.1 is the listing of the `SessionBean`.

Example 22.1 Listing of our implementation of a `SessionBean`

```
package com.jadol.budgetpro;
import net.multitool.util.*;

import javax.ejb.*;

/**
 * Actual implementation of the EJB
 */
public class
MoneyEJBean
  implements SessionBean
{
  protected SessionContext sessionContext;
  // typical; just not used now

  public Cost
  save(double amt, double rate, double paymnt)
    throws java.rmi.RemoteException
  {
    return SAMoney.save(amt, rate, paymnt);
  } // save
```

```
public Cost
debt(double amt, double rate, double paymnt)
  throws java.rmi.RemoteException
{
  return SAMoney.debt(amt, rate, paymnt);
} // debt

public void
setSessionContext(SessionContext context)
{
  sessionContext = context;

} // setSessionContext

public void
ejbCreate() { }

public void
ejbRemove() { }

public void
ejbActivate() { }

public void
ejbPassivate() { }

} // interface MoneyEJBean
```

22.2.2 `EJBObject`

At the other end of the chain of EJB objects used to accomplish all this distributed computing is the object that our application is actually going to touch. When our application creates an EJB, it, acting as a client, won't actually get its hands on the distant session (or entity) bean because that session bean is running somewhere out in the network. There will be, however, a proxy object, acting on behalf of the distant EJB. It is described as the *remote interface*, because it is remote from the EJB (though very close to the application). It is an interface because J2EE supplies a class that does the hidden work of marshaling the data, contacting the EJB, sending the data and receiving the results; the application developer only adds a few additional application-specific methods, via this interface (Example 22.2).

Example 22.2 Sample remote interface

```
package com.jadol.budgetpro;
import javax.ejb.*;
import java.rmi.*;
import net.multitool.util.*;

/**
 * Remote Interface for the Money EJB
 */
public interface
Money
  extends EJBObject
{
  // the methods from the remote object which we will call
  public Cost
  save(double amt, double rate, double paymnt)
    throws java.rmi.RemoteException;

  public Cost
  debt(double amt, double rate, double paymnt)
    throws java.rmi.RemoteException;

} // interface Money
```

The crucial thing to note with this interface is that we have defined two methods that match the two methods in our SessionBean—the save() and debt() methods. These are the methods that will actually be called by our application, and the J2EE mechanisms will do their work behind the scenes to connect to the methods of our SessionBean implementation and send back the results.

22.2.3 EJBHome

Between the SessionBean and its remote interface lies the *home interface*, also called the *remote home interface*, since it pairs with the remote interface. An object that implements the home interface is the kind of object that is returned after the lookup() and then narrow() method calls. It is used to create a reference to the EJB. The home interface for a stateless session bean needs only implement a single method, the create() method with no arguments. The body of the method needs do nothing. All the real work is done by the underlying object supplied by J2EE.

Example 22.3 is a listing of our home interface. It looks like an empty shell, but it is all that we need. The rest is handled by J2EE.

Example 22.3 Sample (remote) home interface

```
package com.jadol.budgetpro;
import javax.ejb.*;
import java.rmi.*;

/**
 * Remote Home Interface
 */
public interface
MoneyHome
  extends EJBHome
{
  public Money
  create()
    throws CreateException, RemoteException
  ;

} // interface MoneyHome
```

22.2.4   Summarizing the Pieces

With these three pieces—the session bean, the remote interface, and the home interface—we can see the structure of the key pieces of an EJB. Let's review what we have:

Application object	Extends/implements	Talked about as
Money	EJBObject	remote interface
MoneyHome	EJBHome	home interface
MoneyBean	SessionBean	the implementation

22.2.5   `EJBLocalHome` **and** `EJBLocalObject`

When the session or entity bean is going to be referenced by application code that resides on the same host as the bean, there are variations on the home and remote interfaces that allow for more efficient execution. When you know that the beans are local to this host, you should use a *local interface* (Example 22.4)

Example 22.4 Sample local interface

```
package com.jadol.budgetpro;
import javax.ejb.*;
import java.rmi.*;

/**
 * Local Interface for the Money EJB
 */
public interface
MoneyLocal
  extends EJBLocalObject
{
  // the methods which we will call

} // interface MoneyLocal
```

Example 22.5 Sample local home interface

```
package com.jadol.budgetpro;
import javax.ejb.*;
import java.rmi.*;

/**
 * Local Home Interface
 */
public interface
MoneyLocalHome
  extends EJBLocalHome
{
  public MoneyLocal
  create()
    throws CreateException;

} // interface MoneyLocalHome
```

and a *local home interface* (Example 22.5). The local interface is in place of the
remote interface and extends EJBLocalObject. The local home interface is in
place of the remote home interface and extends EJBLocalHome.

Why bother? Well, there's no need to marshal and unmarshal all that data
if the calls are staying on the same host. This saves execution time. Perhaps
more importantly, since the arguments don't have to be marshaled and

unmarshaled, they don't have to be serializable. For some applications, this is the only way that they can use beans.

Finally, keep in mind that the choice of local versus remote interfaces is not necessarily an either-or choice. For our session bean we have defined both kinds of interfaces. Then the deployment can determine which one will be used.

22.2.6   Compiling Your Beans

In order to compile these bean-related Java classes, you need to have a J2EE JAR in your classpath. If you've installed JBoss into `/usr/local/jboss`, you could add the JAR to your classpath this way:

```
export CLASSPATH="/usr/local/jboss/client"\
"/jboss-j2ee.jar:.:${CLASSPATH}"
```

If you have the Sun J2EE reference implementation installed on your system (in `/usr/local`), then you could use:

```
export CLASSPATH="/usr/local/SUNWappserver"\
"/lib/j2ee.jar:.:${CLASSPATH}"
```

If you have Geronimo installed on your system (with an environment variable GHOME to hold its location), then you would use:[1]

```
export CLASSPATH="${GHOME}/repository/geronimo-spec/jars"\
"/geronimo-spec-j2ee-1.0-M1.jar:.:${CLASSPATH}"
```

In any case, the point is to have in your classpath the JAR file which contains the `javax/ejb/` classes, such as `EJBObject.class`. If you haven't installed one of these containers on your machine, then download a copy of the JAR from the machine where that container is installed. Put your copy somewhere in your classpath, as in the examples above.

---

1. Our JAR is named `geronimo-spec-j2ee-1.0-M1.jar` but yours will likely have a different name by the time the J2EE-certified version of Geronimo is available. It may likely just have the trailing `-M1` dropped from the name; check in the `geronimo-spec/jars` directory. Another option is to use any of the J2EE JARs, for example, from the Sun reference implementation. That's the advantage of standards. Any of them should work for this compilation step. The resulting compiled code should be deployable to any server. "Compile once, run anywhere," right?

If you are using Ant (and why wouldn't you be?) you will need to put the path to the J2EE JAR in the classpath which Ant uses. Since Ant can define its own classpath, you may want to define your compile task as something like this:

```
<target name="compile" >
<javac srcdir="${src}"
    destdir="${build}"
    classpath="/usr/local/SUNWappserver/lib/j2ee.jar:${stdpath}" />
</target>
```

Now it's a simple matter to compile. The basic Java compile command:

```
$ javac com/jadol/budgetpro/*.java
```

will compile all the various classes and interfaces that make up the EJB. There may be other classes in your source tree that need to be compiled as well. With all that going on, you can see why so many people use Ant. With the `compile` target defined as in our example above, you would need only the command:

```
$ ant compile
```

22.3 REVIEW

There are many pieces involved in the construction of an EJB. Besides writing the session bean implementation, there are the remote and home interfaces to be written. The local and local home interfaces are optional, but useful, especially in cases where arguments cannot be serialized or where you know that the beans and the client will reside on the same host. Compiling an EJB is not different from any other Java compile, but it requires a special JAR in your classpath, one that contains the definitions of the J2EE objects and interfaces.

22.4 WHAT YOU STILL DON'T KNOW

We still haven't shown you how to deploy the EJB, now that you have one compiled. In the next chapter we'll show you how to assemble the pieces of the EJB into an Enterprise Archive and then deploy and run it.

More importantly, though, we haven't covered how to write the code for stateful session beans or entity beans. Stateful session beans are one-to-a-client-session, rather than taking all comers, so there is a little more to code, and a few small changes required in the `ejb-jar.xml` config file. (What is the `ejb-jar.xml` config file? It is part of the configuration information used to deploy your EJB, the topic of the next chapter.) But there are some serious complications with entity beans that involve retrieving the bean's data from a "backing store"—for example, a database—and writing it back. There are many good references on these topics, and we mention our favorites in the next section.

22.5 RESOURCES

These are some of our favorite resources for learning about and dealing with EJBs. All of these give much more extensive examples that we have space for, and we encourage you to look at one or more of them.

- *J2EE and Beyond* by Art Taylor (Prentice Hall PTR, ISBN 0-13-141745-2) gives a very good overview of all of the pieces of J2EE. At over 1,000 pages, it's no small book, but it covers a lot more than just EJBs.

- *Enterprise JavaBeans Component Architecture: Designing and Coding Enterprise Applications* by Gail Anderson and Paul Anderson, Sun Microsystems Press, ISBN 0-13-035571-2. At only 435 pages it is the most concise of the three, with the tightest focus and an emphasis on the code.

- *Applied Enterprise JavaBeans Technology* by Kevin Boone, Sun Microsystems Press, ISBN 0-13-044915-6. At just over 700 pages, it is midway between the other two titles. Like the Taylor book, it covers some related technologies, but gives more depth to EJBs than Taylor, as that is its focus. It provides more examples than the Andersons, but its examples are not any deeper, just broader.

Chapter 23

Deploying EJBs

In this chapter we take apart an EAR, put it together, and then send it out into the world.

23.1 WHAT YOU WILL LEARN

- What is in an EAR.
- How to build an EAR by hand.
- How to integrate some of the tools we've covered before (CVS and Ant) to automate this and avoid having to build an EAR by hand.
- How to deploy an EAR to JBoss.
- How to deploy an EAR to Geronimo.

Some people may wonder why anyone would want to describe to you how to build an EAR by hand. The task of constructing such things is increasingly automated, often performed by IDEs, Ant, or J2EE containers or related tools. So why the grubby details of doing it yourself? Two reasons, really. First, if you hide behind the tool, you never fully understand what is happening. It looks too much like magic, and you're helpless if the magic fails. Secondly, seeing how it works inside out gives you a better understanding of what is going on and even empowers you to do a custom version for your project. If this discussion sounds familiar, it may be because you read something similar about IDEs in Chapter 10.

23.2 LEND ME YOUR EAR: ENTERPRISE PACKAGING AND DEPLOYMENT

There are lots of pieces that are needed to make Enterprise JavaBeans (EJBs) work—not only the classes and interfaces that we have defined, but supporting classes and other Web application pieces (e.g., JSP files) as well. They all have to be in the right place. The distributed nature of EJBs means that we need a way to distribute them across (potentially) several machines. And its not just a matter of putting a single Enterprise JavaBean on a single host. A single bean is typically part of a larger collection of classes and other files (properties, images, JSP, HTML) that work together to make an application. The mechanism to manage all this is the Enterprise Archive, or EAR file.

Let's take a look inside an EAR and examine its pieces. Knowing what it's made of will make an EAR look less intimidating, but will also help us understand what we'll need for our application.

> **TIP**
>
> An EAR file (whose name ends with `.ear`) is nothing more than a JAR file with particular expected contents. So you can easily look inside an EAR with the **jar** command. Use the `-tvf` options for table of contents, verbose, and file (meaning that the next argument is the filename).

The `budgetpro.ear` file will be our example. We haven't yet discussed building this file, but let's peek ahead, to see how it will be put together (Example 23.1).

Notice that, at the top level, there are two files and a directory, and inside the directory there are two other files (Table 23.1).

From the standpoint of building an EAR yourself, you need to create all the files listed in Table 23.1 and then put them all together into a JAR file. So we need to understand those pieces.

Example 23.1 Contents of a sample EAR file

```
$ jar -tvf budgetpro.ear
     0 Wed May 19 05:58:02 CDT 2004 META-INF/
   110 Wed May 19 05:58:00 CDT 2004 META-INF/MANIFEST.MF
   295 Wed May 19 05:58:00 CDT 2004 META-INF/application.xml
 11498 Wed May 19 05:58:02 CDT 2004 budgetpro.jar
 12626 Wed May 19 05:58:02 CDT 2004 budgetpro.war
$
```

Table 23.1 Files inside an EAR archive

Name	Type	Content
budgetpro.jar	JAR	The EJB-JAR file—the JAR file that contains our EJB.
budgetpro.war	WAR	The Web application with servlet and JSP files.
MANIFEST.MF	text	A standard JAR manifest; at a minimum, it gives the version number of the JAR file format—for example, Manifest-Version: 1.0.
application.xml	XML	The *deployment descriptor*, an XML description of what's what.
META-INF	directory	A directory with other files.

The plain files that appear in the META-INF directory are simple. The MANIFEST.MF file is like any JAR manifest and can contain simply the JAR version number:

```
Manifest-Version: 1.0
```

The application.xml file is shown in Example 23.2

Two JAR files are mentioned in this XML description file. This tells the container that we have two modules, an EJB and a Web application. The Web module also defines a context root, which is the portion of the URL pathname that is intended to direct requests to this Web application. For example, if your host is www.bighost.com, then the context root of /budgetpro means that the URL you will use to access the Web application in this EAR is www.bighost.com/budgetpro/ followed by whatever other filename you might need to append, such as a JSP file—or, if left blank, the default index.html file.

Example 23.2 Sample `application.xml` file

```
<?xml version="1.0" encoding="ISO-8859-1"?>

<application>
  <display-name>BudgetPro</display-name>
  <module>
  <web>
    <web-uri>budgetpro.war</web-uri>
    <context-root>/budgetpro</context-root>
  </web>
  </module>

  <module>
    <ejb>budgetpro.jar</ejb>
  </module>

</application>
```

That takes care of the two plain files. Let's also look inside the other two archives, the JAR file and the WAR file, and see what they hold.

23.2.1 What's in an EJB-JAR File

Let's look first at the content of the JAR file. After that we'll look at the specifics of the XML descriptor files.

```
$ jar xf budgetpro.ear      # unjar the EAR
$ ls                        # see what we got
META-INF
budgetpro.ear
budgetpro.jar
budgetpro.war
$ jar tf *.jar              # list the JAR contents
META-INF/
META-INF/MANIFEST.MF
com/
com/jadol/
com/jadol/budgetpro/
net/
net/multitool/
net/multitool/util/
com/jadol/budgetpro/MoneyLocal.class
com/jadol/budgetpro/SessionTestServlet.class
```

```
com/jadol/budgetpro/MoneyEJBean.class
com/jadol/budgetpro/MoneyHome.class
com/jadol/budgetpro/Money.class
com/jadol/budgetpro/MoneyLocalHome.class
com/jadol/budgetpro/TestMoneyEJBean.class
net/multitool/util/Save.class
net/multitool/util/Cost.class
net/multitool/util/Debt.class
net/multitool/util/SAMoney.class
META-INF/ejb-jar.xml
META-INF/jboss.xml
$
```

The EJB-JAR file contains the specifics for our EJB file (Table 23.2).

To keep Table 23.2 simpler and shorter, we didn't list each of the directories in the tree of directories down to each class file. When we show, for example, `com/jadol/budgetpro/*`, realize that each directory that is part of that structure (`com`, `com/jadol`, and so on) is part of the JAR file. The class files are located in that tree.

So what are the two XML files?

These XML files provide the EJB container with information on how the bean parts are wired together. Let's look at the contents of each.

Table 23.2 Contents of the EJB-JAR file

Name	Type	Content
`MANIFEST.MF`	text	A standard JAR manifest; besides defining the JAR version it can be empty.
`ejb-jar.xml`	XML	A description of the EJB, most importantly the mapping between the name of the EJB and the actual Java class file.
`jboss.xml`	XML	This file is specific to JBoss (well, duh!). It describes a mapping between the JNDI name used in the `locate()` and the name of the EJB. The equivalent file for Geronimo (which uses OpenEJB) is `openejb-jar.xml`.
`net/multitool/util/*`	class files	Various classes.
`com/jadol/budgetpro/*`	class files	Various classes.
`META-INF`	directory	A directory with other files.

The `ejb-jar.xml` file (Example 23.3) is part of the J2EE standard. It specifies the names of the home and remote (and local, if any) interfaces, the implementation class (i.e., the real bean) and the name for the bean.

Example 23.3 Sample `ejb-jar.xml` file

```xml
<?xml version="1.0" encoding="UTF-8"?>
<!DOCTYPE ejb-jar PUBLIC
  "-//Sun Microsystems, Inc.//DTD Enterprise JavaBeans 2.0//EN"
  "http://java.sun.com/dtd/ejb-jar_2_0.dtd">

<ejb-jar>

  <description>BudgetPro</description>
  <display-name>BudgetPro</display-name>

  <enterprise-beans>

    <!-- Session Beans -->
    <session id="test_Money">
      <display-name>Test Money Bean</display-name>
      <ejb-name>test/Money</ejb-name>
      <home>com.jadol.budgetpro.MoneyHome</home>
      <remote>com.jadol.budgetpro.Money</remote>
      <ejb-class>com.jadol.budgetpro.MoneyEJBean</ejb-class>
      <session-type>Stateless</session-type>
      <transaction-type>Container</transaction-type>
    </session>

  </enterprise-beans>

  <assembly-descriptor>

  </assembly-descriptor>

</ejb-jar>
```

The name of the bean defined in the `ejb-jar.xml` file is not, however, the name we will use in our JNDI lookup. Rather, there is one more level of mapping used by JBoss. Look at the contents of the `jboss.xml` file (Example 23.4).

Example 23.4 Sample `jboss.xml` file

```
<?xml version="1.0" encoding="UTF-8"?>
<!DOCTYPE jboss PUBLIC "-//JBoss//DTD JBOSS//EN"
  "http://www.jboss.org/j2ee/dtd/jboss.dtd">

<jboss>

  <enterprise-beans>

    <session>
      <ejb-name>test/Money</ejb-name>
      <jndi-name>ejb/Money</jndi-name>
    </session>

  </enterprise-beans>

  <resource-managers>
  </resource-managers>

</jboss>
```

The two tags define the mapping: You use the `jndi-name` in the `lookup()` method and it will (try to) find the EJB named with the `ejb-name` tag. The `ejb-name` tag is also used in the `ejb-jar.xml` file. This provides the association between the two, and the mapping from the JNDI name to EJB is thereby defined.

To summarize, if we want to build an EJB-JAR file, we will need to gather all the class files in their appropriate classpath directory structures. Then we will need to write two XML files and place them in the `META-INF` directory along with the `MANIFEST.MF` file. The two XML files will define the EJB pieces and provide a name mapping for locating this bean. Then put all these pieces together into a JAR file, and you have an EJB-JAR file.

23.2.2   Using Our Bean

We have put a lot of pieces in place to get a bean that we can call from across the enterprise. But what does that call look like? How might we make use of the bean?

The first step is to make contact with the JNDI service and locate the home interface for the bean. It looks like the section of code in Example 23.5.

Example 23.5 Locating the home interface

```
//Look up home interface
InitialContext initctxt = new InitialContext();
Object obj = initctxt.lookup("ejb/Money");
MoneyHome homer = (MoneyHome) PortableRemoteObject.narrow(obj, MoneyHome.class);
```

We're putting this code in the init() method of a servlet; it could also
be in a test program, or in a JSP. It needs to happen only once for our servlet
(which is why we put it in the init() method) and then the connection can
be used many times, once for each contact with the bean.

We get to the actual bean this way:

```
Money mrbean;
mrbean = homer.create();
```

We then use the bean, making the calls on its remote interface (a Money
object, that extends EJBObject) as if it were just a simple method call on an
ordinary class:

```
car = mrbean.save(20000.00, 0.04, 250.00);
```

The math is done in the actual SessionBean, out there in the network,
and the results are sent back to this application. Our application goes on to
display this number as part of an HTML page.

Then when we're done with the bean, we need to clean up:

```
mrbean.remove();
```

23.2.3   Packaging the Servlet

We will now package up the servlet, along with a simple startup page to invoke
it. We'll look at the WAR file and see how it's built.

23.2.3.1   What Is in the WAR File

The other JAR-like file in the EAR is the WAR file. Let's see what is in one of
those (Table 23.3).

Notice that the WAR file puts its XML descriptor not in the META-INF
directory but in a WEB-INF directory along with the classes.

Table 23.3 Contents of the WAR file

Name	Type	Content
MANIFEST.MF	text	A standard JAR manifest; it can be empty or list the contents.
web.xml	XML	XML description of the Web application—servlet definitions, and so on.
jboss-web.xml	XML	Empty in our example—no JBoss-specific directives are used.
classes	directory	Directory structure for the Java class files.
classes/.../*.class	class	The various class files.
*.jsp	JSP	These are the JSP files that run as part of the Web application; note that they are in the top level of this directory structure, not in any subdirectory.
*.html	HTML	Any static HTML pages, too.
META-INF	directory	A directory with other files.
WEB-INF	directory	A directory with other files.

23.2.3.2 Weaving the Web

The web.xml file is the descriptor for the Web application part of all this. Using the servlet tag, it defines a servlet associating a name with this servlet (a name which can be used elsewhere in this XML file) and stating which Java class file is that servlet.

Then the servlet-mapping tag is used to map a URL pattern to a servlet. The URL pattern is the portion of the URL that signals to the server that the request is not for a simple HTML page, but rather for our servlet.

Example 23.6 is a sample web.xml; notice in particular how the mapping from URLs to the Java class is accomplished.

23.2.3.3 Connecting the Pieces

So now that you have seen all the pieces, know that you can edit the XML files with your favorite editor, and can build the JAR/WAR/EAR files with the **jar** command, it's not that hard to put it all together. It is, however, tedious, and is well worth automating, at least with Ant.

The key to making it work, whether by hand or by automation, is a workable directory structure. The easiest way to construct JAR files is to have

Example 23.6 Sample `web.xml` file

```
<?xml version="1.0" encoding="UTF-8"?>
<!DOCTYPE web-app PUBLIC
  "-//Sun Microsystems, Inc.//DTD Web Application 2.3//EN"
  "http://java.sun.com/dtd/web-app_2_3.dtd">

<web-app>
  <servlet>
    <servlet-name>SessionServlet</servlet-name>
    <display-name>Simple Session Servlet</display-name>
    <servlet-class>com.jadol.budgetpro.SessionTestServlet</servlet-class>

    <load-on-startup>1</load-on-startup>

  </servlet>

  <servlet-mapping>
    <servlet-name>SessionServlet</servlet-name>
    <url-pattern>/servlet/test</url-pattern>
  </servlet-mapping>

  <session-config>
    <session-timeout>0</session-timeout>
  </session-config>

</web-app>
```

a directory structure that mirrors the structure of the JARs that you are building. But that arrangement is often not helpful for source management purposes.
It is therefore not uncommon to have a source tree that reflects the project
structure and a separate build directory that mirrors the JAR file directory layout. As classes are compiled, the class files are copied into the build directory
along with copies of the XML, JSP, and other files. As a last step in the build
process, the build directories are "jarred up" into WAR/JAR/EAR files.

23.3 DEPLOYING THE EAR

Deploying means getting your file(s) into the right place and dealing with the
Web server to get your application up and running. For EJBs this includes the

automatic construction of various components by the server. It's not as daunting as it sounds—at least not any more.

23.3.1 JBoss

One of the great things about JBoss is its dynamic or "hot" deployment. The only work involved in deploying your application, if you have the EAR file built properly, is to copy the EAR file to the deployment directory. JBoss does all the rest.

Here is a listing of a very simple shell script that does what is needed, followed by an invocation of that shell script to install our BudgetPro example EAR file.

```
$ cat ejbinstall
cp $* /usr/local/jboss-3.2.3/server/default/deploy
$ ejbinstall budgetpro.ear
$
```

Of course, this assumes that execute permission has been given to the script and it is located in the search path. Furthermore, it assumes that JBoss (version 3.2.3) was installed in /usr/local.

23.3.2 Geronimo

Geronimo will be undergoing lots of change between the time that we write this and the time that you read this. Be sure to check the Geronimo Web site[1] for the latest information.

Geronimo deployment is done as a separate executable step and is not folded into the server. This separation of functions keeps the server smaller and quicker on startup. The deployer has the smarts for reading in all the XML configuration information for your bean, building all the needed classes, and serializing it to package it up.

To deploy our EAR, we execute the following command from the Geronimo home directory:

```
$ java -jar bin/deployer.jar --install --module budgetpro.ear
```

---

1. http://geronimo.apache.org/

Although not available in the early releases, Geronimo may add a "hot deploy" feature where the EAR file can just be put into a deploy directory and the rest will happen automatically. Even so, what will be happening behind the scenes is this same deploy step.

23.4 MAINTAINING A DISTRIBUTED APPLICATION

The deployment is easy if you have the EAR file built properly. But as you just saw, that can be a big "if"—the EAR consists of several layers of files that must be in the right place and have the right contents. There are tools to help with all this, though. Ant is widely used to automate many of these tasks.

23.4.1   Ant and CVS

In previous chapters we've talked about CVS for managing sources and Ant for automating our builds. The first step to making all this work together is something that we should have covered sooner—using CVS with Ant.[2]

Example 23.7 is a simple Ant buildfile (`build.xml`) that will let you get the source from your CVS repository by supplying a particular CVS tag. You name the tag (which you would have previously applied to your sources) and this Ant target will check out that version. The files are put in the `srctree` directory off of the `basedir` of the Ant project.

You will have to modify this script to make it fit your environment. The `cvsRoot` and `csvRsh` values correspond to the `CVSROOT` and `CVS_RSH` environment variables that you would otherwise have set for working with CVS. The `package` attribute should be set to the project directory that you would specify when you check out sources. The directory specified by the `dest` attribute will be created if it doesn't exist.

The next task to accomplish with Ant is the construction of the EAR, WAR, and JAR files. Since all three files are essentially just JAR files, we can use the Ant `jar` task. The EAR contains a WAR and a JAR, and those in turn contain Java class files (and a few miscellaneous files). Using the `depends` attribute, we can build them in steps.

---

2. So, aren't you glad that you've kept reading and gotten this far? Ah, the rewards of persistence!

Example 23.7 An Ant target for checking out source from CVS

```xml
<?xml version="1.0"?>
<!-- ++++++++++++++++++++++++++++++++++++++++++++++ -->
<!--        retrieve our sources by tag name         -->
<!--        invoke with: ant -DTAG=puttaghere         -->
<!-- ++++++++++++++++++++++++++++++++++++++++++++++ -->

<project name="sources" default="src" basedir=".">

  <!-- src target  -->
  <target name="src">
    <cvs cvsRoot=":ext:user@hostaddress:/usr/lib/cvs/cvsroot"
         cvsRsh="/usr/bin/ssh"
         package="projectdir/subproj"
         dest="srctree"
         tag="${TAG}">
    </cvs>
  </target>

</project>
```

Our example (see the book's Web site[3] for the full listing) only copies prebuilt XML files (the deployment descriptors) into place to be included in the JAR, WAR, and EAR files. For small examples like ours, building the deployment descriptors by hand is not a difficult task. But larger, more complex projects will benefit from further automation. Most J2EE servers come with tools to help build such things. These tools tend to be specific to the particulars of their products. Since the J2EE specification allows for certain vendor variations and configuration differences, they can be helpful in configuring things for your specific vendor's version. But being dependent on them for your deployment is a subtle way to become locked into their product. Another good choice—one that avoids this vendor lock-in—is the Open Source tool XDoclet.

23.4.2 XDoclet

XDoclet is an important tool to help with the automation of EJB-related tasks. Working in conjunction with Ant, it uses the Javadoc mechanism of Java to

---

3. http://www.javalinuxbook.com/

automate the building of many of the EJB files and deployment descriptors. Recall that Java comments can include special Javadoc tags, such as `@author` and `@param`. Javadoc uses these tags to generate HTML files that are the documentation of your Java classes and methods based on the text associated with these tags. XDoclet takes this a step further and defines tags like `@ejb.bean` and a few dozen more. Then, using the Javadoc mechanism, it can generate all the various pieces required for an EJB. Used this way, you can write a single source file for your EJB, and have XDoclet generate the various home, remote, and local interfaces as well as the deployment descriptors.

So why aren't we all using XDoclet? It has been around for a few years and is gaining a following in the development community. We may be moving in that direction, but it will take some time. It adds yet another layer to what is needed to build an EJB application, albeit a layer that brings some simplification. Later releases of EJB specifications from Sun may subsume its EJB functionality. However, it is still very important to understand the pieces that go together to make an EJB application. One of the favorite quotes from *XDoclet in Action* by Craig Walls and Norman Richards says it well: "Don't generate what you don't understand."

23.5 ABSTRACTING LEGACY APPLICATIONS

One of the best uses of J2EE technology, particularly the EJB technology, is to provide a single common interface to heterogenous systems. If an application provides any sort of file, data, pipe, or network access to its data, you can wrap an EJB interface around it and make it available to an entire distributed network. This can be a powerful way to leverage investments in legacy systems with modern multitier architectures.

While it is commonplace for EJB applications to interface directly to a relational database back end, there is no requirement that such a system be the back end. IBM, for example, provides Java interfaces to their mainframe legacy data systems, such as CICS.

23.6 REVIEW

We've looked at the contents of an EAR file—not that you'll need to be digging inside them or even building them by hand, but you'll want to know what's inside so as to understand what it takes to put one together. We took a look at

Ant and CVS and how they can be used together to make building and deployment easier. We even mentioned XDoclet, another tool worth knowing something about.

23.7 WHAT YOU STILL DON'T KNOW

JBoss has an IDE plug-in for Eclipse which uses XDoclet to provide an integrated development environment for writing EJBs. If you are working with Eclipse and are going to be doing a lot of EJB development, you should definitely explore this option.

The EJB 3.0 specification, due out within a year, promises to change all this, at least somewhat. With support for metadata in Java 1.5 there will be a standardized mechanism available for use in EJB class construction and deployment. Look for some significant improvements in usability.

23.8 RESOURCES

- Visit `http://geronimo.apache.org` for the latest information on Geronimo.
- Visit `http://www.jboss.org` for the latest information on JBoss.

For more information about all the tags that can be put into the various XML configuration files, look at the DTD files which define them, for example:

- `http://java.sun.com/dtd/ejb-jar_2_0.dtd`
- `http://www.jboss.org/j2ee/dtd/jboss.dtd`
- `http://www.jboss.org/j2ee/dtd/jboss-web.dtd`

XDoclet in Action by Craig Walls and Norman Richards (Manning Publications, ISBN 1932394052) covers the Open Source XDoclet tool for automating the generation of Java code and related files (e.g., deployment descriptors).

Chapter 24

Parting Shots

We try to wrap this whole thing up, talk about the future, and beg for your help.

24.1 THE FUTURE'S SO BRIGHT, I SQUINT AND LOOK CONFUSED

Our crystal ball is a bit foggy, though. Linux is a moving target, and so is Java. In a twist of fate that few could have predicted, the Mono project has a .NET development platform for Linux (and, in fact, for most UNIX-like operating systems). Sun has been talking about open-sourcing Java.[1] New languages and tools emerge all the time. Heck, Geronimo popped up during the research and writing of this very book, while JBoss was the first to pass the Compatibility Test Suite for J2EE. Two minor and one major Java release happened during the writing of this book. A major Linux kernel release occurred. Naught endures but mutability. (The only constant is change.)

---

1. And may we drop all pretense of objectivity and say "Go, Sun! Go! Open it up!"

The three things we can say with confidence are that with Java, Linux, and Open Source, the platform and the tools only get better, the price doesn't go up, and everyone has the chance to play on an level field.

We wouldn't dream of predicting the future, but we're sure that both Linux and Java will have a significant place in it.

24.2 OUR BOOK IS YOURS

This is an Open Content book (as we explained in Preface). You will be able to take it and do with it what you please. We plan to keep improving the book online, and we'd like to invite you all to join in. The authors (who like to refer to themselves in the third person) have the book set up on public servers at `http://www.javalinuxbook.com/` and we welcome comments, suggestions, even patch files.

Don't be afraid to participate. Credit of some sort will be given to every accepted contribution.

24.3 CAME THE REVOLUTION

A lot of people write about Free Software and Open Source in terms ranging from economic history to political revolutionary rhetoric. One of your present humble authors has even written the phrase "economic inevitability" in a weak moment. And while there is ample room to speculate on the future by looking at the past, and while there actually are legitimate issues of liberty, rights, and politics in the mix, it is always shaky when an argument veers close to tautology ("Free Software is right because it is right").

Some people will actually choose Free Software for political reasons, just as some Americans chose rebellion for political reasons. But the majority of Americans in 1776 were not revolutionaries, and the majority of people using Linux are not either. We have other concerns. In both cases, keeping bread on the table is a greater concern for most than the revolutionary issue.

Read Richard Stallman's writings if you are interested in the revolution. Read Lawrence Lessig[2] if you are interested in the politics and legal issues.

---

2. A Stanford Law School professor and founder of the Center for Internet and Society, Lessig is the author of three remarkable books: *Code and Other Laws of Cyberspace*, *The Future of Ideas:*

Most of us, however, will be asking how these technologies can put bread on our table.

The key is lifelong learning. And that is where Open has a distinct advantage. You want to know how it works? Look. There is a lot of good code (and some very bad code) out there, free for the taking, analyzing, and for certain uses. One of the arguments made for closed code is a quality argument. But as programmers who have worked on closed systems, we can tell you that we have seen plenty of bad code out that is closed and proprietary. You just have to look at news about viruses and worms to know that. The point is that Open Source and Free Software are a safer investment. In closed systems there is always pressure to "churn" the APIs so that new OS versions and new development tools can be sold. There is some of that in Free Software too, but you can watch it as it happens, and if a program is your bread and butter, you can participate.

In any revolution, there are the brave and foolhardy rushing to the barricades, banners in hand. But the sensible are keeping their heads down and trying to figure out how to get through it all. We hope our modest contribution helps the latter.

24.4 WHAT YOU STILL DON'T KNOW

This is a book about writing Java applications on Linux systems. We hope we've given you enough to get started, and pointed you to some tools and techniques that, while they've been around a while, may not all be well known or documented.

We've said it before, but each of our chapters tried to cover in a small space what really takes volumes. Our aim has been to give you a flavor, and a start, and a direction.

24.5 RESOURCES

This book that you are reading is part of the Bruce Perens' Open Source Series, "a definitive series of Linux and Open Source books" according to the publisher

---

The Fate of the Commons in a Connected World, and *Free Culture: How Big Media Uses Technology and the Law to Lock Down Culture and Control Creativity.*

Prentice Hall PTR; and who are we to disagree? Seriously though, we encourage you to check out any or all of the titles in the series.

We have already mentioned the more philosophical works by Stallman and by Lessig. As a final reference we offer one that covers not the political philosophy of Open Source but the practical philosophy of what makes Linux so successful. It's called *Linux and the UNIX Philosophy* by Mike Gancarz, published by Digital Press (ISBN 1555582737). It gives practical examples of the way Linux does things, which makes it so useful, so usable, and so enduring. If you're going to be developing on Linux, we encourage you to read it. It is easier to swim with the tide, and understanding the design approaches behind Linux will give you that advantage.

Appendix A

ASCII Chart

All our favorite computer books have an ASCII chart. We wanted one, too.

Int	Oct	Hex	ASCII	Int	Oct	Hex	ASCII
0	000	00	^@	19	023	13	^S
1	001	01	^A	20	024	14	^T
2	002	02	^B	21	025	15	^U
3	003	03	^C	22	026	16	^V
4	004	04	^D	23	027	17	^W
5	005	05	^E	24	030	18	^X
6	006	06	^F	25	031	19	^Y
7	007	07	^G	26	032	1a	^Z
8	010	08	^H	27	033	1b	^[
9	011	09	^I	28	034	1c	^\
10	012	0a	^J	29	035	1d	^]
11	013	0b	^K	30	036	1e	^^
12	014	0c	^L	31	037	1f	^_
13	015	0d	^M	32	040	20	
14	016	0e	^N	33	041	21	!
15	017	0f	^O	34	042	22	"
16	020	10	^P	35	043	23	#
17	021	11	^Q	36	044	24	$
18	022	12	^R	37	045	25	%

Int	Oct	Hex	ASCII		Int	Oct	Hex	ASCII
38	046	26	&		83	123	53	S
39	047	27	'		84	124	54	T
40	050	28	(		85	125	55	U
41	051	29	)		86	126	56	V
42	052	2a	*		87	127	57	W
43	053	2b	+		88	130	58	X
44	054	2c	,		89	131	59	Y
45	055	2d	-		90	132	5a	Z
46	056	2e	.		91	133	5b	[
47	057	2f	/		92	134	5c	\
48	060	30	0		93	135	5d	]
49	061	31	1		94	136	5e	^
50	062	32	2		95	137	5f	_
51	063	33	3		96	140	60	`
52	064	34	4		97	141	61	a
53	065	35	5		98	142	62	b
54	066	36	6		99	143	63	c
55	067	37	7		100	144	64	d
56	070	38	8		101	145	65	e
57	071	39	9		102	146	66	f
58	072	3a	:		103	147	67	g
59	073	3b	;		104	150	68	h
60	074	3c	<		105	151	69	i
61	075	3d	=		106	152	6a	j
62	076	3e	>		107	153	6b	k
63	077	3f	?		108	154	6c	l
64	100	40	@		109	155	6d	m
65	101	41	A		110	156	6e	n
66	102	42	B		111	157	6f	o
67	103	43	C		112	160	70	p
68	104	44	D		113	161	71	q
69	105	45	E		114	162	72	r
70	106	46	F		115	163	73	s
71	107	47	G		116	164	74	t
72	110	48	H		117	165	75	u
73	111	49	I		118	166	76	v
74	112	4a	J		119	167	77	w
75	113	4b	K		120	170	78	x
76	114	4c	L		121	171	79	y
77	115	4d	M		122	172	7a	z
78	116	4e	N		123	173	7b	{
79	117	4f	O		124	174	7c	|
80	120	50	P		125	175	7d	}
81	121	51	Q		126	176	7e	~
82	122	52	R		127	177	7f	^?

Appendix B

A Java Swing GUI
for BudgetPro

This is the listing of the GUI for BudgetPro. For a discussion, see Chapter 16.

```
1 package net.multitool.gui;
2
3 import java.awt.*;
4 import java.awt.event.*;
5 import javax.swing.*;
6 import javax.swing.event.*;
7 import javax.swing.table.*;
8 import java.util.*;
9 import net.multitool.core.*;
10
11 /**
12  * This class is the main application class for the BudgetPro gui
13  */
14
15 public class
16 BudgetPro
17 {
18   Account top;
19   Account current;
20
```

```
21   // gui components
22   private JFrame frame;   // needed by dialogs to root themselves
23   private JLabel nam;
24   private JLabel tot;
25   private JLabel val;
26   private JButton upton = new JButton(
                        new ImageIcon("net/multitool/gui/back.gif"));
27   private JButton creat = new JButton("New Subaccount");
28   private JButton view  = new JButton("View Subaccount");
29   private JButton clos  = new JButton("Quit");
30
31   private JTable list;
32   private AbstractTableModel model;
33
34   private AcctDialog askem;    // make once, use often
35
36   // Set Up an Action for a Button
37   private ActionListener upAction = new ActionListener()
38   {
39     public void
40     actionPerformed(ActionEvent e)
41     {
42       // this is the action for UP arrow icon;
43       Account next;
44       next = current.getParent();
45       if (next != null) {
46         current = next;
47         setStatus();
48         // TODO: notify the table, too
49         model.fireTableDataChanged();
50       } // TODO: else infodialog or Beep.
51     }
52   } ;
53
54   private ActionListener cdAction = new ActionListener()
55   {
56     public void
57     actionPerformed(ActionEvent e)
58     {
59       // this is the action for VIEW subdirectory;
60       // a "cd" into the subaccount.
61       int row = list.getSelectedRow();
62       // System.out.println("Row="+row); // DEBUG; TODO: REMOVE
63       if (row > -1) {                // only if a row was selected
64         String subname = (String) model.getValueAt(row, 0); // name column
65         Account next = current.getSub(subname);
66         if (next != null) {
67           current = next;
68           // System.out.println("cd to:"+current.getName());
```

```
69                 setStatus();
70                 // notify the table, too
71                 model.fireTableDataChanged();
72            } // TODO: else infodialog or Beep.
73          }
74        }
75      } ;
76
77      // TEST ONLY:
78      int testid = 0;
79
80      BudgetPro(JFrame frame, String username, String value)
81      {
82        this.frame = frame;
83        top = new Account("TopLevel", new User(username), value);
84        current = top;
85
86      } // constructor
87
88      private Component
89      createStatus()
90      {
91        JPanel retval = new JPanel();   // default: flow layout
92
93        upton.addActionListener(upAction);
94
95        nam = new JLabel("Account: Name");
96        tot = new JLabel("Total: $");
97        val = new JLabel("Remaining: $");
98
99        retval.add(upton);
100       retval.add(nam);
101       retval.add(tot);
102       retval.add(val);
103
104       setStatus();
105
106       return retval;
107     } // createStatus
108
109     /**
110      * Set the values of the status fields,
111      * as when the account has changed.
112      */
113     private void
114     setStatus()
115     {
116       nam.setText("Account: "+current.getName());
117       tot.setText("Total: $"+current.getTotal());
```

```
118     // tot.setText("SubAccounts: "+current.size());
119     val.setText("Remaining: $"+current.getBalance());
120
121     // disable the button if there is no "up" to go
122     if (current.getParent() == null) {
123         upton.setEnabled(false);
124     } else {
125         upton.setEnabled(true);
126     }
127
128   } // setStatus
129
130   private Component
131   createList()
132   {
133     JScrollPane retval;
134
135     model = new AbstractTableModel()
136       {
137         private String [] columnNames = {"Account", "Owner", "Value"};
138
139         public String
140         getColumnName(int col) {
141           return columnNames[col];
142         } // getColumnName
143
144         public int
145         getRowCount()
146         {
147           int retval;
148
149           if (current != null) {
150               retval = current.size();
151           } else {
152               retval = 1;      // testing only
153           }
154
155           return retval;
156
157         } // getRowCount
158
159         public int getColumnCount() { return columnNames.length; }
160
161         public Object
162         getValueAt(int row, int col) {
163           Object retval = null;
164           Account aa = null;
165           // return "---";    // rowData[row][col];
166           int count = 0;
```

```
167            for (Iterator itr=current.getAllSubs(); itr.hasNext(); )
168            {
169              count++;
170              aa = (Account) itr.next();
171              if (count > row) { break; }
172            } // next
173            switch (col) {
174            case 0:
175                    retval = aa.getName();
176                    break;
177            case 1:
178                    retval = aa.getOwner();
179                    break;
180            case 2:
181                    retval = aa.getTotal();
182                    break;
183            } // endswitch
184            return retval;
185          } // getValueAt
186
187        public boolean
188        isCellEditable(int row, int col)
189        {
190          return false;
191        } // isCellEditable
192      };
193    list = new JTable(model);
194    list.setSelectionMode(ListSelectionModel.SINGLE_SELECTION);
195
196    list.getSelectionModel().addListSelectionListener(
197      new ListSelectionListener()
198      {
199        public void
200        valueChanged(ListSelectionEvent e)
201        {
202          ListSelectionModel lsm = (ListSelectionModel)e.getSource();
203          if (lsm.isSelectionEmpty()) {
204              view.setEnabled(false);
205          } else {
206              view.setEnabled(true);
207          }
208        } // valueChanged
209      }
210    );
211
212    retval = new JScrollPane(list);
213
214    return retval;
215
```

```
216   } // createList
217
218   private Component
219   createButtons(JRootPane root)
220   {
221     JPanel retval = new JPanel();    // default: flow layout
222
223     //Lay out the buttons from left to right.
224     retval.setLayout(new BoxLayout(retval, BoxLayout.X_AXIS));
225     retval.setBorder(BorderFactory.createEmptyBorder(10, 10, 10, 10));
226     retval.add(Box.createHorizontalGlue());
227     retval.add(creat);
228     retval.add(Box.createRigidArea(new Dimension(10, 0)));
229     retval.add(view);
230     retval.add(Box.createRigidArea(new Dimension(10, 0)));
231     retval.add(clos);
232
233     // ------------------------------------- Define some actions
234     ActionListener closAction = new ActionListener()
235     {
236       public void
237       actionPerformed(ActionEvent e)
238       {
239           System.exit(0);
240       }
241     } ;
242     clos.addActionListener(closAction);
243
244     ActionListener creatAction = new ActionListener()
245     {
246       public void
247       actionPerformed(ActionEvent e)
248       {
249         Account child;
250         // get the info via a Dialog (of sorts)
251         if (askem == null) {
252             askem = new AcctDialog(frame, "New Subaccount");
253         } else {
254             askem.clear();
255             askem.setVisible(true);
256         }
257         String subName = askem.getName();
258         String subAmnt = askem.getAmnt();
259
260         // if empty, assume the operation was cancelled, else:
261         if ((subName != null) && (subName.length() > 0)) {
262             child = current.createSub(subName, subAmnt);
263             setStatus();
264             model.fireTableDataChanged(); // notify the table
```

```
265            }
266          }
267        };
268        creat.addActionListener(creatAction);
269
270        // function is to get selection from table and cd there
271        view.addActionListener(cdAction);
272        // but it starts off disabled, since there is no data yet
273        view.setEnabled(false);
274
275        // ------------------------------------------------------------
276        frame.getRootPane().setDefaultButton(creat);
277        clos.grabFocus();
278
279        return retval;
280
281    } // createButtons
282
283    public static void
284    main(String[] args)
285    {
286        BudgetPro app = null;
287
288        //Create the top-level container
289        JFrame frame = new JFrame("BudgetPro");
290
291        // ---------- set up the account/app based on the command line args
292        try {
293            String username = System.getProperty("user.name", "default");
294            if (args.length > 0) {
295                app = new BudgetPro(frame, username, args[0]);
296              } else {
297                System.err.println("usage: BudgetPro dollar_amt");
298                System.exit(1);
299            }
300        } catch (Exception e) {
301            System.err.println("Error on startup.");
302            e.printStackTrace();
303            System.exit(2);
304        }
305
306        // ---------- now set up the UI and get things going
307        try {
308            UIManager.setLookAndFeel(
309                        UIManager.getCrossPlatformLookAndFeelClassName());
310        } catch (Exception e) {
311            System.err.println("Can't set the desired look and feel.");
312            e.printStackTrace();
313            System.exit(3);
```

```
314      }
315
316      // build the pieces and add them to the top-level container
317
318      Component status = app.createStatus();
319      frame.getContentPane().add(status, BorderLayout.NORTH);
320
321      Component list = app.createList();
322      frame.getContentPane().add(list, BorderLayout.CENTER);
323
324      Component buttons = app.createButtons(frame.getRootPane());
325      frame.getContentPane().add(buttons, BorderLayout.SOUTH);
326
327      frame.setDefaultCloseOperation(JFrame.EXIT_ON_CLOSE);
328      frame.pack();
329      frame.setVisible(true);
330    } // main
331
332 } // class BudgetPro
```

Here is the code for the dialog for creating new accounts, `AcctDialog.java`:

```
 1 package net.multitool.gui;
 2
 3 import java.awt.*;
 4 import java.awt.event.*;
 5 import javax.swing.*;
 6 import javax.swing.table.*;
 7 import java.util.*;
 8 import net.multitool.core.*;
 9
10 class
11 AcctDialog
12   extends JDialog
13 {
14   JDialog dialog;   // for reference from the buttons' actions
15   JTextField nameField;
16   JTextField amntField;
17
18   AcctDialog(JFrame frame, String title)
19   {
20     super(frame, title, true);
21     dialog = this;
22     nameField = new JTextField(25);
23     amntField = new JTextField(9);
```

```
24
25       // right justify the numeric field
26       amntField.setHorizontalAlignment(JTextField.RIGHT);
27
28       // TODO: so that <Enter> will do a create
29       // this.getInputMap().put(KeyStroke.getKeyStroke("Enter"), "create");
30       /*
31         Action myAction = new AbstractAction("doSomething") {
32           public void actionPerformed() {
33             doSomething();
34           }
35         };
36         myComponent.getActionMap().put(myAction.get(Action.NAME), myAction);
37       */
38
39       //----------------------------------------------------Label on top----
40       JLabel label = new JLabel("<html><p align=left><i>"
41                     + "Enter the info to create a subaccount.<br>"
42                     + "</i>");
43       label.setHorizontalAlignment(JLabel.LEFT);
44       Font font = label.getFont();
45       label.setFont(label.getFont().deriveFont(font.PLAIN, 14.0f));
46
47       //---------------------------------------------------Text Fields-----
48       String[] labels = {"(Sub)Account Name: ", "Dollar Amount: "};
49       JTextField [] fields = {nameField, amntField};
50       int numPairs = fields.length;
51
52       //Create and populate the panel.
53       JPanel textes = new JPanel(new SpringLayout());
54       for (int i = 0; i < numPairs; i++) {
55         JLabel l = new JLabel(labels[i], JLabel.TRAILING);
56         textes.add(l);
57         l.setLabelFor(fields[i]);  // not nec. since we have no kb shortcuts
58         textes.add(fields[i]);
59       }
60
61       //Lay out the panel.
62       SpringUtilities.makeCompactGrid(textes,
63                                       numPairs, 2, //rows, cols
64                                       6, 6,        //initX, initY
65                                       6, 6);       //xPad, yPad
66
67
68       //---------------------------------------------------Buttons on bottom
69       JButton createButton = new JButton("Create");
70       createButton.addActionListener(new ActionListener() {
71         public void actionPerformed(ActionEvent e) {
72           nameField.grabFocus(); // before leaving, ready for next time.
```

```
73            dialog.setVisible(false);    // go away
74       }
75     });
76
77     JButton cancelButton = new JButton("Cancel");
78     cancelButton.addActionListener(new ActionListener() {
79       public void actionPerformed(ActionEvent e) {
80         clear(); // toss out any entry
81         dialog.setVisible(false);
82       }
83     });
84     getRootPane().setDefaultButton(createButton);
85
86     JPanel closePanel = new JPanel();
87     closePanel.setLayout(new BoxLayout(closePanel, BoxLayout.LINE_AXIS));
88     closePanel.add(Box.createHorizontalGlue());
89     closePanel.add(createButton);
90     closePanel.add(Box.createRigidArea(new Dimension(5, 0)));
91     closePanel.add(cancelButton);
92     closePanel.setBorder(BorderFactory.createEmptyBorder(10,0,5,5));
93
94     JPanel contentPane = new JPanel(new BorderLayout());
95     contentPane.add(label, BorderLayout.PAGE_START);
96     contentPane.add(textes, BorderLayout.CENTER);
97     contentPane.add(closePanel, BorderLayout.PAGE_END);
98     contentPane.setOpaque(true);
99     setContentPane(contentPane);
100
101    //Show it.
102    setSize(new Dimension(300, 160));
103    setLocationRelativeTo(frame);
104    setVisible(true);
105
106  } // constructor
107
108  public String
109  getName()
110  {
111    String retval = null;
112    if (nameField != null) {
113      retval = nameField.getText();
114    }
115    return retval;
116  } // getName
117
118  public String
119  getAmnt()
120  {
121    String retval = null;
```

```
122      if (amntField != null) {
123        retval = amntField.getText();
124      }
125      return retval;
126   } // getAmnt
127
128   public void
129   clear()
130   {
131     nameField.setText(null);
132     amntField.setText(null);
133   } // clear
134
135 } // class AcctDialog
```

Appendix C

GNU
General Public License

Version 2, June 1991

Copyright © 1989, 1991 Free Software Foundation, Inc.
59 Temple Place, Suite 330, Boston, MA 02111, USA

Everyone is permitted to copy and distribute verbatim copies
of this license document, but changing it is not allowed.

PREAMBLE

The licenses for most software are designed to take away your freedom to share
and change it. By contrast, the GNU General Public License is intended to
guarantee your freedom to share and change free software—to make sure the
software is free for all its users. This General Public License applies to most of
the Free Software Foundation's software and to any other program whose authors commit to using it. (Some other Free Software Foundation software is
covered by the GNU Library General Public License instead.) You can apply
it to your programs, too.

When we speak of free software, we are referring to freedom, not price. Our General Public Licenses are designed to make sure that you have the freedom to distribute copies of free software (and charge for this service if you wish), that you receive source code or can get it if you want it, that you can change the software or use pieces of it in new free programs; and that you know you can do these things.

To protect your rights, we need to make restrictions that forbid anyone to deny you these rights or to ask you to surrender the rights. These restrictions translate to certain responsibilities for you if you distribute copies of the software, or if you modify it.

For example, if you distribute copies of such a program, whether gratis or for a fee, you must give the recipients all the rights that you have. You must make sure that they, too, receive or can get the source code. And you must show them these terms so they know their rights.

We protect your rights with two steps: (1) copyright the software, and (2) offer you this license which gives you legal permission to copy, distribute and/or modify the software.

Also, for each author's protection and ours, we want to make certain that everyone understands that there is no warranty for this free software. If the software is modified by someone else and passed on, we want its recipients to know that what they have is not the original, so that any problems introduced by others will not reflect on the original authors' reputations.

Finally, any free program is threatened constantly by software patents. We wish to avoid the danger that redistributors of a free program will individually obtain patent licenses, in effect making the program proprietary. To prevent this, we have made it clear that any patent must be licensed for everyone's free use or not licensed at all.

The precise terms and conditions for copying, distribution, and modification follow.

TERMS AND CONDITIONS FOR COPYING, DISTRIBUTION, AND MODIFICATION

0. This License applies to any program or other work which contains a notice placed by the copyright holder saying it may be distributed under the terms of this General Public License. The "Program," below, refers to any such program or work, and a "work based on the Program" means either

the Program or any derivative work under copyright law: that is to say, a work containing the Program or a portion of it, either verbatim or with modifications and/or translated into another language. (Hereinafter, translation is included without limitation in the term "modification.") Each licensee is addressed as "you."

Activities other than copying, distribution and modification are not covered by this License; they are outside its scope. The act of running the Program is not restricted, and the output from the Program is covered only if its contents constitute a work based on the Program (independent of having been made by running the Program). Whether that is true depends on what the Program does.

1. You may copy and distribute verbatim copies of the Program's source code as you receive it, in any medium, provided that you conspicuously and appropriately publish on each copy an appropriate copyright notice and disclaimer of warranty; keep intact all the notices that refer to this License and to the absence of any warranty; and give any other recipients of the Program a copy of this License along with the Program.

    You may charge a fee for the physical act of transferring a copy, and you may at your option offer warranty protection in exchange for a fee.

2. You may modify your copy or copies of the Program or any portion of it, thus forming a work based on the Program, and copy and distribute such modifications or work under the terms of Section 1 above, provided that you also meet all of these conditions:

    a) You must cause the modified files to carry prominent notices stating that you changed the files and the date of any change.

    b) You must cause any work that you distribute or publish, that in whole or in part contains or is derived from the Program or any part thereof, to be licensed as a whole at no charge to all third parties under the terms of this License.

    c) If the modified program normally reads commands interactively when run, you must cause it, when started running for such interactive use in the most ordinary way, to print or display an announcement including an appropriate copyright notice and a notice that there is no warranty (or else, saying that you provide a warranty) and that users may redistribute the program under these conditions, and telling the user how to view a copy of this License. (Exception: if the Program itself is interactive but does not normally print such an announcement, your work based on the Program is not required to print an announcement.)

These requirements apply to the modified work as a whole. If identifiable sections of that work are not derived from the Program, and can be reasonably considered independent and separate works in themselves, then this License, and its terms, do not apply to those sections when you distribute them as separate works. But when you distribute the same sections as part of a whole which is a work based on the Program, the distribution of the whole must be on the terms of this License, whose permissions for other licensees extend to the entire whole, and thus to each and every part regardless of who wrote it.

Thus, it is not the intent of this section to claim rights or contest your rights to work written entirely by you; rather, the intent is to exercise the right to control the distribution of derivative or collective works based on the Program.

In addition, mere aggregation of another work not based on the Program with the Program (or with a work based on the Program) on a volume of a storage or distribution medium does not bring the other work under the scope of this License.

3. You may copy and distribute the Program (or a work based on it, under Section 2) in object code or executable form under the terms of Sections 1 and 2 above provided that you also do one of the following:

   a) Accompany it with the complete corresponding machine-readable source code, which must be distributed under the terms of Sections 1 and 2 above on a medium customarily used for software interchange; or,

   b) Accompany it with a written offer, valid for at least three years, to give any third party, for a charge no more than your cost of physically performing source distribution, a complete machine-readable copy of the corresponding source code, to be distributed under the terms of Sections 1 and 2 above on a medium customarily used for software interchange; or,

   c) Accompany it with the information you received as to the offer to distribute corresponding source code. (This alternative is allowed only for noncommercial distribution and only if you received the program in object code or executable form with such an offer, in accord with Subsection b above.)

The source code for a work means the preferred form of the work for making modifications to it. For an executable work, complete source code means all the source code for all modules it contains, plus any associated interface definition files, plus the scripts used to control compilation and installation of the executable. However, as a special exception, the source code distributed need not include anything that is normally distributed (in either source or binary form) with the major components (compiler, kernel, and so on) of the operating system on which the executable runs, unless that component itself accompanies the executable.

If distribution of executable or object code is made by offering access to copy from a designated place, then offering equivalent access to copy the source code from the same place counts as distribution of the source code, even though third parties are not compelled to copy the source along with the object code.

4. You may not copy, modify, sublicense, or distribute the Program except as expressly provided under this License. Any attempt otherwise to copy, modify, sublicense or distribute the Program is void, and will automatically terminate your rights under this License. However, parties who have received copies, or rights, from you under this License will not have their licenses terminated so long as such parties remain in full compliance.

5. You are not required to accept this License, since you have not signed it. However, nothing else grants you permission to modify or distribute the Program or its derivative works. These actions are prohibited by law if you do not accept this License. Therefore, by modifying or distributing the Program (or any work based on the Program), you indicate your acceptance of this License to do so, and all its terms and conditions for copying, distributing or modifying the Program or works based on it.

6. Each time you redistribute the Program (or any work based on the Program), the recipient automatically receives a license from the original licensor to copy, distribute or modify the Program subject to these terms and conditions. You may not impose any further restrictions on the recipients' exercise of the rights granted herein. You are not responsible for enforcing compliance by third parties to this License.

7. If, as a consequence of a court judgment or allegation of patent infringement or for any other reason (not limited to patent issues), conditions are imposed on you (whether by court order, agreement or otherwise) that contradict the conditions of this License, they do not excuse you from

the conditions of this License. If you cannot distribute so as to satisfy simultaneously your obligations under this License and any other pertinent obligations, then as a consequence you may not distribute the Program at all. For example, if a patent license would not permit royalty-free redistribution of the Program by all those who receive copies directly or indirectly through you, then the only way you could satisfy both it and this License would be to refrain entirely from distribution of the Program.

If any portion of this section is held invalid or unenforceable under any particular circumstance, the balance of the section is intended to apply and the section as a whole is intended to apply in other circumstances.

It is not the purpose of this section to induce you to infringe any patents or other property right claims or to contest validity of any such claims; this section has the sole purpose of protecting the integrity of the free software distribution system, which is implemented by public license practices. Many people have made generous contributions to the wide range of software distributed through that system in reliance on consistent application of that system; it is up to the author/donor to decide if he or she is willing to distribute software through any other system and a licensee cannot impose that choice.

This section is intended to make thoroughly clear what is believed to be a consequence of the rest of this License.

8. If the distribution and/or use of the Program is restricted in certain countries either by patents or by copyrighted interfaces, the original copyright holder who places the Program under this License may add an explicit geographical distribution limitation excluding those countries, so that distribution is permitted only in or among countries not thus excluded. In such case, this License incorporates the limitation as if written in the body of this License.

9. The Free Software Foundation may publish revised and/or new versions of the General Public License from time to time. Such new versions will be similar in spirit to the present version, but may differ in detail to address new problems or concerns.

Each version is given a distinguishing version number. If the Program specifies a version number of this License which applies to it and "any later version," you have the option of following the terms and conditions either of that version or of any later version published by the Free Software Foundation. If the Program does not specify a version number of this License, you may choose any version ever published by the Free Software Foundation.

10. If you wish to incorporate parts of the Program into other free programs whose distribution conditions are different, write to the author to ask for permission. For software which is copyrighted by the Free Software Foundation, write to the Free Software Foundation; we sometimes make exceptions for this. Our decision will be guided by the two goals of preserving the free status of all derivatives of our free software and of promoting the sharing and reuse of software generally.

NO WARRANTY

11. BECAUSE THE PROGRAM IS LICENSED FREE OF CHARGE, THERE IS NO WARRANTY FOR THE PROGRAM, TO THE EXTENT PERMITTED BY APPLICABLE LAW. EXCEPT WHEN OTHERWISE STATED IN WRITING THE COPYRIGHT HOLDERS AND/OR OTHER PARTIES PROVIDE THE PROGRAM "AS IS" WITHOUT WARRANTY OF ANY KIND, EITHER EXPRESSED OR IMPLIED, INCLUDING, BUT NOT LIMITED TO, THE IMPLIED WARRANTIES OF MERCHANTABILITY AND FITNESS FOR A PARTICULAR PURPOSE. THE ENTIRE RISK AS TO THE QUALITY AND PERFORMANCE OF THE PROGRAM IS WITH YOU. SHOULD THE PROGRAM PROVE DEFECTIVE, YOU ASSUME THE COST OF ALL NECESSARY SERVICING, REPAIR OR CORRECTION.

12. IN NO EVENT UNLESS REQUIRED BY APPLICABLE LAW OR AGREED TO IN WRITING WILL ANY COPYRIGHT HOLDER, OR ANY OTHER PARTY WHO MAY MODIFY AND/OR REDISTRIBUTE THE PROGRAM AS PERMITTED ABOVE, BE LIABLE TO YOU FOR DAMAGES, INCLUDING ANY GENERAL, SPECIAL, INCIDENTAL OR CONSEQUENTIAL DAMAGES ARISING OUT OF THE USE OR INABILITY TO USE THE PROGRAM (INCLUDING BUT NOT LIMITED TO LOSS OF DATA OR DATA BEING RENDERED INACCURATE OR LOSSES SUSTAINED BY YOU OR THIRD PARTIES OR A FAILURE OF THE PROGRAM TO OPERATE WITH ANY OTHER PROGRAMS), EVEN IF SUCH

HOLDER OR OTHER PARTY HAS BEEN ADVISED OF THE POSSIBILITY OF SUCH DAMAGES.

END OF TERMS AND CONDITIONS

HOW TO APPLY THESE TERMS TO YOUR NEW PROGRAMS

If you develop a new program, and you want it to be of the greatest possible use to the public, the best way to achieve this is to make it free software which everyone can redistribute and change under these terms.

To do so, attach the following notices to the program. It is safest to attach them to the start of each source file to most effectively convey the exclusion of warranty; and each file should have at least the "copyright" line and a pointer to where the full notice is found.

```
one line to give the program's name and an idea of what it does.
Copyright (C) year  name of author

This program is free software; you can redistribute it and/or
modify it under the terms of the GNU General Public License
as published by the Free Software Foundation; either version 2
of the License, or (at your option) any later version.

This program is distributed in the hope that it will be useful,
but WITHOUT ANY WARRANTY; without even the implied warranty of
MERCHANTABILITY or FITNESS FOR A PARTICULAR PURPOSE.  See the
GNU General Public License for more details.

You should have received a copy of the GNU General Public License
along with this program; if not, write to the Free Software
Foundation, Inc., 59 Temple Place, Suite 330, Boston, MA 02111, USA.
```

Also add information on how to contact you by electronic and paper mail.

If the program is interactive, make it output a short notice like this when it starts in an interactive mode:

```
Gnomovision version 69, Copyright (C) year name of author
Gnomovision comes with ABSOLUTELY NO WARRANTY; for details
type `show w'.  This is free software, and you are welcome
to redistribute it under certain conditions; type `show c'
for details.
```

The hypothetical commands 'show w' and 'show c' should show the appropriate parts of the General Public License. Of course, the commands you use may be called something other than 'show w' and 'show c'; they could even be mouse-clicks or menu items—whatever suits your program.

You should also get your employer (if you work as a programmer) or your school, if any, to sign a "copyright disclaimer" for the program, if necessary. Here is a sample; alter the names:

```
Yoyodyne, Inc., hereby disclaims all copyright
interest in the program `Gnomovision'
(which makes passes at compilers) written
by James Hacker.

signature of Ty Coon, 1 April 1989
Ty Coon, President of Vice
```

This General Public License does not permit incorporating your program into proprietary programs. If your program is a subroutine library, you may consider it more useful to permit linking proprietary applications with the library. If this is what you want to do, use the GNU Lesser General Public License instead of this License.

Index

http://www.phptr.com/

Prentice Hall PTR   InformIT   InformIT Online Books   Financial Times Prentice Hall   ft.com   PTG Interactive   Reuters

TOMORROW'S SOLUTIONS FOR TODAY'S PROFESSIONALS

Prentice Hall **Professional Technical Reference**

| Browse | Book Series | What's New | User Groups | Alliances | Special Sales | Contact Us |

Search | Help | Home

Quick Search

PTR Favorites

Find a Bookstore

Book Series

Special Interests

Newsletters

Press Room

International

Best Sellers

Solutions Beyond the Book

Shopping Bag

Keep Up to Date with

PH PTR Online

We strive to stay on the cutting edge of what's happening in professional computer science and engineering. Here's a bit of what you'll find when you stop by **www.phptr.com**:

What's new at PHPTR? We don't just publish books for the professional community, we're a part of it. Check out our convention schedule, keep up with your favorite authors, and get the latest reviews and press releases on topics of interest to you.

Special interest areas offering our latest books, book series, features of the month, related links, and other useful information to help you get the job done.

User Groups Prentice Hall Professional Technical Reference's User Group Program helps volunteer, not-for-profit user groups provide their members with training and information about cutting-edge technology.

Companion Websites Our Companion Websites provide valuable solutions beyond the book. Here you can download the source code, get updates and corrections, chat with other users and the author about the book, or discover links to other websites on this topic.

Need to find a bookstore? Chances are, there's a bookseller near you that carries a broad selection of PTR titles. Locate a Magnet bookstore near you at www.phptr.com.

Subscribe today! Join PHPTR's monthly email newsletter! Want to be kept up-to-date on your area of interest? Choose a targeted category on our website, and we'll keep you informed of the latest PHPTR products, author events, reviews and conferences in your interest area.

Visit our mailroom to subscribe today! **http://www.phptr.com/mail_lists**